Gospel Advocate

The Christian System

In Reference to the Union of Christians, and a Restoration of Primitive Christianity, as Plead in the Current Reformation.

Alexander Campbell

Gospel Advocate Company
P.O. Box 150
Nashville, Tennessee 37202

The Christian System
Gospel Advocate Restoration Reprints, 2001

Printed 1980, Gospel Advocate Co.
First Published 1835

Published by Gospel Advocate Co.
P.O. Box 150, Nashville, TN 37202
www.gospeladvocate.com

ISBN: 0-89225-479-3

INDEX

PAGE

A

Abraham 111
Address to Belligerent Aliens 305
      Citizens of the Kingdom 295
Ascension of the Messiah 143
Attributes of a Real Sin-Offering 30

B

Baptist 198
Baptism 39
     Action of 40
     Subject of 42
     Meaning of 42
Barnabas 189
Bible 2
Blessing of Abraham 114
Breaking the Loaf 266
     Proposition i 267
        "   ii 268
        "   iii 269
        "   iv 270
        "   v 271
        "   vi 274
        "   vii 275
Body of Christ 55

C

Christ the Light of the World 34
Christian Ministry 60
     Hope 50
     Discipline 67
     System 114
Christians Are Persons Pardoned, etc. 46
Clement and Hermas 190
Concluding Addresses 295
Confession of Faith 43
Confirmation of the Testimony 95
Conversion 44
Coronation of the Messiah 144
Covenant of Circumcision 112
Cyprian 195

D

Doom of the Wicked 52

PAGE

E

Effects of Modern Christianity 213
Episcopalian 196
Expediency 71

F

Fact 89
Faith 92
Faith in Christ 37
Foundation of Christian Union 84
Fundamental Fact 99

G

Gift of the Holy Spirit 47
God 6
    Son of 9
    Spirit of 11

H

Heresy 75

I

Immersion Not a Mere Bodily Act 215

J

Jewish Institution 115
Justification Ascribed to Seven Causes 216
Justin Martyr 192

K

Kingdom of Heaven 106
    Coming of 137
    Constitution of 127
    Elements of 124
    Induction into 135
    King of 130
    Laws of 132
    Manners and Customs of 135
    Name of 125
    Present Administration of 146
    Subjects of 131
    Territory of 134

L

Lordship of the Messiah 36

M

Man as he was 13
Man as he is 14
Methodist 198

N

New Birth 232
    Life 234

O

Origen 194

P

Patriarchal Age of the World 106
Peter in Jerusalem, and Paul in Philippi, Reconciled 217
Preface vii
Preface to Second Edition xvii
Presbyterian 197
Purity of Speech 102
Purposes of God Concerning Man 16
Physical Regeneration 236

R

Reformation 225
Regeneration 219
          Extra on 228
          Bath of 230
          of the Church 240
                Heavens and the Earth 257
                World 257
          Physical 236
          Use of the Theory of 237
Religion for Man 20
Remission of Sins 153
     Proposition I 154
          "   II 156
          "   III 156
          "   IV 157
          "   V 157
          "   VI 158
          "   VII 163
          "   VIII 165
          "   IX 166
          "   X 171
          "   XI 189
          "   XII 196
     Recapitulation 204
     Conclusion 206
Renewing of the Holy Spirit 233

PAGE

Repentance 38, 222
Rules of Interpretation 3

S

Sacrifice for Sin 21
Sin-offering 30
Sinaitic Covenant 113
Son of God 9
Spirit of God 11
Summary of Christian Facts 54

T

Tertullian 193
Testimony 91
    Confirmation of the 95
Two Promises 112
    Seeds 114

U

Universe 1

W

Wall, Dr. W. W., Testimony of 191
Wesley, John, Testimony of 286
Word to Friendly Aliens 302
Word to Moral Regenerators 258

PREFACE

Since the full development of the great apostasy foretold by Prophets and Apostles, numerous attempts at reformation have been made. Three full centuries, carrying with them the destinies of countless millions, have passed into eternity since the Lutheran effort to dethrone the *Man of Sin.* During this period many great and wonderful changes have taken place in the political, literary, moral, and religious conditions of society. That the nations composing the western half of the Roman Empire have already been greatly benefited by that effort, scientifically, politically, and morally, no person acquainted with either political or ecclesiastical history can reasonably doubt. Time, that great arbiter of human actions, that great revealer of secrets, has long decided that all the reformers of the Papacy have been public benefactors. And thus the Protestant Reformation is proved to have been one of the most splendid eras in the history of the world, and must long be regarded by the philosopher and the philanthropist as one of the most gracious interpositions in behalf of the whole human race.

We Americans owe our national privileges and our civil liberties to the Protestant reformers. They achieved not only an imperishable fame for themselves, but a rich legacy for their posterity. When we contrast the present state of these United States with Spanish America, and the condition of the English nation with that of Spain, Portugal, and Italy, we begin to appreciate how much we are indebted to the intelligence, faith, and courage of Martin Luther and his heroic associates in that glorious reformation.

He restored the Bible to the world A.D. 1534, and boldly defended its claims against the impious and arrogant pretensions of the haughty and tyrannical See of Rome. But, unfortunately, at his death there was no Joshua to lead the people, who rallied under the banners of the Bible, out of the wilderness in which Luther died. His tenets were soon converted into a new state religion, and the spirit of reformation which he excited and inspired was soon quenched by the broils and feuds of the Protestant princes and the collisions of rival political interests, both on the continent and in the islands of Europe.

While Protestant hatred to the Roman Pontiff and the Papacy continued to increase, a secret lust in the bosoms of Protestants for ecclesiastical power and patronage worked in the members of the Protestant Popes, who gradually assimilated the new church to the old. Creeds and manuals, synods and councils, soon shackled the minds of men, and the spirit of reformation gradually forsook the Protestant church, or was supplanted by the spirit of the world.

Calvin renewed the speculative theology of Saint Augustine, and Geneva in a few years became the Alexandria of modern Europe. The power of religion was soon merged in debates about forms and ceremonies, in speculative strifes of opinion, and in fierce debates about the political and religious right of burning heretics. Still, however, in all these collisions much light was elicited; and had it not been for these extremes, it is problematical whether the wound inflicted upon the Man of Sin would have been as incurable as it has since proved itself to be.

Reformation, however, became the order of the day; and this, assuredly, was a great matter, however it may have been managed. It was a revolution, and revolutions seldom move backward. The example that Luther set was of more value than all the achievements of Charles V., or the literary and moral labors of his distinguished contemporary, the erudite Erasmus.

It is curious to observe how extremes begot extremes in every step of the reformation cause, to the dawn of the present century. The penances, works of faith and of supererogation, of the Roman church, drove Luther and Calvin to the ultraism of "faith alone."

After the Protestants had debated their own principles with one another till they lost all brotherly affection, and would as soon have "communed in the sacrament" with the Catholics as with one another; speculative abstracts of Christian Platonism, the sublime mysteries of Egyptian theology, became alternately the bond of union and the apple of discord, among the fathers and friends of the Reformation.

The *five* great dogmas of the Geneva reformer were carried to Amsterdam, and generated in the mind of James Arminius, in 1591, five opposite opinions; and these at the Synod of Dort, in 1618, formed a new party of Remonstrants.

Into Britain, with whose history we are more immediately concerned, Lutheranism, Calvinism, and Arminianism were soon imported; and, like all raw materials there introduced, were immediately manufactured anew. They were all exotics, but easily acclimated, and soon flourished in Britain more luxuriantly than in their native soil. But the beggarly elements of opinions, forms, and ceremonies to which they gave rise, caused the "*Spirit alone*" to germinate in the mind of George Fox, in little more than half a century after the introduction of the Leyden theology.

In Lord Chatham's days, the Episcopal church, as his Lordship declares, was a singular compound—"A Popish liturgy, Calvinistic articles, and an Arminian clergy." But every few years caused a new discussion and reformation, until the kirk of Scotland and the church of England have been compelled to respect, in some good degree, the rights of conscience, even in dissenters themselves.

Abroad it was no better. The Saxon reformer had his friends; John of Picardy lived in the grateful remembrance of the Geneva family; and James of Amsterdam speculated in a very liberal style among all the Remonstrants at home and abroad. In Sweden, Holland, Germany, England, Scotland, the debate varied not essentially: the Pope against the Protestants—the Lutherans against the Calvinists—the Calvinists against the Arminians—the Bishops against the Presbyters—and the Presbyterians among themselves; until, by the potency of metaphysics and politics, they are now frittered down to various parties.

While philosophy, mysticism, and politics drove the parties to every question into antipodal extremes; while justification by metaphysical faith alone; while the forms and ceremonies of all sects begat the "Spirit alone" in the mind of George Fox; while the Calvinian five points generated the Arminian five points; and while the Westminster Creed, though unsubscribed by its makers, begot a hundred others,—not until within the present generation did any sect or party in Christendom unite and build upon the Bible alone.

Since that time, the first effort known to us to abandon the whole controversy about creeds and reformations, and to *restore* primitive Christianity, or to build alone upon the Apostles and Prophets, Jesus Christ himself the chief corner-stone, has been made.

Tired of new creeds and new parties in religion, and of the numerous abortive efforts to reform the reformation; convinced from the Holy Scriptures, from observation and experience, that the union of the disciples of Christ is essential to the conversion of the world, and that the correction and improvement of no creed, or partisan establishment in Christendom, could ever become the basis of such a union, communion, and co-operation, as would restore peace to a church militant against itself, or triumph to the common salvation; a few individuals, about the commencement of the present century, began to reflect upon the ways and means to restore primitive Christianity.

This led to a careful, most conscientious, and prayerful examination of the grounds and reasons of the present state of things in all the Protestant sects. On examination of the history of all the platforms and constitutions of all these sects, it appeared evident as mathematical demonstration itself, that neither the Augsburg articles of faith and opinion, nor the Westminister, nor the Wesleyan, nor those of any state creed or dissenting establishment, could ever improve the condition of things, restore union to the church, peace to the world, or success to the gospel of Christ.

As the Bible was said and constantly affirmed to be the religion of Protestants, it was for some time a mysterious problem why the Bible alone, confessed and acknowledged, should work no happier results than the strifes, divisions, and retaliatory excommunications of rival Protestant sects. It appeared, however, in this case, after a more intimate acquaintance with the details of the inner temple of sectarian Christianity, as in many similar cases, that it is not the acknowledgment of a good rule, but the walking by it, that secures the happiness of society. The Bible in the lips, and the creed in the head and in the heart, will not save the church from strife, emulation, and schism. There is no moral, ecclesiastical, or political good, by simply acknowledging it in word. It must be obeyed.

In our ecclesiastical pilgrimage we have occasionally met with some vehement declaimers against human written creeds, and pleaders for the Bible alone, who were all the while preaching up the opinions of *saint* Arius or *saint* Athanasius. Their sentiments, language, style, and general views of the gospel were as human as auricular confession, extreme unction, or purgatorial purification.

The Bible alone is the Bible only, in word and deed, in profession and practice; and this alone can reform the world and save the church. Judging others as we once judged ourselves, there are not a few who are advocating the Bible alone, and preaching their own opinions. Before we applied the Bible alone to our views, or brought our views and religious practice to the Bible, we plead the old theme, —"The Bible alone is the religion of Protestants." But we found it an arduous task, and one of twenty years' labor, to correct our diction and purify our speech according to the Bible alone; and even yet we have not wholly practically repudiated the language of Ashdod. We only profess to work and walk by the rules which will inevitably issue in a pure speech, and in right conceptions of that pure, and holy, and celestial thing called Christianity,—in faith, in sentiment, and in practice.

A deep and an abiding impression that the power, the consolations, and joys—the holiness and happiness—of Christ's religion were lost in the forms and ceremonies, in the speculations and conjectures, in the feuds and bickerings of sects and schisms, originated a project many years ago for uniting the sects, or rather the *Christians* in all the sects, upon a clear and scriptural bond of union,—upon having a

"thus saith the Lord," either in express terms, or in approved precedent, "for every article of faith, and item of religious practice." This
was offered in the year 1809, in the "Declaration and Address" of the
Washington Association, Pennsylvania. It was first tendered to the
parties that confessed the Westminster creed; but equally submitted
to the Protestants of every name, making faith in Christ and obedience to him that only *test* of Christian character, and the only *bond*
of church union, communion, and co-operation. It was indeed approved by all; but adopted and practiced by none, except the few, or
part of the few, who made the future.

None of us who either got up or sustained that project was then
aware of what havoc that said principle, if faithfully applied, would
have made of our views and practices on various favorite points.
When we take a close retrospective view of the last thirty years (for
we have a pretty distinct recollection of our travel's history for that
period), and on the workings of that principle in heart and life, with
which we commenced our public career in the work of the Lord, we
know not how to express our astonishment better than in the following parable:—

A citizen of the West had a very promising young vineyard on a
fruitful hill. He had no practical knowledge in the cultivation of the
grape, but had read much and largely upon the dressing, pruning,
and managing of the vine. He built himself a wine-vat, and prepared all the implements for the vintage. But he lacked practical
skill in using the pruning-knife. His vines flourished exceedingly,
and stretched forth their tendrils on every side; but he had no vintage.

A vine-dresser from Oporto one day presented himself as he was
musing upon his disappointments. He was celebrated in his profession, and the most skilful in all the affairs of the vineyard. The
owner of the vineyard, having employed him to dress and keep his
vineyard, set out on a long journey for a few weeks. On his return
and visit to his farm, he walked out one day to his vineyard, when, to
his amazement, he saw the ground literally covered with prunings of
his vines. The vine-dresser had very skillfully and freely used the
pruning-hook, and had left little more than the roots and naked stems
of the vines standing by the frames.

"My vineyard is ruined! My hopes blighted! I am undone! I
am ruined!" exclaimed the unhappy husbandman. "Unhappy
wretch! you have deceived me; you have robbed me of the labors of
five years, and blasted in one single moon all my bright hopes for
years to come!" The vine-dresser stood appalled; but, as soon as the
tempest subsided, ventured to say: "Master, I will serve you five

years for nothing, if we gather not more grapes and have not a better vintage this year than you have gathered in all the years since you planted these vines." The proprietor of the vineyard withdrew, saying, "It is impossible! It is impossible!" and visited it not again till invited by his vine-dresser, about the middle of autumn; when, to his still greater astonishment, and much more to his gratification, he found incomparably more grapes than he had hitherto gathered from his vines, and of a much more delicious quality.

So, in the case before us, the application of the principle already stated trimmed us so naked that we strongly inclined to suspect its fallacy, and had well-nigh abandoned it as deceitful speculation. Time, however, that great teacher, and Experience, that great critic, have fully assured us that the principle is a salutary one; and that, although we seemingly lose much by its application, our loss consists only of barren opinions, fruitless speculations, and useless traditions, that only cumber the ground and check the word, so that it is in a good measure unfruitful.

We flatter ourselves that the principles are now clearly and fully developed by the united efforts of a few devoted and ardent minds, who set out determined to sacrifice everything to truth, and follow her wherever she might lead the way: I say, the principles on which the church of Jesus Christ—all believers in Jesus as the Messiah—can be united with honor to themselves, and with blessings to the world; on which the gospel and its ordinances can be restored in all their primitive simplicity, excellency, and power, and the church shine as a lamp that burneth to the conviction and salvation of the world:—I say, *the principles* by which these things can be done are now developed, as well as the *principles themselves*, which together constitute *the original gospel* and *order of things* established by the Apostles.

The object of this volume is to place before the community in a plain, definite, and perspicuous style, the *capital principles* which have been elicited, argued out, developed, and sustained in a controversy of *twenty-five years*, by the tongues and pens of those who rallied under the banners of the Bible alone. The principle which was inscribed upon our banners when we withdrew from the ranks of the sects was, "*Faith in Jesus as the true Messiah, and obedience to him as our Lawgiver and King, the* ONLY TEST *of Christian character, and the* ONLY BOND *of Christian union, communion, and co-operation, irrespective of all creeds, opinions, commandments, and traditions of men.*"

This cause, like every other, was first plead by the tongue; afterwards by the pen and the press. The history of its progress corresponds with the history of every other religious revolution in this re-

spect—that different points, at different times, almost exclusively engrossed the attention of its pleaders. We began with the *outposts*
and *vanguard* of the opposition. Soon as we found ourselves in the
possession of one post our artillery was turned against another; and
as fast as the smoke of the enemy receded we advanced upon his
lines.

The first piece that was written on the subject of the great position
appeared from the pen of THOMAS CAMPBELL, Senior, in the year
1809. An association was formed that year for the dissemination of
the principles of reformation; and the piece alluded to was styled
"The Declaration and Address of the *Christian Association* of Washington, Pennsylvania."

The constitutional principle of this "Christian Association" and its
object are clearly expressed in the following resolution:—"That this
society, formed for the sole purpose of promoting simple evangelical
Christianity, shall, to the utmost of its power, countenance and support such ministers, and such only, as exhibit a manifest conformity
to the *Original Standard*, in conversation and doctrine, in zeal and
diligence; only such as reduce to practice the *simple original* form of
Christianity, expressly exhibited upon the sacred page, without attempting to inculcate any thing of human authority, of private opinion, or inventions of men, as having any place in the constitution,
faith, or worship of the Christian church; or anything as matter of
Christian faith or *duty* for which there can not be produced a *'thus
saith the Lord,'* either in express terms or by approved precedent."

The ground occupied in this resolution afforded ample documents
of debate. Every inch of it was debated, argued, canvassed for several years, in Pennsylvania, Virginia, and Ohio. On this bottom we
put to sea, with scarcely hands enough to man the ship. We had
head-winds and rough seas for the first seven years, a history of
which would be both curious and interesting.

But, to contradistinguish this plea and effort from some others almost contemporaneous with it, we would emphatically remark, that
while the Remonstrants warred against human creeds, evidently because those creeds warred against their own private opinions and favorite dogmas, which they wished to substitute for those creeds,—
this enterprise, so far as it was hostile to those creeds, warred against
them, not because of their hostility to any private or favorite opinions
which were desired to be substituted for them, but because those
human institutions supplanted the Bible, made the word of God of
none effect, were fatal to the intelligence, union, purity, holiness, and
happiness of the disciples of Christ, and hostile to the salvation of the
world.

Unitarians, for example, have warred against human creeds, because those creeds taught Trinitarianism. Arminians, too, have been hostile to creeds, because those creeds supported Calvinism. It has, indeed, been alleged that all schismatics, good and bad, since the days of John Wickliffe, and long before, have opposed creeds of human invention because those creeds opposed them. But so far as this controversy resembles them in its opposition to creeds, it is to be distinguished from them in this all-essential attribute,—viz.: that *our opposition to creeds arose from a conviction that, whether the opinions in them were true or false, they were hostile to the union, peace, harmony, purity, and joy of Christians, and adverse to the conversion of the world to Jesus Christ.*

Next to our personal salvation, two objects constituted the *summum bonum,* the supreme good, worthy of the sacrifice of all temporalities. The first was the union, peace, purity, and harmonious co-operation of Christians, guided by an understanding enlightened by the Holy Scriptures; the other, the conversion of sinners to God. Our predilections and antipathies on all religious questions arose from, and were controlled by, those all-absorbing interests. From these commenced our campaign against creeds. We had not at first, and we have not now, a favorite opinion or speculation which we would offer as a substitute for any human creed or constitution in Christendom.

We were not, indeed, at first apprized of the havoc which our principles would make upon our *opinions.* We soon, however, found our principles and opinions at war on some points; and the question immediately arose, *Whether shall we sacrifice our principles to our opinions, or our opinions to our principles?* We need not say that we were compelled to the latter, judging that our principles were better than our opinions. Hence, since we put to sea on board this bottom, we have been compelled to throw overboard some opinions once as dear to us as they now are to those who never thought of the difference between principle and opinion.

Some of those opinions (as the most delicate and tender buds are soonest blighted by the frost) immediately withered, and died under the first application of our principles. Infant baptism and infant sprinkling, with all infantile imbecility, immediately expired in our minds, soon as the *Bible alone* was made the only measure and standard of faith and duty. This foundation of the pedobaptist temple being instantly destroyed, the whole edifice leaning upon it became a heap of ruins. We explored the ruins with great assiduity, and collected from them all the materials that could be worked into the

Christian temple; but the piles of rubbish that remained were immense.

Other topics became the theme of discussion; and, as the public mind became more intelligent and candid, the great principles of the Law and Gospel, the Patriarchal, the Jewish, and Christian institutions, were gradually unfolded. To the development of these, other publications in 1816 and 1820 greatly contributed; and so fully explored were ancient and modern Christianity that, in 1823, the design was formed of commencing a periodical and establishing a press to contend for the original faith and order, in opposition to all the corruptions of fifteen centuries.

As we are not writing a history of this struggle from its commencement to the present time, but simply informing the reader that the principles stated in the following pages have been maturely considered, and have passed through a long, complicated, and vigorous opposition, we shall hasten to the object of this book, which is to lay before the reader a miniature view of the principles already noticed.

To say nothing of the periodicals which have already been commenced, and which have been for some time our fellow-laborers, in this all-important work, besides our debates of 1820, 1823, and 1829, four editions of the new version of the New Testament, with prefaces, various tables, notes, criticisms, etc., there have been issued from our press *twelve volumes* in illustration and defence of these principles, in hearing and answering objections from all sects, and from many of the most learned and talented of our country.

The CHRISTIAN BAPTIST, in seven annual volumes, being the first of these publications, and affording such a *gradual* development of all these principles as the state of the public mind and the opposition would permit, is, in the judgment of many of our brethren who have expressed themselves on the subject, better adapted to the whole community as it now exists, than our other writings. In this judgment I must concur; and to it especially, as well as to all other publications since commenced, I would refer the reader who may be solicitous to examine these principles more fully, and to consider the ordeal through which they have passed.

Having paid a very candid and considerate regard to all that has been offered against these principles, as well as having been admonished from the extremes into which some of our friends and brethren have carried some points, I undertake this work with a deep sense of its necessity, and with much anticipation of its utility, in exhibiting a concentrated view of the whole ground we occupy, of rectifying some extremes of furnishing new means of defence to those engaged in contending with this generation for primitive Christianity.

Having also attentively considered the most vulnerable side of every great question, and re-examined the terms and phrases which have occasioned most opposition and controversy, whether from our own pen or that of any of our brethren, our aim is now to offer to the public a more matured view of such cardinal principles as are necessary to the right interpretation of the Holy Scriptures, both in acquiring and communicating a correct knowledge of the Christian Institution of the principal Extras of the Millennial Harbinger, to lay before the exposure of error, as well as in a revised and corrected republication of the principal Extras of the Millenial Harbinger, to lay before the reader the elements of the gospel itself, and of the worship most acceptable to God, through Jesus Christ our Lord.

The work, then, naturally divides itself into three parts:—The first, THE PRINCIPLES BY WHICH THE CHRISTIAN INSTITUTION MAY BE CERTAINLY AND SATISFACTORILY ASCERTAINED; the second, THE PRINCIPLES ON WHICH ALL CHRISTIANS MAY FORM ONE COMMUNION and the third, THE ELEMENTS OR PRINCIPLES WHICH CONSTITUTE ORIGINAL CHRISTIANITY. Whether this argument be most in the order of nature, or of importance, is not the question; it is the order in which we have from necessity been compelled to consider these subjects.

A. CAMPBELL

Bethany, Va., January 2, 1835

PREFACE TO THE
SECOND EDITION

The present edition substitutes, for the first part of the last, a series of essays on the Christian System, and somewhat enlarges on the second. The continual misconception of our views on some very fundamental points of the Christian System seem at the present crisis to call for a very definite, clear, and connected view of the great outlines and elements of the Christian Institution, and more especially with a reference to a great question, which we anticipate soon to be the all-absorbing question of Protestant Christendom—viz.: *How may schisms cease, and all Christians unite, harmonize and co-operate in one great community, as at the beginning?*

Things ecclesiastic are moving forward to a new issue. The Christian system is undergoing an examination in the pesent day, both as to its evidences and signification, wholly unprecedented since the days of the grand defection. Such an age is always an age of extremes; but things will regulate themselves and settle down on the true foundation. "Many are running to and fro;" and certainly knowledge is on the increase.

The Christian System, as unfolded in the following essays, would, but for the special essays on the "Kingdom of Heaven," "Remission of Sins," "Regeneration," and "Breaking the Loaf," have been more systematically and fully developed. Sundry points are meagerly discussed in the new essays, because of their recurrence in those elaborate articles which have been so often published. We have, indeed. aimed first at giving a general view, leaving the important details on the most disputable points for those essays.

Instead of the "Dialogue on the Holy Spirit," so generally read and so fully discussed, we have added a few essays, on CHURCH ORDER as a part of the Christian system; thus endeavoring to give to the book all the chances of being as useful as possible to those who are desirous of a more perfect understanding of our attainments in Christian knowledge. We speak for ourselves only; and, while we are always willing to give a declaration of our faith and knowledge of the Christian system, we firmly protest against dogmatically propounding our own views, or those of any fallible mortal, as a condition or foundation of church union and co-operation. While, then, we would, if we could, either with the tongue or the pen, proclaim all that we believe, and all that we know, to the ends of the earth, *we take the Bible, the whole Bible, and nothing but the Bible, as the foundation of all Christian union and communion.* Those who do not like this will please show us a more excellent way.

A. CAMPBELL

Bethany, Va., June 13, 1839

THE CHRISTIAN SYSTEM

CHAPTER I

I. One God, one system of nature, one universe. That universe is composed of innumerable systems, which, in perfect concert, move forward in subordination to one supreme end. That one end of all things is the sovereign and infinite pleasure of him who inhabits eternity and animates the universe with his presence. So worship and adore the heavenly hierarchies, saying, "Thou art worthy, O Lord, to receive glory, and honor, and power; for thou hast created all things, and for thy pleasure they were created."

II. The universe is a system of systems, not only as respects the seventy-five millions of suns and their attendant planets, which fill up the already-discovered fields of ethereal space, but in reference to the various systems, separate, though united; distinct, though amalgamated; heterogeneous, though homogeneous; which are but component parts of every solar system, of every planet in that system, and of every organic and inorganic mass on each planet. Thus, in the person of a single individual man, we have an animal system, an intellectual system, a moral system, running into each other, and connecting themselves with everything of a kindred nature in the whole universe of God, just as we have in the human body itself a system of solids, and a system of fluids; and these again forming themselves into a system of bones, a system of nerves, a system of arteries, a system of veins, etc.

III. Now, as no one system is insular and independent, no system can be understood abstractly. Every particular system must be viewed in reference to that system which is proximate to it in nature and use. Thus we view the bones in the human body as connected with the muscles; the muscles as connected with the nerves; the nerves as connected with the arteries; the arteries as connected with the veins; and this all as connected with all the human frame, and with the fluids evolved by them, or circulated through them, etc.

1

IV. As, then, the systems of the universe, and the sciences which treat of them, run into each other and mutually lend and borrow light, illustration, and development, it is a mark of imbecility of mind rather than of strength—of folly rather than of wisdom—for any one to dogmatize with an air of infallibility, or to assume the attitude of perfect intelligence on any one subject of human thought, without an intimate knowledge of the whole universe. But, as such knowledge is not within the grasp of feeble mortal man, whose horizon is a point of creation, and whose days are but a moment of time, it is superlatively incongruous for any son of science, or of religion, to affirm that this or that issue is absolutely irrational, unjust, or unfitting the schemes of eternal Providence or the purposes of the supreme wisdom and benevolence, only as he is guided by the oracles of infallible wisdom or the inspirations of the Almighty. Who could pronounce upon the wisdom and utility of a single joint without a knowledge of the limb to which it belongs; of that limb, without understanding of the body to which it ministers; of that body, without a clear perception of the world in which it moves, and of the relations which it sustains; of that world, without some acquaintance with the solar system of which it is but a small part; of that particular solar system, without a general and even intimate knowledge of all the kindred systems; of all these kindred systems, without a thorough comprehension of the ultimate design of the whole creation; of that ultimate design, without a perfect intelligence of that incomprehensible Being by whom and for whom all things were created and made? How gracefully, then, sits unassuming modesty on all the reasonings of man! The true philosopher and the true Christian, therefore, delight always to appear in the unaffected costume of humility, candor, and docility.

"He who through vast immensity can pierce,
See worlds on worlds compose one universe;
Observe how system into system runs,
What other planets circle other suns,
What varied beings people every star—
May tell why God has made us as we are."
—*Pope.*

CHAPTER II

THE BIBLE

I. One God, one moral system, one Bible. If nature be a system, religion is no less so. God is "a God of order," and that is the same as to say he is a God of system. Nature and religion, the offspring of the same supreme intelligence, bear the image of one father—twin-sisters of the same divine parentage. There is an intellectual and a moral universe as clearly bounded as the system of material nature. Man belongs to the whole three. He is an animal, intellectual, and moral being. *Sense* is his guide in nature, *faith* in religion, *reason* in both. The Bible contemplates man primarily in his spiritual and eternal relations. It is the history of nature so far only as is necessary to show man his origin and destiny, for it contemplates nature—the universe—only in relation to man's body, soul, and spirit.

II. The Bible is to the intellectual and moral world of man what the sun is to the planets in our system—the fountain and source of light and life, spiritual and eternal. There is not a spiritual idea in the whole human race that is not drawn from the Bible. As soon will the philosopher find an independent sunbeam in nature, as the theologian a spiritual conception in man, independent of *The One Best Book*.

III. The Bible, or the Old and New Testaments, in Hebrew and Greek, contains a full and perfect revelation of God and his will, adapted to man as he now is. It speaks of man as he was, and also as he will hereafter be; but it dwells on man *as he is*, and *as he ought to be*, as its peculiar and appropriate theme. It is not, then, a treatise on man as he was, nor on man as he will be; but on man as he is, and as he ought to be; not as he is physically, astronomically, geologically, politically, or metaphysically; but as he is and ought to be, *morally* and *religiously*.

IV. The words of the Bible contain all the ideas in it. These words, then, rightly understood, and the ideas are clearly perceived. The words and sentences of the Bible are to be translated, interpreted, and understood according to the same code of laws and principles of interpretation by which other ancient writings are translated and understood; for, when God spoke to man in his own language, he spoke as one person converses with another—in the fair, stipulated, and well-established meaning of the terms. This is essential to its character, as a revelation from God; otherwise it would be no revelation, but would always require a class of inspired men to unfold and reveal its true sense to mankind.

V. We have written frequently and largely upon the principles and rules of interpretation, as of essential importance and utility in this generation of remaining mysticizing and allegorizing. From our former writings we shall here only extract the naked rules of interpretation, deduced from extensive and well-digested premises; fully sustained, too, by the leading translators and most distinguished critics and commentators of the last and present centuries.

VI. RULE 1. On opening any book in the sacred Scriptures, con-

sider first the historical circumstances of the book. These are the order, the title, the author, the date, the place, and the occasion of it.

The *order* in historical compositions is of much importance; as, for instance, whether the first, second, or third, of the five books of Moses, or of any other series of narrative, or of even epistolary, communications.

The *title* is also of importance, as it sometimes expresses the *design* of the book. As *Exodus*—the departure of Israel from Egypt; *Acts of Apostles,* etc.

The peculiarities of the *author,* the age in which he lived, his style, mode of expression, illustrate his writings. The date, place, and occasion of it, are obviously necessary to a right application of any thing in the book.

RULE 2. In examining the contents of any book, as respects precepts, promises, exhortations, etc., *observe who it is that speaks, and under what dispensation he officiates.* Is he a Patriarch, a Jew, or a Christian? *Consider also the persons addressed, their prejudices, character, and religious relations.* Are they Jews or Christians, believers or unbelievers, approved or disapproved? This rule is essential to the proper application of every command, promise, threatening, admonition, or exhortation, in Old Testament or New.

RULE 3. To understand the meaning of what is commanded, promised, taught, etc., *the same philological principles, deduced from the nature of language, or the same laws of interpretation which are applied to the language of other books, are to be applied to the language of the Bible.*

RULE 4. *Common usage, which can only be ascertained by testimony, must always decide the meaning of any word which has but one signification;* but when words have, according to testimony (*i. e.,* the Dictionary), more meanings than one, whether literal or figurative, *the scope, the context, or parallel passages must decide the meaning;* for if common usage, the design of the writer, the context, and parallel passages fail, there can be no certainty in the interpretation of language.

RULE 5. *In all tropical language ascertain the point of resemblance, and judge of the nature of the trope, and its kind, from the point of resemblance.*

RULE 6. In the interpretation of symbols, types, allegories and parables, this rule is supreme:—*Ascertain the point to be illustrated; for comparison is never to be extended beyond that point—to all the attributes, qualities, or circumstances of the symbol, type, allegory, or parable.*

Rule 7. For the salutary and sanctifying intelligence of the Oracles of God, the following rule is indispensable:

We must come within the understanding distance.

There is a distance which is properly called *the speaking distance,* or *the hearing distance;* beyond which the voice reaches not, and the ears hear not. To hear another, we must come within that circle which the voice audibly fills.

Now we may with propriety say, that as it respects God, there is an understanding distance. All beyond that distance can not understand God; all within it can easily understand him in all matters of piety and morality. God himself is the center of that circle, and humility is its circumference.

The wisdom of God is as evident in adapting the light of the Sun of Righteousness to our spiritual or moral vision, as in adjusting the light of day to our eyes. The light reaches us without an effort of our own, but we must open our eyes, and if our eyes be sound, we enjoy the natural light of heaven. There is a sound eye in reference to spiritual light, as well as in reference to material light. Now, while the philological principles and rules of interpretation enable many men to be skilful in biblical criticism, and in the interpretation of words and sentences, who neither perceive nor admire the *things* represented by those words; the sound eye contemplates the things themselves, and is ravished with the moral scenes which the Bible unfolds.

The moral *soundness* of vision consists in having the eyes of the understanding fixed solely on God himself, his approbation and complacent affection for us. It is sometimes called a *single* eye because it looks for one thing supremely. Every one, then, who opens the Book of God, with *one aim,* with one ardent desire—intent only to know the will of God—to such a person the knowledge of God is easy; for the Bible is framed to illuminate such, and only such, with the salutary knowledge of things celestial and divine.

Humility of mind, or what is in effect the same, contempt for all earth-born pre-eminence, prepares the mind for the reception of this light; or, what is virtually the same opens the ears to hear the voice of God. Amidst the din of all the arguments from the flesh, the world, and Satan, a person is so deaf that he can not hear the still small voice of God's philanthropy. But, receding from pride, covetousness, and false ambition; from the love of the world; and in coming within that circle, the circumference of which is unfeigned humility, and the center of which is God himself—the voice of God is distinctly heard and clearly understood. All within this circle are taught by God; all without it are under the influence of the wicked one. "God resisteth the proud, but he giveth grace to the humble."

He, then, that would interpret the Oracles of God to the salvation of his soul, must approach this volume with the humility and docility of a child, and meditate upon it day and night. Like Mary, he must sit at the Master's feet, and listen to the words which fall from his lips. To such a one there is an assurance of understanding, a certainty of knowledge, to which the man of letters alone never attained, and which the mere critic never felt.

VII. The Bible is a book of facts, not of opinions, theories, abstract generalities, nor of verbal definitions. It is a book of awful facts, grand and sublime beyond description. These facts reveal God and man, and contain within them the reasons of all piety and righteousness, or what is commonly called religion and morality. The meaning of the Bible facts is the true biblical doctrine. History is, therefore, the plan pursued in both Testaments; for testimony has primarily to do with faith, and reasoning with the understanding. History has, we say, to do with facts—and religion springs from them. Hence, the history of the past, and the anticipation of the future, or what are usually called history and prophecy, make up exactly four-fifths of all the volumes of inspiration.

CHAPTER III

GOD

I. "I am that I am." "I lift up my hand to heaven and say, *I live forever.*" "The *everlasting God*, the Lord, the Creator of the ends of the earth, fainteth not, neither is weary; there is no searching of his *understanding.*" "His understanding is infinite." "Do not I *fill* heaven and earth, saith the Lord." "For thus saith the *high* and *lofty* One that *inhabiteth eternity*, whose name is *Holy*, I dwell in the high and holy place; with him also that is of a contrite and humble spirit, to revive the spirit of the humble, and to revive the heart of the contrite ones." "I beseech thee show me thy *glory;* and he said, I will make all my goodness pass before thee, and I will proclaim the name of the Lord before thee; and will be gracious to whom I will be gracious, and will show mercy on whom I will show mercy." "And the Lord passed by before him,[1] and proclaimed, The Lord, the Lord God, merciful and gracious, long-suffering, abundant in goodness and in truth, keeping mercy for thousands, forgiving iniquity, and trans-

---

[1] Moses.

gression, and sin, and that by no means acquits the guilty; visiting the iniquity of the fathers upon the children, and upon the children's children, unto the third and to the fourth generation"—"and showing mercy unto thousands of them that love me and keep my commandments." "O Lord God of Israel, who dwellest between the cherubims, thou art the God, even *thou alone;* thou hast made heaven and earth. Hear, O Israel, Jehovah our Aleim is one Jehovah[1]—the Lord our God is one Lord." "Holy, holy, holy, Lord God Almighty, which wast, and art, and art to come." "Great and marvellous are thy works, Lord God Almighty; just and true are thy ways thou king of saints." "Who shall not fear thee, O Lord, and glorify thy name, for thou alone art holy?" "He is the Rock: his work is perfect, for all his ways are judgment; a God of truth and without iniquity: just and right is he." "Glorious in holiness, fearful in praise, doing wonders."

II. Such are a few—a specimen of the Divine declarations concerning himself, repeated and re-echoed by the purest and most intellectual beings in heaven and earth. It is from his word and his works we learn the being and perfections of God. As we form a character of man from what he says and what he does, so learn we the Divine character. "The heavens declare his glory, and the firmament showeth forth his handiwork: day unto day uttereth speech, and night unto night showeth knowledge." Creation reveals the power, the wisdom, and the goodness of God—Providence proclaims also his justice, truth, and holiness. Redemption develops his mercy, condescension, and love; and all these are again characterized by infinity, eternity, immutability. Nature, then, attests and displays the knowledge, wisdom, power, and goodness of God. The law and the providence of God especially declare his justice, truth, and holiness; while the gospel unfolds his mercy, condescension, and love: and all these proclaim that God is infinite, eternal, and immutable. God appears before the universe of intellectuals in the threefold attitude of Creator, Lawgiver, and Redeemer; and, although each of these involves and reveals many of his excellencies, still in each department three are most conspicuous. As Creator, wisdom, power, and goodness; as Lawgiver, justice, truth, and holiness; as Redeemer, mercy, condescension, and love. In each and all of which departments he is infinite, immutable, and eternal.

III. But the Scriptures speak of his divinity, or godhead, as well as of the unity, spirituality, and eternity of his being. We have not, indeed, much said upon this incomprehensible theme; for who by searching can find out God, or know the Almighty to perfection? "The knowledge of him is high as heaven: what canst thou do?

---

[1] So reads the Hebrew. (Deut. 5:4.)

Deeper than hell: what canst thou know? The measure thereof is longer than the earth, and broader than the sea."

IV. Paul and Peter indeed speak of the divine nature in the abstract, or of the divinity or godhead. These are the most abstract terms found in the Bible. Eternity and divinity are, however, equally abstract and almost equally rare in Holy Writ. Still they are necessarily found in the divine volume; because we must abstract *nature* from *person* before we can understand the remedial system. For the divine nature may be communicated or imparted in some sense; and, indeed, while it is essentially and necessarily singular, it is certainly plural in its personal manifestations. Hence we have the Father, Son, and Holy Spirit equally divine, though personally distinct from each other. We have, in fact, but one God, one Lord, one Holy Spirit; yet these are equally possessed of one and the same divine nature.

V. Some conceive of God as a mathematical unit; and as a thing can not be both mathematically singular and plural—one and three, at the same time and in the same sense—they deny the true and proper divinity of the Son of God and of the Spirit of God. But it would seem to us that they reason not in harmony with the sacred style of inspiration. But why should we imagine that there can not be a plurality of personal manifestations in the divine nature any more than in the angelic or human, especially as man was created in the image of God?

VI. The *relations* in human plurality are indeed limited to *three:* for while all the human nature was at one time originally and wholly in the person of Adam, it was afterwards found equally in the person of Eve; and again in the person of their first-born. Now, as to its derivation and mode of existence, it was diverse in the three. In Adam it was underived as respected human nature, in Eve it was derived from Adam, and in Cain it was again derived from Adam and Eve. Here the matter ends; for while Eve proceeded from Adam in one mode, and Cain proceeded from Adam and Eve in another, all the residue of human nature is participated without any new relation or mode of impartation. While, then, our nature is plural as to its participation, it is limited to three relations or modes of existence. Now, as man was made in the image of God, we must conceive of him as having plurality, relation, and society in himself—though far be it from us to suppose that the divine nature either is or can be fairly or fully exhibited by any resemblance or illustration drawn from angel or from man, or from any created thing. Still there is a resemblance between God and the sun that shines upon us—between God and an angel—between God and man; and even in the mode of his existence, and in the varieties of relation and personal manifestation, there is so much resemblance as to peremptorily forbid all dogmatism as to what is, or is not, compatible with the unity, spirituality, and immutability of God. But of this more fully and intelligibly when we shall have examined the record concerning the Word and the Spirit of God.

CHAPTER IV

THE SON OF GOD

I. "The holy progeny [or thing] which shall be born of thee shall be called *the Son of God.*" "Unto us a child is born; unto us a son is given, and the government shall be upon his shoulder, and his name shall be called Wonderful, Counsellor, the Mighty God, the Everlasting Father, the Prince of Peace." "This is my Son, the Beloved; hear him." "No person has ascended into heaven, but he that came down from heaven, even the Son of Man, who is in heaven," or whose abode is in heaven. "God so loved the world that he gave his *only begotten* Son, the only begotten of the Father, full of grace and truth." "No man has seen God at any time; the only begotten Son, who is the bosom of the Father, has declared him." "Rabbi, thou art the Son of God, thou art the King of Israel." "Glorify thou me with thine own self, with the glory which I had with thee before the world was." "In him dwells all the fulness of the godhead[1] bodily," or substantially. "He is the first and the last." "All things were created by him and for him." "In the beginning was the Word, and the Word was with God, and the Word was God. All things were made by him, and without him was not any thing made that was made." "The Word was made flesh and dwelt among us; and we beheld his glory, the glory as of an only begotten of the Father, full of grace and truth."

II. So speak the Divine Oracles of the supreme deity and excellency of the author and perfecter of the Christian system. "By him

---

[1] The Apostle here uses the word *Theotees* (Col. 2:9), which is but once found in the New Testament. We have, indeed, *Theiotees* (Rom. 1:20), from the same Apostle, also found but once, translated *godhead*. We have also *Theios, Theion*, three times; once (Acts 16:29), translated *divinity:* and by Peter (2 Pet. 1:3, 4), twice; once in connection with *power*, and once with *nature*—"his divine power"; a "divine nature." "The fulness of the Deity," or godhead, indicates all divine excellency—all the perfections of God. "The *fulness*" of that divine nature is here contrasted with an *empty* and deceitful philosophy (verse 8), and the term *bodily* superadded, shows that God is in Christ, not, as he was in the tabernacle or temple, typically, but substantially, literally, and truly.

and for him" all things were created and made; and "he is before all things, and by him all things consist." But "he became flesh." Who? He that existed before the universe, whose mysterious, sublime, and glorious designation was the *Word of God.* Before the Christian system, before the *relation* of Father, Son, and Holy Spirit began to be, his rank in the divine nature was that of the *Word of God.* Wonderful name! Intimate and dear relation! The relation between a word and the idea which it represents is the nearest of all relations in the universe: for the idea is in the word, and the word is in the idea. The idea is invisible, inaudible, unintelligible, but in and by the word. An idea can not be without an image or a word to represent it; and therefore God was never without his word, nor was his word without him. "The Word was with God, and the Word was God"; for a word is the idea *expressed:* and thus the "Word that was made flesh" became "the brightness of his glory," and "the *express* image of his person"—insomuch that "he who has seen the Son has seen the Father also."

III. While, then, the phrase "Son of God" denotes a temporal relation, the phrase "the Word of God" denotes an eternal, unoriginated relation. There was *a word of God* from eternity, but the Son of God began to be in the days of Augustus Caesar. "Thou art my Son, this day have I begotten thee." He was by his resurrection from the dead declared to be the Son of God with a power and evidence extraordinary and divine. The Word incarnate or dwelling in human flesh, is the person called our Lord and Redeemer, Jesus Christ; and while in the system of grace the Father is the *one God* in all the supremacy of his glory, Jesus is the *one Lord* in all the divine fulness of sovereign, supreme, and universal authority. The Lord of Shem, of Abraham, Isaac, and Jacob, is the God and the Lord of Christians: for "the child" that has been born to us, and "the son" that has been given according to another Prophet, came from eternity: "His goings forth have been from of old, from everlasting."[1] Such is the evangelical history of the author of the Christian system as to his antecedent nature and relation in the deity or godhead.

IV. He became a true and proper "Son of Man." "A body hast thou prepared me." But the "me" was before "the body." It dwelt forever "in the bosom of the Father." "I came forth from God," said "the incarnate Word." Great beyond expression and "without controversy, great is the mystery—the secret of godliness." "God was manifest in the flesh." "He that has seen me has seen the Father also." The Son of Man was and is the Son of God—"Emanuel, God

---

[1] Micah 5:2.

with us." Adored be his name! The one God in the person of the Father has commanded all men to worship and honor the one Lord, as they would honor him that sent him: for now in glorifying the Son we glorify the Father that sent him and that dwells in him. "Know ye not that I am in the Father, and the Father in me?" Thus spake our Lord Jesus Christ.

CHAPTER V

THE SPIRIT OF GOD

I. As there is man and the spirit of man, so there is God and the Spirit of God. They are capable of a separate and distinct existence. "What man knoweth the things of a man," says Paul, "but the spirit of man that is in him? even so the things of God knoweth no man but the Spirit of God." There is in this case an image of God in man —not, indeed, an exact image, but an image; for as Paul says of the law, so say we of man—"For the law had a shadow [a resemblance] of good things to come, and not the very [or exact] image of the things." So man was made an image of God, though not the exact image. The active power of man is in his spirit. So John the Baptist came in the *power* of Elijah, because he came in his *spirit*. The Spirit of God is therefore often used for his power; though it is not an impersonal power, but a living, energizing, active, personal existence. Hence in all the works of God the Spirit of God is the active, operating agent. Thus in the old creation, while ancient chaos yet remained—when "the earth was without form and void, and darkness brooded on the bosom of the vast abyss," the Spirit of God "moved [incubated and energized] upon the face of the waters." "The hand of the Lord has made me, and the Spirit of the Almighty has given me life." "The Holy Spirit shall come upon thee, and the *power* of the Highest shall overshadow thee." And thus was chaos subdued, man vitalized, "the heavens garnished," and the body of Jesus made by the Spirit of God.

II. The Spirit is said to do, and time have done, all that God does and all that God has done. It has ascribed to it all divine perfections and works; and in the New Testament it is designated as the immediate author and agent of the new creation, and of the holiness of Christians. It is therefore called *the Holy Spirit*. In the sublime and ineffable relation of the deity, or godhead, it stands next to the Incarnate Word. Anciently, or before time, it *was* God, the *Word* of God, and the *Spirit* of God. But now, in the development of the

Christian scheme, *it is* "the Father, the Son, and the Holy Spirit"—one God, one Lord, one Spirit.   To us Christians there *is*, then, but one God, even the Father; and one Lord Jesus Christ, even the Saviour; and one Spirit, even the Advocate, the Sanctifier, and the Comforter of Christ's body—the church.   Jesus is the *head*, and the Spirit is the *life* and animating principle of that body.

III. The whole systems of creation, providence, and redemption are founded upon these relations in the Deity.   Destroy these, blend and confound these, and nature, providence, and grace are blended, confounded, and destroyed.   The peerless and supreme excellency of the Christian system is, that it fully opens to the vision of mortals the divinity—the whole godhead—employed in the work of man's regeneration and ultimate glorification.   God is manifest in human flesh, and is justified and glorified by the Spirit, in accomplishing man's deliverance from ruin.   Each name of the sacred three has its own peculiar work and glory in the three great works of Creation, Government, and Redemption.   Hence we are, by divine authority, immersed into the name of the Father, the Son, and the Holy Spirit, in coming into the kingdom of grace; and while in that kingdom the supreme benediction is, "The *grace* of the Lord Jesus Christ, and the *love* of God, and the *communion* of the Holy Spirit, be with you!" Indeed, in the old church that was in the wilderness, while matters were comparatively in the shadows of a moonlight age, the High-Priest of Israel was commanded to put the *name* of God upon the children of Israel, in the same relation of the sacred three—"The Lord[1] bless thee and keep thee—The Lord make his face shine upon thee, and be *gracious* unto thee—The Lord lift up his countenance upon thee, and give thee peace."[2] "Jehovah bless thee" is equal to "the love of God."   "Jehovah be gracious unto thee" answers to "the grace of our Lord Jesus Christ."   And "Jehovah lift up his countenance upon thee, and give thee peace," corresponds to "the communion of the Spirit."

IV. The divine doctrine of these holy and incomprehensible relations in the Divinity is so inwrought and incorporated with all the parts of the sacred book—so identified wth all the dispensations of religion—and so essential to the mediatorship of Christ, that it is impossible to make any real and divine proficiency in the true knowledge of God, of man, of reconciliation, or remission of sins, of eternal life, or in the piety and divine life of Christ's religion, without a clear and distinct perception of it, as well as a firm and unshaken faith and confidence in it, as we trust still to make more evident in the sequel.

---

[1] In the Hebrew Bible it is Jehovah each time.   [2] Numbers 6:24-28.

CHAPTER VI

MAN AS HE WAS

I. The original man was the rational and moral ultimatum of the mundane system. Naturally, or as he came from God's hand, he was the perfection of all terrestrial creations and institutions. In the elements of his constitution he was partly celestial and terrestrial—of an earthly material as to his body, but of spiritual intelligence and divine life. Made to know and to enjoy his Creator, and to have communion with all that is divine, spiritual, and material in the whole universe, he was susceptible of an almost boundless variety of enjoyments.

II. And God said, "Let us make man in our image, after our likeness, and let them have dominion over the fish of the sea, and the fowl of the air, and over the cattle, and over all the earth, and over every creeping thing that creepeth upon the earth. So God created man in his own image, in his own image created he him; male and female created he them." (Gen. 1:26, 27.) Man, then, was a companion of his Father and Creator, capable of admiring, adoring, and enjoying God. Having made the earth for him, God was fully glorified in all his sublunary works when they made man happy, grateful, and thankful to himself. Man, then, in his natural state was not merely an animal but an intellectual, moral, pure, and holy being.

III. His position or state in this creation was that of a *lord tenant*. The earth is, indeed, the Lord's; but he gave it to man on a very easy and liberal lease, and so it became his property. He was therefore, a free and responsible agent, capable of managing his estate and paying his rent; and consequently was susceptible of virtue and of vice, of happiness and misery. In order to freedom, virtue, and happiness, it was expedient and necessary to place him under a law; for where there is no law there can be no liberty, virtue, or happiness. The law became a test of his character, a guarantee of his continued enjoyment of the life and property which God had leased to him on the condition of his obedience to that precept.

IV. That the temptation to disobedience might be weak, and the motive to obedience strong, single, and pure, the precept given here was simple, positive, and clear. It could not be a moral precept, because other reasons than simple submission to the will of his Lord and King might have co-operated and prevented that display of pure loyalty by which his character was to be tried and his future fortunes governed. It was therefore a positive law. The requisition was so little as to present the least conceivable restraint upon liberty of thought and of action, and yet it was the most infallible test of his

loyalty. The Adamic constitution was therefore admirably designed
and adapted to happiness. It placed only one restriction in the way
of universal liberty, and that at such a distance as to make the circle
of his free and unrestrained movements within a single step of the
last outpost of all intellectual, moral, and sensible enjoyment. The
whole earth was his to use, one single fruit alone excepted. Truly,
God was superlatively good and kind to man in his peculiar constitution and state. "Thou madest him a little lower than the angels, and hast crowned him with glory and honour. Thou madest
him to have dominion over the works of thy hands. Thou hast put
all things under his feet: all sheep and oxen; yea, and the beasts of
the field, the fowls of the air, and the fish of the sea, and whatsoever
passes through the paths of the sea. O Lord, our Lord, how excellent is thy name in all the earth!" (Psalm 8:5-9.)

CHAPTER VII

MAN AS HE IS

I. "God made man upright, but they have sought out many inventions." Adam rebelled. The natural man became preternatural.
The animal triumphed over the human elements of his nature. Sin
was born on earth. The crown fell from his head. The glory of the
Lord departed from him. He felt his guilt, and trembled; he saw his
nakedness, and blushed. The bright candle of the Lord became a
dimly-smoking taper. He was led to judgment. He was tried, condemned to death, divested of his patrimonial inheritance; but re-
spited from immediate execution. A prisoner of death, but permitted
to roam abroad and at large till the king authorized his seizure and
destruction.

II. The stream of humanity, thus contaminated at its fountain,
can not in this world ever rise of itself to its primitive purity and excellence. We all inherit a frail constitution physically, intellectually,
but especially morally frail and imbecile. We have all inherited our
father's constitution and fortune; for Adam, we are told, after he fell
"begat a son in his own image," and that son was just as bad as any
other son ever born into the world; for he murdered his own dear
brother because he was a better man than himself. Thus "by one
man sin entered into the world, and death by that one sin; and so
death, the wages of sin, has fallen upon all the offspring of Adam,"
because in him they have all sinned, or been made mortal, and conse-

quently are born under condemnation to that death which fell upon our common progenitor because of his transgression.

III. In Adam all have sinned; therefore "in Adam all die." Your nature, gentle reader, not your person, was in Adam when he put forth his hand to break the precept of Jehovah. You did not personally sin in that act; but your nature, then in the person of your father, sinned against the Author of your existence. In the just judgment, therefore, of your heavenly Father, your nature sinned in Adam, and with him it is right that all human beings should be born *mortal*, and that death should lord it over the whole race as he has done in innumerable instances even "over them that have not sinned after the similitude of Adam's transgression," i.e., by violating a positive law. Now it must be conceded that what God can righteously and mercifully inflict upon a part of mankind, he may justly and mercifully inflict upon all; and therefore, those that live onescore or fourscore years on this earth, for the sin of their nature in Adam, might have been extinguished the first year as reasonably as those who have in perfect infancy perished from the earth. Death is expressly denominated by an apostle, "*the wages of sin.*" Now this reward of sin is at present inflicted upon at least *one-fourth* of the human race who have never violated any law, or sinned personally by any act of their lives. According to the most accurate bills of mortality, from one-third to one-fourth of the whole progeny of man die in infancy, under two years, without the consciousness of good or evil. They are thus, innocent though they be as respects actual and personal transgression, accounted as sinners by him who inflicts upon them the peculiar and appropriate wages of sin. This alarming and most strangely pregnant of all the facts in human history proves that Adam was not only the common father, but the actual representative of all his children.

IV. There is, therefore, a sin of our nature as well as personal transgression. Some inappositely call the sin of our nature our "original sin," as if the sin of Adam was the personal offence of all his children. True, indeed, it is; our nature was corrupted by the fall of Adam before it was transmitted to us; and hence that hereditary imbecility to do good, and that proneness to do evil, so universally apparent in all human beings. Let no man open his mouth against the transmission of a moral distemper, until he satisfactorily explain the fact, that the special characteristic vices of parents appear in their children as much as the colour of their skin, their hair, or the contour of their faces. A disease in the moral constitution of man is as clearly transmissible as any physical taint, if there be any truth in history, biography, or human, observation.

V. Still, man, with all his hereditary imbecility, is not under an invincible necessity to sin. Greatly prone to evil, easily seduced into transgression, he may or may not yield to passion and seduction. Hence the differences we so often discover in the corruption and depravity of man. All inherit a *fallen,* consequently a *sinful* nature, though all are not equally depraved. Thus we find the degrees of sinfulness and depravity are very different in different persons. And, although without the knowledge of God and his revealed will—without the interposition of a mediator and without faith in him—"it is impossible to please God," still there are those who, while destitute of this knowledge and belief, are more noble and virtuous than others. Thus admits Luke when he says, "The Jews in Berea were more noble than those in Thessalonica, in that they received the word with all readiness of mind, and searched the Scriptures daily whether these things were so. Therefore, many of them believed." (Acts 17:11.) But, until man in his present preternatural state believes the gospel 'report of his sins, and submits to Jesus Christ as the only Mediator and Saviour of sinners, it is impossible for him to do any thing absolutely pleasing or acceptable to God.

VI. Condemned to natural death, and greatly fallen and depraved in our whole moral constitution though we certainly are, in consequence of the sin of Adam, still, because of the interposition of the second Adam, none are punished with everlasting destruction from the presence of the Lord but those who actually and voluntarily sin against a dispensation of mercy under which they are placed: for this is the "condemnation of the world, that light has come into the world, and men *choose darkness* rather than the light, because their deeds are evil."

CHAPTER VIII

THE PURPOSES OF GOD CONCERNING MAN

I. The universe issued from the goodness of God. Not to display his power and wisdom, but to give vent to his benignity, God created the heavens and the earth, and peopled them with all variety of being. Infinite wisdom and almighty power do but execute the designs of eternal love. Goodness is the impulsive attribute which prompted all that the counsel and hand of the Lord have executed. The current of the universe all runs on the side of benevolence. "Abundant in goodness and truth," all God's designs are for the diffusion of bliss on the largest possible scale. Evil there is; but, under the benevolent administraton of the Father of mercies, there will be as much good, with as little evil, as almighty power, guided by infinite wisdom, can achieve.

II. We may conjecture much, but can know little of the origin of moral evil in God's dominions. Its history on earth is faithfully detailed in the Bible; and that, in the divine prudence, is all that is necessary to our successful warfare against its power, and blissful escape from its penal consequences. It is not necessary that we should analyze and comprehend the origin and nature of darkness in order to enjoy the light of the sun. The influences of light and darkness upon our system are quite sufficient, without any theory, to induce us to eschew the former, and delight in the latter. "By one man sin entered into the world," says Paul; and "by one tempter sin entered into man," says Moses; and "lust when it conceives brings forth sin, and sin when it is perfected brings forth death," says James the apostle; and these are the landmarks of our knowledge of the matter.

III. To limit contagion of sin, to prevent its recurrence in any portion of the universe, and to save sinners from its ruinous consequences, are the godlike purposes of the common Father of all. The gospel, or Christian system, is that only scheme which infinite intelligence and almighty love could devise for that benignant and gracious end. This purpose, like all God's purposes, is eternal and immutable. The scheme or theory was, therefore, not only arranged before the Jewish and patriarchal ages, but before the foundation of the world.

IV. The promises made to Eve, to Noah, Abraham, Isaac, Jacob, Judah, David, etc., are positive proofs that the plan was laid and the purposes perfected before the world began. For why, we ask, could God promise the conquest of Satan by the son of Eve, the blessing of all nations by the son of Abraham, etc., etc., if a scheme of this import had not been previously established? The moment that Adam, Eve, and the serpent were judged, dates the first promise of a glorious conquest over our adversary by a descendant of Eve. That promise, and the consequent institution of sacrifice—the altar, the victim, and the priest—are ample proofs that the plan was completed and a remedial system adopted antecedent to the trial of our first parents.

V. But this is not to be inferred even from premises clear and forcible as these are. It is expressly and repeatedly declared. Two things are evident as demonstration itself. The first—that all the *purposes* and *promises* of God are in Christ—in reference to him, and consummated in and by him; and, in the second place, they were all contemplated, covenanted, and systematized in him and through him *before the foundation of the world.* These two propositions are so intimately connected, that they are generally asserted in the same portions of Scripture. For example: "He hath saved us and called us with a holy calling, not according to our works, but according to his own purpose and grace which was given us *in* Christ Jesus before the world began; but is *now* made manifest by the appearing of our Saviour Jesus Christ." (2 Tim. 1:9.) Again, "Paul, an apostle of Jesus Christ, in hope of eternal life, which God, that can not lie, *promised before the world began;* but has in due time manifested his word through preaching." (Titus 1:1, 2.)[1] "He has chosen us *in him before the foundation of the world,* that we should be holy and without blame before him in love." (Eph. 1:4.) Indeed, Jesus himself intimates that the whole affair of man's redemption, even to the preparation of the eternal abodes of the righteous, was arranged ere time was born: for, in his own parable of the final judgment, he says, "Come, you blessed of my Father, inherit a *kingdom prepared for you from the foundation of the world.*" (Matt. 25:34.) And Peter settles the matter forever by assuring us that we "were redeemed by the precious blood of Christ, as of a lamb without blemish and without spot, who verily was foreordained *before the foundation of the world.*" Christ, then, is the Lamb that was *foreordained,* and "slain from the foundation of the world." "Therefore," says Jesus to his Father, speaking doubtless in contemplation of his work, "Thou lovedst me before the foundation of the world"; and thus, as Matthew quotes a Prophet speaking of him, "he uttered things which had been kept secret from the foundation of the world."

VI. Evident then it is, that the whole remedial or gospel system was purposed, arranged, and established upon the basis of the revealed distinctions of Father, Son, and Holy Spirit; and by these, in reference to one another, before the foundation of the world; and that all the institutions and developments of religion in the different ages of the world were, in pursuance of that system, devised in eternity, and consummated some two thousand years ago.

VII. Jesus of Nazareth, the promised Messiah, was elected, or rather was always the elect, the beloved of God, and appointed to be

---

[1] In the original the phrase in these two passages is *pro chronoon aionoon,* translated sometimes, "before the time of the ages"—before the Jewish jubilees or ages began: and means that God's purpose to call the Gentiles was antecedent to the covenants with Abraham and the Jews. Thus understood, it only proves that the purposes and promises of God in Christ were formed and expressed before the days of Abraham. But it is equally true as respects the beginning of time: for the phrase *pro* and *apo katabole kosmou,* found *ten times* in the New Testament, literally indicates the foundation of the world. We quote Ephesians 1:4; Matthew 25:31; 1 Peter 1:9 as unequivocally declarative of this.

the foundation of this new creation. "Behold," said Jehovah, seven centuries before his birth, "I lay in Zion for a foundation a stone, a tried stone, a precious corner, a sure foundation," called by Peter "an elect stone," though disallowed by the Jewish builders. Again, by the same prophet he is called the elect of God: "Behold my servant whom I uphold, mine *elect* in whom my soul delights! I have put my spirit upon him: he shall bring forth judgment to the Gentiles," etc. "He shall be for salvation to the ends of the earth."

VIII. In consequence of these gracious purposes of God, the Word was made flesh, and dwelt among us—the Son of God was *sent* by his Father—became a Prophet, a High-Priest, and a King over men, that he might be the mediator and administrator of an institution of grace. He became the righteous servant of Jehovah, a voluntary sacrifice for us—died, was buried, and rose again—ascended where he had been before—then, in union with his Father, sent the Holy Spirit, who proceeded forth from the presence and by the authority of the Father and the Son, to consummate the sanctification of his people. He is now placed upon the throne of God—head over all things to complete the triumphs of his cause—to lead many sons to glory—to raise the dead, judge the world, and revenge Satan and all that took part with him in his rebellion, whether angels or men—to create new heavens and a new earth, and to establish eternal peace, and love, and joy through all the new dominions which he shall have gained, and over which he shall have reigned: for he must reign till all his and our enemies shall have been subdued forever. Then he shall resign into the hands that gave him his empire all that species of authority which he exercised in this great work of human deliverance. Then God himself, in his antecedent character and glory, as he reigned before sin was born and his administration began, shall preside over all things in all places forever and ever.

IX. The present elect of God are, then, those who are *in Christ*, and not those out of him: for it was *in him* that God has set his affection upon them, and chose them to eternal life before the world began. God is not, indeed, in this whole affair a respecter of persons. It is at character, and not at person, that God looks. He has predestinated all that are in Christ "to be holy and without blame before him in love," and, at his coming, to be conformed to him in all personal excellency and beauty and to share with him the bliss of a glorious immortality. So that "we shall be like him"—he the *first-born*, and we his junior brethren, bearing his image in our persons as exactly as we now bear the image of the earthly Adam, the father of us all.

X. In all these gracious purposes of God, two things are most remarkable:—First, that he has elected and called certain persons to high and responsible stations as parts of a grand system of practical philanthropy—such as Abraham, Isaac, Jacob, Joseph, Moses, Aaron, Joshua, David, Paul, etc., etc. These were chosen and elevated not for their own sakes, so much as for public benefactors and blessings to the human race. It is not for its own sake that the eye is so beautiful, or performs the functions of vision; nor that the ear is so curiously fashioned, and performs the office of hearing; but for the general comfort and safety of the whole body. So stand in the family of God—in the body of Christ—all apostles, prophets, preachers, reformers, and all specially called and chosen persons. As the Lord said to Saul of Tarsus, so may it be said of all those sons of oil— those elect ones—"I have appeared to you to make you a minister and a witness for me—to send you to the Gentiles," etc.—*to make you a public benefactor.* Next to this remarkable fact is another still more remarkable;—that, according to the purposes of God in reference to the whole human race, things are so arranged and set in order, that all enjoyments shall be, as respects human agency, *conditional;* and that every man, in reference to spiritual and eternal blessings, shall certainly and infallibly have his own choice. Therefore life and death, good and evil, happiness and misery, are placed before man as he now is, and he is commanded to make his own election and take his choice. Having chosen the good portion, he is then to "give all diligence to make his *calling* and *election* sure."

CHAPTER IX

RELIGION FOR MAN, AND NOT MAN FOR RELIGION

I. Religion, as the term imports, began after the Fall; for it indicates a previous apostasy. A remedial system is for a diseased subject. The primitive man could love, wonder, and adore as angels now do, without religion; but man, fallen and apostate, needs religion in order to his restoration to the love, and worship, and enjoyment of God. Religion, then, is a system of means of reconciliation—an institution for bringing man back to God—something to bind man anew to love and delight in God.[1]

II. It consists of two departments:—the things that God has done for us, and the things that we must do for ourselves. The whole proposition of necessity in this case must come from the offended party. Man could propose nothing, do nothing to propitiate his Creator,

---

[1] *Religo,* with all its Latin family, imports a *binding again,* or *tying fast* that which was dissolved.

after he had rebelled against him. Heaven, therefore, overtures; and man accepts, surrenders, and returns to God. The Messiah is a *gift*, sacrifice is a gift, justification is a gift, the Holy Spirit is a gift, eternal life is a gift, and even the means of our personal sanctification is a gift from God. Truly, we are saved by *grace*. Heaven, we say, *does* certain things for us, and also *proposes* to us what we should do to inherit eternal life. It is all of God; for he has sent his Son; he has sent his Spirit; and all that they have done, or shall do, is of free favor; and the proposition concerning our justification and sanctification is equally divine and gracious as the mission of his Son. We are only asked to accept a sacrifice which God has provided for our sins, and then the pardon of them, and to open the doors of our hearts, that the Spirit of God may come in and make its abode in us. God has provided all these blessings for us, and only requires us to accept of them freely, without any price or idea of merit on our part. But he asks us to *receive* them cordially, and to give up our hearts to him.

III. It is in the kingdom of grace, as in the kingdom of nature. Heaven provides the bread, the water, the fruits, the flowers; but we must gather and enjoy them. And if there be no merit in eating the bread which Heaven has sent for physical life and comfort, neither is there merit in eating the bread of life which came down from heaven for our spiritual life and consolation. Still, it is true, in grace, as in nature—that he that eats shall not die. Hence, there are conditions of enjoyments, though no conditions of merit, either in nature or grace. We shall therefore speak in detail of *the things which God has done*, and of *the things that we must do*, as essential to our salvation. First of the things that God has done:—

CHAPTER X

SACRIFICE FOR SIN

I. The history of sacrifice is the history of atonement, reconciliation, redemption, and remission of sins. These are not, at least in the Jewish and Christian style, exactly synonymous terms. Sacrifice atones and reconciles. It propitiates God, and reconciles man. It is the cause, and these are its effects on heaven and earth, on God and man.

II. For form's sake, and, perhaps, for the sake of perspicuity, four questions ought here to be propounded and resolved, at the very threshold of our inquiries. 1. What *is* sacrificed? 2. *To whom* is it to be offered? 3. *For whom* is it to be offered? 4. *By whom* is it to be offered? The answers are as prompt and as brief as the interrogations. 1. In its literal primary acceptance, it is *"the solemn and religious infliction of death upon an innocent and unoffending victim, usually by shedding its blood."* Figuratively, it means the offering of anything living or dead, person, or animal, or property, to God. 2. Religious sacrifice is to be offered to God alone. 3. It is to be offered for man. 4. It is to be offered by a priest.

III. The greater part of sacrifices were lambs. Hence Christ is called the Lamb of God, not because of his innocence or patience, but because "he taketh away," or beareth, "the sin of the world." It is rather, then, with a reference to his *death* than his *life*, that he is called the *Lamb* of God. Neither his *example* nor his *doctrine* could expiate sin. This required the shedding of blood: for without shedding of blood, there never was remission of sin.

IV. Priests are mediators in their proper place and meaning. But at first every man was his own priest. For as it was once right for a man to marry his sister, because he could find no other person for a wife, so was it lawful and expedient for every man to be his own priest. Thus, Adam, Abel, Noah, etc., were their own priests. In the next chapter of time, the eldest sons—then the princes of tribes— were priests of their respective tribes and people. But finally, God called and appointed such persons as Melchizedek and Aaron to these offices.

V. Sacrifice, doubtless, is as old as the Fall. The institution of it is not recorded by Moses. But he informs us, that God had respect for Abel's offering, and accepted from him a *slain lamb*. Now had it been a human institution, this could not have been the case; for a divine warrant has always been essential to any acceptable worship. The question, "Who has required this at your hands?" must always be answered by a *"thus saith the Lord,"* before an offering of mortal man can be acknowledged by the Lawgiver of the universe. "In vain," said the Great Teacher, "do you worship God, teaching for doctrines the commandments of men." God accepted the sacrifices of Noah, Abraham, Isaac, Jacob, etc., and in the Jewish system gave many laws and enactments concerning it.

VI. Now as sacrifice may be contemplated in different aspects, in reference to what it is in itself, to whom it is rendered, for whom and by whom it is offered; so in each of these relations, it may be represented under different names. Hence, it is a *"sin-offering,"* a *thank-*

offering, a *propitiation,*[1] a *reconciliation,* a *redemption.* Contemplated in reference to God, it is a propitiation; in reference to mankind, it is a reconciliation; and in another point of view, it may even be regarded as a redemption or ransom. On each of these it may be expedient to make a few remarks.

VII. Sacrifice, as respects *God,* is a *propitiation;* as respects *sinners,* it is a *reconciliation;* as respects *sin,* it is an *expiation;* as respects the *saved,* it is a *redemption.* These are aspects of the thing of cardinal value in understanding the Scriptures. As a *propitiation* or atonement[2] it is offered to God: not, indeed, to move his benevolence or to excite his mercy, but to render him propitious *according to law and justice.* It sprang from everlasting love, and is the *effect* and not the *cause* of God's benevolence to sinners. But without it God could not be propitious to us. The indignity offered his person, authority, and government, by the rebellion of man, as also the good of all his creatures, made it impossible for him, according to justice, eternal right, and his own benevolence, to show mercy without sacrifice. True, indeed, he always does prefer mercy to sacrifice, as he prefers the end to the means. But divine mercy forever sits upon the propitiatory; upon law and justice. Thus affirms Paul of Jesus, "Whom God has set forth as a *propitiatory* through faith in his blood, for a declaration of his justice—that he *might be just,* and *the justifier of the ungodly,* or of him that believeth in Jesus." In this sense only, God could not be gracious to man in forgiving him without a propitiation, or something that could justify him both to himself and all his creatures. In this acceptation of the term *atonement,* it *is found* often in the law, not less than twenty-five times in the single book of Leviticus.

VIII. As respects the sinner, we have said it is a *reconciliation.* Indeed, the term reconciliation very appropriately applies to sacrifice

---

[1] The Hebrew term *copher,* translated in the Greek Old Testament by *ilasmos,* and in the common English version, by *atonement* or propitiation, signifies a *covering.* The verb *copher,* "to *cover,"* or "to *make atonement,"* denotes the object of sacrifice; and hence Jesus is called the *ilasmos,* the covering, propitiation or atonement for our sins. (1 John 2:2 and 4:10.) It is a curious and remarkable fact, that God covered Adam and Eve with the skins of the first victims of death, instead of their *fig-leaf* robes. This may have prefigured the fact, that while sin was atoned or expiated as respects God by the life of the victim, the effect as respects man was a covering for his nakedness and shame, or his sin, which divested him of his primitive innocence and beauty, and covered him with ignominy and reproach.

[2] *Katallagee,* translated once *atonement* (Rom. 5:11), occurs in the New Testament four times. In Romans 5:11, it ought to have been *reconciliation,* as in Romans 11: 15; 2 Corinthians 5:18, 19. It is not *ilasmos, atonement* in the Jewish sense, but *katallagee, reconciliation.* God receives the atonement. and men the reconciliation. It is preposterous, then, to talk of the extent of the atonement, but not so of the reconciliation.

inasmuch as it brings forth the offended and the offender together. So far as it honors law and justice, it reconciles God to forgive; and so far as it displays to the offender love and mercy, it reconciles him to his offended Sovereign. It is, in this view, a reconciliation indeed. It propitates God and reconciles man. God's "anger is turned away" (not a turbulent passion, not an implacable wrath); but *"that moral sentiment and justice,"* which demands the punishment of the violated law, is pacified or well pleased; and man's hatred and animosity against God are subdued, overcome, and destroyed in and by the same sacrifice. Thus, in fact, it is, in reference to both parties, a reconciliation. Still, however, when we speak according to scriptural usage, and with proper discrimination, sacrifice, as respects God, is atonement or propitiation, and, as respects man, it is reconciliation. These are its reasons and its effects. "For this cause," says Paul, "Jesus is the mediator of a new institution, that *by means of death for the redemption of the transgressions* under the first institution, those who had been called might receive the promise of the eternal inheritance."[1] Again, the same writer makes the death of Christ the basis of reconciliation, saying, "Be reconciled to God," for he has made Christ a sin-offering for us; and now "God is in Christ, reconciling the world to himself."[2]

IX. As respects sin, it has been observed, sacrifice is an *expiation.* The terms purification or cleansing are in the common version preferred to *expiation.* Once, at least (Num. 35:33), we have need of a better word to represent the original than the term *cleansing.* "There can be no expiation for the land" polluted with blood "but by the blood of him that shed it." Still, if any one prefer *purification to* expiation, or even *cleansing* to either, so long as we understand each other, it is indeed a matter of very easy forbearance. The main point is, that sacrifice cancels sin, atones for sin, and puts it away. *"He put away sin,"* says Paul, *"by the sacrifice of himself."* This is expiation.

X. "The redemption, then, which is in Christ Jesus," is a *moral* and not a *commercial* consideration. If sin were only a *debt,* and not a *crime,* it might be forgiven without atonement. Nay, if sin were a debt, and sacrifice a payment of that debt, then there could be no forgiveness at all with God! For, if the Redeemer or Ransomer of man has paid the debt, justice, and not mercy or forgiveness, commands the *release,* not the *pardon* of the debtor. Some there are, however, who from inattention to the sacred style, and the meaning of biblical terms, have actually represented the death of Christ rather

---

[1] Hebrews 9:15.   [2] 2 Corinthians 5:20.

as the payment of an immense debt than as an expiation of sin, or a purification from guilt, and have thus made the pardon of sin wholly unintelligible, or rather, indeed, impossible. Every one feels, that when a third person assumes a debt, and pays it, the principal must be discharged, and can not be forgiven. But when sin is viewed in the light of a crime, and atonement offered by a third person, then it is a question of grace, whether the pardon or acquittal of the sinner shall be granted by him against whom the crime has been committed; because, even after an atonement or propitiation is made, the transgressor is yet as deserving of punishment as before. There is room, then, for both justice and mercy; for the display of indignation against sin, and the forgiveness of the sinner; in just views of sin, and of the redemption there is in and through the Lord Jesus Christ.

XI. Redemption, however, is the *deliverance from sin*, rather than the expiation or atonement for it. Thus, Christ is said "by his own blood to have obtained an eternal redemption for us."[1] Thus pardon, sanctification, and even the resurrection of the bodies of the saints, are severally contemplated as parts of our redemption, or deliverance from guilt to sin, from the power of sin, and from the punishment of sin.[2]

XII. There is a number of incongruities and inaccuracies in the controversy about the nature and extent of the atonement, which, as the mists of the morning retire from the hills before the rising sun, disappear from our mental horizon when the light of scriptural definition breaks in upon our souls. The atonement or propitiation has no "*extent*," because God alone is its object. It contemplates sin as a unit in the divine government, and therefore the "*Lamb of God* beareth away the sin of the world," and his death is a "*sin-offering*." As to its value, it is unspeakable. Commensurate it is, indeed, with the sin of the world; for it makes it just on the part of God to forgive and save every one that believeth in Jesus. Reconciliation and redemption have, however, a certain limited extent. Reconciliation is not universal, but partial. All do not believe in Jesus; all are, therefore, not reconciled to God through him. Redemption, or deliverance from the guilt, pollution, power, and punishment of sin, is only commensurate with the elect of God; i.e., with those who believe in Jesus and obey him.

XIII. They who affirm that one drop of Christ's blood could expiate the sin of the whole world, teach, without knowing it, that Christ has died in vain: for, surely the Messiah might have shed

---

[1] Hebrews 9:12.
[2] See Ephesians 1:7; Colossians 1:14; 1 Peter 3:18; Isaiah 59:20; Romans 8:23; Ephesians 1:14; 4:30.

many drops of blood and still have lived. They make his death an unmeaning superfluity or redundancy who reason thus. They also agree, without intending it, with those who view sin merely as a debt, and not a crime, and therefore say that there is no need of sin-offerings, or sacrifice, or of a divine Saviour, in order to its forgiveness.

XIV. They, too, seem to mistake the matter, and I am sorry to find such names among them as Butler, Whitby, and Macknight, who, while they contend that the death of Christ was a sacrifice, or a propitiation for sin, wholly resolve its efficacy into the mere appointment of God. According to them, God might have saved the whole world without the appearance of his Son; for the merit of efficacy of Christ's death arises not from his dignity of person, but from the mere appointment or will of God! Now we can not think that it was possible for God himself to save sinners in any other way than he has chosen; for to have paid an overprice for our redemption savors rather of prodigality than of divine wisdom and prudence. And if mere appointment was sufficient, why not, then, have continued the legal sacrifices, and have made the blood of bulls and of goats efficacious to take it away?

XV. To conclude, sacrifice is essential to remission of sins, and is therefore old as the fall of man. But the sacrifices of the patriarchal and Jewish dispensations could not and did not take away sin. They were but types of the real sacrifice; for, as Paul says, "It was not possible that the blood of bulls and goats could take away sin." And again, "If the blood of bulls and of goats, with the ashes of a heifer, did cleanse to the purification of the flesh, how much more shall the *blood of Christ*, who through an eternal spirit offers himself to God, cleanse your conscience from dead works to serve the living God?" Christ's death is, therefore, a real and sufficient sacrifice for sin, and stands in the attitudes of *propitiation, reconciliation, expiation,* and *redemption;* from which spring to us justification, sanctification, adoption, and eternal life.

XVI. The sacrifice of Christ, as before affirmed, is, as respects God, a propitiation; as respects man, a reconciliation; as respects sin, an expiation; as respects the penitent, a redemption; but the attributes that apply to it in any of these aspects do not apply to it in the others; and this oversight has, in our opinion, been the fruitful source of interminable controversies concerning the *"atonement,"* as it is most usually denominated. It is, indeed, *infinite* in value, as respects the expiation of sin, or its propitiatory power; but as respects the actual reconciliation and redemption of sinners, it is limited to those only who believe on and obey the Saviour. While, also, it is as universal as the sin of the world, the peculiar sins only of the obedient are expiated by it. Its *design,* then, is necessarily limited to all who come to God by it; while its value and efficacy are equal to the salvation of the whole world, provided only they will put themselves under the covering of its propitiatory power.

XVII. The "doctrine of the cross" being the great central doctrine of the Bible, and the very essence of Christianity—which explains all the peculiarities of the Christian system, and of the relation of Father, Son, and Holy Spirit, as far as mortals can comprehend them, and as it has been, to skeptics and to many professors, "a stone of stumbling, and a rock of offence," for the sake of some of the speculative and cavilling, who ask *why are these things so?* I subjoin an extract from the writings of Mr. Watson, on this point, which may suggest to them some useful reflections on this cardinal and all-absorbing subject:—

XVIII. "How sin may be forgiven," says Mr. Watson, "without leading to such misconceptions of the divine character as would encourage disobedience, and thereby weaken the influence of the divine government must be a problem of very difficult solution. A government which admitted no forgiveness, would sink the guilty in despair; a government which never punishes offence, is a contradiction; it can not exist. Not to punish the guilty, is to dissolve authority; to punish without mercy is to destroy, and where all are guilty, to make the destruction universal. That we can not sin with impunity, is a matter determined. The Ruler of the world is not careless on the conduct of his creatures: for that penal consequences are attached to the offence, is not a subject of argument, but it is matter of fact, evident by daily observation of the events and circumstances of the present life. It is a principle, therefore, already laid down, that the authority of God must be preserved; but it ought to be remarked, that in that kind of administration which restrains evil by penalty, and encourages obedience by favor and hope, we and all moral creatures are the interested parties, and not the Divine Governor himself, whom, because of his independent and all-sufficient nature, our transgressions can not injure. The reasons, therefore, which compel him to maintain his authority, do not terminate in himself. If he treats offenders with severity, it is for our sake, and for the sake of the moral order of the universe, to which sin, if encouraged by a negligent administration, or by entire and frequent impunity, would be the source of endless disorder and misery; and if the granting of pardon to offence be strongly and even severely guarded, so that no less a satisfaction could be accepted than the death of God's own Son, we are to refer this to the moral necessity of the case, as arising out of the general welfare of accountable creatures, liable to the deep evil of sin, and not to any reluctance on the part of our Maker to forgive,

much less to any thing vindictive in his nature, charges which have
been most inconsiderately and unfairly said to be implied in the doctrine of Christ's sacrificial sufferings. If it then be true, that the release of offending man from future punishment, and his restoration to
the divine favor, ought, for the interest of mankind themselves, and
for the instruction and caution of other beings, to be so bestowed,
that no license shall be given to offence; that God himself, while he
manifests his compassion, should not appear less just, less holy than he
really is; that his authority should be felt to be as compelling, and
that disobedience should as truly, though not unconditionally, subject
us to the deserved penalty, as though no hope of forgiveness had
been exhibited;—we ask, On what scheme, save that which is developed in the New Testament, are those necessary conditions provided
for? Necessary they are, unless we contend for a license and an impunity which shall annul all good government in the universe, a point
for which no reasonable man will contend; and if so, then we must
allow, that there is strong internal evidence of the truth of the doctrine
of Scripture, when it makes the offer of pardon consequent only upon
the securities we have mentioned. If it be said, that sin may be pardoned, in the exercise of the divine prerogative, the reply is, that if
this prerogative were exercised towards a part of mankind only, the
passing by of the rest would be with difficulty reconciled to the divine
character; and if the benefit were extended to all, government would
be at an end. This scheme of bringing men within the exercise of a
merciful prerogative does not, therefore, meet the obvious difficulty
of the case; nor is it improved by confining the act of grace only to
repentant criminals. For if repentance imply a 'renewal in the spirit
of the mind,' no criminal would of himself thus repent. But if by
repentance be meant merely remorse and terror in the immediate
view of danger, what offender, surrounded with the wreck of former
enjoyments, feeling the vanity of guilty pleasures, now past forever,
and beholding the approach of the delayed penal visitation, but
would repent? Were the principle of granting pardon to repentance
to regulate human governments, every criminal would escape, and ju-
dicial forms would become a subject of ridicule. Nor is it recognized
by the Divine Being, in his conduct to men in the present state, although in this world punishments are not final and absolute.
Repentance does not restore health injured by intemperance; property
wasted by profusion; or character once stained by dishonorable practices. If repentance alone could secure pardon, then all must be pardoned, and government dissolved, as in the case of forgiveness by the
exercise of mere prerogative; but if a merely arbitrary selection be
made, then different and discordant principles of government are in-

troduced into the divine administration, which is a derogatory supposition.

XIX. "The question proposed abstractedly, How may mercy be extended to offending creatures, the subjects of the divine government, without encouraging vice by lowering the righteous and holy character of God, and the authority of his government in the maintenance of which the whole universe of beings are interested? is, therefore, at once one of the most important and one of the most difficult that can employ the human mind. None of the theories which have been opposed to Christianity affords a satisfactory solution of the problem. They assume principles either destructive of moral government, or which can not, in the circumstances of man be acted upon. The only answer is found in the holy Scriptures. They alone show, and indeed, they alone profess to show, how God may be 'just,' and yet the 'justifier' of the ungodly. Other schemes show how he may be merciful; but the difficulty does not lie there. The gospel meets it, by declaring 'the righteousness of God,' at the same time that it proclaims his mercy. The voluntary sufferings of the divine Son of God, 'for us,' 'the just for the unjust,' magnify the justice of God; display his hatred to sin; proclaim 'the exceeding sinfulness' of transgression, by the deep and painful manner in which they were inflicted upon the Substitute; warn the persevering offender of the terribleness, as well as the certainty, of his punishment; and open the gates of salvation to every penitent. It is a part of the same divine plan, also, to engage the influence of the Holy Spirit, to awaken penitence in man, and to lead the wanderer back to himself; to renew our fallen nature in righteousness, at the moment we are justified through faith, and to place us in circumstances in which we may henceforth 'walk not after the flesh, but after the Spirit.' All the ends of government are here answered—no license is given to offence—the moral law is unrepealed—a day of judgment is still appointed—future and eternal judgments still display their awful sanctions—a new and singular display of the awful purity of the divine character is afforded —yet pardon is offered to all who seek it; and the whole world may be saved.

XX. "With such evidence of the suitableness to the case of mankind, under such lofty views of connexion with the principles and ends of moral government, does the doctrine of the atonement present itself. But other important considerations are not wanting to mark the united wisdom and goodness of that method of extending mercy to the guilty, which Christianity teaches us to have been actually and exclusively adopted. It is rendered, indeed, 'worthy of all acceptation,' by the circumstance of its meeting the difficulties we

have just dwelt upon—difficulties which could not otherwise have
failed to make a gloomy impression upon every offender awakened to
a sense of his spiritual danger; but it must be very inattentively considered, if it does not further commend itself to us, by not only removing the apprehensions we might feel as to the severity of the Divine Lawgiver, but as exalting him in our esteem, as 'the righteous
Lord, who loveth righteousness'; who surrendered his beloved Son to
suffering and death, that the influence of moral goodness might not
be weakened in the hearts of his creatures; and as a God of love, affording in this instance a view of the tenderness and benignity of his
nature, infinitely more impressive and affecting than any abstract description could convey; or than any act of creating or providential
power and grace could exhibit, and therefore most suitable to subdue
that enmity which had unnaturally grown up in the hearts of his
creatures, and which, when corrupt, they so easily transfer from a law
which restrains their inclination, to the Lawgiver himself. If it be
important to us to know the extent and reality of our danger, by the
death of Christ it is displayed, not in description, but in the most impressive action; if it be important that we should have an assurance
of the divine placability toward us, it here receives a demonstration
incapable of being heightened; if gratitude be the most powerful motive of future obedience, and one which renders command on the one
part, and active service on the other, 'not grievous, but joyous,' the
recollection of such obligations as those which the 'love of Christ' has
laid us under is a perpetual spring to this energetic affection, and will
be the means of raising it to higher and more delightful activity forever. All that can most powerfully illustrate the united tenderness
and awful majesty of God, and the odiousness of sin; all that can win
back the heart of man to his Maker and Lord, and render future obedience a matter of affection and delight, as well as duty; all that can
extinguish the angry and malignant passions of man to man; all that
can inspire a mutual benevolence, and dispose to a self-denying charity for the benefit of others; all that can arouse by hope, or tranquil-
lize by faith, is to be found in the sacrificed death of Christ, and the
principles and purpose for which it was endured."

CHAPTER XI

THE ATTRIBUTES OF A REAL SIN-OFFERING

I. A single action or event often involves, in weal or woe, a family, a nation, an empire. Who can count the effects or bearings of the
elevation or fall of a Caesar, a Hannibal, a Napoleon? A single victory,

like that of Zama, or of Waterloo, a single revolution, like that of England or America, sometimes involves the fortunes of a world. Neither actions nor events can be appreciated but through their bearings and tendencies upon every person and thing with which they come in contact. The relations, connections, and critical dependencies in which persons and actions stand are often so numerous and so various that it is seldom, or, perhaps, not at all, in the power of man to calculate the consequences or the value of one of a thousand of the more prominent actions of his life.

II. Who could have estimated, or who can estimate, the moral or the political bearings of the sale of Joseph to a band of Ishmaelites —of the exposure of Moses in a cradle of rushes on the Nile—of the anointing of David King of Israel—of the schism of the twelve tribes under Rehoboam—of the treachery of Judas—of the martyrdom of Stephen, the conversion of Paul, the accession of Constantine the Great, the apostasy of Julian, the crusades against the Turks, the reformation of Luther, the revival of letters, or any of the great movements of the present day? How difficult, then, is it to estimate the rebellion of Satan, the fall of Adam, the death of Christ, in all their bearings upon the destinies of the universe!

III. Before a remedy for sin could either be devised or appreciated, a knowledge of its bearings upon God and man, upon time and eternity, upon heaven and earth, is an indispensable prerequisite. But who possesses this knowledge, or what uninspired man can attain it? At best we know but in part; and, therefore, can but partially explain any thing. How difficult, then, to form a satisfactory view of sin and its remedy—of the fall of Adam and the death of Christ!

IV. It would, however, greatly aid our conceptions of the death of Christ, and illustrate the nature and use of *sin-offerings*, could we obtain just and scriptural views of sin in its necessary consequences, or in its prominent bearings upon the universe. Indeed, some knowledge of these aspects of sin is essential to our perception and appreciation of the wisdom, justice, and grace of the Christian system. It is not enough that we entertain a few vague and indistinct notions of its tendencies, or of the attitudes in which it stands to God, ourselves, and our fellows: we must have clear and definite views of the relations in which God stands to us, and we to him and to one another, and how sin affects us all in these relations: for that it bears a peculiar aspect to each of us in all these relations will, we doubt not, be conceded without debate.

V. God stands in diverse relation to the intellectual and moral creation. He is our Father, our Lawgiver, and our King. Now his feelings as a father, and his character as a lawgiver and sovereign, are equally involved in the bearings and aspects of sin. The influence of sin upon ourselves is also various and multiform. It affects the heart, the conscience, the whole soul and body of man. It alienates our affections, and even works hatred in our minds both towards God and man. As an ancient adage says, "We hate those we have injured"; and, having offended God our Father, we are for that very reason filled with enmity against him. It also oppresses and pollutes the conscience with its guilt and dread, and enslaves the passions as well as works the destruction of the body. It also alienates man from man, weakens the authority and destroys the utility of law, and, if not subdued, would ultimately subvert the throne and government of God. If not restrained and put down, it would fill the universe with anarchy and disorder—with universal misery and ruin.

VI. To go no further into details, it may, on the premises already before us, be observed:—First: That every sin wounds the affection of our heavenly Father. Second: Insults and dishonors his law and authority in the estimation of his other subjects. Third: Alienates our hearts from him. Fourth: Oppresses our conscience with guilt and dread. Fifth: Severs us from society by its morbid selfishness and disregard for man. Sixth: Induces to new infractions and habitual violations of right. And Seventh: Subjects us to shame and contempt —our bodies to the dust, and our persons to everlasting destruction from the presence of the Lord.

VII. Not as the full tale, but rather as a specimen of the loss sustained, and of the mischief done, by our transgression, we have made these seven specifications. These only serve to show in how many aspects sin must be contemplated before we can form a just estimate of a suitable and sufficient sin-offering or remedy.

VIII. Now, so far as we have been able to trace the tendencies and bearings of transgression in the above enumeration, we must find in the *sin-offering* a remedy and an antidote which will fully meet all these aspects; otherwise it will be utterly valueless and unavailing in the eye of enlightened reason, as well as in the righteous judgment of God, to expiate sin, to put it away, and to prevent its recurrence.

IX. Need we demonstrate that man himself can not furnish such a sin-offering? Need we again propound Micah's question, "Wherewith shall I come before the Lord, and bow myself before the high God? Shall I come before him with burnt-offerings—with calves of a year old? Will the Lord be pleased with thousands of rams, or with ten thousands of rivers of oil? Shall I give my first-born for my transgression; the fruit of my body for the sin of my soul?" Will repentance for the past, and future amendment, place things as they were, raise the murdered dead, repair wasted fortunes, and recruit broken constitutions? Will tears, and groans, and agonies, honor a violated law, sustain a righteous government, vindicate the divine character, and prevent further enormities? Have they ever done it? Can they ever do it? Surely, we shall be excused for not attempting to prove that we have neither a tear, nor a sigh, nor an agony, nor a lamb, nor a kid of our own creation, to offer to the Lord, even were such a sacrifice available to meet all the bearings of the case!

X. Every transgression, even the least, the eating of a forbidden apple, subjects the transgressor to destruction. One sin, of one man, has involved the whole race in death. The life of the transgressor is demanded in the very mildest accents of insulted justice. Hence, in the law of the typical sin-offerings, we find it thus written: "The *life* of the flesh is in the *blood*: and I have given it to you upon the altar, to make an atonement for your souls: *for it is the blood that maketh an atonement for the soul*."[1] But such blood, such lives as the law required could not, Paul and Common Sense being judge, take away sin. They could only prefigure a *life* and a *blood* that could truly, and justly, and honorably expiate it. Thus, *the death of Christ* is forced upon our attention by the law, by the prophets, and by the necessity of the case, enlightened Reason being in the chair, as the only real, true, and proper sin-atoning offering. It does, indeed, meet not only the above seven particulars, but all others which have occured to the human mind; and thus secures the union and harmony of things on earth, and of things in heaven, in the inviolable bonds of an everlasting brotherhood.

XI. First: "In bringing many sons to glory," it soothes and delights the wounded love of our kind and benignant heavenly Father. Second: "It magnifies and makes honorable" his violated law and insulted government. Third: It reconciles our hearts thoroughly and forever to God, as a proof and pledge incontrovertible of his wonderful and incomprehensible love to us. Fourth: It effectually relieves our conscience by "cleansing us from all sin," and produces within us a divine serenity, a peace and joy "unspeakable and full of glory." Fifth: It also reconciles us to our fellows, and fills us with brotherly affection and universal benevolence, because it makes us all one in faith, in hope, in joy, as joint heirs of immortality and eternal life. Sixth: It is the most effectual guard against new infractions of the divine law, and superlatively deters from sin, by opening to us its diabolical nature and tremendous consequences, showing us, in the person of God's only begotten and well-beloved Son, when a sin-of-

---

[1] Leviticus 17:11.

fering, the impossibility of escape from the just and retributive punishment of insulted and indignant Heaven. And Seventh: It is a ransom from death, a redemption from the grave, such a deliverance from the guilt, pollution, power, and punishment of sin, as greatly elevates the sons of God, above all that they could have attained or enjoyed under the first constitution. It presents a new creation to our view:—new heavens, new earth, new bodies, new life, new joys, new glories. He that vanquished death by dying, who now sits upon the throne says, "Behold, I make all things new." "He has become the Author of an eternal salvation to all that obey him."

XII. Let no one imagine that in this exemplification of the aspects in which sin and sin-offerings must be contemplated before we can rationally judge of the necessity, the suitableness, and the sufficiency of the death of Christ, we have attempted to present a full view of these aspects. We are incompetent to the task. This life is too short, and our opportunities too limited, to learn all the bearings of transgression upon ourselves, the throne and government of God, and his other subjects. We only intend a specimen of the points to be met in a proper sin-offering. These put it out of the reach of all human, of all angelic, of all created mediators, victims, or sacrifices to expiate sin. So far as we can comprehend this wonderful subject, that nothing inferior to the voluntary sacrifice of the Son of God, could put away sin; and make it both just, and merciful, and honorable, and safe, on the part of his God and Father, to forgive and save one of his rebel race. Nor could it then have been just, according to our conception, to have compelled him to bear our iniquities, or to suffer the just for the unjust; to inflict on an innocent person, the chastisement of our offences; but it was both just and kind on the part of our heavenly Father, to accept for us the voluntary surrender of his Son, as a willing sacrifice for our sins. "Thanks be to God for his unspeakable gift!"

CHAPTER XII

CHRIST THE LIGHT OF THE WORLD

I. As Abraham said to Isaac on his way to Mount Moriah, "My son, God will provide himself a lamb for a burnt-offering," so has it come to pass. In order to the redemption of man from sin and all its penal consequences, God has provided a lamb for a sin-offering. He sent his Son, who, on coming into the world, said, "Sacrifice and offering thou wouldst not, but a body has thou prepared me; in burnt-offerings and sacrifices for sins thou hast had no pleasure; then said I, Lo, I come to do thy will, in the volume of the book it is written of me." But he did more than offer himself as a sin-offering; he was more than the Lamb of God; he was the "Prophet of Jehovah," and revealed to man the character and the will of God. He disclosed secrets hid from the foundation of the world. In one word, he is *The Oracle, as well as the Sacrifice,* which God has provided for us.

II. As the *Incarnate Word,* he is the interpreter of his will. The New Testament is, then, the gift of Christ—and was written by his guidance and inspiration. For all that the Spirit of God has done has been through his instrumentality. The Spirit is Christ's gift. Jesus is now as much "Lord of the Spirit" as he is the Lord of life and glory. The New Testament is a volume written by his servants. Six of his apostles and two of his evangelists wrote it all. That book is to us now in the stead of the personal presence of the Lord and his apostles. He gave gifts to men after he left their abode. "He gave apostles, prophets, evangelists, pastors, teachers." As a means of our salvation; as one of the things which God has done for us, we place the New Testament, the living oracles, or gospel of Christ, as next in order, as it is in importance, to his sacrifice.

III. To the sacrifice of Christ, we always look for the basis of our pardon; to his blood that cleanses from all sin, for justification and personal acceptance; and to his Word we look for counsel and instruction in Christian piety and righteousness. We are as dependent on his *Word* for light, as we are upon his *blood* for pardon. "I am," said he, "*the light of the world; he* that followeth me shall not walk in darkness, but shall have the *light of life.*" "In him was life, and the life was the light of men." "That was the true light," said John, "which, coming into the world, enlighteneth every man." "As long as I am in the world," says Jesus, "I am the light of the world." Thus Isaiah spake of him: "I will also give thee as a light to the Gentiles, that thou mayest be my salvation to the ends of the earth." "I will give thee for a covenant of the people, or light of the Gentiles, to open the blind eyes, to bring out the prisoners from the prison; and them that sit in darkness out of the prison-house." "His going forth is prepared as the morning." "The Sun of Righteousness will arise with healing under his wings." "I witness," said Paul, "both to small and great, that the Messiah should show light to the people and to the Gentiles." The word of Christ is the light of Christ; and therefore the Christian Scriptures are the light of the world; and he that followeth them shall have the light of life. "If you continue in my doctrine," says the Messiah, "you shall know the truth, and the truth shall make you free." "If the Son makes you free, you shall be free indeed."

CHAPTER XIII

THE LORDSHIP OF THE MESSIAH

I. We are seeking to apprehend *the things done for us* in the Christian system. "Christ, our passover, has been sacrificed for us." As such "not a bone of him was broken." Yet, "he died for us." In the second place, he has become our *prophet*, as well as our *priest;* and has declared to us the will of God, the whole will of God concerning us. He is our *light*, as well as our *sin-offering*. But in the third place, he has been made *Lord* for us. To make Christ Lord *for* us, as well as *of* us—was the last act of the sublime drama of man's redemption from sin. The last secret of the mystery of Christ, which Peter promulgated on the day of Pentecost, was, "Let all the house of Israel know, that God has made that same Jesus, whom you crucified, both Lord and Christ." To make him Lord for us, was to invest him with *universal authority*, that he might have it in his power to give eternal life to all his people. Jesus, in one of his prayers, in anticipation of his investiture, says, "Thou hast given him *power over all flesh* that he might give eternal life to as many as thou hast given him." But after his resurrection from the dead, and ascension into heaven, he was crowned Lord of angels, as well as Lord of men; and therefore he said, "all authority," or lordship, "in heaven and on earth is given to me." He is now the Lord of hosts: legions of angels, the armies of the skies, are given to him:—for what? That he might be able to do all for us that our condition needs. It was for *us* he became a Prophet, *for us* he became a Priest, *for us* he has been made Lord of hosts, King of the universe, Judge and avenger of all. He is Lord of life, Lord of the Spirit, Lord of all.

II. We need sacrifice—and therefore we need a priest. We need a Leader, a Luminary, a Sun of Righteousness; and we want one who can always help us in time of need, when we wrestle not with flesh and blood, but with the rulers of the darkness of this world; with wicked spirits living in the air. If Jesus himself, in one of these conflicts, needed an angel to minister to him, we need it more.

III. Three things are done for us: a sin-offering is presented; a lamp of life is put into our hands; and all the active powers and energies in the wide universe are placed at the command of our King whenever he needs them. These are things already done. Hence, the Holy Spirit, and all the angels of heaven are now at the disposal of our Saviour: for in him all the promises of God are laid up; all the treasures of wisdom and knowledge, and all the fulness of the Deity, reside fully and truly in him. All these things, it is true, might be comprehended in one gift—the gift of Jesus as our Mediator; our

Prophet, Priest, and King. Still it is expedient to view the things done for us, severally and distinctly in the Christian system.

IV. Other things are promised *to be done* for us: but these are the things already done for us, and before we shall speak of the things yet to be done for us, and done in us, we shall summarily consider the things to be done by us, before any thing more can be done for us, or done in us.

CHAPTER XIV

FAITH IN CHRIST

I. The things done for us will truly be to us as though they were not, unless they are believed. Hence to the untutored and unbelieving barbarian or infidel, the universe is without a sin-offering, a Sun of Righteousness, a Lord, Redeemer, and a Holy Spirit. Faith is necessary only as a means of attainment; as a means of enjoyment. It is not, then, an arbitrary enactment or requisition, but a gracious means of salvation.

II. Faith in Christ is the effect of belief. Belief is the *cause*, and trust, confidence, or faith *in* Christ, the *effect*. "*The faith*," sometimes means *the truth* to be believed. Sometimes it means "*the belief of the truth*"; but here we speak of it metonymically, putting the effect for the cause—or calling the effect by the name of the cause. To believe what a person says, and to trust in him are not always identical. True, indeed, they often are; for if a person speaks to us concerning himself, and states to us matters of great interest to ourselves, requiring confidence in him, to believe what he says, and to believe or trust *in* him, are in effect, one and the same thing. Suppose a physician present himself to one that is sick, stating his ability and willingness to heal him: to believe is to trust in him, and to put ourselves under his guidance; provided, only, we love health rather than sickness, and life rather than death.

III. While, then, faith is the simple belief of testimony, or of the truth, and never can be more nor less than that; as a *principle of action* it has respect to a person or thing interesting to us; and is confidence or trust in that person or thing. Now the belief of what Christ says of himself, terminates in trust or confidence in him: and as the Christian religion is a personal thing, both as respects *subject* and *object*, that faith in Christ which is essential to salvation is not the belief of any doctrine, testimony, or truth, abstractly, but belief *in*

Christ; trust or confidence in him as a person, not a thing.[1] We take Paul's definition of the term and of the thing as perfectly simple, intelligible, and sufficient. For the term faith, he substitutes *the belief of the truth.* "God has from the beginning chosen you to salvation through the sanctification of the Spirit; through the belief of the truth."[2] And of the thing, he says, "Faith is the *confidence* of things hoped for, the *conviction* of things not seen."[3] And John says, it is "receiving testimony," for "if we receive the testimony of man," as a principle of action, or put trust in it, "the testimony of God is greater," and of course will produce greater confidence.[4] Any belief, then, that does not terminate in our personal confidence in Jesus as the Christ, and to induce trustful submission to him, is not faith unfeigned; but a dead faith, and can not save the soul.

CHAPTER XV

REPENTANCE

I. Repentance is an effect of faith: for who that believes not that God exists, can have "repentance towards God"? Repentance is sorrow for sins committed; but it is more. It is a resolution to forsake them; but it is more. It is actual "ceasing to do evil, and learning to do well." This is *"repentance unto life,"* or what is truly called *reformation.* Such is the force of the command, *"Repent, every one of you."* It is not merely, Be sorry for what you have done wrong; nor is it, Resolve to do better; nor even, Try to amend your ways: but it is actual amendment of life from the views and the motives which the gospel of Christ exhibits. Gospel repentance is the offspring of gospel light and gospel motive, and therefore, it is the effect, and not the cause, of belief of the testimony of God.

II. True repentance is, then, always consummated in actual reformation of life. It therefore carries in its very essence, the idea of restitution. For no man can cordially disallow or reprobate his sinful course of life, who does not redress the wrongs he has done, to the utmost limit of his power. To God he can make no restitution, only as he refunds to his creatures, whom he has injured. If, then, any one is convicted in his own mind, that he has injured the person, character, or the property of his neighbor, by word or deed, and has it in his power, by word or deed, to undo the evil he has done, or to re-

---

[1] See the Essay on the Foundation of Christian Union, on the terms, *fact, testimony, faith, etc.,* where this subject is treated at large.
[2] 2 Thessalonians 2:13.
[3] Hebrews 11:1.   [4] 1 John 5:9.

store what he has unjustly taken away, he will certainly do it, if his repentance be according to either the law of Moses or the gospel of Christ. Otherwise his repentance is of no value; for God can not, without trampling on his own law, and dishonoring his own character, forgive any man who is conscious of any sin he has done to any man, unless to the utmost extent of his power he make good the injury he has done. Thus saith the Lord, "If a soul sin and commit a trespass against the Lord, and lie unto his neighbor in that which was delivered him to keep, or in fellowship [*i.e.*, trading], or in anything taken away by violence, or has deceived his neighbor, or has found that which was lost, and lieth concerning it, or sweareth falsely; in any or all these that a man doeth, sinning therein: then it shall be, because he hath sinned and is guilty, that he shall *restore* that which he took violently away, or the thing which he has *deceitfully gotten*, or that which was delivered him to keep, or that lost thing which he found, or all that about which he has sworn falsely, he shall even restore in the principal, and shall add a fifth part more thereto, and give it to him to whom it appertaineth, in the day of his trespass-offering, and he shall bring his trespass-offering to the Lord, and the priest shall make atonement for him before the Lord, and it shall be forgiven him." (Lev. 6:1-7.) Sin-offerings without repentance, and repentance without sin-offerings, are equally ineffectual before God. We sin against God always, when we sin against man; and therefore, after making all things right with man, we can only, through sacrifice, which makes the matter right with God, obtain forgiveness. To the same effect, Jesus speaks (Matt. 5:23, 24), "Be reconciled to your brother," first make the matter right with him, "and then come and offer your gift."[1]

CHAPTER XVI

BAPTISM

I. There are three things to be considered in baptism:—1. The action commanded to be done;—2. The subject specified;—3. The meaning or design of that action. Jesus commanded a certain *character* to be the subject of a certain *action*, for a certain specific purpose or *design*. The questions, then, are, What that action? What that subject? What that design?

---

[1] See my Essay on *Regeneration*, on the words *repentance* and *reparation*.

OF THE ACTION

II. The action is indicated by a word as definite, clear, and unequivocal, as any word in any language ever spoken by the many-
tongued sons of Adam. Besides, in all laws and institutions, and more
especially in those that are of a *positive*, rather than a *moral* nature,
all words having both a literal and a figurative meaning, a common
and a special signification, are to be understood in their literal and
common, and not in their figurative and uncommon import and acception. So have decided all the judges of law and language, from
time immemorial.

III. That definite and unambiguous word, as almost universally
known in these days of controversy, is *baptisma*, or *baptismos*, anglicized, not translated, *baptism*. The primary means by which the
meaning of this word is ascertained are the following:—1. The ancient lexicons and dictionaries;—2. The ancient and modern transla-
tions of the New Testament;—3. The ancient customs of the church;
—4. The place and circumstances of baptizing, as mentioned in the
New Testament;—and 5. The allusions to this ordinance and the expositions of it in the apostolic epistles. To each of these we shall do
little more than simply advert on the present occasion.

1. The ancient lexicons with one consent give *immersion* as the
natural, common, and primary sense of this word. There is not
known to us a single exception. Nor is there a received lexicon, ancient or modern, that does ever translate this word by the terms
sprinkling, or pouring. And as there are but three *actions* allowed to
be Christian baptism; and as the original words, both verbs and
nouns, are translated *immerse* and *immersion*, in all lexicons, and
never *sprinkle* or *pour;* follows it not, then, that neither sprinkling nor
pouring is Christian baptism? The question is not whether these
words are ever, like other words, used figuratively: whether they may
not *metonymically* mean, *wetting* or *washing*: for these may be the
effects of either sprinkling, pouring, or dipping. The question is not,
whether these words may be so used: but the question is, whether
the action commanded in *baptizo*, be sprinkling, pouring, or immersing a person. All authorized Greek dictionaries, ancient and modern,
with one consent, affirm that action to be immersion; and not sprinkling or pouring.

2. All Latin, English, German and French versions which we
have seen, and we believe on the testimony of others, all that we have
not seen, sometimes translate these words, their derivatives, or compounds, by words equivalent to *immersion*: but on *no occasion* ever
translate them by sprinkling, or pouring, or any word equivalent to

these terms. This is an evidence of great moment: for if these versions have nineteen times in twenty been made by those who practice sprinkling or pouring in the name of the Lord: and if these words occur about one hundred and twenty times in the New Testament, is it not very singular that never once have such translators rendered the words by sprinkling, or pouring? a decisive proof in our judgment that it could not be so translated. Indeed, a mere English scholar, who has only heard that *baptism* is a Greek word, may indubitably ascertain that it means neither sprinkling nor pouring, by substituting the definition of the term, and trying its sense in all places where the ordinance is spoken of. This is an infallible canon interpretation. *The proper definition of a term substituted for it will always make as good senses as the term itself.* Now, if an English reader will try *sprinkling* or *pouring* in those places where he finds the word *baptism*, he will soon discover that neither of these words can possibly represent it, if the above canon be true. For instance, we are told, that all Judea and Jerusalem went out to John and were *baptized* of him in the Jordan. Sprinkled them *in* the Jordan! poured them *in* the Jordan! immersed them *in* the Jordan! Can any one doubt which of these truly represents the original in such passages? I may sprinkle or pour water upon a person; but to sprinkle or pour them into water is impossible. It is not said he baptized water upon them, but he baptized them in water, in the river.

3. The ancient church, it is admitted on all hands, practised immersion. It did so, Roman, Greek and English historians being worthy of any credit.

4. The places where baptism was anciently administered, being rivers, pools, baths, and places of much water, show that it was not sprinkling or pouring. They went down *into* the water, and came up *out* of it, etc. And John baptized where there were many waters or much water. And even Paul and Silas went out of the Philippian jail to baptize the jailer at night, rather than send for a cup of water!

5. It is also alluded to and explained under the figure of a burial and resurrection, as relating to the death, burial, and resurrection of Jesus, etc. (Rom. 6 and Col. 2.)

From these topics many clear and conclusive arguments may be drawn, on which it is not now our business to dwell. If, indeed, any one of these five topics be correct, the action that Christ commands is forever decided. How much more, when they all concur in asserting the same interpretation! There is, then, but one baptism, and not two, under the Christian administration.

IV. *Characters*, not *persons*, as such, are the subjects of baptism. *Penitent believers*—not infants nor adults, not males nor females, not Jews nor Greeks; but professors of repentance towards God, and faith in Christ—are the proper subjects of this ordinance. "To as many as received him, to them he granted privilege of becoming the sons of God, to them that believed on his name, which were born not of flesh, nor of blood, nor of the will of man, but of God." "He that believeth, and is baptized [not he that is baptized and believeth], shall be saved." "Many of the Corinthians hearing, believed and were baptized," not many of the Corinthians were baptized and then believed, and finally heard the gospel! "for without faith it is impossible to please God," etc.

V. "In those days came John the Baptist, preaching in the wilderness of Judea, the baptism of repentance, for the remission of sins." "And Jesus said that repentance and remission of sins should be preached in his name among all nations, beginning at Jerusalem." Therefore, Peter said to the penitent Pentecostians, "Repent, and be baptized every one of you in the name of the Lord Jesus, for the remission of sins." Again, "As many of you as have been baptized or immersed into Christ, have put on Christ, have been immersed into his death"; "have risen with him."

VI. Baptism is, then, designed to introduce the subjects of it into the participation of the blessings of the death and resurrection of Christ; who "died for our sins," and "rose again for our justification." But it has no abstract efficacy. Without previous faith in the blood of Christ, and deep and unfeigned repentance before God, neither immersion in water, nor any other action, can secure to us the blessings of peace and pardon. It can merit nothing. Still to the believing penitent it is the *means* of receiving a formal, distinct, and specific absolution, or release from guilt. Therefore, none but those who have first believed the testimony of God and have repented of their sins, and that have been intelligently immersed into his death, have the full and explicit testimony of God, assuring them of pardon. To such only as are truly penitent, dare we say, "Arise and be baptized, and wash away your sins, calling upon the name of the Lord," and to such only can we say with assurance, "You are washed, you are justified, you are sanctified in the name of the Lord Jesus, and by the Spirit of God." But let the reader examine with care our special essay on the Remission of Sins, in which this much-debated subject is discussed at considerable length.

CHAPTER XVII

THE CHRISTIAN CONFESSION OF FAITH

I. The only apostolic and divine confession of faith which God, the Father of all, has laid for the church—and that on which Jesus himself said he would build it, is the sublime and supreme proposition: *That Jesus of Nazareth is the Messiah, the Son of the living God.* This is the peculiarity of the Christian system: its specific attribute. The antediluvian Abel, Enoch, etc., believed that a son of Eve would bruise Satan's head. Abraham, Isaac, and Jacob believed that a peculiar son of theirs would be the child of blessings, the Son of promise to the human race. Indeed, Jesse, David, and all the prophets, looked for one from the sceptred *tribe*, who would be king of all the earth, and a benefactor of humanity. John the Baptist in his day preached and believed that the Messenger of the covenant of eternal peace was immediately to appear. But the disciples of Jesus, the son of Mary, believed and confessed that he was the identical person. "We have found him of whom Moses in the law, and all the prophets did write: Jesus of Nazareth, the Son of David, the King of Israel." "Rabbi," said Nathanael, "thou art the Son of God, thou art the King of Israel." But yet it remained for Peter to speak fully and expressly, the very proposition which contains the whole matter. "We believe and are sure that thou art the Messiah, the Son of the living God." "On this rock," responded he, with a blessing upon Peter's name and head: "on this rock I will build my church, and the gates of Hades shall not prevail against it." Of this foundation Paul has said, "Other foundation can no man lay than that which is already laid, which is Jesus Christ." God himself laid this corner, this tried and precious stone, as the foundation of the temple of grace; and therefore with his own lips pronounced him his beloved Son; and sealed him by the visible descent and impress of his Spirit, as his Messiah, the Messenger of life and peace to a condemned and rebellious world.

II. This confession of faith has in it two distinct ideas—the one concerning the *person*, the other concerning the *office*, of the Son of Man. The one asserts his divine relations, the other his official rank and glory. No one can intelligently believe this proposition, and not turn to God with all his heart: for there is in it a thousand thoughts and motives to bind the soul to God, and melt it into the most affec-

tionate devotion. There is also in it the strongest bond to secure the
affections of all Christians to one another. There is no other confession of faith on which the church can be built, on which it can possibly stand one and undivided, but on this one. With the heart man
believes this proposition in order to justification; and with his mouth
he maketh this confession of it in order to his salvation. So Paul explains it (Rom. 10) and thus we have one Lord, one faith, and one
baptism, among the immutable reasons why Christians should maintain unity of spirit in the bonds of peace.[1]

CHAPTER XVIII

CONVERSION, REGENERATION

I. The change which is consummated by immersion is sometimes
called in sacred style, *"being quickened,"* or *"made alive," "passing
from death to life," "being born again," "having risen with Christ,"
"turning to the Lord," "being enlightened," "conversion," "reconcilation," "repentance unto life."* These, like the words propitiation,
atonement, reconciliation, expiation, redemption expressive of the
various aspects which the death of Christ sustains, are expressive of
the different relations in which this great change, sometimes called a
"new creation," may be contemplated. The entire change effected in
man by the Christian system, consists in four things:—a change of
views; a change of affections; a change of state; and a change of
life. Now, in respect of each of these separately or in combination,
it is called by different names. As a change of *views,* it is called
"being enlightened"; "Once you were darkness, now are you light in
the Lord; walk as children of the light"; "After that you were enlightened," etc. As a change of the *affections,* it is called "being reconciled"; thus, "for if when we were enemies we were reconciled to
God by the death of his Son, much more being reconciled we shall
be saved through his life." As a change of *state,* it is called a "being
quickened"; "passing from death to life," "being born again," "having
risen with Christ"; "And you *hath he quickened* who were dead in
trespasses and sins"; "By this we know we have *passed from death to
life,* because we love the brethren"; "Being *born again,* not of corruptible, but of incorruptible seed, the word of God, which liveth
and abideth forever." "If you be," or "since you *are risen with
Christ,* set your affections on things above, not on things on the
earth." As a change of *life* it is called "repentance unto life," "turn-

---

[1] See the Essay on the Foundation of Christian Union and Communion.

ing to the Lord," "conversion"; "Then God has granted to the Gentiles repentance to life." "And all that dwelt in Lydda and Sharon saw Eneas and *turned to the Lord.*" "Except you be converted, and become as children, you shall not enter the kingdom of heaven." "When thou art converted, strengthen thy brethren." "He that converts a sinner from the error of his way shall save a soul from death and hide a multitude of sins."

II. Great confusion has been introduced into the Christian community by a confounding of these terms, making only one of them to mean all the others. Witness the controversy about *regeneration;* as if that word were used by the sacred Scripture in reference to the entire change effected by the Christian system; whereas in strict propriety, it is never used by itself in the Bible to represent any part of this change, much less the whole of it. We have the phrase *"washing of regeneration"* once, in contradistinction from the "renewal of the Holy Spirit" (Tit. 3:5), but never, by itself, as indicative of this fourfold change. But suppose it should be conceded that the term *regeneration* might be just equivalent to *"being born again,"* it could even then only represent so much of this change as respects mere *state:* for the figure of a new birth applies merely to admission into a family or nation, and not to the process of quickening or making alive of the person so admitted. It can, then, in strict propriety, only apply to the fourth part of that change which the gospel of salvation proposes and effects. Being *born again* is, or may be, the *effect* of a change of views, of a change of affections, or it may be the *cause* of a change of life; but certain it is, it is not identical with any of them, and never can represent them all.

III. But may it not include them all? It is impossible: for however we might extend the figure and suppose it to include its causes, it can not also include its effects. If it should include a change of views, a change of affections, and a change of state, it can not include a change of life or of character. We ought, then, to use this word in its strict and scriptural acceptance, if we would escape the great confusion now resting upon this subject. The sophistry or delusion of this confusion is, that making *regeneration* equivalent to the entire change, instead of to be one-fourth part of it, the community will be always imposed on and misled by seeking to find the attributes of conversion in the new birth, or of the new birth in conversion; and so of all the others. Being born again is not *conversion,* nor a *change of views,* nor a *change of affections,* but a *change of state.* True, indeed, that of the person who is born again we may suppose a change of views, a change of heart, and we may infer a change of character, and may therefore say he is enlightened, renewed in heart, converted as well as born again; but this license respecting the *person*, the subject of the change, is not allowed in talking of the *change* itself. A Christian is, indeed, one whose views are enlightened, whose heart is renewed, whose relations to God and the moral universe are changed, and whose manner of life is according to righteousness and true holiness.

CHAPTER XIX

CHRISTIANS ARE PERSONS PARDONED, JUSTIFIED, SANCTIFIED, ADOPTED, SAVED

I. While adjusting the most important terms and phrases in the Christian system, in order to a more perspicuous and comprehensive intelligence of it, it is expedient that we should also advert to other predicates of the genuine Christian. The five terms at the head of this chapter are all indicative of his *state;* and do not include any attributes of his *character.*

II. These predicates are but so many counterpart aspects of a new state in reference to an old one; or they represent the gospel as affecting the position of man in the universe in all those points in which sin affected him. Was he guilty, condemned, unholy, alien, and lost, in Adam the first? When in Adam the second, he is just in an opposite state;—he is pardoned wherein he was guilty—justified wherein he was condemned—sanctified wherein he was unholy—adopted wherein he was alien—and saved wherein he was lost. Sin, then, condemns, pollutes, alienates, and destroys its subjects. Grace justifies, sanctifies, adopts, and saves its subjects in reference to these points. Pardon has respect to guilt; justification, to condemnation; sanctification, to pollution; adoption, to alienation; and salvation, to destruction. Those *out of Christ* are, then, in their sins, condemned, unholy, alien, and lost; while those *in Christ* are pardoned, justified, sanctified, adopted into the family of God, and saved.

III. In former dispensations, and in the present, two things are immutable as respects the preparation for a change of state, while the act by which that change is formally consummated is not necessarily immutable. Thus, in reference to actual transgression, faith and repentance, in all dispensations of religion, were necessary to forgiveness, justification, sanctification, adoption, salvation. In one word, God can not forgive an impenitent and unbelieving transgressor. But whether this or that act shall consummate a change of state, as respects man's relations to the moral universe—whether that act shall be circumcision, animal sacrifice, baptism, confession, prayer, etc., is not from any necessity, either in the divine or human nature, immutable. It has been changed; but faith in God's appointments, and repentance for past transgressions, are now, always were, and evermore shall be, necessary to forgiveness.

IV. The philosophy or reason of this is, that faith and repentance change the state of man's heart to God; and if there was a universe beyond God and the sinner, all further acts respecting it would be uncalled for. But as respects the condition of sinners in the universe, and their views, affections, relations, and manner of life, more than faith and repentance, or a change of views and feelings, is necessary to actual, and sensible, and formal pardon, justification, sanctification, adoption, and the salvation of the soul from sin. Hence came the ordinances of baptism, confession, prayer, fasting, and intercession.

V. It is wise and kind on the part of Heaven to ordain such acts or to institute such ordinances as will assure ourselves and others of our new relations; and to suspend our *enjoyment* of the favor and love of God, not merely upon faith and penitence, or any other mental operation, but upon certain clear overt acts, such as baptism, confession, prayer, etc., which affect ourselves and others much more than they possibly can affect God himself, being the fruit of our faith, or perhaps, rather, only the perfecting of our faith in the promises of God.

CHAPTER XX

THE GIFT OF THE HOLY SPIRIT

I. Having spoken of three things which God has done for us, and of three things which we must do for ourselves, we are now come to the proper place to consider other aids which our heavenly Father tenders to us, just at this point. "He has provided a Lamb for a sin-offering," and "Jesus has full atonement made." He has also given to us "the *light of life*"—the words of Jesus faithfully written out; and he has invested him as the Son of Man, with all authority, celestial and terrestrial, that he may lead many sons to glory, and give eternal life to all that are given him.

II. We also have believed all this, repented of our sins, and been immersed into Christ. We have assumed him as our Leader, our Prophet, Priest, and King; and put ourselves under his guidance. Having disowned the great apostate and his ranks, and enlisted under the Messiah, and taken sides with the Lord's Anointed, he now proposes to put his Holy Spirit within us, to furnish us for the good fight of faith, and to anoint us as the sons and heirs of God.

III. Some will ask, Has not this gift been conferred on us to make us Christians? True, indeed, no man can say that Jesus is Lord but by the Holy Spirit. As observed in its proper place, the Spirit of God is the perfecter and finisher of all divine works. "The Spirit of God moved upon the waters"; "The hand of the Lord has made me, the Spirit of the Almighty has given me life"; "By his Spirit he has garnished the heavens, his hand has formed the crooked serpent,"— the milky way; "The Spirit descended upon him"; "God himself bore the Apostle witness, by divers miracles and gifts of the Holy Spirit according to his will"; "Holy men of old spake as they were moved by the Holy Spirit"; "When the Spirit of truth, the Advocate, is come, he will convict the world of sin, because they believe not on me, and of justification, because I go to my Father"; "God was manifest in the flesh and justified by the Spirit."

IV. The Spirit of God inspired all the spiritual ideas in the New Testament, and confirmed them by miracles; and he is ever present with the word that he inspired. ·He descended from heaven on the day of Pentecost, and has not formally ascended since. In the sense in which he descended he certainly has not ascended; for he is to animate and inspire with new life the church or temple of the Lord. "Know you not," you Christians, "that your bodies are temples of the living God?" "The temple of God is holy, which temple you are"; "If the Spirit of him that raised up Jesus from the dead dwell in you, God shall quicken your mortal bodies by *his Spirit that dwelleth in you*," etc.

V. Now we can not separate the Spirit and word of God, and ascribe so much power to the one and so much to the other; for so did not the apostles. Whatever the word does, the Spirit does; and whatever the Spirit does in the work of converting men, the word does. We neither believe nor teach abstract Spirit nor abstract word, but word and Spirit, Spirit and word.

VI. But the Spirit is not *promised to any persons out of Christ.* It is promised only to them that believe in and obey him. These it actually and powerfully assists in the mighty struggle for eternal life Some, indeed, ask, "Do Christians need more aid to gain eternal life than sinners do to become Christians? Is not the work of conversion a more difficult work than the work of sanctification?" Hence, they contend more for the work of the Spirit in conversion, than for the work of the Spirit in sanctification. This, indeed, is a mistaken view of the matter, if we reason either from analogy or from divine testimony. Is it not more easy to plant than to cultivate the corn, the vine, the olive? Is it not more easy to enlist in the army, than to be a good soldier, and fight the battles of the Lord; to start in the race, than to reach the goal; to enter the ship, than cross the ocean; to be naturalized, than to become a good citizen; to enter into the matrimonial compact, than to be an exemplary husband; to enter into life, than to retain and sustain it for threescore years and ten? And while the commands *"believe,"* *"repent,"* and *"be baptized,"* are never accompanied with any intimation of peculiar difficulty; the commands to the use of the means of spiritual health and life; to form the Christian character; to attain the resurrection of the just; to lay hold on eternal life; to make our calling and election sure, etc., are accompanied with such exhortations, admonitions, cautions, as to make it a difficult and critical affair, requiring all the aids of the Spirit of our God, to all the means of grace and untiring assiduity and perseverance on our part; for it seems, "the called" who enter the stadium are many, while "the chosen" and approved "are few"; and many, says Jesus, "shall seek to enter into the heavenly city, and shall not be able"; "Let us labor, therefore, to enter into that rest, lest any man fall after the same example of unbelief."

VII. Sanctification, in one point of view, is unquestionably a progressive work. To sanctify is to set apart; this may be done in a moment, and so far as mere *state or relation* is concerned, it is as instantaneous as baptism. But there is the formation of a holy character: for there is a holy *character* as well as a holy state. The formation of such a character is the work of means; "Holy Father," said Jesus, "sanctify them [my disciples] through the truth, thy word is the truth"; "And the very God of peace sanctify you wholly," says Paul to the Thessalonians, "and I pray God your whole spirit and soul and body be preserved blameless to the coming of our Lord Jesus Christ." Christians, then, are to "follow peace with all men, and sanctification, without which no one shall see the Lord." Therefore, it is the duty and the work of Christians, "to *perfect* holiness in the fear of the Lord."

VIII. This requires aid. Hence, assistance is to be prayed for; and it is promised. Now as the Spirit of God, under the administration of Christ, is the author of all holiness in us—he is called the "Holy Spirit," "the Spirit of holiness." Hence, while we have the phrase "Holy Ghost" or Spirit, *ninety-four times* in the Christian Scriptures, it is found only three times in all the Jewish writings. The Holy Spirit is, then, the author of all our holiness; and in the struggle after victory over sin and temptation, *"it helps our infirmities,"* and comforts us by seasonably bringing to our remembrance the promises of Christ, and "strengthens us with all might, in the new or inner man." And thus "God works in us to will and to do of his own benevolence," "while we are working out our own salvation with fear and trembling." Christians are, therefore, clearly and unequivocally temples of the Holy Spirit; and they are quickened, animated, encouraged, and sanctified by the power and influence of the Spirit of God, working in them through the truth.

IX. God "gives his Holy Spirit to them who ask him," according to his revealed will; and without this gift no one could be saved or ultimately triumph over all opposition. He knows but little of the deceitfulness of sin, or of the combating of temptation, who thinks himself competent to wrestle against the allied forces of the world, the flesh, and the devil. Hence, the necessity of "supplications, deprecations, intercessions and thanksgivings," of praying always with all prayer and supplication in the Holy Spirit, and watching thereunto with all perseverance, and of making supplication for all saints, our fellow-soldiers in this good warfare.

X. To those, then, who believe, repent, and obey the gospel, he actually communicates of his Good Spirit. The fruits of that spirit in them are "love, joy, peace, long-suffering, gentleness, goodness, fidelity, meekness, temperance." The attributes of character which distinguish the new man are each of them communications of the Holy Spirit, and thus are we the sons of God in fact, as well as in title, under the dispensation of the Holy Spirit.

XI. We have, then, every thing done for us, after our conversion, which we need in order to that "holiness without which no one shall see the Lord." Thus God has provided for us a sin-offering; a *prophet* to expound it; a *priest* to present it; a *king*, with universal dominion, to govern and protect all that by it are reconciled to God. And when through faith, repentance, and baptism, we have assumed him as our rightful Sovereign, by his Holy Spirit, in answer to our prayers, he worked in us, and by us, and for us, all that is needful to our present, spiritual, and eternal salvation.

CHAPTER XXI

THE CHRISTIAN HOPE

I. "Beloved, now are we the sons of God; and it does not yet appear what we shall be, but we know that when he shall appear, we shall be like him—that we shall see him as he is. And every one that has this hope in him, purifies himself even as he is pure." "God has predestinated us to be conformed to the image of his Son." "I reckon that the sufferings of this life are not worthy to be compared with the glory that shall be revealed in us." "He hath begotten us again to a lively hope; to an inheritance incorruptible, undefiled, and that fadeth not away." So testify three apostles—John, Paul and Peter. The whole hope of the Christian may, indeed, be summed up in one sentence: "If children, then *heirs*—heirs of God, *joint heirs with Christ.*" Immortality, eternal life, the riches of Christ, the glory, honor, wealth, and bliss of God's only begotten Son are to be equally participated with all his saints.

II. The remedial system is, therefore, a moral creation in progress —a new creation of men unto good works, still advancing; but its termination will be the stereotyping of individual moral excellence by an instantaneous physical new creation of men at the resurrection of the just: or a manifestation of the sons of God in full redemption from the whole entail of sin; raised, refined, immortalized, glorified, and invested with eternal life.

III. Hope differs from faith, in that it looks only forward to future objects. It looks not back, nor does it contemplate the present: "for," says Paul, "what a man sees, why does he yet hope for?" Nor looks it on all the future; but only on future *good*. It desires and expects good and nothing else. There is not one dark cloud, not one dark speck, in all the heavens of Christian hope. Every thing seen in its wide dominions, in the unbounded prospect yet before us, is bright, cheering, animating, transporting. It is all desirable and desired. It is all expected. It is all "earnest expectation"; not a doubtful, but a "confident expectation of things" desirable and to be "hoped for."

IV. It is not what some in this age call "*the hope*," *i.e.*, the desirable expectancy of pardon of their past transgressions; for none but those who are actually pardoned are the subjects of this hope. "If our heart condemn us, then, indeed, we have no confidence"; so no confident expectation, no hope of eternal life. The mere possibility of an event is no foundation of hope. Hope deals not in possibilities, nor indeed much in probabilities—unless they are very strong probabilities. Conjectures, peradventures, possibilities, probabilities, are not of the essence of Christian hope. It rests on covenants, charters, promises, oaths, tendered by the Eternal Source of almighty truth and love. These are good securities; and produce assurance. Hence, hope is the assurance of future good in expectation.

V. There are, indeed, various degrees of hope; but in the least degree of it there is desire combined with expectation. Things expected are not always desirable, nor are things desirable always to be expected: but hope embraces promises that are desirable, and also expects the enjoyment of them. Hence, hope, like faith and love, may grow exceedingly. When based on the promises of God, and on the habitual patient conformity to his will, it will keep pace with our growing intelligence of the character of God; of the fulness and richness of the promises, and in the persuasion of our actual devotion to the manifestations of that will.

VI. But *the things hoped for* by the Christian are beyond description. Eye, indeed, has not seen, ear has not heard, the human heart has not conceived the glories of the resurrection of the just;— the new bodies, the new heavens, the new earth, the new Jerusalem, the new society, the new pleasures: for according to his promise we look for (expect) new heavens and new earth in which righteous persons shall alone dwell. Thus terminates the remedial system on all its happy subjects. "It lifts the beggar from the dust, and the wretched from the dunghill, and sets them among princes, amongst the nobles of the universe"; the thrones, hierarchies, and lordships of the skies; in the presence of God, too, "where there is fulness of joy, and at his right hand, where there are pleasures for evermore." Such are the things to be done for those, for whom such things have already been done as constitute the remedial system: for with Paul we must say: "He that spared not his own Son, but delivered him up to the death for us all; how shall he not with him also freely give us all things?" "All things are yours, whether Paul, or Apollos, or Cephas, or the world, or life, or death, or things present, or things to come, all are yours; and you are Christ's, and Christ is God's."

CHAPTER XXII

THE DOOM OF THE WICKED

I. There are two classes of men in this world. They are often and in various manners contradistinguished from each other. They are called the righteous and the wicked, the saints and the sinners, the holy and the unholy, the good and the bad, he that feareth God and he that feareth him not. Of the one class many things are predicated which are not predicated of the other. Of the one it is said, that they "in Christ," justified, sanctified, saved, children of God, heirs of God, joint heirs with Christ, an elect race, a royal priesthood, a peculiar people. Of the other class, these things are never predicated in the Bible. They are not in Christ, not justified, not sanctified, not saved; children of the devil, "children of wrath," not an elect race, not a royal priesthood, not a peculiar people.

II. These have not been reconciled to God through the propitiation of his Son. They are still enemies of God in heart. And for them that loved darkness rather than light, and would not have God's Son to be their Saviour, he has appointed a day of judgment; a day for the ultimate perdition of ungodly men. Then they shall perish "with an everlasting destruction from the presence of the Lord, and from the glory of his power, when he shall come to be glorified in all his saints, and to be admired by all the believers." Then will the King say to them on his left hand, "Depart, ye cursed, into everlasting fire prepared for the devil and his angels." They are the allies of Satan in his rebellion against God, and have spent all their energies and fortunes on his side of the question; and therefore it is reasonable that they should have their ultimate portion with him.

III. Of this judgment, Enoch, the seventh from Adam, prophesied, saying, "Behold the Lord cometh with ten thousand of his saints, to execute judgment upon all, and to convict all that are ungodly among them of all their ungodly deeds, which they have ungodly committed, and of all their hard speeches which ungodly sinners have spoken against him." God had, then, long before the Christian era— from the foundation of the world, "*appointed a day* in which he will judge *the world* [the whole world] righteously by Jesus Christo," whom he has constituted Judge of all the dead as well as of all the living.

IV. "It is, indeed, appointed to men once to die, and after this the judgment." The judgment consequent upon death is not the general but the particular judgment of individuals, as the phrase would seem to indicate, whose spirits returning to God are judged and instantly rewarded, so far as in a separate state they can be the subjects of reward or punishment. But the "*judgment of the great day*" is for another purpose: not, as some profanely say, "to bring men out of heaven and hell to judge and remand them back again"; but in the presence of an assembled world to vindicate the administrations of the moral government and providence of God, to develop the real characters of angels and of men, and to pronounce an irrevocable sentence upon all according to their works. For, says Paul, "we must all appear before the tribunal of Christ, that every one may receive, *in his body,* the things he has done, whether good or bad." It is, then, because of the actual and public pronunciation and execution of this judgment, that the last day is called "*the day of judgment,*" and that the judgment itself is called "*the judgment of the great day.*"

V. This final judgment and *"perdition of ungodly men"* is set forth by the Lord himself, as well as by his apostles, in the clearest and strongest terms, and in the boldest and most appalling imagery which human speech and human knowledge can afford. Indeed, to place this awfully sublime and glorious day in full array before the perceptive powers of man, is impossible. The best efforts have exhausted the powers of nature in all her wonted energies. John, in his sublime visions of the last acts of the great drama of human existence, says, "I saw a great white throne, and him that sat on it, from whose face earth and heaven fled away, and there was found no room for them. And I saw the dead, small and great, stand before God; and the books were opened: and another book was opened, which is called the Book of Life; and the dead were judged out of the things that were written in those books, according to their works. And the sea gave up the dead which were in it, and death and the grave[1] gave up the dead which were in them; and they were judged every one according to his works: and death and the grave were cast into the lake of fire. This is the second death. And whosoever was not found written in the Book of Life was cast into the lake of fire." Surely, "it is a fearful thing to fall into the hands of the living God."

CHAPTER XXIII

SUMMARY OF THE CHRISTIAN SYSTEM OF FACTS

I. God alone is self-existent and eternal. Before earth and time were born he operated by his Word and his Spirit. God, the Word of God, and the Spirit of God, participants of one and the same nature, are the foundations of *Nature, Providence,* and *Redemption.* In *Nature* and *Providence,* it is God, the Word, and the Spirit. *In Grace,* it is the Father, the Son, and the Holy Spirit. All creation, providences, and remedial arrangements display to us the cooperations of *Three Divine Participants,* of one self-existent, independent, incommunicable nature. These are fundamental conceptions of all the revelations and developments of the Divinity, and necessary to all rational and sanctifying views of religion.

II. In the *Law* and in the *Gospel* these sacred and mysterious relations and personal manifestations of God are presupposed and assumed as the basis of the whole procedure. "God created *all things* by Jesus Christ, and for him." "The Word was in the beginning with God," "before all things," and "by him all things consist." "God

---

[1] Hades.

created man upright." Man sinned: all became mortal: our nature became susceptible of evil. It is in this respect fallen and depraved. "There is none righteous—no, not one." God the Father has chosen men in Christ to salvation "through the sanctification of the Spirit unto obedience, and sprinkling of the blood of Jesus"; and "promised," to such, "eternal life before the foundation of the world."

III. Therefore, in "the fulness of time"—"in *due* time, God sent forth his Son, made of a woman"—for "the Word became flesh, and dwelt among us; and we beheld his glory, the glory as of an only begotten of the Father, full of grace and truth." "He showed us the Father." He died as a sin-offering—was buried, rose again the third day—ascended to heaven—presented his offering in the true Holy Place—made expiation for our sins—"forever sat down on the right hand of the Supreme Majesty in the heavens"—set down his Holy Spirit—inspired his apostles, who "preached with the Holy Spirit sent down from heaven"—persuaded many Jews and Gentiles that he was made "the author of an eternal salvation to all who obeyed him." He commanded faith, repentance, and baptism to be preached in his name for remission of sins to every nation and people under heaven.

IV. All who "believe in him are justified from all things"; because this faith is living, active, operative, and perfected by "obeying from the heart that mould of doctrine delivered to us." Hence such persons repent of their sins, and obey the gospel. They receive the Spirit of God, and the promise of eternal life—walk in the Spirit, and are sanctified to God, and constituted heirs of God and joint heirs with Christ. They shall be raised from the dead incorruptible, immortal, and shall live forever with the Lord; while those "who know not God, and obey not the gospel of his Son, shall perish with an everlasting destruction from the presence of the Lord and from the glory of his power."

CHAPTER XXIV

THE BODY OF CHRIST

I. That institution which separates from the world, and consociates the people of God into a peculiar community; having laws, ordinances, manners and customs of its own, immediately derived from the Saviour of the world, is called the *congregation* or *church* of the Lord. This is sometimes technically called the *mystical* body of Christ, contradistinguished from his literal and natural body. Over this spiritual body he is the head, the king, lord, and lawgiver, and they are severally members of his body, and under his direction and government.

II. The *true* Christian church, or house of God, is composed of all those in every place that do publicly acknowledge Jesus of Nazareth as the true Messiah, and the only Saviour of men; and, building themselves upon the foundation of the apostles and prophets, associate under the constitution which he himself has granted and authorized in the New Testament, and are walking in his ordinances and commandments—and of none else.

III. This institution, called *the congregation of God*, is a great community of communities—not a community representative of communities, but a community composed of many particular communities, each of which is built upon the same foundation, walk according to the same rules, enjoys the same charter, and is under the jurisdiction of no other community of Christians, but is to all other communities as an individual disciple is to every other individual disciple in any one particular community meeting in any given place.

IV. Still, all these particular congregations of the Lord, whether at Rome, Corinth, or Ephesus, though equally independent of one another as to the management of their own peculiar affairs, are, by virtue of one common Lord, one faith, one baptism, and one common salvation, but one kingdom or church of God, and, as such, are under obligations to co-operate with one another in all measures promotive of the great ends of Christ's death and resurrection.

V. But, in order to this holy communion and co-operation of churches, it is indispensable that they have an intimate and approving knowledge of one another, which can only be had and enjoyed in the form of districts. Thus the "congregations in Judea" intimately knew one another, and co-operated. Those in Galatia also knew one another, and co-operated. And while some of the churches or brethren in each district, being mutually acquainted with some in another, made the churches of both districts acquainted with one another, they were enabled to co-operate to the ends of the earth.

VI. These districts are a part of the *circumstances* of Christ's kingdom, as well as the *manner* of maintaining correspondence and co-operation among them, and the occasions and incidents requiring concert and conjoint action. For these, as well as for the circumstances of any particular community, the apostles gave no specific directions. It was, indeed, impossible they could; for, as the circumstances of particlar communities, and of the whole church, vary at different times and places, no one set of particular, sectional, or intersectional regulations could suit all these peculiarities and emergencies. These, then, are necessarily left to the wisdom and discretion of the whole community, as the peculiar exigencies and mutations of society may require.

VII. But in granting to the communities of the saints this necessary license of deciding what is expedient, orderly, decent, and of public and practical utility in the circumstantials of Christianity, no allowance is implied authorizing any interference with a single item of the Christian institution. Hence the necessity of a very clear discrimination, not between "the essentials and the non-essentials," for in Divine Christianity there are no non-essentials, but between the family of God and its circumstances—between the Christian institution and its accidents. Certain it is that there is a very manifest difference between any individual man, family, community, or institution, and its circumstances. What is more evident than the difference between a man and his apparel, his house, his neighborhood, his associations and connections?

VIII. The Christian institution has its facts, its precepts, its promises, its ordinances, and their meaning or doctrine. These are not matters of policy, of arrangement, of expediency, but of divine and immutable ordination and continuance. Hence the faith, the worship, and the righteousness, or the doctrine, the piety, and the morality of the gospel institution, are not legitimate subjects of human legislation, alteration, or arrangement. No man nor community can touch these and be innocent. These rest upon the wisdom and authority of Jehovah; and he that meddles with these presumes to do that which the cherubim and seraphim dare not. Whatever, then, is a part of the Christian faith or the Christian hope—whatever constitutes ordinances or precepts of worship, or statutes of moral right and wrong, like the ark of the covenant, is not to be touched with uninspired and uncommissioned hands.

IX. But whether we shall register the churches in a given district, or the members in a particular church; whether we shall meet oftener than once on the Lord's day, or at what hour and in what sort of house; whether we shall commemorate the Lord's death forenoon or afternoon, before day or after night; whether we shall sit round one board, or in our respective pews; whether we shall sing from book or from memory, prose or verse, etc., etc., are matters in which our conceptions of expediency, decency, and good order may have free scope. Also whether the churches in a given district shall, by letter, messengers, or stated meetings, once or twice per annum, or oftener, communicate with one another; whether they shall send one, two, or twenty persons, or all go and communicate face to face, or send a letter; and whether they shall annually print, write, or publish their statistics, etc., etc., etc., are the mere circumstantials of the Christian institution.

X. But, co-operation itself is one thing, and the manner of co-operation another. Co-operation, as much as the intercommunion of Christians, is a part of the Christian institution. We must "*strive together* in our prayers" for one another, and for the salvation of men; and this, if there were no scriptural example nor precept on the subject, is enough. To pray for one another as individuals or communities implies that we shall assist one another in every way for which we pray for one another; otherwise our prayers and thanksgivings for each other are mere hypocrisy. He that would pray for the progress of the truth at home and abroad, having it in his power to contribute a single dollar to that end, and yet withholds it, shows how little value he sets upon his own prayers, and how much upon his money.

XI. From the days of the apostles till now co-operative associations of churches have uniformly followed the political distributions of the earth. Those in "Judea, Galatia, Achaia, Pontus, Cappadocia, Macedonia, Asia, Bithynia," etc., etc., are designations of churches and brethren familiar to all New Testament readers. This is a matter of convenience, rather than of necessity; just as the churches in Pennsylvania, Virginia, Ohio, Kentucky, etc., can generally more conveniently and successfully co-operate by states and territories, than by any other divisions or precincts. I say, this is matter of convenience, rather than of necessity. It is of necessity that we co-operate, but of convenience that the churches in one county, state, or nation, form regular ways and means for co-operation.

XII. The necessity of co-operation is felt everywhere and in all associations of men. It is a part of the economy of Heaven. What are mountains, but grains of sand! What are oceans, but drops of water! And what the mightiest and most triumphant armies, but collections of individual men! How much more good or ill can be done by co-operation than by individual enterprise, the history of the world, both civil and ecclesiastic, does little more than detail. One hundred churches, well disciplined, acting in concert, with Christian zeal, piety, humanity—frequently meeting together in committees of ways and means for building up Zion, for fencing in the deserts, cultivating the enclosed fields, watering the dry and barren spots, striving together mightily in prayer, in preaching the word, in contributing to the necessities of the saints, in enlightening the ignorant, and in devising all practicable ways of doing good—would, in a given period, do more than twice the same number acting in their individual capacity, without concert, without co-operation, and that united energy always the effect of intelligent and cordial combination.

XIII. But, in order to this, Christians must regard the church, or body of Christ, as one community, though composed of many small communities, each of which is an organized member of this great national organization; which, under Christ, as the supreme and sole head, king, lord, and lawgiver, has the conquest of the whole world in its prayers, aims, plans, and efforts. Hence, there must be such an understanding and agreement between these particular congregations as will suffice to a recognition and approval of their several acts; so that the members or the measures of one community shall be treated with the respect due to them at home, in whatever community they may happen to be presented. On this principle only can any number of independent and distinct communities of any sort—political, commercial, literary, moral, or religious—act in concert with mutual advantage to themselves, and with a proper reference to the general good.

XIV. Any one who seeks apostolic sanctions for these views of co-operation will find ample authority in the Acts and Epistles of the Apostles. Paul addresses *all the saints* in Rome" in his Epistle to the Romans. Now in Rome there were sundry churches, as appears from chapter 16:5, 10, 11, 14, 15. These all he addresses as one single community. Again he represents "all the churches of the Gentiles" as uniting in thanks to Priscilla and Aquila. (16:4.) He also represents "the churches of Christ" as uniting in salutations by him to the Romans. (Verse 16.) In his letters to the Corinthians he addresses the church of Corinth, "All the saints which are in all Achaia," and "all them in every place who call upon the name of Jesus Christ." (1 Cor. 1: 2; 2 Cor. 1:1.) These he exhorts to "be perfectly joined together in the same mind and in the same judgments." (1 Cor. 1:10.) "The churches in Asia united in their salutations to the Corinthians." (16:19.) He speaks in the Second Epistle of all the churches in Achaia, as "helping together in prayer for him" and his companions, and of their helping him on his way in the work of the Lord. In the eighth chapter he informs them of the grace of God bestowed on "all churches in Macedonia," evinced by the liberality of their united contributions for the saints. He also speaks of an equality in the mutual contributions of churches in one co-operation—and of a brother chosen by sundry communities to travel with the apostles (8:14, 18, 19): and of his accompanying brethren as "messengers of the churches." The whole ninth chapter of this epistle speaks of the co-operation of the churches in public contributions for common objects. Paul, and all the brethren with him, unite in the epistle to "all the churches in Galatia." These he commands to "bear one another's burdens, and thus to fulfil the law of Christ."

But, indeed, all the *catholic epistles* are unequivocal proofs that co-operation is of the very essence of the Christian institution. Such are some of Paul's epistles, both the epistles of Peter, the First of John, and that of James and Jude. The very basis of such general or universal letters is the fact that all the communities of Christ constitute but one body, and are individually and mutually bound to co-operate in all things pertaining to a common salvation.

CHAPTER XXV

THE CHRISTIAN MINISTRY

I. "He gave some apostles, some prophets, some evangelists, some pastors and teachers, for the perfecting of the saints for *the work of the ministry,* for the edifying of the body of Christ; till we all come in the unity of the faith, and of the knowledge of the Son of God, unto the measure of the stature of the fulness of Christ," etc. For the setting up of the Christian institution, officers extraordinary were needed. So was it in the Jewish, and so is it in every institution, human and divine. But when an institution is set up, it only requires an ordinary ministry or administration of its affairs. All the extraordinary gifts vouchsafed to Moses, and to the apostles and prophets of the gospel institution, ceased when these institutions were fully developed and established. Still a regular and constant ministry was needed among the Jews, and is yet needed among the Christians; and both of these by divine authority.

II. Natural gifts for a natural state of things, and supernatural gifts for a supernatural state of things, are, in the wisdom of both God and man, opposite and needful. Hence, even in the apostolic age, there were officers without, as well as with miraculous endowment. "Having, then, gifts differing according to the office or grace that is given to us—if prophecy, let us prophesy according to the measure of our faith; or ministry, let us attend on our ministering; he that teacheth, on teaching; he that exhorteth, on exhortation; he that distributeth, with simplicity; he that ruleth, with diligence." God has therefore conferred various gifts on the church for the effectual administration of its affairs. He has placed in it *"helps and governments,"* as well as apostles and prophets.

III. The standing and immutable ministry of the Christian community is composed of bishops, deacons, and evangelists. Of each of these there is but one order, though possessing great diversities of gifts. There have been bishops, deacons, and evangelists, with both ordinary and extraordinary gifts. Still the office is now, and ever was, the same. In ancient times official and unofficial persons sometimes possessed miraculous gifts. Those in high office were also generally of those most eminently gifted with extraordinary powers. Superficial readers have, therefore, sometimes concluded that, inasmuch as bishops, deacons and especially evangelists, frequently possessed these manifestations of the Holy Spirit, with the ceasing of those gifts the offices themselves also expired. This is a great mistake. Officers there must be while there are offices, or services to be performed. So long as the human system needs sight, hearing, and feeling, there will be eyes, ears, and hands. So long, also, as the Christian body is an organized body, having many services to perform, it must have organs or officers by which to enjoy itself and operate on society.

IV. There are, indeed, necessarily as many offices in every body as there are services to be performed to it, or by it. This is the root and reason of all the offices in all the universe of God. Our planet needs diverse celestial services to be performed to it. Hence, the sun, moon, and stars, are celestial officers ministering to it. The eye, the ear, the tongue, the hand, the foot, are, for the same reason, officers in the human body, essentially serving it in its vital interests and enjoyments; and by means of these organs it performs important functions to other bodies.

V. Experience, as well as observation, has taught us that "practice makes perfect," and that "whatever is every person's business is no person's business." Hence arose the custom among men of communicating certain offices to particular individuals. The philosophy of such elections and ordinances is found in the fact, that special services are best performed by special organs or agents, whose special province and duty it is to attend to them.

VI. As the Christian system is a perfect system, it wisely provides for its own perpetuity and prosperity by creating all necessary offices and filling them with suitable persons. We have said these offices are three, and of perpetual because of necessary existence. *Bishops,* whose office it is to preside over, to instruct, and to edify the community—to feed the church of the Lord with knowledge and understanding—and to watch for their souls as those that must give account to the Lord at his appearing and his kingdom, compose the first class. *Deacons,* or servants—whether called treasurers, almoners, stewards, doorkeepers, or messengers—constitute the second. For the term *deacon* originally included all public servants whatever, though now most commonly confined to one or two classes; and improperly, no doubt, to those only who attend to the mere temporal interests of the community. They are distinguished persons, called and commissioned by the church (and consequently are always responsible to it) to serve in any of these capacities. *Evangelists,* however, though a class of public functionaries created by the church, do not serve it directly; but are by it sent out into the world, and constitute the third class of functionaries belonging to the Christian system.

VII. As there is more scrupulosity on some minds concerning the third class of evangelists than concerning either bishops or deacons, we shall take occasion to speak more explicitly and fully upon the nature and necessity, as well as upon the authority of this office. Evangelists, as the term indicates, are persons devoted to the preaching of the word, to the making of converts, and the planting of churches. It is, indeed, found but three times in the New Covenant; but the verb from which it comes—viz.: *to evangelize*—is in some of its branches found almost sixty times in that volume. "To evangelize" and "to do the work of an evangelist" are phrases of equal import, and indicate the same duties, rights, and privileges.

VIII. Among the offices which were comprehended in the apostleship, none required more varied endowments than that of the evangelist. The gift of tongues was amongst the qualifications necessary to those who, after the ascension, first undertook this work. But the qualifications for this office, so far as the gift of tongues or the knowledge of language is concerned, are not immutably fixed. It depends upon the field of labor which the evangelist is to occupy, whether he must speak one language or more. His work is to proclaim the word intelligibly and persuasively—to immerse all the believers, or converts of his ministry—and to plant and organize churches wherever he may have occasion; and then teach them to keep the commandments and ordinances of the Lord.

IX. Take, for example, the sketch given us by Luke of the labors of Philip the evangelist, one of the first who wore that designation. One of the seven ministers of the Jerusalem church, after his diaconate was vacated by the dispersion of that community, he commenced his evangelical labors. He turned his face towards Samaria, and preached and baptized among the Samaritans: for, we are told, when the Samaritans believed Philip preaching the things concerning the kingdom of God and the Lord Jesus, they were baptized, both men and women. He also converted the Ethiopian eunuch; and then, passing from Azotus, he "preached *in all the cities* till he came to Caesarea," where he afterwards resided. The next notice we have of him is found in Acts 21:8. "We," says Luke, "who were of Paul's company, departed, and came into Caesarea, and entered into the house of Philip the evangelist, one of the seven, and abode with him. He had four virgin daughters that did prophesy." Evident, then, it is that he obtained the title of *evangelist* from his itinerant labors in the gospel and in the converting of men. His possession of the gift of the Holy Spirit was no more peculiar to him as an evangelist than as deacon of the church in Jerusalem; for while in the diaconate of that church he seems to have been as full of the Holy Spirit as when visiting all the cities from Azotus to Caesarea.

X. Convening converts into societies, and organizing them into worshiping assemblies, are inseparably connected with the right of converting men. Casually, in his letters to Timothy, Paul seems to define the work of an evangelist. He says, "Preach the word; be instant in season, out of season; endure affliction; *do the work of an evangelist;* fulfil thy ministry." "Let no man despise thy youth. Till I come, give attendance to reading, to exhortation, to teaching. Neglect not the gift that is in thee [or cultivate and exercise the office conferred upon thee], according to prophecy—by the laying on the hands of the presbytery [or eldership]. Meditate upon these things; give thyself wholly to them, that thy profiting may appear to all: take heed to thyself and to thy teaching; continue in them: for in doing this, thou shalt both save thyself and them that hear thee."[1] This seems to be the office of an Evangelist which the Lord gave the church after his ascension.

XI. Setting things in order in the churches—the committing the same office to faithful men, who shall be able to instruct others—the ordaining of elders, and a general superintendence of the affairs of churches, seem to have been also lodged in the hands of Timothy and Titus as agents of the apostles. How far these works are yet necessary, and how far the superintendence of them may be safely lodged in the hands of select evangelists as *respects infant communities,* may be, with many, a question of dubious interpretation. But that evangelists are to separate into communities their own converts, teach and superintend them till they are in a condition to take care of themselves, is as unquestionably a part of the office of an evangelist, as praying, preaching, or baptizing.

XII. But we shall be asked, "Is not preaching, and baptizing, and even teaching, the common privilege of all disciples, as they have opportunity?" And we also ask in answer, "Is it not the privilege of all fathers to teach their own children, and to preside over their own families?" But who will thence infer, that all fathers are teachers and presidents, does not more shock common sense, than he who in-

_____
[1] 1 Timothy 4; 2 Timothy 4.

fers that all disciples, as such, are evangelists, pastors, and teachers, because we concede that in certain cases it is the privilege of all the citizens of Christ's kingdom to preach, baptize, and teach. Every citizen of Christ's kingdom has, in virtue of his citizenship, equal rights, privileges, and immunities. So has every citizen of the United States. Yet all citizens are not legislators, magistrates, judges, governors, etc. Before any community, civil or religious, is organized, every man has equal rights to do what seemeth good in his own eyes. But when organized, and persons appointed to office, then whatever rights, duties, privileges are conferred on particular persons, can not of right belong to those who have transferred them; any more than a person can not both give and keep the same thing.

XIII. But there are some duties and privileges we can not wholly communicate to others. Parents can not wholly transfer the education of their children to others; neither can a master transfer all his duties to a steward or overseer. No more can the citizens of Christ's kingdom wholly transfer their duties to preach and teach Christ. To enlighten the ignorant, persuade the unbelieving, to exhort the disobedient when they fall in our way and we have the ability or opportunity, is an intransferable duty. Even the Church of Rome, with all her clerical pride, commands and authorizes *lay baptism*, when a priest is not convenient. A Christian is by profession a preacher of truth and righteousness, both by precept and example. *He may of right preach, baptize, and dispense the supper, as well as pray for all men, when circumstances demand it.* This concession does not, however, either dispense with the necessity of having evangelists, bishops, and deacons; nor, having them, does it authorize any individual to assume to do what has been given in charge to them. Liberty without licentiousness, and government without tyranny, is the true genius of the Christian institution.

XIV. While, then, the Christian system allows every man "as he has received a gift to minister as a good steward of the manifold grace of God," it makes provision for choosing and setting apart qualified persons for all its peculiar services, necessary to its own edification and comfort, as well as to its usefulness in the world. It provides for its own perpetuity and its growth in the wisest and most practical manner. Its whole wisdom consists in four points:—First: It establishes the necessary offices for its perpetuity and growth. Second: It selects the best-qualified persons for those offices. Third: It consecrates or sets those persons apart to those offices. Fourth: It commands them to give themselves wholly to the work, that their improvement may keep pace with the growth of the body, and be apparent to all. Can any person point out an imperfection in this plan?

XV. All its officers, whether for its services at home or abroad, when fully proved, are to be formally and solemnly set apart by the imposition of the hands of the presbytery or eldership of the church. The whole community chooses—the seniors ordain. *This is the apostolic tradition.* Let those unacquainted with the volume examine the apostolic law and usage. (Acts 6:2-6.) So the Christian system in its elections and ordinations began. *It is immutable.* Therefore this system obtains in all cases. The qualifications for any office are always founded in the nature of the office. They are generally detailed, but not always, because the *work to be done* is the best guide in ascertaining the qualifications of the doer of it.

XVI. We say the seniors or elders always ordain. Popery says, "None but those on whom the apostolic hands have been laid can of right ordain." *Such an idea is not in the Christian system.* The seniors always lay on hands, whether hands have been laid on them or not. This is true Protestantism. Better still, it is true Bibleism. *Nay, it is the Christian system.* The apostles laid on hands because *seniors,* and not because *apostles.* This is the gist of a controversy of fifteen hundred years' standing. It has been very generally, almost universally, misstated and overlooked. Protestants are as much Papists in this, as the Papists are Protestants in disowing Protestantism. It is assumed by Romanists, and conceded by Protestants, that *"holy hands"* are official hands by a *jure divino.* They are sometimes, but not always. But *Christian elders* (for I do not mean mere old men), who have long walked in the ways of the Lord, have holy hands, and much more power with and from the Lord, than ever dwelt in any pontiff or pretended vicar of Christ, in twelve hundred and sixty years.

XVII. In proof that seniors lay on hands, we appeal to the fact (Acts 6), for the apostles were the oldest converts in Jerusalem. We appeal also to the fact that the presbytery or eldership laid hands on Timothy, and gave him the gift or office of an evangelist. And are there two rules of ordination in one system? Paul and Barnabas, though *apostles,* were themselves ordained by the church of Antioch by its presbytery. Consequently, *seniors in Christ,* as such, can, of divine warrant, lay hands on any persons, for any office to which the church has elected them. It must be done also by prayer and fasting. See Acts 6:6; 13:3; 16:23.

XVIII. Persons may be juniors in years and seniors in Christ. Timothy, says Paul, *"lay hands suddenly on no man."* This implies that the ordained were juniors in the Lord; and, until they had attained some character and standing as seniors (even Timothy himself), were not to consent to their ordination. Perhaps it may be necessary to say that classic presbytery and the presbytery of a single church are very different institutions. The apostles ordained *elders* (a presbytery) in every church. They did not make young men old, but set apart those that were seniors in the Lord to the office of overseers. They did not make juniors *seniors*, but they made elders *bishops*.

XIX. The community, the church, the multitude of the faithful, are the fountain of official power. This power descends from the body itself—not from its servants. Servants made by servants are servants of servants; and such are all the clergy of the man of sin. But the body of Christ, under him as its head, animated and led by his Spirit, is the fountain and spring of all official power and privilege. How much surer and purer is ecclesiastic authority thus derived from Christ the head, immediately through his body, than when derived through a long, doubtful, corrupt dynasty of bishops or pontiffs! The church is the mother of all the sons and priests of God; and to look for authority to her servants or creatures, as do all sorts of Papists, whether Catholic or Protestant, is to worship and serve the creature more than the Creator—a species of idolatry worthy only of the darkest night of the darkest day of the dark ages.

XX. But the church needs messengers for special occasions—not only her stated deacons and ministers, but ministers extraordinary. These, too, are selected by the church or churches in a given district, and *commissioned by their letters*. They are not consecrated by imposition of hands, but *approved by letters* from the community. Are we asked for authority? We produce it with pleasure. First Corinthians 16:3 is just to the point. "And," says Paul to the saints in Corinth, "when I come, *whomsoever you shall approve by letters,* them will I send to bring your liberality to Jerusalem." This is the apostolic usage in such cases. In the second epistle Paul says, "We have sent Titus the brother (Luke, we opine) whose praise is in the gospel (written by him), throughout all the churches—who was also *chosen by the churches* to travel with us this bounty," etc.

XXI. The Christian system demands for its perpetuity and for its prosperity at home and abroad, bishops, deacons, and evangelists. Its bishops teach, preside, and execute the laws of Christ in all its convocations. The deacons, a large and diverse class of functionaries, composed of stewards, treasurers, almoners, doorkeepers, etc., as the case may require, wait continually upon its various services. Its evangelists, possessed of proper qualifications, ordained and consecrated to the work of the Lord in converting sinners and planting churches, by a presbytery, or a board of seniors competent to the prudent discharge of this duty, are constantly engaged in multiplying its members. These ministers of the word are commanded to be wholly engrossed in this work, and consequently to be fully sustained by their brethren in it. They are held responsible to all the holy brethren, and to the Lord at his appearing and his kingdom, for the faithful discharge of that sacred trust confided in them.

XXII. What an efficient institution is that over which Christ presides, when well understood and fully carried out in all its details! With its bishops and deacons at home, and its evangelists abroad, wholly devoted to the faithful discharge of their respective trusts; men of experience, faith, piety, morality, full of zeal, energy, benevolence, co-operating with all similar institutions, supported by the prayers and freewill offerings of all the united people, having the love of God in their hearts, and heaven in their eye, what may they not achieve of glory to God, of good to men, and honor to themselves! Of such an army of the faith, in full operation and concert, it might indeed be asked, "Who is this that looketh forth as the morning, fair as the moon, bright as the sun, and terrible as an army with banners?"

CHAPTER XXVI

THE CHRISTIAN DISCIPLINE

I. Members should be publicly received into all societies. They are so in the state. It is matter of record. When a person is regenerated, and desires to be enrolled among the disciples meeting in any one place, if his confession to salvation or immersion has not been publicly known to all the brethren, reason says those who have been privy to the fact, who can attest his confession, ought to introduce him to the congregation, and he ought to be saluted or received as such by the brethren with whom he unites. This the slightest attention to propriety, the reason and nature of things, fully and satisfactorily demonstrates. Letters of recommendation are the expedient which, in apostolic times, was submitted for this formal introduction, when a citizen of the kingdom visited any community where he was unknown personally to the brethren.

II. A person can not be under the oversight or under the discipline of a congregation, unless he voluntarily associate with the brethren meeting in that place, and unless it be a matter of notoriety or of record among the brethren that he is one of them. There can be no formal exclusion if there be no formal reception. If there be no visible and formal union, there can be no visible and formal separation. In truth, there can be no discipline in any congregation, unless it be an organized body; and no body can be organized unless it is known who are members of it. On a matter of such plain, common-sense perception we have seldom thought it necessary to say a word, and should not now have noticed it at all, had we not found some societies which could not tell their own members, which even hesitated about the necessity of a formal reception of any person into them, or of having it on record who belonged to them. They demanded a positive commandment or precedent for such a reception. They might as pertinently have demanded a positive commandment for persons to be formally married before they could be recognized as husband and wife, as to ask for a positive commandment for one of the most common dictates of reason, though, indeed, every commandment addressed to the Christian congregations on relative duties and privileges assumes the principle that those who belong to any society are known to each other to belong to it, else they could not even perform the first duty to one another—they could not know when they were assembled—they could not "tarry for one another."

III. Whether there shall be a record in print, in writing, or on the memory of all the congregation, is a question which must depend on circumstances. If all the members are blessed with infallible memories, so as never to forget who are members, when they became such, when any one was received, when any one was rejected—I say, if every brother and sister can so well remember these matters, as, when the discipline of the congregation or any particular question respecting any case of discipline may arise, they can infallibly remember all about it; then, and in that case, it is unnecessary to have any record, church-book, secretary, or any thing written or printed. But if otherwise, there must be a record; because question involving peace and good order of society may arise, and have arisen, which require infallible testimony, of the most satisfactory evidence on questions of fact, such as, Was A B ever a member of your community? When did he become a member of it? When was he excluded? When was he restored? When did he forsake the assembly of the brethren? Was he a husband at the time of his removal? etc.

IV. Two things are paramount in all cases of discipline before brought into the congregation—*the fact and the law*. The fact is always to be established by good testimony or by the confession of the transgressor. The thing said to have been done, or the fact being established, the next question is, *What is the law in the case?* This the elders of the congregation must decide. They are to be judges both of the fact and the law. If they are not they are unfit for the office and unworthy the name of *"the rulers"* of the congregation. When they have fully examined and decided the case, they lay it before the congregation. If they acquiesce, the matter ends, and the accused is retained or excluded as the case may be. If they do not acquiesce, or if the accused appeals to the congregation, the case must be reconsidered; and if, on further examination, both the elders, the congregation and the accused retain the same views and the same position, helps must be called either from the congregation or from some other. This indeed must be a rare occurrence; and is the only ultimatum that Christianity contemplates.

V. "Offences must come"; and, if possible, they must be healed. To cut off an offender, is good; to cure him, is better; but to prevent him falling, is best of all. The Christian spirit and system alike inculcate vigilance in preventing; all expedition in healing offences; and in firmness in removing in corrigible offenders. Its disciplinary code is exceedingly simple, rational, and benevolent. It teaches us to regard all offences as acts of impiety or acts of immorality; sins against our brethren, or sins against God alone; the omission of right, or the commission of wrong.

VI. Trespasses against our brethren are all matters of aggression upon their person, property, or character. They are either private or public. We can only offend against the person, the property, or the character of a brother; and we can do this only privately or publicly. Christ's legislation on private or personal offences, as recorded in the eighteenth chapter of Matthew, commends itself to the approbation of Jew and Gentile all over the world. It is as plain and as excellent as his golden rule of moral feeling.

VII. Without giving any rules to decide who is the aggressor, or the aggrieved, allowing either of the parties to view the matter as he pleases, he commands him that supposes himself to be aggrieved to go to the aggressor and tell him his fault privately. If restitution is made and reconciliation effected, the matter ends. If not, he takes with him a second or a third person, states the facts of the case, reasons and remonstrates. If this also fails, then he is commanded to inform the church of the matter; and if the aggressor will not hear the church, then he is to be as a heathen man or a publican.

VIII. Some, indeed, imagine a difficulty in this case; for after *"teli"* there is no *it* in the original; and ask, *"What is to be told to the church—the original fault, or simply that the aggressor will not make restitution?"* The most natural construction of the sentence favors the simple statement of the fact—that an offence had been committed and restitution refused, without going into the details of the trespass. But a second difficulty has been suggested on the manner in which the congregation is to be informed. Is it to be told to the whole community in full assembly met? or to those appointed by the congregation to hear and adjudicate such matters? Certainly the congregation has ears as well as a tongue, and it is not all ears nor all tongue. Every well-organized church has its eldership, who hear all such matters, and who bring them before the whole assembly only when it is absolutely necessary, and even then at a convenient season.

IX. The elders hear the matter; and if the case be one that requires a special committee, which Paul calls "secular seats of judicature" (1 Cor. 6:4), they appoint it; then, and not till then, if their decision of the matter be refused, they bring it before the whole congregation, and he is excluded from among them, that he may be as a heathen man and a publican—one entitled only to civil and not to Christian respect—one whose company is to be eschewed rather than courted.

X. The whole community can act, and ought to act, in receiving and in excluding persons: but in the aggregate, it can never become judges of offences and a tribunal trial. Such an institution was never set up by divine authority. No community is composed only of wise and discreet full-grown men. The Christian church engrosses old men, young men, and babes in Christ. Shall the voice of a babe be heard, or counted as a vote, in a case of discipline? What is the use of bishops in a church, if all are to rule—of judges, if all are judges of fact and law? No wonder that broils and heartburning, and scandals of all sorts, disturb those communities ruled by a democracy of the whole—where every thing is to be judged in public and full assembly. Such is not the Christian system. It ordains that certain persons shall judge and rule,[1] and that all things shall "be done decently and in order."

XI. Besides matters of private trespass between brethren, there are matters of public wrong, or acts of injustice towards the whole Christian community, and also towards them that are without. Drunkenness in a professor, for example, is a sin against God and against all the Christian brotherhood. It is, moreover, a public nuisance to all men, so far as it is witnessed or known. The transgressor in such a case, if he be not penitent and reform, must be convicted of the offence. An attempt at convicting him of the offence is not to be made till he fail to acknowledge it. A failure to acknowledge, or an attempt to deny, calls for conviction, and precludes the idea of repentance.

XII. In all cases of conviction the church is to be addressed through its rulers. No private individual has a right to accuse any person before the whole community. The charge, in no case, is to be preferred before the whole congregation. Such a procedure is with-

---

[1] 1 Timothy 3:5; 5:17; Acts 20:28-31; Hebrews 13:17, etc., etc.

)ut precedent in the law or in the gospel—in any well-regulated soci-ty, church, or state. If, then, any brother fall into any public of-:ence, those privy to it notify the elders of the church, or those for :he time-being presiding over it, of the fact, and of the evidence on ,vhich they rely. The matter is then in the hands of the proper per-;ons. They prosecute the investigation of it; and, on the denial of :he accused, seek to convict him of the allegation.

XIII. When a person is convicted of any offence, he is unworthy of the confidence of the brethren; for conviction supposes conceal-ment and denial; and these, of course, are evidence of impenitence. We do not say that such a one is never again to be worthy of such confidence; but that until he has given satisfactory proofs of genuine repentance, he is to be treated as one not of the body of Christ.

XIV. In all cases of hopeful repentance the transgressor is to be restored with admonition. The acknowledgment of an offence, and of repentance for it, are, in all cases, to be as public as the sin itself. Peter's sin and repentance are as public as his name. So was Da-vid's. So should be those of all transgressors. Those who have caused the Saviour and his faithful followers to blush ought them-selves to be made to blush before the world; and if their sorrow and amendment be genuine, they will do it cheerfully and fully. "Them that sin rebuke before all, that others also may fear." (1 Tim. 5:29.)[1]

XV. Whether it may be always prudent in the incipient stages of every case of discipline to have open doors, or whether some cases may not require closed doors, are questions referred to human pru-dence; but in the case of the ultimate decision of the congregation, and in that of exclusion, there can be but one opinion on the neces-sity and utility of its being done in the presence of all who may please to attend.

CHAPTER XXVII

EXPEDIENCY

I. "All things lawful are not expedient, because all things lawful edify not." So Paul substantially affirmed. A position of licentious tendency, if not well qualified. As defined by its author, it is per-fectly safe. He only assumed that there were many things which he might lawfully do, which were not *expedient* for him to do. He might, for example, have married a wife, eaten the flesh of either Jewish or Pagan sacrifices, or drunk the wine of their libations, etc.,

---

[1] By a reference to an Extra on Order, published 1835, the curious reader may find other useful hints on the subject of discipline.

etc., according to the Christian law; but, in the circumstances of his peculiar vocation and localities, to have done these things would have been inexpedient.

II. Law itself is, indeed, at best but an expedient—a means, supposed, at the time of its promulgation, suitable to some rational end. But, owing to the mutability of things, laws often fail to be the best means to the ends proposed; and are therefore abolished, or, for the time-being, suspended. This is true of all laws and institutions prescribing *modes* and *forms* of action, whether in religion or morality. Moral laws, properly so called, are, indeed, immutable; because the principle of every moral law is *love*, and that never can cease to be not only a way and means, but the *only way and means*, to rational, to human happiness. Positive precepts, however, prescribing the *forms* of religious and moral action, emanating from God himself, have been changed, and may again be changed, while all the elements of piety and morality are immutable. It would now, for example, be immoral to marry a natural sister; yet it was for a time done by divine authority. It became inexpedient to continue the practice, and the law was changed.

III. There is, therefore, *a law of expediency*, as well as the expediency of law. This law of expediency, as it is, indeed, the basis of the expediency of law in the divine government, has been, as in the case of David eating the loaves of the presence, and the priests profaning the Sabbath by the labors of the temple, occasionally elevated above the precepts that prescribe the forms of religious and moral action. True, indeed, that such cases are exceedingly rare; and they are rare reasoners who can safely decide when any particular precept prescribing the *form* of action may, for the sake of the action itself, be waived or suspended. It is, moreover, exceedingly questionable, whether, under the more perfect institution of Christianity, the law of expediency can ever clash with any moral or religious precept in the New Covenant.

IV. Still, there are many things left to the law of expediency, concerning which no precepts are found in the apostolic writings. To ascertain these is the object of this chapter. They are then, in one sentence, those things, or forms of action, which it was impossible or unnecessary to reduce to special precepts; consequently they are not faith, piety, nor morality; because whatever is of the faith, of the worship, or of the morality of Christianity, was both possible and necessary to be promulgated; and is expressly and fully propounded in the sacred Scriptures. The laws of expediency, then, has no place in determining the articles of faith, acts of worship, nor principles of morality. All these require a *"thus saith the Lord"* in express statenents, and the sacred writings have clearly defined and decided them. But in other matters that may be called the circumstantials of the gospel and of the church of Christ, the people of God are left to their own discretion and to the facilities and exigencies of society.

V. Many things, indeed, that are of vital importance to the well-being and prosperity of the kingdom of Christ, are left to the law of expediency. A few examples will suffice:—Can any one imagine any measures of more consequence than the safe-keeping of the apostolic writings, the multiplication of copies, the translation of them into different languages, and the mode of distributing them throughout the whole world? Now, who can show a positive or special precept on any one of these four vital points? Scribes or copyists, paper-makers, printers, bookbinders, and vendors of the oracles of God, are as unknown to the apostolic writers as mails, post-offices, railroads, and steam-engines. So negligent, too, has the kingdom of Christ been on some of these points, that she has not at this hour a *received copy* of the living oracles. We American and English people have a *received version* by authority of a king; but we have not a *received original* by the authority of any king or government, civil or ecclesiastic. A startling fact, truly! But who dares to deny it?

VI. Next to these are meeting-houses, baptisteries, Lord's tables, the emblematic loaf and cup, times of convocation, arrangements for the day, etc., etc. Acts of parliament, decrees of synods and councils, but no apostolic enactments, statutes, or laws, are found for any of these important items. There is neither precept nor precedent in the New Testament for building, hiring, buying, or possessing a meeting-house; for erecting a baptismal basin, font, or bath; for chancel, altar, table, leavened or unleavened bread, chalice, cup, or tankard, and many other things of equal value.

VII. There is no law, rule, or precedent for the *manner* of eating the Lord's supper, no hint as to the quantity of bread and wine to be used by each participant; nothing said about who shall partake first, or how it shall be conveyed from one to another. These are all discretionary matters, and left to the prudence and good sense of the Christian communities—in other words, to the law of expediency.

VIII. Touching these and very many other such matters and things, nothing is enacted, prescribed, or decided by apostolic authority; but all the things to be done are enjoined in very clear and broad precepts, or in very striking and clear apostolic precedents. General laws and precepts, embracing the whole range of religious and moral action, are often found in the sayings of the Lord and his ministers of the new institution, from which also our duties and obligations may be clearly ascertained. That "marriage is honorable in all" is clearly taught; but who ever read a verse on the *manner* in which this most important of all social institutions is to be performed? No age is fixed at which the covenant shall be made or ratified—on time of life prescribed for its consummation—nothing said about who shall perform the service, the formula, the witnesses, the record, etc. And, still more singular, there is no table, no law, or statute in all the new covenant saying who may, or who may not, enter into that relation on any principle of consanguinity or affinity. By the consent of the Christian church the Jewish law obtains in this matter.

IX. The communion of saints, of all Christian churches—the co-operation of churches as one holy nation, a kingdom of priests, as a peculiar people in all common interests and benefits—an efficient gospel ministry, supported justly and honorably by the whole community —are matters clearly and fully taught by both apostolic precept and authority; but the forms, the ways and means by which these ends shall be attained, are left to the law of expediency.

X. But here arises a practical and all-important question, viz.: *Who shall ascertain and who shall interpret this law of expediency?* We all agree that expedients are to be chosen with regard to times, seasons, and other circumstances. Changes in these must always change expedients. The mariner's compass, the art of printing, new modes of traveling, banks and their commercial operations, new forms of government, etc., etc., have changed the order of society and all human expedients. Now the law of expediency is the law of adopting the best present means of attaining any given end. But this is a matter which the wisdom and good sense of individuals and communities must decide. This is not, this can not be, a matter of standing revelation. Now if the church was always unanimous in opinion as in faith—if all the accumulated wisdom gave one uniform decision on all such questions—then the whole church is by one voice to ascertain the law of expediency on any given point. But this is not the case. No class of men, apostles, teachers, privates, ever did agree on questions of expediency. Paul and Barnabas dissented and differed, *without any breach of communion,* on a question of this sort. Hence arises the necessity of the spirit of concession, subordination, bearing, forbearing, submitting to one another. When there are two views or opinions on any question of expediency entertained by two parties, one of them must yield, or there are two distinct systems of operation, and ultimately two distinct parties. According to the law of expediency, then, the minors in age, experience, or numbers, must give place to the majors in age, experience, or numbers. But as numbers are supposed to represent the ratios of age, wisdom, and knowledge, it is expedient that a clearly ascertained majority of those whose province it is to decide any matter shall interpret the law of expediency; or, in other words, the minority shall peaceably and cordially acquiesce in the decisions of the majority. Since the age of social compacts began, till now, no other principle of co-operation, no other law of expediency, can secure the interests, the union, harmony, and strength of any people, but that of the few submitting to the many.

XI. He that asks for unanimity asks for what is not often attainable in a small number of persons. He asks for the liberty of one or two to govern or to control a whole community—for the government of a minority, however small, over a majority, however large. This is virtually, though not formally, and not often intentionally, the demand of all the advocates of unanimity in ascertaining or interpreting the law of expediency in any given case. The law of expediency enacts that a majority of the seniors shall decide in all cases what is most expedient to be done in attaining any of the ends commanded in the Christian institution, the means to which are not divinely ordained in the written laws of that institution; and that the miniority shall cheerfully and conscientiously acquiesce in such decisions.

XII. *The law of love is the supreme law of religion, morality, and expediency. No code of laws, without it, could make or keep any people pure, peaceable, and happy; and with it, we only want, in most matters, but general laws.* This is the spirit, and soul, and body of the Christian institution. We can not love by law, but we can walk in love with no other law but that of love. The Christian system contemplates love as supreme, and makes no arrangements nor provisions for keeping together a carnal, worldly, selfish, self-willed population. Better such a confederacy had burst into as many particles as persons, by the repellent principle of selfishness, than to be hooped together by all the laws of expediency from Noah to John Wesley.

CHAPTER XXVIII

HERESY

I. Schisms and heresies are matters strongly reprobated in the Christian Scriptures. That they may be guarded against with due care, they must be contemplated and understood in their true and proper scriptural attributes. We shall therefore first attempt to define them.

II. The term *schism* is found but eight times in the apostolic writings. When applied to a garment (Matt. 9:16; Mark 20:21), it is properly translated *rent;* applied to a concourse of people (John

7:43; 9:16; 10:19), it is translated *division;* when applied to the church by Paul (1 Cor. 1:10; 9:18; 12:25), it denotes *division* or *alienation*—not on account of faith, doctrines, or opinions—but on account of men as leaders or chiefs among the brethren. So the connections in which it is found always indicate. It is a division as respects *internal union,* or the union of heart and affection, only tending to a breach of visible or outward union, and therefore reprobated by the apostle. Such are its New Testament acceptations.

III. Schisms may then exist where there is the most perfect agreement in faith, in doctrine, in all religious tenets. Undue attachment to certain persons, to the disparagement of others, partial regards because of personal preferences, are the true elements of schism or division as it appeared in Corinth, and as the word is used in the New Testament. But few persons, nowadays, can correctly appreciate the force of the word *schism* in the apostolic age, because but a very few experimentally know the intimacies, the oneness of heart and soul, that obtained and prevailed in the Christian profession while all was genuine and uncorrupt. A union formed on Christian principles—a union with Christ and his people, in views, sentiments, feelings, aims, and pursuits—a real copartnery for eternity—almost annihilated individuality itself, and inseparably cemented into one spirit all the genuine members of Christ's body. Kindred drops do not more readily mingle into one mass, than flowed the souls of primitive Christians together in all their aspirations, loves, delights, and interests. Hence arose the jealousy in the apostle Paul when first he learned that particular persons in Corinth began to attract to themselves the notice and attachment for mere personal, individual, and fleshly considerations, as leaders or chiefs in the Christian family. In these indications he already saw the dissolution of the church. Although yet but one visible community, having one Lord, one faith, one baptism, one table, one ostensible supreme and all-controlling interest; still, in these attachments to particular persons, he not only saw a real division or breach in the hearts of the people, but foresaw that it would issue in positive, actual, and visible disunion or heresy. And here we are led to inquire into the scriptural import of this word *heresy.*

IV. *Hairesis,* strictly and literally indicative of *choice* or *option,* is anglicized *heresy,* and properly rendered *sect* or *faction,* and by implication *discord* and *contention.* It is found only *nine* times in the New Testament. In the Acts of the Apostles (5:17), we have it rendered "the sect of the Sadducees"; (15:5), "the sect of the Pharisees"; (24:5), "the sect of the Nazarenes"; (24:14), "after the way which they call *heresy* [a sect], so worship I," says Paul; (26:5), 'after the most strict *sect* of our religion I lived a Pharisee"; (28:22), 'as for this *sect* [of the Christians] we know that it is everywhere spoken against." Besides these six occurrences, we find it twice used by Paul in his epistles, and once by Peter. First Corinthians 11:19, 'For there must be *heresies* [sects] among you." Galatians 5:20, 'Seditions, heresies." Second Peter 2:1, "Shall bring in damnable heresies." In the common version it is, then, five times rendered *sect*, and four times *heresy*.

V. As the word *sect* or *heresy*, found only in the Acts of the Apostles and Epistles, does always in the former simply mean a *party*, without any regard to its tenets, the term has nothing in it either reproachful or honorable—nothing virtuous or vicious. Hence it is equally applied to Pharisees, Sadducees, Nazarenes, or Christians, without any insinuation as to the character of the party. It is only once rendered *heresy* in the Acts, and in that place it ought most obviously to have been *sect*. Paul had been accused by Tertullus (Acts 24:6) with the crime of being "a ringleader of the *sect* of the Nazarenes." Now, in vindicating himself from any censure in this case, he ought to have met the charge under the same title. This he did in the original; for in verse 5, in the indictment, and in verse 14, in his defence, we have the same word *hairesis*. How injudicious, then, was it on the part of our translators and the Vulgate to make Tertullus accuse Paul of a *sect*, and to make Paul defend himself of a *heresy*, when both Tertullus and Paul used the same word in their speeches as reported by Luke in the original!

V. In the new version this word is, as it should be, uniformly rendered *sect*. In the Epistles, and apparently once in the Acts, it is used as though it included an idea of censure or guilt. Paul defends himself from the accusation of Tertullus. Here, then, a question arises:—Why should the term *hairesis* import blame in its *Christian* and none in its *Jewish* acception? We answer, Because among the Jews sects or parties did not terminate, as among Christians, in separate communities or communions. They resembled the high and low church parties in the Episcopalian communion; or the different and numerous sects among the Romanists—viz.: Benedictines, Franciscans, Dominicans, Jesuits, etc., which never terminate in a breach of communion or co-operation as one church. Thus the Pharisees, Sadducees, Herodians, etc., frequented the same temple, altar, priesthood, and united in all the same acts of worship. Not so the Jews and Samaritans; they were real *sects* in the Christian sense. Again, among the Jews the bond of union was national and fleshly; and, therefore, parties could not destroy it. With us it is spiritual, social, cordial—

one faith, one hope, one spirit; and parties are destructive of this in the superlative degree.

VII. To this view there is but one plausible objection; and that we meet in the answer to the question, *Why did Paul defend himself from the accusation of Tertullus as indicating censure, if sects among the Jews were such harmless and inoffensive things?* We answer, There is no blame in the simple imputation of a sect, but in the ideas which Tertullus connected with it. The Romans had agreed to protect the Jews in the enjoyment of their religion, and they wished in the presence of Felix to make Paul appear an apostate from that religion—"a pestilent fellow, a mover of *sedition,* a ringleader of the sect of the Nazarenes"—that he might be from under the protection granted to the Jews' religion. From this view only can we see the wisdom of Paul's defence. He admits the charge of being a *sectary,* but in no criminal sense—worshiping the same God with them, believing every word in their law and prophets, and cherishing the same hope of a future life in the resurrection of the dead, and thus evinces that nothing offensive or criminal could be imputed to him on account of his being a ringleader of the sect of the Nazarenes.

VIII. In the Christian epistles it is, however, used in a bad sense, and is always connected with censure. This may have been the reason why King James's version changes the translation into *heresies,* or, as in the case of *baptism, bishop,* etc., anglicizes rather than translates the word. It is not, however, a good or a sufficient reason, because it necessarily imposes upon the English reader that *heresy* in the epistles, and *sect* in the Acts of the Apostles, are two distinct and different things; and this, of course, not only obscures those passages, but also prevents the clear intelligence of a matter essential to our duty and our happiness. That acceptation, however, is not materially different in the epistles, except in the relation of things. When the word *sect* is connected with a proper name, such as the *sect* of the Pharisees, the *sect* of the Sadducees, or the *sect* of the Christians, it is used in a middle sense, neither as intimating truth or error, good or evil; but if it be applied to a party formed in a community which admits of no division or subdivision in its nature, because necessarily tending to its corruption and destruction, then, in that relation and sense, a sect is a destructive and condemnable thing. Now, in the Epistles it is always taken in this sense, and is ranked with *factions,* as a work of the flesh, carnal and destructive, and doomed to the judgments of heaven.

IX. Still, in its scriptural application, whether used by Luke, Paul, or Peter (and it is found in no other writer), it never relates to doctrine, tenet, opinion, or faith. There is not, in sacred usage, any *tenet*, or *doctrine*, which is called *heresy*, or *sect*. Hence that ecclesiastical definition, viz.: "*Heresy denotes some erroneous opinion, tenet, or doctrine obstinately persisted in*," is without any countenance from the New Testament. *Heresy* and *heretical*, in the lips of Paul and Peter, and in the lips of an ancient or modern schoolman or churchman, are two very different things.

X. But some allege that any doctrine that makes division is heretical, and therefore condemnable. It may be admitted, for the sake of argument, that any doctrine or action that makes division is heretical or divisive; but on this account it is not condemnable; because in that sense Jesus Christ was a heretic and his gospel heresy: for he came to make divisions on earth, and did make a sect; and, of course, his doctrine is divisive or heretical.

XI. Now, if we say Jesus was a *heretic*, and his gospel *heresy*, and his followers *sectaries*, does not this divest the word of any bad or culpable significance, and make both heretics, heresies, and sects innocent things? It does, so far as all without Christ's kingdom or institution are concerned. But this is the all-important difference in this place; Christians, contradistinguished from Jews, Mussulmans, Pagans, Infidels, are lawfully, righteously, and innocently a sect, a heresy: but a sect among these is corrupt, treasonable, and most reprehensible, according to every precept, doctrine, and saying of the new institution. Thus a man may be a Christian, or of the sect of the Nazarenes, but not a Lutheran, a Calvinist, an Arminian, without blame.

XII. The words *schism* and *heresy* so far explained, may we not regard schism as the cause, and heresy as the effect? or, in other words, must we not regard sects as the effects of schisms? The philosophy of the whole matter, then, is, that separation is the effect of alienation of heart, alienation the fruit of rival attachments, which in the church generally begin in personal sympathies or personal antipathies, and end in detaching the subjects of them from the body of Christ. In this view of the matter Paul seems to reason (1 Cor. 11:18, 19):—"There are *schisms* among you—for there must be *sects* among you, that the approved may be made manifest'" The schisms in Corinth began in particular predilections for great teachers; such as Paul, Apollos, Cephas. These preferences violated that *unity of spirit*, that oneness of heart, essential to one body in Christ; and that led to parties in the church, displayed in the manner they celebrated the supper. This same spirit in other communities ultimately led to visible separations and distinct sects, as among the professed members of Christ's body at the present day.

XIII. Paul, in commenting on this most ancient schism, further observes, that there *must*, of necessity, be sects in such a state of things, that "the *approved* may be made manifest." So true it is that all strifes, contentions, parties, and sects grow out of corruption. Sects are the egress of corruptions. The approved hold to Christ, and thus become manifest; the disapproved follow human leaders, and are also made manifest. There appears no other cure for a corrupt and mixed community than heresies or sects. It is as wise and benevolent a provision in a remedial system, that incurable corruption should work out in this way, as that law in the animal kingdom which forces to the surface all unfriendly humors, and congregates into swellings and biles those vicious particles which would otherwise vitiate the whole system and fatally terminate in the ruin of the body.

XIV. Men, indeed, do not fall in love with Paul, Peter and Cephus, in the partisan sense, till they have lost some of their love for Christ. Hence the first indication of personal regards, or of sectarian attachment, is the first proof of declension, backsliding, or apostasy. The partisan attachment is of the essence of the first sin, and carries deeply concealed in its core the first element of hatred. Thus we observe that he that loves Wesley for any sectarian attribute hates Calvin just in the ratio of his attachment to his leader; as he who loves Calvin for his humanisms hates Wesley for opposing them. While he that loves only what is Christian in the two in no sense hates either; but grieves for the errors and delinquencies of both. If for no other reason, we ought most devoutly and ardently to eschew partyism; for this it ought to be abjured, viz.: that our hatred of one party will always be in the ratio of our love for its antagonist; and in all such cases both our love and our hatred are obnoxious to the reprobation of God, and lie, indeed, under the doom of his express condemnation.

XV. On this account we presume it is that the next place we find this word *hairesis*, and the only time it is again found in Paul's epistles, it stands immediately after *"factions"* and before *envyings* and *murders*," in Paul's enumeration and classification of the works of the flesh (Gal. 5:20), the perpetrators of which Paul strongly and repeatedly affirmed, shall not "enter the kingdom of God." He says, "The works of the flesh are manifest, which are these—fornication, uncleanness, lasciviousness, sorcery, enmities, strifes, emulations, wraths, brawlings, *factions, sects,* envyings, murders, intoxication," etc., etc. Every sectary is, then, Paul being in the chair of judgment, a fleshly man, and without the precincts of the kingdom of God. A severe judgment, truly! How shall we understand it?

XVI. It is now still more evident that *heresies* are not mere opinions, tenets, doctrines, or theories; for who will affirm that opinions, tenets, or theories, as such, are works of the flesh? Or who will say that fleshly principles are the roots or reasons of mere opinions, tenets, or theories, etc.? Corrupt opinions, indeed, may be more naturally propagated or received by corrupt men; but to make opinions or tenants, even those sectarian opinions on which some parties are founded, works of the flesh, is to confound mental imbecility, or a defective education, with depravity of the heart; for nothing can be called a work of the flesh that partakes not of the corruptions of the heart. *Hairesis* in this place, then, means sects, as it always does in the New Testament.

XVII. Still the question recurs, Are all religious sects works of the flesh? Paul makes no exceptions. We dare not. He speaks not of philosophic, political, or foreign factions and sects; but of those pertaining to the Christian institution. Among the Jews Paul himself was a *Pharisee;* among the political castes he was a *Roman;* but in religion he was a Christian; not a Calvinist, Arminian, or Methodist; but a Christian. Indeed, Paul himself, in his history of sectaries, or of the founders and makers of religious parties, traces all their zeal and effort to the stomach, rather than to the conscience, or love of truth. "Mark them," says he, "who cause divisions and offenses contrary to the doctrine which you have received, and avoid them; for such persons do not serve our Lord Jesus Christ, but their own *belly;* and by flattery and fair speeches deceive the hearts of the simple." Surely such sectaries and sects are "the works of the flesh."

XVIII. But here we ought to define a *factionist* and a *sectary,* since nowadays we have some sectarians that are not factionists, and some factionists and factions that are more than mere sectaries. The factionist, or, as Paul calls him, the "heretic," makes the faction. The faction are those who take part with him. While the ordinary sectaries are those who are simply led by the heretic, beguiled by his flatteries and fair speeches, without any sinister motive impelling their course. There are many sectarians who, in the simplicity of their hearts, imagine their party to be the true and only church of Christ, and therefore conscientiously adhere to it. There are others who think that no party is the church of Christ, but that he has a church in all parties—an invisible church—to which they think themselves to belong, and therefore fraternize with all of a similar stamp in all parties so far as known to them. These differ much from the schismatics, heretics, and factionists of Paul. Those either made, or labored to keep up, a party or a sect; and all such persons are corrupt, fleshly men; because, from pride of their own opinion, from emulation, ambition, or the love of money, they are prompted to create or to keep up a faction or sect favorable to their views and interests. These serve their own appetites and mind earthly things. But a great mass of sectaries are following, as they imagine, Jesus Christ and his apostles, under the name and tenets of Luther, Calvin, Wesley, etc. They are, without knowing it, the mere followers of men; for they examine nothing for themselves by a constant and habitual reference to the Bible.

XIX. Now, what may be the amount of carnality and fleshly or wordly influence that keeps them there, and what may be the amount of long-suffering and forgiveness exercised towards them from heaven, I presume not to dogmatize; but that the factionist,—the person who makes a party,—and he who labors to keep it up, are certainly earthly, sensual, and demoniacal; and, as such, not of the kingdom of God, we can not but assert as a conviction deep and rational, derived from the most impartial examination of the sacred Scriptures —from the clearest and most ample testimony of the Holy Spirit, speaking to us in the words of prophets and apostles.

XX. The Christian party are "built on the foundation of the apostles and prophets, and on Jesus the Messiah, himself the chief corner-stone," and therefore *on the Christian Scriptures alone,* not, indeed, as contradistinguished from the Jewish, but as the development and full revelation of all that concerns Christ and his kingdom contained in those Scriptures. Now, all other parties that are in any way diverse from the Christian party are built upon some alloy— some creed, formula, or human institution supplementary to the apostolic laws and customs. This alloy is what makes the party. So many items of the apostles' doctrine and so many notions of Calvin combined produce the compound called Calvinism. So many items of Luther's opinions, compounded with the apostles' teaching, make Lutheranism. And so many portions of Wesley's speculations, compounded with certain portions of the New Testament, make the compound called Methodism. The Christian ingredients in these compounds, so far as they are not neutralized by the human alloy, make the Christians among them; while the alloy makes the sectary. Take away all that belongs to the founder of the sect in all these parties, and they would certainly coalesce and form one community.

XXI. Now, we do not suppose that there is the same guilt in forming a new Protestant party that there was in first of all forming the Roman Catholic, the Greek, or any of the ancient sects. The modern sects have been got up with the desire of getting back to primitive Christianity; the ancient sects arose directly from the lust of power,—from fleshly, selfish, and worldly motives. Now, however, since we have so largely eaten of the gall and wormwood, of the bitter fruits of sects and parties, and have learned the cause, the cure, and the preventive of sectarianism, alas for all that are found keeping up the old landmarks of strife, or laying the foundation for new rivalries, partialities, and antipathies, to arise and pollute many, to retard the progress of the gospel abroad, and to foster the spirit of infidelity at home!

XXII. There remains another occurrence of *hairesis* (sect) in the writings of Peter, not yet formally examined. We shall now specially consider it. This apostle says, "There shall be false teachers among you, who will privately introduce *destructive sects,* denying even the Lord that bought them, bringing on themselves swift destruction; and many will follow their bad practices." Paul, in his valedictory to the Ephesians, also speaks, of "grievous wolves devouring the flock, and of men rising out of their own society to draw away disciples after them, speaking perverse things." From these intimations we learn the apostles Paul and Peter foresaw the rise of sectaries and sects; and both of them, it is worthy of remark, distinctly connected the sects with sectarian teachers: for all sects have been originated by false teachers or by corrupt men. Sectaries, it would appear, occupy the same place under Christ that false prophets filled under Moses. Need we, then, infer the danger of keeping up religious sects, or go on to prove that every one who builds up a party is a partaker of the crime with him who set it up?

XXIII. It behooves all men, then, who wish to be approved by the Lord at his coming, to be up and doing to purge and cleanse the Christian profession from every root and branch of sectarianism, and to endeavor to destroy those destructive sects that have been a sort of Pandora's box to the human race; that have filled the profession with hypocrites, the world with infidels, and retarded for so many centuries the conversion of both Jews and Gentiles to the Christian faith.

XXIV. Finally, while endeavoring to abolish the old sects, let us be cautious that we form not a new one. This may be done by either adding to, or subtracting from, the apostolic constitution a single item. Our platform must be as long and as broad as the New Testament. Every person that the apostles would receive, if present, we must receive; and therefore the one faith, one Lord, one baptism, one hope, one body, one Spirit, one God and Father of all, must be made the reason of one, and only one, table.

XXV. Factionists, or opinionists, or those who seek to attach men to themselves because of their opinions or talents or personal accidents, whatever they may be, are to be guarded as the very roots of bitterness in the Christian church—as seeking their own interests, honors, and profits, and not the things of Jesus Christ. By such spirits as these the ancient schisms and sects began; and by kindred spirits, of which every generation can furnish its proper ratios, they are kept alive. All such persons have not the power of effecting much; but now and then one arises and succeeds in drawing away disciples after him. We can suggest no better remedies or preventives than those commanded by the apostles. Let us hold fast their traditions; contend only for the faith; allow differences of opinion; suffer no dogmatics; countenance none of the disciples of Diotrephes; and walk in love, guided by that wisdom which is "first pure, then peaceable, gentle, easy to be persuaded, full of mercy and of good fruits, without partiality and without hypocrisy."

XXVI. From the preceding inductions it will appear, we presume, very evident to all, that we need neither telescopes nor microscopes to detect *heresies* in the New Testament sense of that word. They are neither more nor less than sects—plain, palpable sects and parties. Every party in Christendom, without respect to any of its tenets, opinions, or practices, is a *heresy*, a schism—unless there be such a party as stands exactly upon the apostles' ground. Then, in that case, it is a sect just in the sense of the old sect of the Nazarenes, afterwards called *Christians*, and all others are guilty before the Lord, and must be condemned for their opposition to Christ's own party, whose party we are, provided we hold fast all, and only all, the apostolic traditions, and build upon the Bible, the whole Bible, and nothing but the Bible.

FOUNDATION OF CHRISTIAN UNION

"I pray . . . for those who shall believe on me through their teaching, *that all may be one;* that as thou, Father, art in me, and I in thee, *they also may be in us, that the world may believe* that thou hast sent me, and that thou gavest me the glory, which I have given them, that *they may be one,* as we are one; I in them, and thou in me, *that their union may be perfected*: and that *the world may know* that thou hast sent me, and that thou lovest them as thou lovest me." Thus Messiah prayed; and well might he pray thus, seeing he was wise enough to teach that, "If a kingdom be torn by factions, that kingdom can not subsist. And if a family be torn by factions, that family can not subsist. By civil dissensions any kingdom may be desolated; and no city or family, where such dissensions are, can subsist."

If this be true,—and true it is, if Jesus be the Messiah,—in what moral desolation is the kingdom of Jesus Christ! Was there at any time, or is there now, in all the earth, a kingdom more convu 'sed by internal broils and dissensions, than what is commonly called the church of Jesus Christ? Should any one think it lawful to paganize both the Greek and Latin churches—to eject one hundred millions of members of the Greek and Roman communions from the visible and invisible precincts of the Christian family or kingdom of Jesus Christ, and regard the Protestant faith and people as the only true faith and the only true citizens of the kingdom of Jesus; what then shall we say of them, contemplated as the visible kingdom over which Jesus presides as Prophet, Priest, and King? Of forty millions of Protestants shall we constitute the visible kingdom of the Prince of Peace? Be it so for the sake of argument; and what then? The Christian army is forty millions strong; but how do they muster? Under forty ensigns? Under forty antagonistic leaders? Would to God there were but forty! In the Geneva detachment alone there is almost that number of petty chiefs. My soul sickens at the details!

Take the English branch of the Protestant faith—I mean England and the United States and all the islands where the English Bible is read; and how many broils, dissensions, and anathemas may we compute? I will not attempt to name the antagonizing creeds, feuds, and parties, that are in eternal war, under the banners of the Prince of Peace. And yet they talk of love and charity, and of the conversion of the Jews, the Turks, and Pagans!!!

Shall we turn from the picture, lay down our pen, and languish in despair? No: for Jesus has said, "Happy the *peacemakers,* for they shall be called *sons of God."* But who can make peace when all the elements are at war? Who so enthusiastic as to fancy that he can stem the torrent of strife or quench the violence of sectarian fire? But the page of universal history whispers in our ears, "If you tarry till all the belligerent armies lay down their arms and make one spontaneous and simultaneous effort to unite, you will be as very a simpleton as he that sat by the Euphrates waiting till all its waters ran into the sea."

We are so sanguine—perhaps many will say, so visionary—as to imagine that a *nucleus* has been formed, or may be formed, around which may one day congregate all the children of God. No one, at all events, can say that it is either impious or immoral— that it is inhuman or unchristian—to think about the present state of Christ's kingdom, or to meditate upon the possibility or practicability of any scheme of gathering together the children of God under the ensign of the cross alone. No one can say that such an enterprise is absolutely chimerical, unless he affirms the negative of the Messiah's proposition, and declares that the present wars and strifes must extend and multiply through all time, and that God will convert the whole world *without answering the prayer of his Son;* or, rather, on a plan adverse to that promulgated by him, and in despite of all the moral desolations which have ensued upon all the broils and battles of five hundred sects and fifteen hundred years!

Dare any one say, or even think it unphilanthropic or malevolent to make an effort to rally the broken phalanxes of Zion's King, and to attempt to induce them to turn their arms from one another against the common foe? With such a one it were worse than hopeless to reason, or to exchange a single argument. Shall we not rather esteem it to be the most honorable, acceptable, and praiseworthy enterprise that can be dared or undertaken by mortal man on this earthly stage of action? And, as God has ever effected the most splendid revolutions by the most humble agents, and by means the most unlikely in the wisdom of all human schools, we think it not amiss or incongruous to make an effort, and to put our hands to the work of peace and love.

From Messiah's intercession above quoted, it is incontrovertible that union is strength, and disunion weakness; that there is a plan founded in infinite wisdom and love, by which, and by which alone, the world may both *believe* and *know* that God has sent his Son to be the Saviour of the world; and, like all the schemes of Heaven, it is simple to admiration. No mortal need fancy that he shall have the honor of devising either the plan of uniting Christians in one holy band of zealous co-operation, or of converting Jews and Gentiles to the faith that Jesus is that *seed* in whom all the families of the earth are yet to be blessed. The plan is divine. It is ordained by God; and, better still, it is already revealed. Is any one impatient to hear it? Let him again read the intercessions of the Lord Messiah, which we have chosen for our motto. Let him then examine the two following propositions, and say whether these do not express Heaven's own scheme of augmenting and conserving the body of Christ.

First: *Nothing is essential to the conversion of the world but the union and co-operation of Christians.*

Second: *Nothing is essential to the union of Christians but the apostles' teaching or testimony.*

Or does he choose to express the plan of the Self-Existent in other words? Then he may change the order, and say—

First: *The testimony of the apostles is the only and all-sufficient means of uniting all Christians.*

Second: *The union of Christians with the apostles' testimony is all-sufficient and alone sufficient to the conversion of the world.*

Neither truth alone nor union alone is sufficient to subdue the unbelieving nations; but truth and union combined are omnipotent. They are *omnipotent*, for God is in them and with them, and has consecrated and blessed them for this very purpose.

These two propositions have been stated, illustrated, developed (and shall I say proved?), in the *Christian Baptist*, and *Millennial Harbinger*, to the conviction of thousands. Indeed, one of them is as universally conceded as it has been proposed, viz.: *That the union of Christians is essential to the conversion of the world;* and though, perhaps, some might be found who would question whether, if all Christians were united, the whole world could be converted to God; there is no person, of whom we have heard, who admits a general or universal prevalence of the gospel, in what is usually called the millennial age of the world, and who admits that moral means will have any thing to do with its introduction, who does not also admit that the union of Christians is essential to that state of things. Indeed, to suppose that all Christians will form one communion in that happy age of the world, and not before it, is to suppose a moral effect without a cause.

The second proposition, viz.: *That the word or testimony of the apostles is itself all-sufficient and alone sufficient to the union of all Christians,* can not be rationally doubted by any person acquainted with that testimony, or who admits the competency of their inspiration to make them infallible teachers of the Christian institution. And, indeed, all who contend for those human institutions called creeds contend for them as necessary only to the existence of a party, or while the present schisms, contentions, and dissensions exist. Therefore, all the defences of creeds, ancient and modern, while they assert that the Bible alone is the only perfect and infallible rule of faith and morals, not only concede that these symbols called *creeds* are imperfect and fallible, but also that these creeds never can achieve what the Bible, without them, can accomplish.

But how to do without them appears to be an insuperable difficulty to many well-disposed Christians. To labor this point would be foreign to our present purpose; especially as it has already been fully discussed in the present controversy.[1]

It is, perhaps, altogether sufficient at present to propose the question, How has what is called *the church* done with them? Have they not been the fruitful cause or occasion of all the discords, schisms, and parties now existing in Christendom? And will not a very superficial observation and a little experience convince every man that the

---

[1] *Christian Baptist,* vol. 2, pp. 66, 67.—Essays on the Westminster Creed, vol. 2.—Review of Dr. Noel's Circular, vol. 5.

rivers tend not more certainly to the sea, than creeds and human devices in religion tend to discords and divisions? Take, for example,
two of the most popular creeds of the present day—the Westminster,
and that of the Methodists, with whose history American society is
better acquainted than with that of any other, and test the tree of its
fruits—judge their tendency by their practical effects upon society.
To say nothing of the lesser schisms in the party that once formed
one communion on the platform of the Westminster creed, we can
now enumerate no less than nine separate communions, all professing
the Westminster Articles in substance or in form. These are the
General Assembly in Scotland and the United States, the Cameroni-
ans or Solemn League and Covenant Presbyterians, the Burghers or
Unionists, the Anti-Burghers or Seceders, the Relief Presbyterians,
the Cumberland Presbyterians, and the New School, now upon
the eve of being born. To these might be added those called English Presbyterians, who are now more generally known by the name
of Independents and Congregationalists; and, indeed the Glassites or
Sandemanians, who came out of the Synod of Angus and Mearns in
the year 1728. Thus, in one hundred and ninety years have nine or
ten distinct communions originated out of the Westminster creed,—
some of them, too, as discordant and aloof from each other as were
the Jews and Samaritans.

Nor have the Methodists in England, Canada, and the United
States done much better for their age. They now form five or six
separate communions, under different names. To say nothing of the
Whitefieldite Methodists, those of John Wesley are—the Wesleyan
Methodists, the New Connection of Methodists, the Methodist Epis-
copal Church, the O'Kelly Methodists, the Protestants, etc.

And what shall I say of the twelve or fourteen sects of Baptists,
many of whom have as much affection for the Greek and Roman
church as for one another? It were useless to furnish other evidence
in proof that human opinions, inferential reasonings, and deductions
from the Bible, exhibited in the form of creeds, can never unite
Christians; as all their fruits are alienation, repulsion, bickering, and
schism. *No human creed in Protestant Christendom can be found
that has not made a division for every generation of its existence.*
And I may add, the more thinking, inquisitive, and intelligent the
community which owns a creed, the more frequent their debates and
schisms.

But the Bible will do no better if men approach it with a set of
opinions or a human symbol in their minds. For then it is not the
Bible, but the opinions in the mind, that form the bond of union.
Men, indeed, had better have a *written* than an *unwritten* standard

of orthodoxy, if they will not abandon speculation and abstract notions as any part of Christian faith or duty.

But all these modes of faith and worship are based upon a mistake of the true character of Revelation, which it has long been our effort to correct. With us Revelation has nothing to do with opinions or abstract reasonings; for it is founded wholly and entirely upon facts. There is not one abstract opinion, not one speculative view, asserted or communicated in Old Testament or New. Moses begins with asserting facts that had transpired in creation and providence; and John ends with asserting prophetic or prospective facts in the future displays of providence and redemption. Facts, then, are the *Alpha and the Omega* of both Jewish and Christian revelations.

But that the reader may have before his mind in one summary view the whole scheme of union and co-operation, which the living oracles and the present state of the Christian religion in the world demand; which has been, at different times and in various manners, illustrated and sustained, in the present controversy, against divisions, —we shall here submit it in one period.

Let THE BIBLE *be substituted for all human creeds;* FACTS, *for definitions;* THINGS, *for words;* FAITH, *for speculation;* UNITY OF FAITH, *for unity of opinion;* THE POSITIVE COMMANDMENTS OF GOD, *for human legislation and tradition;* PIETY, *for ceremony;* MORALITY, *for partisan zeal;* THE PRACTICE OF RELIGION, *for the mere profession of it:* and the work is done.

For the illustration of the leading terms, and their correlates found in this *project,* and for a full development of our meaning (as we may not be understood if interpreted by the polemic vocabulary of this age), we shall introduce some extracts from the *Christian Baptist* and *Millennial Harbinger,* developing our meaning, and containing some of the capital positions which have been fully elicited and canvassed in a controversy of twelve years.

FACT

Fact means something done. The term *deed,* so common in the reign of James I, is equivalent to our term *fact.* Truth and fact, though often confounded, are not the same. All facts are truths, but all truths are not facts. That God exists is a truth, but not a fact; that he created the heavens and the earth is a fact and a truth. That Paul was the apostle of the Gentiles is a truth, but not a fact; and that he preached Christ to the Gentiles is both a fact and a truth. The simple agreement of the terms of any proposition with the subject of that proposition, or the representation of any thing as it exists, is a truth. But something must be done or effected before we have a fact. There are many things true in religion, morals, politics, and general science, which are not facts; but these are all but the correspondence of words and ideas with the things of which they treat.

Facts have a power which logical truth has not; and therefore we say that facts are stubborn things. They are *things*, not *words*. The power of any fact is the meaning; and therefore the measure of its power is the magnitude of its import. All moral facts have a moral meaning; and those are properly called moral facts which either exhibit, develop, or form moral character. All those facts, or works of God, which are purely physical, exhibit what have been commonly called his natural or physical perfections; and all those facts or works of God, which are purely moral, exhibit his moral character. It so happens, however, that all his works, when properly understood, exhibit both his physical and moral character, when viewed in all their proper relations. Thus, the deluge exhibited his power, his justice, and his truth; and therefore displayed both his physical and moral grandeur. The turning of water into wine, apart from its design, is purely a demonstration of physical power; but, when its design is apprehended, it has a moral force equal to its physical majesty.

The work of redemption is a system of works, or deeds, on the part of Heaven, which constitute the most splendid series of moral facts which man or angel ever saw. And they are the proof, the argument, or the demonstration, of that regenerating proposition which presents God and *Love* as two names for one idea.

When these facts are understood, or brought into immediate contact with the mind of man, as a moral seal or archetype, they delineate the image of God upon the human soul. *All the means of grace are, therefore, only the means of impressing this seal upon the heart,—of bringing these moral facts to make their full impression on the soul of man.* Testimony and faith are but the channel through which these facts, or the hand of God, draws the image on the heart and character of man. If, then, the fact and the testimony are both the gift of God, we may well say that faith and eternal life are also the gift of God, through Jesus Christ our Lord.

To enumerate the gospel facts would be to narrate all that is recorded of the sayings and doings of Jesus Christ from his birth to his coronation in the heavens. They are, however, concentrated in a few prominent ones, which group together all the love of God in the gift of his Son. He died for our sins—he was buried in the grave—he rose from the dead for our justification—and is ascended to the skies to prepare mansions for his disciples—comprehend the whole, or are the heads of the chapters which narrate the love of God and display his moral majesty and glory to our view.

These moral facts unfold all the moral grandeur of Jehovah, and make Jesus the effulgence of his glory, the express image of his substance. These are the moral seal which *testimony* conveys to the understanding, and *faith* brings to the hearts of sinners, by which God creates them anew and forms them for his glory. It is the Spirit which bears witness—the Spirit of God and of Christ which gives the testimony and confirms it in the disciples. But let us next proceed to *testimony*.

TESTIMONY

The Romans, from whom we have borrowed much of our language, called the witness the *testis*. The declaration of this *testis* is still called *testimony*. In reference to the material system around us, to all objects and matters of sense, the eye, the ear, the smell, the taste, the feeling, are the five witnesses. What we call the evidence of sense, is, therefore, the testimony of these witnesses, which constitute the five avenues to the human mind from the kingdom of nature. They are figuratively called *witnesses,* and their evidence *testimony.* But the report or declaration of intelligent beings, such as God, angels, and men, constitute what is properly and literally called *testimony.*

As light reflected from any material object upon the eye brings that object into contact with the eye, or enables the object to make its image on the eye; so testimony concerning any fact brings that fact into contact with the mind, and enables it to impress itself or to form its image upon the intellect or mind of man. Now, be it observed, that, as by our five external senses we acquire all information of the objects of sense around us; so by testimony, human or divine, we receive all our information upon all facts which are not the objects of immediate exercise of our five senses upon the things around us.

To appreciate the full value of testimony in divine work of regeneration, we have only to reflect that all the moral facts which can form moral character, after the divine model, or which can effect a moral or religious change in man, are found in the testimony of God; and that no fact can operate at all where it is not present, or where it is not known. The love of God in the death of the Messiah never drew a tear of gratitude or joy from any eye, or excited a grateful emotion in any heart among the nations of our race to whom the testimony never came. No fact in the history of six thousand years, no work of God in creation, providence, or redemption, has ever influenced the heart of man or woman to whom it has not been testified. Testimony is, then, in regeneration, as necessary as the facts of which it speaks.

The real value of any thing is the labor which it cost, and its utility when required. If reason and justice arbitrated all questions upon the value of property, the decision would be, that every article is worth the amount of human labor which is necessary to obtain it; and when obtained it is again to be tried in the scales of utility. Now, as all the facts and all the truth which can renovate human nature are in the testimony of God, and as that testimony cost the labor and the lives of the wisest and best that ever lived, that testimony, to us, is just as valuable as the facts which it records and the labors and the lives which it cost, and just as indispensable in the process of regeneration as were the labors and the lives of prophets, apostles, and the Son of God.

History, or narrative, whether oral or written, is only another name for testimony. When, then, we reflect how large a portion of both Testaments is occupied in history, we may judge of how much importance it is in the judgments of God. Prophecy, also, being the history of future facts, or a record of things to be done, belongs to the same chapter of facts and record. Now, if all past facts and all future facts, or all the history or testimony concerning them, were erased from the volumes of God's inspiration, how small would the remainder be! These considerations, added together, only in part exhibit the value and utility of testimony in the regeneration of mankind. But its value will be still more evident when the proper import of the term *faith* is fully set before us.

FAITH

No testimony, no faith: for faith is only the belief of testimony, or confidence in testimony as true. To believe without testimony is just as impossible as to see without light. The measure, quality, and power of faith are always found in the testimony believed.

Where testimony begins, faith begins; and where testimony ends, faith ends. We believe Moses just as far as Moses speaks or writes; and when Moses has recorded his last fact, or testified his last truth, our faith in Moses terminates. His five books are, therefore, the length and breadth, the height and depth, or in other words, the *measure*, of our faith in Moses. The *quality* or value of faith is found in the quality of value of the testimony. If the testimony be valid and authoritative, our faith is strong and operative. "If," says John, "we receive the testimony of men, the testimony of God is greater,"—stronger and more worthy of credit. The value of a bank-bill is the amount of the precious metals which it represents, and the indisputable evidence of its genuineness; so the value of faith is the importance of the facts which the testimony presents, and the assurance afforded that the testimony is true. True or unfeigned faith may be contrasted with feigned faith; but true faith is the belief of truth; for he that believes a lie believes in vain.

The *power* of faith is also the power or moral meaning of the testimony, or of the facts which the testimony represents. If by faith I am transported with joy, or overwhelmed in sorrow, that joy or sorrow is in the facts contained in the testimony, or in the nature and relation of those facts to me. If faith purifies the heart, works by love, and overcomes the world, this power is in the facts believed. If a father has more joy in believing that a lost son has been found, than in believing that a lost sheep has been brought home to his fold, the reason of this greater joy is not in the nature of his believing, but in the nature of the facts believed.

Here I am led to expatiate on a very popular and pernicious error of modern times. That error is, that the nature or power and saving efficacy of faith is not in the truth believed, but in the *nature* of our faith, or in *the manner of believing* the truth. Hence all that unmeaning jargon about the nature of faith, and all those disdainful sneers at what is called "historic faith"—as if there could be any faith without history, written or spoken. Who ever believed in Christ without hearing the history of him? *"How shall they believe in him of whom they have not heard?"* Faith never can be more than the receiving of testimony as true, or the belief of testimony; and if that testimony be written it is called history, though it is as much history when flowing from the tongue as when flowing from the pen.

Let it be again repeated and remembered that there is no other manner of believing a fact than by receiving it as true. If it is not received as true, it is not believed; and, when it is believed, it is no more than regarded as true. This being conceded, then it follows that the efficacy of faith if always in the fact believed or the object received, and not in the nature or manner of believing.

> "Faith was bewilder'd much by men who meant
> To make it clear, so simple in itself.
> A thought so rudimental and so plain,
> That none by comment could it plainer make.
> All faith was one. In object, not in kind,
> The difference lay. The faith that saved a soul,
> And that which in the common truth believed,
> In essence were the same. Hear, then, what faith,
> True Christian faith, which brought salvation, was:

Belief in all that God reveal'd to men;
Observe:—in all that God reveal'd to men,
In all he promised, threaten'd, commanded, said,
Without exception, and without a doubt."[1]

This holds universally in all the sensitive, intellectual, and moral powers of man. All our pleasures and pains, all our joys and sorrows, are the effects of the objects of sensation, reflection, faith, etc., apprehended or received, and not in the nature of the exercise of any power or capacity with which we are endowed. We shall illustrate and confirm this assertion by an appeal to the experience of all.

Let us glance at all our sensitive powers. If, on surveying with the eye a beautiful landscape, I am pleased, and on surveying a battlefield strewed with the spoils of death, I am pained,—is it in accordance with truth to say, that the pleasure or the pain received was occasioned by the nature of vision, or the mode of seeing? Was it not *the sight*, the thing seen, the object of vision, which produced the pleasure and the pain? The action of looking, or the mode of seeing, was in both cases the same; but the things seen, or the objects of vision, were different; consequently the effects produced were different.

If on hearing the melody of the grove I am delighted, and on hearing the peals of thunder breaking to pieces the cloud, dark with horror, hanging over my head, I am terrified,—is the delight or the terror to be ascribed to the manner or nature of hearing, or to the thing heard? Is it not the thing heard which produces the delight or the terror?

If I am refreshed by the balmy fragrance of the opening bloom of spring, or sickened by the fetid effluvia of putrid carcasses,—are these effects to be ascribed to the peculiar nature or mode of smelling, or to the thing smelt? Or when the honey and the gall come in contact with my taste, is the sweet or the bitter to be regarded as the effect of my manner of tasting, or of the object tasted? And when I touch the ice, or the blazing torch, is the effect or feeling produced to be imputed to the manner of feeling them, or to the thing felt? May we not, then, affirm that all the pleasures and pains of sense— all the effects of sensation—are the results, not of the manner in which our five senses are exercised, but of the objects on which they are exercised? It may be said, without in the least invalidating this conclusion, that the more intimate the exercise of our senses is with the things on which they are exercised, the stronger and more forcible will be the impressions made; but still it is the object seen, heard, smelt, tasted, or felt, which affects us.

---

[1] Pollok's Course of Time, book 8, p. 189.

Passing from the outward to the inward man, and on examining the powers of intellection one by one, we shall find no exception to the law which pervades all our sensitive powers. It is neither the faculty of perception, nor the manner of perception, but the thing perceived, that excites us to action: it is not the exercise of reflection, but the thing reflected upon: it is not memory, nor the exercise of recollection, but the thing remembered: it is not imagination, but the thing imagined: it is not reason itself, nor the exercise of reason, but the thing reasoned upon, which affords pleasure or pain—which excites to action—which cheers, allures, consoles—which grieves, disquiets, or discommodes us.

Ascending to our volitions and our affections, we shall find the same universality. In a word, it is not choosing, nor refusing; it is not loving, hating, fearing, desiring, nor hoping; it is not the nature of any power, faculty, or capacity of our being, nor the simple exercise of them, but the objects or things upon which they are exercised, which give us pleasure or pain; which induce us to action, or influence our behavior. Faith, then, or the power of believing, must be an anomalous thing—a power *sui generis*—an exception to the laws under which every power, faculty, or capacity of men is placed, unless its measure, quality, power, and efficacy be in the facts which are testified, in the objects on which it terminates.

There is no connection of cause and effect more intimate—there is no system of dependencies more closely linked—there is no arrangement of things more natural or necessary, than the ideas represented by the terms *fact, testimony, faith,* and *feeling.* The first is for the last, and the two intermediates are made necessary by the force of circumstances, as the means for the end. The fact, or the thing said to be done, produces the change in the frame of mind. The testimony, or the report of the thing said or done, is essential to belief; and belief of it is necessary to bring the thing said or done to the heart. The change of heart is the end proposed in this part of the process of regeneration; and we may see that the process on the part of Heaven is, thus far, natural and rational; or, in other words, consistent with the constitution of our nature.[1]

CONFIRMATION OF THE TESTIMONY

All revealed religion is based upon facts. Testimony has respect to facts only; and that testimony may be credible, it must be confirmed. These points are of so much importance as to deserve some illustration, and much consideration. By *facts* we always mean some-

---

[1] *Millennial Harbinger*, Extra, No. 6, pp. 340-345.

thing said or done. The works of God and the words of God, or the things done or spoken by God, are those facts which are laid down and exhibited in the Bible as the foundation of all faith, hope, love, piety, and humanity. All true and useful knowledge is an acquaintance with facts; and all true science is acquired from the observation and comparison of facts. But he that made the heart of man and gave him an intelligent spirit knows that facts alone can move the affections and command the passions of man. Hence the scheme of mercy which he has discovered to the world is all contained in, and developed by, *the works of mercy* which he has wrought.

Facts have a meaning which the understanding apprehends, and the heart feels. According to the meaning or nature of the fact is its effect upon us. If a friend have risked his life or sacrificed his reputation or fortune to relieve us, we can not but confide in him and love him. If any enemy have attempted our life, invaded our property, or attacked our reputation, we can not, naturally, but hate him. Nothing but the command of a benefactor, or the will of some dear friend who has laid us under obligation to himself, can prevent us from hating our enemies. If a beloved relative have sustained some great misfortune, we must feel sorry; or if he have been rescued from some impending calamity, we must feel glad. Our joy in the latter case, and our sorrow in the former, arise from the meaning or nature of the fact. The feelings corresponding with the nature of the fact are excited or called into existence the moment the fact is known or believed. It is *known* when we have witnessed it ourselves, and it is *believed* when reported to us by credible persons who have witnessed it. This is the chief difference between faith and knowledge.

As existences or beings must precede knowledge, so facts must precede either knowledge or belief. An event must happen before it can be known by man—it must be known by some before it can be reported to others—it must be reported before it can be believed—and the testimony must be confirmed or made credible before it can be relied on.

Something must be done before it can be known, reported, or believed. Hence, in the order of nature, there is first the fact; then the testimony; and then the belief. A was drowned before B reported it —B reported it before C believed it—and C believed it before he was grieved at it. This is the unchangeable and universal order of things as respects belief. In this example, when we reason from effect to cause, it is *grief, belief, testimony, fact;* and from cause to effect, it is *fact, testimony, belief, grief.* We ascend from grief to belief—from belief to testimony—from testimony to fact. We descend from fact to testimony—from testimony to belief—and from belief to grief. To this there is no exception, more than against the universality of the law of gravity. If, then, there was nothing said or done, there could be no testimony, and so no faith. Religious affections spring from faith, and therefore it is of importance that this subject should be disintricated from the mysticism of the schools.

Laws call for obedience, and testimony for belief. Where there is no law there an be no obedience, and when there is no testimony there can be no faith. As obedience can not transcend law, so faith can not transcend testimony. John's testimony went to so many facts. On his testimony we can believe only as far as he has testified; and so of all the other witnesses. The certainty of faith depends upon the certainty or credibility of the witnesses. But not so its effects. The *effects* depend upon the facts believed—the *certainty* upon the evidence. I may be equally certain that John was beheaded—that Jesus was crucified. Nay, I may be as certain of the birth of Jesus in Bethlehem as I am of his death on Calvary. The testimony may be equally credible, and the faith equally strong; but the effects produced are not the same. The facts believed have not the same meaning, are not of the same nature, and do not produce the same feelings or effects. I may be as certain of the assassination of Caesar in the Senate House as I am of the crucifixion of Jesus on Calvary; but, as the facts believed are as diverse in their nature, meaning, and bearings upon me, as the East and the West, so the effects or fruits of my faith are as different as Julius Caesar and Jesus Christ.

The more ordinary the fact, the more ordinary the testimony necessary to establish it. That A B, aged 90, and confined for some time with sickness, died last night, requires only the most ordinary testimony to render it credible. But that C D lived to 140, enjoying unabated vigor of mind and body, requires stronger testimony. But still, all facts happening in accordance with the ordinary and natural laws of things require but good human testimony to make them worthy of credence. It is only extraordinary and supernatural facts which require supernatural testimony, or testimony supernaturally confirmed. This is the point to which we have been looking in this essay. And, now that we have arrived at it, I would ask, *How has the testimony of the apostles and evangelists been confirmed?*

To *confirm a testimony* is neither more nor less than to make it credible to those to whom it is tendered; or, to express the same idea in other words, it is to give men power to believe. Now, it will not require the same amount of evidence to persuade an astronomer that the earth's shadow struck the moon last eclipse, as it would to convince an Indian; nor would it require the same amount of evidence to convince a chemist that combustion was effected by pouring water on a certain composition of mineral substances, as it would an unlettered swain. To make any testimony credible to any order of beings, regard must therefore be had to the capacity, attainments, and habits of those beings. To confirm the testimony of the apostles concerning the Messiah's death, resurrection, ascension into heaven, and coronation as the Lord and king of the universe, imports no more nor no less than that it should be rendered everyway credible to such things as we are, or that we should be made able to believe. A testimony *confirmed*, and yet *incredible* to those to whom it is tendered, is a contradiction in terms. But why emphasize on the word *confirmed?* Because the holy apostles have emphasized upon it. It is therefore necessary that we should pay a due regard to the confirmation of the testimony. The testimony is one thing, and the confirmation is another. It is necessary, in all important occasions in human affairs, that the testimony which is received between man and man should be confirmed by some sanction. Hence an oath for confirmation of testimony is an end of all strife. The highest confirmation which men require in all questions of fact is a solemn oath or affirmation that the things affirmed are true.

But supernatural facts require supernatural confirmations. Hence, when the confirmation of the gospel is spoken of in the apostolic writings, it is resolved into the doings or works of the Holy Spirit. "Demonstrations of the Holy Spirit" are the confirmatory proofs of the gospel. When Paul delivered the testimony of God, or the testimony concerning Jesus, to the Corinthians, he says, "*It was confirmed among them.*" And if we examine into the confirmation of the testimony as Paul explained it, we shall find that he makes the spiritual gifts, or those extraordinary and miraculous powers which the apostles themselves displayed, and which so many of their converts also possessed, an assurance or confirmation of what he promulgated.

We shall only attend to the light which one of his epistles to the Corinthians throws upon this subject. After thanking his God for the favor bestowed upon the disciples of Corinth when he first visited them, he proceeds to specify the special favors bestowed upon the disciples in that renowned city. "You were enriched [says he, 1:5] with every gift by him, even with *all speech* and *all knowledge* when the testimony of Christ was confirmed among you: so that you come behind in *no gift*." "There are diversities of gifts [chapter 12], for to one disciple is given *the word of wisdom;* to another, *the word of knowledge;* to another *faith* [to be healed]; to another, *the gift of healing;* to another, *the ability of working in others the power of working miracles;* to another, *prophecy;* to another, *discerning of spirits;* to another, *divers kinds of foreign tongues;* and to another, *the interpretation of foreign tongues.*" Now, the Corinthians were put in possession of these (for they came behind in no gift) "when the testimony of Christ was confirmed among them." "For," says Paul, "I came not to you with the excellency of speech, or the persuasive eloquence of the schools, but with the demonstration of the Spirit and of power; that your belief of my testimony, or your faith, might not rest or be founded upon human wisdom or eloquence; but upon the power of God evinced in the demonstrations of the Spirit which confirmed my testimony among you." For had it not been for these demonstrations of the Spirit and power, your faith could not have rested upon an immovable basis.

To those desirous to understand this subject, an examination of this first letter to the Corinthians can not fail to be most instructive; for it most clearly and unequivocally teaches us that the *visible, audible, sensible* demonstration of the Spirit and of power was that supernatural attestation of the testimony of Christ which made it credible, so that no man could have acknowledged Jesus of Nazareth to be the Almighty Lord, but by this demonstration of the Holy Spirit. Thus was the testimony confirmed—thus was Jesus demonstrated to be the only begotten Son of God—and thus, and thus only, are men enabled to believe in him.[1]

FUNDAMENTAL FACT[2]

Amidst the uncertainty, darkness, and vice, that overspread the earth, the Messiah appears, and lays the foundation of hope, of true religion, and of religious union, unknown, unheard-of, unexpected among men. The Jews were united by consanguinity, and by agreement in a ponderous ritual. The Gentiles rallied under every opinion, and were grouped, like filings of steel around a magnet, under every possible shade of difference of thought, concerning their mythology. So long as union of opinion was regarded as a proper basis of religious union, so long have mankind been distracted by the multiplicity and variety of opinions. To establish what is called a system of orthodox opinions as the bond of union was, in fact, offering a premium for new diversities in opinion, and for increasing, *ad infinitum,* opinions, sects, and divisions. And, what is worse than all, it was establishing self-love and pride as religious principles, as fundamental

---

[1] *Millennial Harbinger,* vol. 1, pp. 8-12.
[2] The fundamental proposition is—*that Jesus is the Christ.* The *fact,* however, contained in this proposition is—that God has anointed Jesus of Nazareth as the only Saviour of sinners. He is the promised Christ: "God has constituted him Lord and Christ."—Peter.

to salvation; or a love regulated by similarity of opinion is only a love to one's own opinion; and all the zeal exhibited in the defence of it is but the workings of the pride of opinion.

When the Messiah appeared as the founder of a new religion, systems of religion consisting of opinions and speculations upon matter and mind, upon God and nature, upon virtue and vice, had been adopted, improved, reformed, and exploded, time after time. That there was always something superfluous, something defective, something wrong, something that could be improved, in every system of religion and morality, was generally felt, and at last universally acknowledged. But the grandeur, sublimity, and beauty of the foundation of hope, and of ecclesiastical or social union, established by the author and founder of Christianity consisted in this,—that THE BE-LIEF OF ONE FACT, *and that upon the best evidence in the world, is all that is requisite, as far as faith goes, to salvation. The belief of this* ONE FACT, *and submission to* ONE INSTITUTION *expressive of it, is all that is required of Heaven to admission into the church.* A Christian, as defined, not by Dr. Johnson, nor any creed-maker, but by one taught from Heaven, is one that believes this *one* fact, and has submitted to *one institution,* and whose deportment accords with the morality and virtue of the great Prophet. The one fact is expressed in a single proposition—*that Jesus the Nazarene is the Messiah.* The evidence upon which it is to be believed is the testimony of *twelve men,* confirmed by prophecy, miracles, and spiritual gifts. The *one institution* is baptism into the name of the Father, and of the Son, and of the Holy Spirit. Every such person is a disciple in the fullest sense of the word, the moment he has believed this one fact, upon the above evidence, and has submitted to the above-mentioned institution; and whether he believes the five points condemned, or the five points approved, by the Synod of Dort, is not so much as to be asked of him; whether he holds any of the views of the Calvinists or Arminians, Presbyterians, Episcopalians, Methodists, Baptists, or Quakers, is never once to be asked of such persons, in order to admission into the Christian community called the church. The only doubt that can reasonably arise upon these points is, whether this *one fact,* in its nature and necessary results, can suffice to the salvation of the soul, and whether the open avowal of it, in the overt act of baptism, can be a sufficient recommendation of the persons so professing to the confidence and love of the brotherhood. As to the first of these, it is again and again asserted, in the clearest language, by the Lord himself, the apostles Peter, Paul, and John, that he that believes the testimony that Jesus is the Christ is begotten by God, may overcome the world, has eternal life, and is, on the veracity of God, saved from his sins. This should settle the first point; for the witnesses agree that whosoever confesses that Jesus is the Christ, and is baptized, should be received into the church; and not an instance can be produced of any person being asked for any other faith, in order to admission, in the whole New Testament. The Saviour expressly declared to Peter that upon this fact, that he was the Messiah, the Son of God, he would *build his church;* and Paul has expressly declared that "other foundation can no man lay [for ecclesiastical union] than that *Jesus is the Christ.*" The point is proved that we have assumed; and, this proved, every thing is established requisite to the union of all Christians upon a proper basis.

It must strike every man of reflection, that a religion requiring much mental abstraction or exquisite refinement of thought, or that calls for the comprehension or even apprehension of refined distinctions and of nice subtleties, is a religion not suited to mankind in their present circumstances. To present such a creed as the Westminster, as adopted either by Baptists or Pedobaptists, such a creed as the Episcopalian, or, in fact, any sectarian creed, composed, as they all are, of propositions deduced by logical inferences and couched in philosophical language, to all those who are fit subjects of the salvation of heaven,—I say, to present such a creed to such for their examination or adoption shocks all common sense. This pernicious course is what has paganized Christianity. Our sects and parties, our disputes and speculations, our orders and castes, so much resemble anything but Christianity, that when we enter a modern synagogue, or an ecclesiastical council, we seem rather to have entered a Jewish sanhedrim, a Mohammedan mosque, a Pagan temple, or an Egyptian cloister, than a Christian congregation. Sometimes, indeed, our religious meetings so resemble the Areopagus, the Forum, or the Senate, that we almost suppose ourselves to have been translated to Athens or Rome. Even Christian orators emulate Demosthenes and Cicero. Christian doctrines are made to assume the garb of Egyptian mysteries, and Christian observances put on the pomp and pageantry of pagan ceremonies. Unity of opinion, expressed in subscription to voluminous dogmas imported from Geneva, Westminister, Edinburgh, or Rome, is made the bond of union; and a difference in the tenth or ten-thousandth shade of opinion frequently becomes the actual cause of dismemberment or expulsion. The New Testament was not designed to occupy the same place in theological seminaries that the carcasses of malefactors are condemned to occupy in medical halls—first doomed to the gibbet, and then to the dissecting-knife of the spiritual anatomist. Christianity consists infinitely more in good works than in sound opinions; and, while it is a joyful truth, that he that believes and is baptized shall be saved, it is equally true that he that says, "I know him, and keeps not his commandments, is a liar, and the truth is not in him."[1]

PURITY OF SPEECH

If I were to classify in *three* chapters the whole Christian institution, after the fashion of the modern schools, for the sake of being understood, I would designate them Christian *faith*, Christian *worship*, and Christian *morality*. To these the moderns have added two others, which, using the same license, I would call human *philosophy* and human *traditions*. Now, in the first chapter, we and all Christians are agreed: for as Christian faith has respect to *the matters of fact* recorded—to the direct testimony of God found in the New Testament concerning himself—concerning his Son and Spirit—concerning mankind—what he has done and what he will do—on it there is no debate. I find all *confessions of* FAITH, properly so called, like the *four* Gospels, tell the same story so far as matters of fact or faith are concerned.

In the second chapter we are also agreed, that God is to be worshiped through the Mediator—in prayer, in praise, public and private —in the ordinances of Christian baptism, the Lord's day, the Lord's supper, and in the devotional study of his word and of his works of creation and providence.

In the third chapter we all acknowledge the same moral code. What is morality is confessed and acknowledged by all; but in the practice of it there are great subtractions.

We repudiate the two remaining chapters as having any place in our faith, worship, or morality; because we think we have discovered that all the divisions in Protestant Christendom—that all the partyism, vain jangling, and heresies which have disgraced the Christian profession—have emanated from human philosophy and human tradition. It is not faith, nor piety, nor morality, but philosophy and tradition, that have alienated and estranged Christians, and prevented the conversion of the world. Socrates, Plato, and Aristotle deserved not the reputation of philosophers, if Calvin, Arminius, and Wesley were not worthy of it. The former philosophized morally on nature and ancient tradition—the latter, on the Bible, and human society.

Religious philosophers on the Bible have excogitated the following doctrines and philosophical distinctions:—

---

[1] *Christian Baptist*, vol. 1, pp. 167-69.

'The Holy Trinity,' 'Three persons of one substance, power, and eternity,' 'Co-essential, co-substantial, co-equal,' 'The Son eternally begotten of the Father,' 'An eternal Son,' 'Humanity and divinity of Christ,' 'The Holy Ghost eternally proceeding from the Father and the Son,' 'God's eternal decrees,' 'Conditional election and reprobation,' 'God out of Christ,' 'Free will,' 'Liberty and necessity,' 'Original sin,' 'Total depravity,' 'Covenant of grace,'[1] 'Effectual calling,' 'Free grace,' 'Sovereign grace,' 'General and particular atonement,' 'Satisfy divine justice,' 'Common and special operations of the Holy Ghost,' 'Imputed righteousness,' 'Inherent righteousness,' 'Progressive sanctification,' 'Justifying and saving faith,' 'Historic and temporary faith,' 'The direct and reflex acts of faith,' 'The faith of assurance, and the assurance of faith,' 'Legal repentance,' 'Evangelical repentance,' 'Perseverance of the saints,'[2] and 'Falling from grace,'[3] 'Visible and invisible church,' 'Infant membership,' 'Sacraments,' 'Eucharist,' 'Consubstantiation,' 'Church government,' 'The power of the keys,' etc., etc., etc.

Concerning these and all such doctrines, and all the speculations to which they have given rise, we have the privilege neither to affirm nor deny—neither to believe nor doubt; because God has not proposed them to us in his word, and there is no command to believe them. If they are deduced from the Scriptures, we have them in the facts and declarations of God's Spirit: if they are not deduced from the Bible, we are free from all the difficulties and strifes which they have engendered and created.

We choose to speak of Bible things by Bible words, because we are always suspicious that if the word is not in the Bible the idea which it represents is not there; and always confident that the things taught by God are better taught in the words and under the names which the Holy Spirit has chosen and appropriated, than in the words which man's wisdom teaches.

There is nothing more essential to the union of the disciples of Christ than *purity* of speech. So long as the earth was of one speech, the human family was united. Had they been then of a pure speech as well as of one speech, they would not have been separated. God, in his just indignation, dispersed them; and before he scattered them *he divided their language.* One of his prophets, who lived in a degenerate age, who prophesied against the corruptions of his day, when he spoke of better times, of an age of union and communion,

---

[1, 2, 3] These are samples of scriptural phrases misapplied; for the corruption of Christianity has been consummated by the incursions of barbarian language, and by the new appropriations of the sacred style.

was commanded to say, in the name of the Lord, "Then will I turn to the people a pure *language*, that they may call upon the name of the Lord, to serve him *with one consent.*"[1] Purity of speech is here declared to be prerequisite to serving the Lord with one consent.

"The words of the Lord are pure words."[2] To have a pure speech we must choose the language of Canaan, and abandon that of Ashdod. And if we would be of one mind we must "speak the same thing." This was Paul's scheme of union, and no man can suggest a better.

It requires but little reflection to discover that the fiercest disputes about religion are about what the Bible does *not* say, rather than about what it *does* say—about words and phrases coined in the mint of speculative theology. Of these the *homoussos* and the *homoousios* of the ever-memorable Council of Nice are a fair sample. Men are neither wiser, more intelligent, nor better, after, than before, they know the meaning of these words. As far as known on earth, there is not, in "the Book of Life of the Lamb slain from the foundation of the world," the name of any person who was either converted or sanctified to God by any of these controversies about human dogmas, nor by anything learned from the canons or creeds of all the Councils, from that of Nice to the last Methodist Conference.

It is a virtue, then, to forget this scholastic jargon, and even the names of the dogmas which have convulsed Christendom. It is a concession due to the crisis in which we live, for the sake of peace, to adopt the vocabulary of Heaven, and to return the borrowed nomenclature of the schools to its rightful owners—to speculate no more upon the opinions of Saint Austin, Saint Tertullian, Saint Origen—to speak of the Father, and the Son, and the Holy Spirit—of the gospel, of faith, of repentance, of baptism, of election of the death of Christ, of his mediation, of his blood, of the reconciliation, of the Lord's supper, of the atonement, of the church of God, etc., etc., in all the phrases found in the Record, without partiality—to learn to love one another as much when we differ in opinion as when we agree, and to distinguish between the testimony of God, and man's reasonings and philosophy upon it.

I need not say much upon the chapter of *human traditions.* They are easily distinguished from the *apostles' traditions.* Those of the apostles are found in their writings, as those of men are found in their own books. Some human traditions may have a show of wisdom, but is only an appearance. So long as it is written, "In vain do they worship me, teaching for doctrines the commandments of men,"

---

[1] Zephaniah 3:9.   [2] Psalm 12:6.

so long will it be presumptuous folly to add the commandments of men to the precepts of Jesus Christ. I know of but one way in which all believers in Jesus Christ, honorably to themselves, honorably to the Lord, and advantageously to all the sons of Adam, can form one communion. All have two chapters too many in their present ecclesiastic constitutions. The contents of the aforesaid two chapters are various and different in all the sects, but they all have these two chapters under some name. In some they are long, and in some they are short; but whether long or short, let every one agree to tear them out of his book and burn them, and be satisfied with *faith, piety,* and *morality.* Let human philosophy and human tradition, as any part of the Christian institution, be thrown overboard into the sea, and then the ship of the church will make a prosperous, safe, and happy voyage across the ocean of time, and finally, under the triumphant flag of Immanuel, gain a safe anchorage in the haven of eternal rest.

I would appeal to every honorable, good, and loyal citizen of the kingdom of heaven,—to everyone that seeks the good of Zion, that loves the kingdom and the appearing of our common Lord and Saviour, whether such a concession be not due to the Lord, to the saints in heaven and on earth, and to the whole human race in the crisis in which we are now placed; and whether we could propose less, or ought to demand more, than to make one whole burnt-offering of all our "empty and deceitful philosophy,"—our "science, falsely so called,"—and our traditions received from our fathers. I would leave it to the good sense of every sane mind to say, whether such a whole burnt-offering would not be the most acceptable peace-offering which, in this our day, could be presented on the altar of the Prince of Peace; and whether, under the teachings of the apostles of the Great Prophet, the church might not again triumphantly stand upon the holy ground which she so honorably occupied before Origen, Austin, Athanasius, or the first pope, was born![1]

---

[1] *Millennial Harbinger,* vol. 6, pp. 139-142.

KINGDOM OF HEAVEN

GENERAL ESSAYS[1]

PATRIARACHAL AGE OF THE WORLD

The world had its infancy as well as man. Families preceded nations. Family worship was, therefore, the first religious institution. At the head of this institution naturally stood the *father of every family*. From necessity and from choice, he was the prophet, the priest and the king. As a *prophet*, he instructed his household in the knowledge of God, and in the history of man. As a *priest*, he officiated at his family altar, interceded for those under his care, and pronounced benedictions upon his children. As a *lawgiver* and *king*, he commanded his children and servants, and rewarded them according to merit. By a divine ordinance, *the first fathers of mankind* were thus constituted prophets, priests and kings. Hence, the first religious and political institution is properly called *"the Patriarchal."*

Family worship was, then, the *first social worship;* and during the first ages of the world (for at least two thousand five hundred years) it was the *only social worship*, of divine authority. Though other institutions have since been added, this has never been superseded. Having its foundation in the matrimonial compact, the most ancient of all religious and political institutions, and this being founded on nature itself, it never can be superseded. While the forms of this worship have always been adapted to the genius of the various revela-

---

[1] These essays do not appear in the order in which they were written and published. We place the last-written first; because, in the natural order of things, general views of the nature of the Christian kingdom ought to precede the special development of its peculiar institutions. They appeared first in the form of *extras* to the regular series of the *Millennial Harbinger;* and, as we thought it expedient to preserve them, as much as possible, in their original form, this will apologize for several repetitions which may appear in them.

All the leading and characteristic principles of that reformation for which we plead, as far as the gospel institution is concerned, may be learned from them. Much, indeed, of the proof of some of the propositions found in these essays, lies scattered over the face of several volumes; but such a miniature view of the evidence by which they are sustained, as, in most cases, is sufficient to the conviction of the reader, will be found embodied in them. Those, however, who may not be perfectly satisfied with the arguments offered, must be referred to the various discussion of these principles found in the *Christian Baptist* and *Millennial Harbinger*.

tions of God vouchsafed to mankind, it has continued through all the changes of six thousand years, and will continue till the day when men, like the angels of God, shall neither marry nor give in marriage.

Family worship, so long as it continued the only social worship, underwent no material change; and this is the period which is properly called the *patriarchal age of the world.* So long as the descendants of one man and one woman continued under the paternal roof, or until they became heads of families themselves, they continued under this religious and political administration. And if, after marriage, they did not migrate to a great distance from the patrimonial inheritance, the paternal authority was still acknowledged and acquiesced in. Thus, in process of time, he who at first was only the head of a single family, if his days were prolonged and his progeny multiplied, became the paternal prince or chief-patriarch of a tribe.

In the youth of time and freshness of human nature, families soon became large; and as the father and head could not always be present while he lived, and as he might die before all his children could have become heads of families, it became necessary that a substitute in his absence, and a successor in case of his premature death, should be appointed to fill his place and administer the affairs of the family. Nature and reason alike pointed to the first-born son, and religion consecrated him his vicegerent. Hence, the privileges and honors of the first-born son were both religious and political; and thus the duties devolving upon him gave him a right to a double portion of the inheritance. Esau was, therefore, both *prodigal* and *profane* in selling his birthright for a meal of pottage.

The antiquity of this arrangement appeared from the envy and jealousy of Cain, roused at the rejection of his offering and the acceptance of that of Abel. That jealousy seems to have been kindled into rage because of his birthright. This is fairly implied in God's address to Cain, when that address is fairly translated and understood:—"If you do well, shall you not have the excellency? and if you do not well, sin precludes you [from the excellency]. And [Abel shall be subject to you] to you shall be his desire, and you shall rule over him."[1]

The moral and religious institutions of the patriarchal or family worship, which continued from the fall of Adam to the convenant of circumcision, were the sabbath, the service of the altar, oral instruction, prayer, praise, and benediction. With the addition of circumcision in the family of one patriarch, for special purposes, these were the parts of that system which continued for two thousand five hundred years.

---

[1] Genesis 4:7.

The religious observance of weeks or sabbaths in commemoration of creation, and prospective of an eternal rest, to arise out of the sacrificial and typical institution, was religiously observed to the giving of the law, or the erection of the Jewish institution. Thus the law of the sabbath commences with the words *"Remember the sabbath."* The righteous always remembered the weeks, and regarded the conclusion of the week as holy to the Lord. Hence, even after the apostasy, which issued in the neglect of family worship, in consequence of the sons of God intermarrying with the daughters of men, and which brought a flood of water upon the world of the ungodly—we find Noah religiously counting his weeks even while incarcerated in the ark. In the wilderness of Sin, before the giving of the law, we also find the Jews observing the sabbath. And to facilitate the observance of it, God wrought three special miracles during the peregrinations of Israel. He gave two days' portion of manna on the sixth day—none on the seventh—and preserved from putrefaction that portion laid up for the sabbath.[1]

Sin-offerings and thank-offerings, on altars both of stone and earth, were presented to the Lord—the former in faith of the promise concerning the bruising the serpent's head by the offspring of the woman—the latter in grateful acknowledgement of the goodness of God in creation and providence. Cain, without faith in the promised redemption, like many deists and natural religionists in our time, did acknowledge the goodness and care of God by a thank-offering; but Abel, *by faith in that promise,* not only offered his thank-offering, but a lamb as a sin-offering: therefore, while God respected not Cain's oblation without faith in that promise, he testified in favor of the *gifts* of Abel—he accepted his sin-offering and his thank-offering.

In the very brief and general outlines of almost two thousand five hundred years given us in the book of Genesis, we find sundry allusions to this part of the patriarchal institution. Immediately after his egress from the ark, we find Noah rearing his altar upon the baptized earth, and of every clean bird and beast offering to the Lord whole burnt-offerings. Thus began Noah, after the deluge, to worship the Lord according to the patriarchal institution. And thus we find Abraham, Isaac, Jacob, Job, and other patriarchs, presenting their sacrifices to the Lord, while the family worship was the only religious institution to the world.

Even libations, drink-offerings, and anointing as token of gratitude and consecration, are found in this most ancient and venerable institution. "Jacob rose up early in the morning, took the stone which he had put for his pillow, set it up for a pillar, and poured oil upon the

---

[1] Exodus 16:15-27.

top of it."[1] "And Jacob set up a pillar in the place where God talked with him, even a pillar of stone, and he poured a drink-offering thereon, and he poured oil thereon."[2]

A beautiful and instructive instance of ancient family worship, and of the sacerdotal functions, as exercised by the patriarchs in reference to *the altar*, we have in that most ancient of books, supposed by many to have been written by Moses while in the land of Midian; but, according to others, by Job himself, who was certainly contemporary with *Eliphaz the Temanite*. Eliphaz was the son of Teman, who was the son of Eliphaz, who was the first son of Esau, the son of Isaac, the son of Abraham. He therefore lived before Moses. Thus we find him also officiating at the altar. We are told that "his sons went and feasted in each other's houses, every one his day, and sent and called for their sisters to eat and drink with them. And it was so that when the days of their feasting had gone about, that Job sent and sanctified them, and rose up early in the morning, and offered burnt-offerings according to the number of them all; for Job said, It may be that my sons have sinned and cursed God in their hearts. Thus acted Job continually."[3]

The same Job, by divine appointment, acted as priest or intercessor in behalf of his three friends, princes of Edom: for, having spoken amiss, they were commanded to take seven bullocks and seven rams, and go to Job, the servant of God, and to offer them up for themselves; and "Job my servant shall pray for you." "Job prayed for them, and the Lord accepted his prayer, and forgave Eliphaz, Bildad, and Zophar." "The Lord also accepted and blessed Job after he had prayed for these his friends, and the Lord turned again the captivity of Job."[4]

During this period of the world, there was but one high or general priest, specially called and sent by God. "He was King of Salem and Priest of the Most High God." To him the patriarch Abraham paid tithes or gave the tenth of the spoils taken in war, and Melchizedek blessed him. He was of an order of his own sort. He had no predecessor, successor, nor equal, in the age of family worship.

From all these facts and documents we learn that the service of the altar belonged first to the father of the family—next, to his eldest son;—that it consisted in presenting sin-offerings and thank-offerings of various sorts in behalf of himself or family;—that all pious sons and individuals might *for themselves* erect altars, offer sacrifices, and pour out libations and drink-offerings to the Lord;— that these sacrificial observances were generally, if not always, accompanied with

---

[1] Genesis 28:18.   [2] Genesis 35:14.   [3] Job 1:4, 5.   [4] Job 13:8-10.

prayer, intercession, and thanksgivings;—and that intercession in behalf of those under the care of any father or patriarch was a part of the first institution.

Benediction also was one of the first duties of this office.—Fathers pronounced blessings on their children. Superiors in age and standing blessed their inferiors. Melchizedek blessed Abraham, Isaac blessed Jacob, and Jacob blessed the twelve patriarchs. The invocation of blessings and the imposition of hands upon the head were parts of the family-worship institution.

Concerning prayer and praise, as we can not imagine a religion without them, it is unnecessary to speak particularly of them as parts of the patriarchal institution. Jubal soon taught men to handle the harp and the organ, and piety soon consecrated them to the praise of God. The melodies of nature soon taught man to tune his voice to God. Isaac went out into the fields at eventide for secret prayer. Abraham interceded for Sodom until he was ashamed to push his importunities further; and for Abimelech, king of Egypt, and his family, he made his requests to God. Of him and his patriarchal character God said, "I know Abraham, that he will command his children, and his household after him, and they shall keep the ways of the Lord, to do justice and judgment, that the Lord may bring upon Abraham that which he has spoken of him."[1]

Prophets of a public character were occasionally raised up to bring men back to the primitive simplicity of the patriarchal institution, as well as to lead them forward to the future developments of God's purposes in reference to this work of redemption. Amongst these the most conspicuous were Enoch, Noah, Abraham, Isaac, Jacob. To all these were given new visions of the future, and thus they were all preachers of righteousness and reformers in their respective generations.

From these gleanings from the book of Genesis one may learn that the family-worship institution, which was divinely instituted in the first age of the world, embraced the observance of the sabbath, the service of the altar, oral instruction, prayer, intercession, thanksgiving, and benediction. It contemplated no other bond of union than the marriage covenant, and the relations springing out of it. Doing justly, loving mercy, and walking humbly with God, were enforced in all its maxims, and in the examples of those whom God honored and approved.

There was, during the long period of this family institution, no community separated from the world larger than a single household

---

[1] Genesis 18:19.

—no public altars—no temples—no established order of public teachers; therefore, there were no initiating or separating institutions. There was no *circumcision* for the infant, nor *washing of regeneration* for the instructed. These institutions of latter times had respect to public professing communities; and therefore for two thousand years there was no initiating rite or ordinance amongst men.

Wherever the family curtains were spread and a tent erected, the devout father built his own altar to the Lord, gathered his own children and domestics around him, instructed them in the knowledge of God the creator and preserver of all; and in the history of man, his origin and destiny, as far as revealed to them. They offered their thank-offerings, acknowledgments of favors received; and, when conscious of sin, they presented their sin-offering, with confessions, and, in faith of God's promise, supplicated pardon. Such are the essential attributes of the patriarchal institution, and of the family worship, as learned from the writings of Moses.

But, as the root of all the subsequent dispensations of God's mercy and favor to man was planted in the patriarchal institution, it is necessary to our plan, before we advance further, to pay some attention to one of these patriarchs, whose fame is eternal, on whom God bestowed an honor above all earthly honor, and who stands enrolled in the annals of time as *The Friend of God.* The intelligent reader needs not to be informed that we now call his attention specially to

ABRAHAM

Reader, attend! "I am the God of Abraham, the God of Isaac, and the God of Jacob: this is my name forever, and this is my memorial to all generations." And shall not the name, the calling, the blessing, and the history of Abraham always occupy a large space in the records of God's government of man, and in all the details of his redemption?

Because of his unprecedented faith in God's promises and exalted piety, he was constituted the *father of all believers;* and his whole life is made a model for all the children of God, as far as walking by faith in God's promises is an ornament to human character.

Sufficient, then, to our present purpose, we observe, that *during the family-worship institution,* a little after the commencement of the third millennium, about the seventy-fifth year of his life, God appeared to Abraham while he yet lived in Ur of Chaldea, and commanded him to depart out of that country, and that he would do for him certain things. Abraham obeyed. God gratuitously tendered him *two promises,* not only interesting and valuable to Abraham himself, but to all the human race.

These two promises were intended to be the basis of a twofold relation to God, and the foundation of two distinct religious institutions, called "the Old Testament and the New," "the Old Covenant and the New," "the Two Covenants," and "the covenants of promise." There are contemplated in them the constitution for a temporal and spiritual kingdom of God—a kingdom of God of this world, and a kingdom of God not of this world. Be it, therefore, always remembered, when we attempt to form correct views of the whole economy of God's redemption, that these two promises were made while the patriarchal institution was yet standing, and several centuries before its close. What then, it will be asked, are these

TWO PROMISES

We find them in their most simple form in the beginning of the twelfth chapter of Genesis. The first—

"I will make of thee a great nation, and I will bless thee and make thy name great, and thou shalt be a blessing. I will bless them that bless thee, curse them that curse thee."

The second—*"In thee shall all the families of the earth be blessed."*

These promises, when fully developed, contained numerous blessings. They are, however, in all their details separate and distinct from each other. Abraham's family alone are personally concerned in the first—all families of the earth in the second. Temporal and earthly are the blessings of the former—spiritual and eternal are the blessings of the latter. Paul calls the second, "The gospel preached to Abraham," and "The covenant confirmed by God in reference to the Messiah four hundred and thirty years before the giving of the law." The Jewish kingdom in all its glory was but the development of the first—the Christian kingdom in its present and future blessings is the consummation of the second.

COVENANT OF CIRCUMCISION

In pursuance of the first promise, and in order to its exact and literal accomplishment, about twenty-four years after its promulgation of *"covenant of circumcision"* was established. This "covenant in the flesh" marked out and defined the natural descendants of Abraham, and gave to the world a full proof of the faithfulness of God, putting it in the power of every one to ascertain how God keeps his covenants of promise with all people. This gave to the descendants of

Abraham the title of *"the circumcision,"* and beautifully represented the separation of God's people from the children of this world.

The land of Canaan, as *the inheritance* of this nation, is repeatedly promised to Abraham; and as soon as Isaac, the child of promise, is born and circumcised, the promise of the "seed" in which all nations were to be blessed is confined to him. Not in Ishmael, but "in Isaac, shall *thy seed* be called."[1]

After the death of Abraham, and towards the close of the life of Isaac, his father's God gave him a second edition of these two promises. The first is considerably amplified in its details, while the second is repeated almost in the same words. That which was first to be accomplished is first developed, and its provisions pointed out. "I will be with thee and will bless thee; for unto thee and to thy seed I will give all these countries, and I will perform all the oath which I sware to Abraham thy father; and I will make thy seed to multiply as the stars of heaven, and will give to thy seed all these countries; and in thy seed shall all the nations of the earth be blessed: because Abraham obeyed my voice, and kept my charge, my commandments, my statutes, and my laws."[2]

The same two promises are repeated in almost the same words to Jacob, the son of Isaac, at the time he had the vision of the ladder reaching from earth to heaven, while, in obedience to a command given him by his parents, he was on his way to Padanaram in quest of a wife. On these *three* great occasions—to Abraham—to Isaac—to Jacob—these two promises are solemnly pronounced; always standing in the same order—never confounded; but as distinct as earth and heaven—as time and eternity.

Four hundred and thirty years after the first solemn declaration of these promises, the descendants of Abraham, Isaac, and Jacob, in virtue of the promise, were redeemed out of bondage in Egypt, and saved from the tyranny and cruelty of Pharaoh. Then, in order to the *full completion* of its stipulations, God, by the hand of Moses, proposed a covenant with all Israel at Sinai; in which he guarantees to do all for them contemplated in the promise, confirmed by an oath to Abraham, in being a God to his seed after him. This

SINAITIC COVENANT

constituted them a kingdom of God, a holy nation, a peculiar people. All the blessings comprehended in the first promise to Abraham, or that could grow out of the relation to God which it contemplated, were in full detail carried out into this transaction and secured to the

---

[1] Genesis 21:12   [2] Genesis 26:3-5.

whole nation. The relation was, however, temporal, and its blessings temporal and earthly. The second promise made no part of the Jewish institution or covenant at Sinai, more than it did of the patriarchal or antecedent institution. The typical or figurative part of the family worship, enlarged and improved, was translated into the *national* institution and made a part of it; and whatever spiritual privilege was enjoyed by the Jew was enjoyed upon the same principle with the patriarch—by faith in the second promise, and by an intelligent and believing attendance upon all the appointed means which either prefigured the coming redemption, or realized the blessings which were to be derived through the promised seed.

THE CHRISTIAN SYSTEM

The *seed* in which all the families of the earth were to be blessed was in the nation, but in no other sense than as it was in the people while in Egypt, or in the patriarchs before they went down into Egypt. It was in the nation, but no element of the national institution. They had the second promise made to their fathers, and all the faithful and approved among them believed that promise, and acted conformably to it. Thus amongst the Jews, even before the coming of the Messiah, there were

TWO SEEDS,

the natural and the spiritual children of Abraham. The whole nation were his literal and natural children; and such of them as believed the second promise and understood it were not only his natural children, but his children in the same sense in which all *believing Gentiles* are by virtue of the second promise constituted the children of Abraham. The first, like Ishmael, were born according to the flesh— the fleshly seed of Abraham; the second, like Isaac, were the children of faith in the promise: and thus Abraham is the constituted father of all who believe in that promise, whether of his flesh or not.

But the second promise was not fulfilled for nearly one thousand five hundred years after the first, or after the national institution was confirmed at Sinai; and therefore

THE BLESSING OF ABRAHAM,

which was to come on the nations through his seed, through faith in the accomplished promises, was to be the basis and the substance of a new institution. This "blessing of Abraham" includes all the spiritual and eternal blessings which are laid up in his seed, who is the ark of this new constitution, in whom all the promises of God are verified, and in whom they are deposited for the comfort and salvation of all the faithful children of God. Whatever concerned the family of Abraham, coming through the first promise, descended upon the family principle which is only *flesh*, but whatever concerns all saints of all nations descends upon the new principle of *faith*. "They who are of faith," says Paul, "are blessed with believing Abraham." And "If you be Christ's, then" (and only then) "are you Abraham's seed, and heirs according to the promise."

The blessing of Abraham was then promised in the patriarchal age antecedent to the Jewish national institution, and independent of it; therefore that institution can not affect, much less disannul, the blessings promised in the covenant, confirmed before by God, respecting the Messiah, in the time of family worship, and four hundred and thirty years before the Jewish institution began.

In calling Abraham and in making him the father of many nations, and the depositary of still more precious promises and revelations, God did not supersede the family worship. He only added to the stock of religious knowledge, strengthened the faith, and enlarged the hopes, of that single family. The family institution continued without the slightest change, except in one particular specified in the covenant of circumcision, as respected the single family of Abraham, for four hundred and thirty years after the charter concerning his seed and that concerning the Messiah were secured to this renowned patriarch. Thus we have traced the continuance of the family religion, or patriarchal economy, for two thousand five hundred years, and are now prepared to make a few remarks on the Jewish national institution, though we have already anticipated almost all that is necessary to our present object. Still, however, we shall make it the object of a distinct notice.

THE JEWISH INSTITUTION

In this age of improvement of divine institutions, we read and hear much of "two dispensations of the covenant of grace"; thus making the Jewish and the Christian institutions dispensations of one "covenant of grace." Why not make the patriarchal (still more venerable for its antiquity, and which continued a thousand years longer than the Jewish) also a dispensation of the covenant of grace, and then we should have had *three* dispensations of one covenant? This is but a "*show* of wisdom." The Holy Spirit calls them "two covenants," or "two institutions," and not two modifications of one covenant; and it speaks of each as established upon promises. The Jewish was established upon temporal and earthly promises, contained in the first promise made to Abraham; but the new, says Paul, "is established upon *better promises,"* growing out of that concerning *the blessing of the nations* in the promised seed.[1]

The Jewish institution commenced and continued about one thousand five hundred years before the reign of heaven began. It was not substituted for the family worship, but added to it; affecting, however, the patriarchal institution in some respects, as far as concerned the single family of Abraham. The individual families of the nation of the Jews, *as such*, had still their family worship—still the worship of God was heard in the dwellings of the righteous; and, like Joshua, every good Israelite said, "As for me and my family, we will serve the Lord."

In four hundred years the family of Abraham had, in the line of Isaac and Jacob, in fulfilment of the first promise, grown up into millions. Not less than two million[2] came up out of Egypt under the conduct of Moses. The heavenly Father, in progressive development of his plan of blessing all nations, leaves all the world under the family-worship institution, and erects the whole progeny of Abraham that came up out of Egypt into one great national institution. He condescends to appear in the character of *king of the Jews*, and to make them a *kingdom of God*, as preparatory to the appearance of his *Son*, who is predestined to be the king of the whole earth, and to have a kingdom which shall ultimately embrace all the nations of the world.

The twelve tribes were brought into the form of one great worshiping family, presenting through the common high priest their united worship to God. This gave rise to the erection of one public house consecrated to the Lord, as the place of meeting in their social and national character. A constitution, political, moral, and religious, was submitted to the people; and on their adoption of it they became the covenanted people of God. This constitutional kingdom was built upon precepts and promises; and its worship, when fully developed, was little more than the extension of the family worship to one great national family. They had one king, one high priest, one national altar, one national house of God, one morning and evening service, one great national sacrifice, and one great annual atonement. The nation was a family of families, and what ever pertained to a single family in its family worship was extended and accommodated to this great confederate family.

Various mystic and significant institutions distinguished this nation from all others; for it was one principal object of its institution to

---

[1] Jeremiah 31:31.
[2] Men fit for war are never more than the third or fourth of any population. There were six hundred thousand men of this class when they came to Mount Sinai.

keep its subjects separate and distinct from all other people till Messiah (the promised seed) should come.   Another object was, to picture out in appropriate types the spiritual worship of the kingdom of heaven, and to exhibit the great doctrines of faith, repentance, remission, adoption, and inheritance, by picturesque images, ingeniously devised to adumbrate the whole doctrine of reconciliation and sanctification to God.

The Jewish institution is not to be regarded only in its political, moral, and religious aspects, but especially in its figurative and prospective character.   God so wisely and benevolently contrived it from its origin to its close, that its whole history—the fates and fortunes of its subjects from their descent into Egypt, their travels thence to Canaan and settlement in the land of promise—their fortunes in that land to their final catastrophe—should exactly and impressively shadow forth the new institution with the fates and fortunes of the subjects of this new and more glorious order of things. "All these things happened to them for *types*" (examples), says Paul, "and they are written for our admonition, upon whom the ends of the world have come." The same great commentator on this institution not only presents the history of its subjects as instructive to the citizens of the new institution, but of the tabernacle he says, "It was a figurative representation for the time then present," and the furniture thereof "the patterns of things in the heavens." "The law," he adds, "contained only a shadow of the good things to come." A shadow, indeed, proceeding from a man, a house, a tree, is not, and can not be, an exact image or representation of them; yet, when explained by a verbal description, it easily facilitates an easy and correct conception of them.

So full of the doctrine of the new institution was the old, that we find all the apostles and Christian writers unceremoniously applying every thing they quote from the law, the prophets, and the Psalms, to the Messiah, his kingdom, and the fortunes of his people; as if the Jewish writings had no other object than to unfold the kingdom of heaven.   Jesus begins with Abraham seeing his day on Mount Moriah in the typical resurrection of Isaac.   Paul regards Hagar, Ishmael, Sarah, Isaac, as the best illustration of the *two institutions;* and John ends with the description of the descent of Jerusalem from heaven.

Every one, then, who would accurately understand the Christian institution must approach it through the Mosaic; and he that would be a proficient in the Jewish must make Paul his commentator. While the mere politician, moralist, or religionist contemplates the one without the other, though he may find much to admire in both, he will never understand either.   A veil, thick as that which concealed the glory of the face of Moses from the Israelites, will hide the glory of the Jewish and Christian institution from his view.

Not only did the tabernacle, the temple, their furniture, the service of both, the priests, the sacrifices, the festivals, the convocations, and all the ordinances of that ritual, together with the history of that people, assume the picturesque and figurative character, but almost all the illustrious and highly-distinguished personages of that institution were made prophetic or typical of the Messiah or of the great incidents of his life, sufferings, and triumphs, and the leading affairs of his government. Amongst *persons* in the patriarchal and Jewish ages who, in one or more prominent characters or incidents, or in their general history, adumbrated the Messiah and his reign, the following group occupy a lofty eminence:—Adam, Abel, Noah, Melchizedek, Isaac, Jacob, Joseph, Moses, Aaron, Joshua, Samson, David, Jonah. Of *things* of this class, as well as persons highly figurative and instructive, are the visions of Jacob's ladder—the burning bush —the pillar of cloud and fire—the manna—the rock Horeb, a fountain of living water in the wilderness—the veil of Moses—the brazen serpent—the victory over the nations of Canaan—and the land of Canaan itself. And of *ordinances*, the passover, the scapegoat, the red heifer, the year of jubilee, the law of the leper, the kinsman redeemer, the cities of refuge; together with all the sacrifices, washings, anointings, and consecrations of the *holy* nation.

But a third object of the Jewish institution, of paramount importance to the world, was the furnishing of a new alphabet and language (the elements of heavenly science), without which it would appear to have been almost, if not altogether, impossible to learn the spiritual things or to make any proficiency in the knowledge of those relations which Christianity unfolds. The language of the new institution is therefore explained by that of the old. No one can understand the dialect of the kingdom of heaven who has not studied the dialect of the antecedent administrations of heaven over the patriarchs and Jews. The most striking and characteristic attribute of the sacred dialect is, that the elements of it are composed of the incidents of history, or what we call *remarkable providences.*

I can not explain myself better, nor render my readers a more essential service, than by illustrating by an actual detail of sacred history the following proposition, viz.:—*That sacred history, or the remarkable instances of God's providence to the Jews and patriarchs, are the foundation of the sacred dialect of the new institution.* Or, if the reader will understand it better, it may be thus expressed:—*All the leading words and phrases of the New Testament are to be ex-*

plained and understood by the history of the Jewish nation and God's government of them. Take the following as a mere specimen:—

God *called* Abram out of Ur, and changed his name into *Abraham*, and the name of his wife Sarai into *Sarah*. He *promised* Isaac as the person in whom his *seed* should be *called*. God did *tempt* Abraham, commanding him to *offer* Isaac for a burnt-offering. Isaac had two sons—Esau the elder, and Jacob the younger. Esau *despised* his *birthright* and *sold* it to Jacob. Jacob wrestled with God, and *prevailed;* he obtained a blessing, and was therefore called *Israel.* He had *twelve* sons: of these Joseph was his favorite. His brethren *envied* him, and *sold* him for twenty pieces of silver. Joseph *found grace* in the sight of his master. *The Lord was with Joseph.* He was cast into prison, and from thence was elevated to the *governor* of Egypt under Pharaoh. A famine in Canaan compelled Jacob and his sons into Egypt for bread, and Joseph was *made known* to his brethren. Joseph died in Egypt and left his father's house in that land. They multiplied exceedingly, and the Egyptians greatly *afflicted* and *oppressed* the Israelites. *Moses* was born and exposed: Pharaoh's daughter found him and *adopted* him for a son. Moses fled into Midian and married the daughter of the priest or prince of Midian, and kept his father-in-law's flock in the *desert,* and came to Horeb, *the mountain of God.* The Lord appeared to him in *a flame of fire* in a bush. The bush burned and was not consumed. Moses *drew near,* and then first stood on *holy ground.* God *sent* him to Egypt to lead *his* people out of *bondage.*

God made him say to the *children of Israel,* "I AM has sent me to you." Gather the *elders* of Israel and say to them, *The Lord God of* your fathers, the God of Abraham," etc., "has sent me to you. I will *smite* Egypt with my *wonders,* and *bring you up out of the afflictions* of Egypt. Tell Pharaoh, Israel is *my son—my first-born.* Take Aaron with thee, and thou shalt *put words into his mouth;* and I will be *with thy mouth* and with his mouth: he shall be to thee instead of a mouth, and thou shalt be to him *instead of God.* Take thy *rod* in thy hand. The Lord *sent* Aaron to Moses: and he met him in the mount and *kissed* him. And the Lord *visited* his people. And the people *believed when they heard* that the Lord had *looked upon* their affliction. Pharaoh oppressed them still more. The Lord said, "With a *strong hand* shall he let them go. I will *redeem* them with a stretched-out arm, and with great *judgments.* I will give you Canaan for a *heritage;* I will take you to me *for a people. I will be your God."*

Moses said, I am a man of *uncircumcised lips,* and how shall Pharaoh *hearken* to me? I have made thee a *god* to Pharaoh, and

Aaron *thy prophet.* I will multiply my *signs,* and bring out *my people,* and *harden* Pharaoh's heart. When he says, "Show me a miracle," cast your rod before him, and *it shall become* a serpent. Still Pharaoh refused, and *hardened his heart.* The magicians, overcome with the *signs,* said, *This is the finger of God.* The *God of the Hebrews* said, Let *my people go.* I have *roused* thee up (as a lion) to show in you my power, and to make *my name known* through *all the earth.* The Lord slew all the *first-born* of Egypt after he had *plagued* them exceedingly. Pharaoh commanded them to depart; but he pursued them to the Red Sea. Israel fainted at the sight before and behind them. Moses said, Stand still and see *the salvation of God.* The sea was divided. Covered with a cloud, Israel marched through as on dry ground. The waters stood on either side as a wall. Pharaoh pursued with his chariots and horsemen, but the waters returned and they were drowned. Thus the Lord *redeemed, saved, delivered, and brought Israel out of bondage.*

After this deliverance, Moses and the children of Israel sang, "The Lord is become *my salvation;* he is *my God.* Thou hast overthrown them that *rose up against thee.* Thou hast *led forth thy people* whom thou *hast redeemed.* Thou *hast guided them* in thy strength to thy *holy habitation.* The inhabitants of Canaan shall be still as a stone till *thy people* pass over, O Lord, the people *thou hast purchased.* Thou shalt plant them in the mountains of *thine inheritance;* in the *sanctuary* which *thy hands* have *established.*"

They came into *the wilderness of Sin.* They cried for bread, and God *rained bread from heaven upon them,* that he might *prove* them whether or not they would *walk in his law,* and they did eat manna forty years till they came to the borders of Canaan.

They complained for water, and tempted God. And Moses *smote the rock* in Horeb, and water gushed out. But Moses was wroth, and smote the rock twice, and he and Aaron thus *rebelled* against God, and fell in the wilderness. The Lord made a covenant with the whole nation at Sinai, and made them a *peculiar treasure* above all people—a *kingdom of priests, a holy nation;* and God spake all the words of the law, written on two tables of stone; and *spake to Israel from heaven.*

The Lord, by Moses, gave them directions for rearing a *tabernacle,* and a pattern for all its furniture. And as *a ransom for his soul,* every man, rich and poor, was to pay half a shekel as an *offering to the Lord to make an atonement* for his soul; and it was given for *the service* of the tabernacle. When the tabernacle was reared and finished, *the glory of the Lord* filled the tabernacle and the *cloud* covered it. And when the cloud *was taken up* they journeyed; but until it was taken up they journeyed not. The *cloud* was in the tabernacle by day, and *fire* was on it by night, in the sight of all Israel throughout all their journeys.

And before Moses died he *laid his hands* upon Joshua, and gave him a *charge* as the *Lord commanded;* and thus put *honor* upon him, that the children of Israel might be *obedient* to him as their *saviour.* "As I was *with Moses,* so will I be *with thee,*" saith God: "I will not fail thee nor *forsake* thee."

Could we thus proceed with the history of this people, and add to their history the observance of their religious institutions, we should find out the true meaning of the sacred style of the New Testament with more accuracy and certainty than from all the commentators of ancient and modern times. This, as a sample, must suffice for our present purpose.

From the premises now before us, the specifications of the outlines of the Sinaitic and national institution, and the terms and phrases found in the history of this people, we may discover in what *relation* they stood to God, and what *favors* be bestowed upon them in that relation.

They were the *called* and *chosen,* or the *elect* of God as a nation. As such, they were *delivered, saved, bought,* or *purchased,* and *redeemed.* God is said to have *created, made, formed,* and *begotten* them. As such he is called their *Father,* their God, their *Redeemer,* their *King,* their *Saviour,* their *Salvation;* and they are called his *children, sons, and daughters; born to him,* his *house, people, inheritance, family, servants.*

As a *chartered* and *congregated* people, they are called *the city, the holy city, the city of the Lord, Jerusalem, Zion, Mount Zion, the city of David.* Other nations in contrast with them are called *not a people, aliens, strangers, enemies, far off, unclean.*

Various similitudes expressive of the kind relation in which they stood to God are also found in the pages of the ancient institutions, —such as *husband* and *wife, shepherd* and *flock, vine* and *vineyard, mother* and *children.* They are said to be *written* or *enrolled* in *the book of God;* to be *planted, washed, sanctified, clean, separated to God;* they are called *the house, buildings, sanctuary, dwelling-place* of God; *a kingdom of priests, a holy nation, a peculiar people,* etc.

Those who are curious to trace these phrases descriptive of the relation and privileges of this ancient kingdom of God had better (in addition to the passages quoted in their history from Egypt to the Jordan) examine the following passages:—Exodus 14:30; 15:16; 19:6; Deut. 4:37; 7:6; 10:15; 14:1; 1:31; 7:5; 32:6, 18, 19; 18:7;

3:18, 20; 12:9; 1 Kings 3:8; Psalms 105:6; 33:13; 105:43; 106:5, 21; 64:2; 149:2; Isaiah 41:8, 9; 43:1, 3, 5, 7; 51:2, 4; 41:1, 6, 7. Jeremiah, Ezekiel, and the Psalms of David throughout, etc.

Unless we should write a full treatise on these antecedent institutions, we can not with propriety descend further into details. The outlines, as far as subordinate to the theme of this essay, are now before the reader; and with this preparation we shall now invite his attention to *the kingdom of heaven.*

And why, an *American* would say, is it not called the *republic* of heaven, and the Chief called the *President* of a celestial Republic? Certainly there were the republics of Greece and Rome before the doctrine of this kingdom was first promulgated, and the Gentiles as well as the Jews could have understood the figure of a republic as well as that of a kingdom. It was not, then, because there was not in society a model or type of this sort; but because such a type would have been inapposite to the nature of this institution.

History testifies that republics are better adapted to peace than war, and that they are forced and unnatural organizations of society. Aristocracies and republics owe all their attractions to the excessive corruptions of the governments under which they have originated. They are the reaction of force and fraud, of cruelty and oppression, and are sustained by the remembrance and apprehension of the evils which occasioned them. They have always been extolled or admired either in contrast with the vices and enormities of degenerate and profligate monarchies, or in the freshness of the recollections of the wrongs and outrages which occasioned them; and men have generally tired of them when they became corrupt and forgetful of the oppressions and crimes which forced them into being. So that the corruptions of monarchies have given birth to republics, and the corruptions of these have originated monarchies again.

In these last days of degeneracy, republics are great blessings to mankind, as good physicians are blessings in times of pestilence; but yet it must be confessed that it would be a greater blessing to be without plagues and doctors. While men are, however, so degenerate, and while selfishness and injustice are so rampant in society, republican officers are better than kings—because we can get rid of them sooner. They are indeed, kings under another name, with a short-leased authority; and our experience fully demonstrates that in these degenerate days the reigns of our republican kings are nearly long enough. Till the King of kings comes, we Christians ought to be good republicans, under the conviction that human governments seldom grow better, and that the popular doctrine of our country is true—that political authority generally makes a man worse, and public favors almost invariably corrupt the heart. Rapid rotation in office is the practical influence of the republican theory; and the experiment proves that, brief as republican authority is, it is sometimes too long for republican virtue to sustain without deterioration. Now, if this be true of republican virtue, the brightest and the best, what earthly virtue can long resist the contamination of long-protracted authority?

Monarchy is the only form of government, however, which nature recognizes. It was the first, and it will be the last. A government with three or thirty heads is a monster; and therefore the beast that represents it comes out of the sea with a plurality of horns as well as heads.

The most approved theory of human nature and of human government now current wherever the English language is spoken, either in the Old World or in the New, is that a monarchy would be always the best government, because the cheapest, the most efficient, and the most dignified; provided only, that the crown was placed on the wisest head, and the scepter wielded by the purest hands. Could we always secure this, we would all be monarchists: because we can not, we are all republicans.

But, after this apology for the phrase *kingdom of heaven*, we would recall the attention of the reader to the concession, made by republicans themselves, that a kingdom is better adapted to a state of war than a republic; and that this beautiful though most appropriate figure, which occurs in the New Testament more than one hundred and fifty times, and very often in the Old, presupposes a state of war as existing in the universe. But, for the reasons assigned in preference of monarchy, the *natural* government of the universe always was, is, and evermore shall be, monarchy. God himself is of necessity absolute monarch of the universe. Had he not essentially sustained that relation to all his creatures, there never could have been rebellion nor sin in his dominions. The systems of nature are all after this model. Every sun is a king over the system which it controls; and in every sphere there is one controlling and supreme principle. It will be the last government; for when the episode in the great drama of *rational* existence which sin occasioned shall have been completed, the government of the universe will assume its ancient order, and God be supreme monarch again. But this will not be till Jesus gives up the kingdom to God which a preternatural state of things put into his hands. This can not be till he has subdued man to his rightful allegiance, or destroyed forever every opponent to the absolute monarchy of the Eternal Supreme; "for Jesus must reign till all his enemies be put under his feet."

The kingdom which Jesus has received from his Father, however heavenly, sublime, and glorious it may be regarded, is only temporal. It had a beginning, and it will have an end; for he must reign only *till* all enemies are put under his feet. But the transition of the scepter into the hands of Emanuel has not changed the government. He is now the hereditary monarch of the universe, as well as the proper king of his own kingdom. He now reigns as absolutely over all principalities, hierarchies, and powers, celestial and terrestrial, as did the great God and Father of the universe, before he was invested with the regal authority.

We have said it was a preternatural state of things which originated the kingdom of Jesus: therefore the object of this remedial reign is to destroy that preternatural state of things—to put down sin. Now, as all human governments presuppose disorder, and as the kingdoms of this world generally have arisen out of confusion and war, the kingdom of heaven of which we are to speak owes its origin to the celestial and terrestrial apostasies—the revolt of Satan and of Adam. Were there no justice within or violence without, civil government would be wholly unnecessary, and its appendages an excrescence upon society. Had there not been such a revolt and rebellion as sacred history records, there would have been no such kingdom of heaven as that over which Jesus the Messiah now presides. Now, as both this King and kingdom, and all that appertains to them, were occasioned by such a preternatural state of things, we must view them in all their attributes and details, with reference to those circumstances which called them into being.

THE ELEMENTS OF A KINGDOM

We must understand the type, or we can not understand the antitype. We must understand that which is natural before we can understand that which is spiritual. What then are the essential elements of a kingdom as existing among men? They are five, viz.: King, Constitution, Subjects, Laws, and Territory. Such are the essential parts of every political kingdom, perfect in its kind, now existing on earth.

In *forming a state,* the essential elements are people and country. The people make a constitution, and this makes a president or king, citizens or subjects, and every thing else belonging to a state. It is, then, the relation into which the people resolve themselves which makes it a republic, an aristocracy, a monarchy. Do they choose a monarchy? They first make a constitution, and this places one upon the throne—makes them subjects, and the gives them laws. Although the constitution is first, in the order of nature, of all the elements of a kingdom (for it makes one man a king and the rest subjects), yet we can not imagine a constitution in reference to a kingdom, without a king and subjects. In speaking of them in detail, we can not then speak of any one of them as existing without the others —we must regard them as correlates, and as coming into existence contemporaneously. There is no husband nor wife before marriage, neither can there be a husband without a wife; yet one of the parties must be made before the other. Marriage makes a husband out of a bridegroom, and a wife out of the bride. So the constitution makes the king or the governor, the citizens or subjects, out of the people, as the case may be; for there never can be a king or subject without a constitution, or, what is the same thing, an agreement, verbal or written, for certain privileges stipulated and conditioned. In every well-regulated political kingdom, *in the order of nature,* the elements stand thus:—1. Constitution; 2. King; 3. Subjects; 4. Laws; 5. Territory.

In the kingdom which God set up by Moses, the elements stood in this order. The constitution was first proposed under which God condescended to be their king, and they were to be regarded as his people or subjects; he then gave them laws and established them in the territory before promised.

But in the kingdom of nature, or in the original kingdom of God, the elements are only four, and the order in which they stand are:—1. King; 2. Subjects; 3. Laws; 4. Territory. As Father and Creator of that kingdom, God himself was absolute Sovereign, whose will is the supreme law of the whole realm of nature.

Having ascertained the essential elements of a *kingdom,* and marked the order in which they stand, before we particularly attend to those elements in order, we shall ask, Why this kingdom is called the kingdom of *heaven.*

THE NAME

Heaven, and the kingdom of heaven, are not one and the same thing. God is not the kingdom of God. But, as the kingdom of God is something pertaining to God, so the kingdom of heaven is something pertaining to heaven, and consequently to God. Whether always the phrases "the kingdom of God" and "the kingdom of heaven" exactly represent the same thing, certain it is that both phrases are often applied to the same institution.[1]

---

[1] If the following passages are carefully examined and compared it will appear that both these phrases often represent the same thing:—Matthew 3:7; Mark 1:14; Luke 4:43.—Matthew 13:12; Mark 4:11; Luke 8:10.—Matthew 11:11; Luke 6:28. To these three distinct evidences many more might be added. What Matthew calls "the kingdom of *heaven*" Mark and Luke call the "kingdom of *God.*"

This is true of them, whether translated *reign* or *kingdom;* and it is very evident that frequently the original word *basileia* ought in preference to be rendered *reign,* inasmuch as this term better suits all those passages where *coming* or *approaching* is spoken of: for, while reigns or administrations approach and recede, kingdoms have attributes and boundaries which are stationary. Reign and kingdom of God, though sometimes applicable to the same subject, never contemplate it in the same light. They are, indeed, as intimately connected as the reign of King William and the kingdom of Great Britain. The former represents the administration of the kingdom, and the latter the state over which this administration extends.

Two good reasons may be offered why Matthew, the oldest Christian writer, generally prefers kingdom or reign of *heaven,* to the phrase kingdom or reign of *God;* I say *generally,* for he occasionally uses *both* designations.[1] He wrote to Jews in Judea who expected a Messiah, a king, and a kingdom of God on *earth,*—a mere improvement of the Jewish system; and therefore to raise their conception he delights to call it the reign or kingdom of *heaven,* in contrast with that earthly kingdom of God of which they were so long in possession.

He also found a good reason in the idiom of the Jewish prophets for using the word *heaven* (both in the singular and plural form) for *God.* Daniel told the Assyrian monarch that his kingdom would be sure to him when he would have learned that "the *Heavens* do rule"; yet in the preceding verse he says, "Till thou knowest that the Most High rules in the kingdom of man,—thus using *Heavens* and *the Most High* as synonymous. The Psalmist says, "The wicked set their mouths against the *Heavens.*" The Prodigal confesses that he had "sinned against *Heaven,*" and Jesus himself asked whether the baptism of John was "from *Heaven* or from men." Thus he was authorized from the Jewish use of the word to regard it as equivalent to *God.* If, then, Matthew had meant no more by the phrase "kingdom of heaven" than the "kingdom of God," he was justified, by the Jewish use of the word *heaven,* to apply it in that sense. Some may object to all these remarks upon Matthew's manner, that it was Jesus Christ and the preachers he commissioned who called it the kingdom of heaven, and not Matthew Levi. To such we reply that the other sacred writers uniformly, in reciting all the same parables and incidents, use the phrase "kingdom of God," and *never* the phrase "the kingdom of heaven."

From the use of the phrase "kingdom of God," we must, I think, regard him as having special reference to the reason first assigned.

---

[1] See chapters 6:33; 12:28; 19:24; 21:31, 43.

He does not say the kingdom of *heaven* shall be taken from the Jews; but "The kingdom of God shall be taken from you, and given to a nation bringing forth the fruits of it"; for although it might with propriety, in his acceptation, he said that the Jews already had the kingdom of God, it could not be said that they had the kingdom of *heaven* as proclaimed by Matthew.[1]

When compared with the earthly kingdom of God among the Jews, it is certainly the kingdom of *heaven;* for Jesus alleges that his kingdom is not of this world; and Daniel affirmed that in the days of the last worldly empire the God of heaven would set up a kingdom unlike all others then on earth; in which, as Paul teaches, men are "blessed with every spiritual blessing in heavenly places in Christ":[2] for he has raised us Jews and Gentiles, and "has set us down together in the heavenly places by Christ Jesus."[3]

There is, in the superior and heavenly privileges and honors bestowed upon the citizens of this kingdom, the best reason why it should have first been presented to the world under this title, rather than any other; and for the same reasons which influenced Matthew to usher it into notice in Judea, under this designation, we ought now to prefer it, because many of our contemporaries, like the ancient Jews, see as much of heaven and glory in the veiled grace of the Mosaic institution as in the unveiled grace of the Christian kingdom. The pertinency of this title will appear still more evident as we develop the constitutional privileges of this kingdom.

But most evidently the kingdom of heaven is *"the kingdom of Christ and of God."*[4] It is the kingdom of God, because he set it up,[5] gave the constitution and king, and all the materials out of which it is erected.[6] It is the kingdom of Christ, because God the Father gave it to him as his Son, and as the *heir of all things;* and therefore, "all that is the Father's is mine," says Jesus, "and I am his."[7] *"God created all things by Jesus Christ and for him."*

Having, then, noticed the reasons for the characteristic *titles* of this kingdom, and having already ascertained what are the elements absolutely essential to a kingdom, distinguished from those merely circumstantial or accidental, we shall now proceed to consider, in the order suggested, the Constitution, King, Subjects, Laws, and Territory of the kingdom of heaven.

CONSTITUTION

God himself, after the gracious counsels of his own will, proposed and tendered the constitution of this kingdom to his own Son. This

---

[1] Matthew 21:43. [2] Ephesians 1:3. [3] Ephesians 2:6.
[4] Ephesians 5:5. [5] Daniel 2:44. [6] Jeremiah 31:31, 34. [7] John 17:10.

"glory he had with the Father before the world was." He that was "in the beginning with God"—"*the wisdom and power of God*"—was set up (constituted) from everlasting, or ever the earth was. "Then was I with God, as one brought up with him; I was daily his delight, rejoicing always before him—rejoicing in the habitable parts of his earth; and my delights were with the sons of men."[1] Therefore, he who was to be "*ruler in Israel*" was with God in counsel "in the beginning of all his ways"; for "his goings forth were from of old, even from the day of eternity."[2]

It was *to do the will*, or fulfil the items in this constitution, that "the *Word* was made flesh and dwelt among us." "I came to *do the will* of him that *sent* me," and to finish "the work *given* me to do." "I have power to lay down my life, and I have power to resume it; this commandment I received from my Father." The Father "commissioned and sent him forth into the world." He "came down from heaven." "Thou hast given me power over all flesh, that I might give eternal life to all that thou hast given me."

These and many other passages, which the reader will easily remember, unequivocally evince that an understanding and agreement existed ere time began between God and the *Word* of God; or, as now revealed, between the Father and the Son, respecting the kingdom. In consequence of which "he divested himself" of his antecedent glory—"took upon him the form of a bond-servant"—"was made in the likeness of sinful flesh"—"took part with us in flesh and blood." In consequence of which agreement, and the promised glory, for "the joy set before him in the promise," of "seeing his seed, the travail of his soul, and being satisfied," he "endured the cross, despising the shame," and was "made perfect through sufferings to lead many sons to glory."

To the stipulations concerning eternal life, propounded in the constitution of the kingdom of heaven, frequent allusions are made in the apostle's writings. Thus the believers were "elected in *him* before the foundation of the world," and "eternal life was promised before the times of the ages," according to the benevolent purposes which *he purposed in himself* for the administration of the fulness of the appointed times, to gather together all under Christ—all in the heavens and all on the earth, under him. He formerly marked us out for an adoption through Jesus Christ to himself, according to his purpose who effectually works all things according to the counsel of his will.[3]

From all these sayings and allusions, we must trace the constitu-

---

[1] Proverbs 8:30, 31.   [2] Micah 5:2.   [3] Ephesians 1:3-12.

tion of this kingdom into eternity—before time began. We must date it from *everlasting,* and resolve it into the absolute gracious will of the eternal God. In reference to all the prospective developments of time, "known to God from the beginning," it proposed to make the *Word* flesh, and then to make the Incarnate Word, called Emanuel, or Jesus Christ, the *king;* to give him all who should be reconciled to God by him for *subjects,* to put under him all the angelic hosts, and constitute him monarch of earth, *lawgiver* to the universe; and thus make him heir and Lord of all things.

As a constitution brings all the elements of a kingdom into a new relation to one another, so it is the measure and guarantee of all the privileges, immunities, and obligations accruing to all the parties in that relation. It prescribes, arranges, and secures all the privileges, duties, obligations, honors, and emoluments of the king and the subjects. Neither of them can claim more than it stipulates and guarantees, and neither of them can rightfully be deprived of any of them.

From the premises now before us, and the light given to us in these Scriptures and those in the margin, we learn—

First. That God is the author of the constitution of the kingdom of heaven; that he propounded it to the *Word* that was made flesh, before the world was, in prospect of all the developments of creation.

Second. That the *Word* accepted it, because the will of God was always his delight; therefore he said, "I come to do thy will, O God!" Hence "*God* has so loved the world as to give his only begotten Son, that whosoever believes on him may not perish, but obtain eternal life."

Third. That in consequence "all *authority* in heaven and earth" was given to Jesus Christ, and all orders of intelligence subjected to him, that he might be *king* over all, and have the power of giving eternal life to his people.[1]

Fourth. That the earth is now the Lord's, the present temporal territory of his kingdom; that the heathen people are given to him for his inheritance, and the uttermost parts of the earth for his possession; that all ends of the earth are his, and all dominions, kindreds, tribes, tongues, and people shall yet serve him on earth and glorify him in heaven.[2]

Fifth. That all that he redeems are his seed—his subjects; that he will have their faith, confidence, esteem, admiration, and gratitude forever; that he will be worshiped, honored, and revered by them in a world without end; that God, angels, and saints will delight in him

---

[1] Matthew 27; 2:44; 7:27. [2] Psalms 2:6-8; 72:2-18.

for ever and ever.[1] He has, therefore, to raise the dead, judge the world, and to present the redeemed pure, holy, happy and triumphant before his Father, and then to give up his kingdom to God.

To comprehend in any adequate idea the constitution of this kingdom, we must learn more than its history, or the way in which it was introduced and propounded. We must regard all the elements of the kingdom as *constitutional* elements; the king as a constitutional king; the subjects, laws, and territory, including the ultimate inheritance, as constitutional subjects, laws, territory, inheritance; and, therefore, we shall speak of them in detail.

THE KING

The Lord Jesus Christ is the constitutional monarch of the kingdom of heaven. The privileges guaranteed to him in reference to the kingdom are as follows:

As king, he is to be the *oracle* of God—to have the disposal of the Holy Spirit—to be prophet and high priest of the temple of God—to have the throne of his Father—to be governor of all nations on earth, and head of all hierarchs and powers in heaven—the supreme lawgiver, the only saviour—the resurrection and the life, the ultimate and final judge of all, and the heir of all things.

These honors, privileges, and powers are secured to him by the irrevocable grant of the God and Father of all; therefore, as said Isaiah, "The Lord cometh with a strong hand, and his arm shall rule for him. Behold, his reward is with him, and his work before him." "I have set my king upon my holy hill of Zion." "Ask of me, and I will give thee the heathen for thine inheritance, and the uttermost parts of the earth for thy possession." "I have made him a leader and commander of the people"—"a light to the Gentiles"—"salvation to the ends of the earth,"—"a priest forever after the order of Melchizedek." "Sit thou at my right hand till I make thy foes thy footstool." "The government shall be upon his shoulders." "All things are delivered to me by my Father." "He is Lord of the dead and living." "Angels, authorities, and powers are subjected to him." "The Father gave the Spirit without measure to him." "He received of the Father the promise of the Holy Spirit.' "The kingdom is the Lord's, and he is the governor among the nations." "He shall have dominion from sea to sea, and from the Euphrates to the ends of the earth." "They shall fear thee as long as sun and moon endure to all generations." "The Father has committed all judgment to the Son."

But, not to weary the reader with quotations and proofs, we shall

[1] Revelation 5:9-14; 14:1-5; 16:3, 4; 21:9-27; Ephesians 1:20, 21.

give but another:—"Behold my servant, whom I uphold; my elect, in whom my soul delights. I have put my Spirit upon him. He shall bring forth judgment unto truth. He shall not fail nor be discouraged till he have set judgment in the earth; and the isles shall wait for his law." "I the Lord have called thee in righteousness, and will hold thy hand and keep thee, and give thee for a *covenant* [a constitution] of the people, for a *light* to the Gentiles—to open the blind eyes, and bring out the prisoners from the prison, and them that sit in darkness out of the prison-house."

THE SUBJECTS OF THE KINGDOM

They are all born again. Their privileges and honors are the following:—

First. Their constitutional king is the only begotten Son of God; whose titles and honors are—Image of the invisible God—Effulgence of the Father's glory—Emanuel—Upholder of the Universe—Prophet of the Prophets—High Priest of the Temple of God—King of kings —Lord of lords—the only Potentate—Commander and covenant of the people—Captain of Salvation—Counsellor, Lawgiver, Redeemer, Deliverer, Mediator, Saviour, Advocate, Judge. He is the Sun of Righteousness, Prince of Peace, Lamb of God, Lion of the tribe of Judah, the Root and Offspring of David, the Bright and Morning Star, Light of the World, the Faithful and True Witness, Bishop of Souls, Great Shepherd of the Sheep, Head of the Church, Lord of all, Heir of the Universe, the Resurrection and the Life, the Son of Man, the Alpha and the Omega, the Beginning and the End, the Amen, etc., etc. Such is the Christian's king, whose assistance in all these characters, offices, and relations, as exhibited under all these figures, is guaranteed to him in the constitution. Indeed, it is all expressed in one promise:—"*I will be your God, and you shall be my people.*"

Second. It is guaranteed that "their sins and iniquities are to be remembered no more." "There is no condemnation to them who are under Christ." "Sin shall not have dominion nor lord it over them." "The Lord imputeth to them no sin." "They are all pardoned, justified, and saved from sin."

Third. They are adopted into the family of God; made sons and daughters of the Lord Almighty, children of God, and heirs—joint heirs—with Christ. They have an advocate in the heavens, through whom their persons and prayers are accepted.

Fourth. They all know the Lord. "All thy children shall be taught of God." The Holy Spirit of God writes the law of God upon their hearts, and inscribes it upon their understanding; so that they need not teach every one his fellow-citizen to know the Lord, "for they all know him, from the least to the greatest." They are sanctified through the truth—separated and consecrated to God.

Fifth. They have the promise of a resurrection from the dead, and eternal life; an inheritance incorruptible, undefiled, and unfading —new heavens and a new earth, in which righteousness alone shall dwell forever.

Such are the constitutional rights and privileges of the citizens of the kingdom of heaven. And these have obtained for them the following titles and honors:—kingdom of heaven; Israel of God; chosen generation; body of Christ; children of God; habitation of God; family of God; Jerusalem from above; Mount Zion; peculiar people; the elect of God; holy nation; temple of the Holy Spirit; house of God; city of the living God; pillar and ground of the truth; living stones; seed of Abraham; citizens of heaven; lights of the world; salt of the earth; heirs of God; joint heirs with Christ, etc.

The privileges, honors, and emoluments belong to every citizen of the kingdom of heaven. Indeed, they are all comprehended in the summary which Paul (from Jeremiah) lays before the believing Hebrews:—"This is the constitution which I will make with the house of Israel after those days: I will put my laws into their mind, and inscribe them upon their hearts; and I will be to them a God, and they shall be to me a people. And they shall not teach every man his fellow-citizen, and every man his brother, saying, Know the Lord; for all shall know me, from the least of them to the greatest of them; because I will be merciful to their unrighteousness, and their sins and iniquities I will remember no more."[1] To this summary the reader may add those scriptures in the margin, as confirmatory of the above.[2]

THE LAWS OF THE KINGDOM

The supreme law of this kingdom is *love*—love to the king and love to each other. From this law all its religious homage and morality flow. Precepts and examples innumerable present this to the mind of all the citizens. The kingdom of heaven is divided into small societies, called *churches*, or *congregations of the Lord*. Each of these communities, in the reception of members, in the education and discipline of them, or in excluding them when necessary, is to be governed by the apostolic instructions; for to the apostles the Saviour

---

[1] Hebrews 8:10-13.
[2] Romans 6:5, 6, 14; 8:1, 33-39; 1 Corinthians 6:11; Ephesians 1:7; 2:6, 19, 21, 22; Colossians 1:13, 14; 1 Peter 2:5, 7; 2 Peter 1:10, 11; 1 John 2:2.

committed the management of his kingdom. After they had made citizens by preaching the gospel and baptizing, they were commanded to teach them to observe whatsoever the Saviour had commanded them.

These laws and usages of the apostles must be learned from what the apostles published to the world, after the ascension and coronation of the king, as they are recorded in the Acts of the Apostles and epistles; for we shall see in the sequel that the gospel was fully developed, and the whole doctrine of the reign of Christ began to be proclaimed in Jerusalem, on the first Pentecost after the ascension.

The old Jewish constitution was promulgated first on Sinai on the first Pentecost after the redemption of Israel from Egyptian bondage; and from that day, and what is written after it in Exodus and Leviticus, Numbers and Deuteronomy, all the laws, manners, and customs authorized by the national constitution are to be found. They are not to be sought after in Genesis, nor in the antecedent economy. Neither are the statutes and laws of the Christian kingdom to be sought for in the Jewish Scriptures, nor antecedent to the day of Pentecost; except so far as our Lord himself, during his lifetime, propounded the doctrine of his reign. But of this when we ascertain the *commencement* of this kingdom.

There is one universal law of naturalization, or for making citizens out of all nations, enjoined upon those citizens of the kingdom who are engaged in the work of proselytism; but the laws of this kingdom, like the laws of every other kingdom, are obligatory only on the citizens.

The weekly celebration of the death and resurrection of Jesus, and the weekly meeting of the disciples of Christ for this purpose, and for the edification of one another in their most holy faith, are the only positive statutes of the kingdom; and, therefore, there is no law, statute, or observance in this kingdom, that in the least retards its extension from east to west, from north to south, or that can prevent its progress in all nations of the world.

It is, however, worthy of observation, that every part of the Christian worship in the small communities spread over the territory of the kingdom of heaven, like so many candlesticks in a large edifice, are designed to enlighten and convert the world; and, therefore, in all the meetings of the family of God, they are to keep this supremely in view; and to regard themselves as the "pillar and ground of the truth."

Concerning the details of the laws of the kingdom we can not now speak particularly. "The favor of God which brings salvation teaches all the citizens of heaven, that, denying all ungodliness and worldly lusts, they should live soberly, righteously, and godly in this present world, expecting the blessed hope—namely, the appearing of the glory of the great God, and of our Saviour Jesus Christ, who gave himself for us, that he might redeem us from all iniquity, and purify to himself a peculiar people, zealous of good works." These things the bishops of every community should teach and enforce; for such is the spirit and such is the object of all the laws and statutes of the kingdom of heaven.

THE TERRITORY

In all other kingdoms, except the kingdom of heaven, the territory is the national domain and inheritance. It was so in the first kingdom of God under the constitution from Sinai. But in the typical kingdom they lived at a distance from their inheritance for one generation. During these forty years, in which they pitched their tents in the wilderness, *God was their inheritance.* He rained bread from heaven upon them, and sent them flesh upon the east wind. He made the flinty rock Horeb a living spring, whose stream followed them all the way to Jordan. He renewed their garments every day, so that for forty years they grew not old, nor needed a single patch. A pillar of fire by night and a cloud by day guided them towards Canaan, the land of their inheritance.

The whole earth is the present territory of the kingdom of heaven, but the new heavens and earth are to be its *inheritance.* The earth, indeed, is the Lord's, and the fulness thereof; but the children of God and the children of the wicked one—the *wheat* and the *darnel* —are both planted in it, and must grow together till the harvest. The righteous have their bread and water guaranteed to them while they live; for "godliness is profitable to all things, *having promise of the life that now is,* as well as of that which is to come." But the joint heirs of Christ are never taught to regard the earth as their inheritance. They may indeed say, though poor and penniless, "All things are ours; whether Paul or Apollos, or Cephas, or the world, or life, or death, or things present, or things to come—all are ours; and we are Christ's, and Christ is God's." But, like the Jews on their journey to Canaan, "they seek a better country"—"they seek a city yet to come." "My kingdom," says Jesus, "is not of this world." And, therefore, in the world, Christians are strangers and pilgrims, and may expect tribulation.

The earth is the present *theater of war;* therefore, all Christians in the territory are *soldiers.* Their expenses, their rations, are allowed, the arms and munitions of war are supplied them from the magazines in Mount Zion, the stronghold and fortress of the kingdom; where the king, the heads of departments, and all the legions of angels, are resident. So that on entering the army of the faith every soldier is panoplied with the armor of God; and when inducted into the heavenly tactics under the captain of salvation, he is expected to be a good soldier of Jesus Christ, and to fight the good fight of faith courageously and victoriously.

The kingdom of heaven on this territory is greatly opposed by the kingdom of Satan, which ever seeks to make an *inheritance* out of the territory of the militant kingdom of righteousness; and therefore the citizens have not to wrestle with flesh and blood, but with the rulers of the darkness of this world—with spiritual wickedness in high places.

Ever since the commencement of this kingdom, the governments of this world have either been directly opposed to it, or, at best, pretended friends; and therefore their influence has always been opposed to the true spirit and genius of the Christian institution. Christians have nothing to expect from them except liberty of conscience and protection from violence, while leading peaceable and quiet lives, in all godliness and honesty, till Jesus take to himself his great power, and hurl all these potentates from their thrones and make his cause triumphant,—a consummation devoutly to be wished, and which can not now be regarded as far distant.

MANNERS AND CUSTOMS

Touching the *manners and customs* of the kingdom of heaven, they are such as generally obtained in the land of Judea and in the East at the time of its erection: or, rather, they are the simple manners and customs of the *family-worship age* of the world. These are consecrated by simply performing them with a regard to Jesus Christ, or from the motives prompted by the doctrine of the reign of heaven. As we treat our natural brothers and sisters in public and in private —as we address, salute, and converse with them—as we transact all family business, and conduct the affairs of the household—so are Christians to treat one another. There is no other virtue or utility in these than as they cherish brotherly kindness and love and are regarded to the Lord.

INDUCTION INTO THE KINGDOM OF HEAVEN

Into every kingdom, human or divine, there is a legal door of admission. This is, in the statute-book of heaven, called a *birth*. Into the kingdom of nature we are born. Into the future and ultimate kingdom of glory we enter, soul and body, by being born from the grave.

As Christ, the first-born from the dead, entered the heavenly kingdom, so must all his brethren.   And as to this kingdom of which we speak, as now existing in this world, Jesus himself taught that into it no person can legally enter who is not born again, or *"born of water and the Spirit."*[1] The analogy is complete between the kingdoms of nature, of grace, and of glory.   Hence we have natural birth, metaphorical or spiritual birth, and supernatural birth.   There is a being born of the flesh—born of the Spirit—born of the grave; and there is a kingdom for the flesh—a kingdom for the Spirit—and a kingdom for the glorified man.

This second or new birth, which inducts into the kingdom of God, is always subsequent to a death and burial, as it will be into the everlasting kingdom of glory.   It is indeed a literal death and burial before a literal resurrecton into the heavenly and eternal kingdom.   It is also a metaphorical or figurative death and burial, before the figurative resurrection or new birth into the kingdom of heaven.   Water is the element in which this burial and resurrection are performed, according to the constitutional laws of the kingdom of heaven.   Hence Jesus connects the water and the Spirit when speaking of entering the kingdom of God.

In naturalizing aliens, the commandment of the king is first—submit to them the constitution, or *preach to them the doctrine of the kingdom.*   Soon as they understand and believe this, and are desirous of being translated into the kingdom of Christ and of God, that "they may receive the remission of sins and inheritance among all that are sanctified," they are to be buried in water into the name of the Father, Son, and Holy Spirit, and raised out of it confessing their death to sin, their faith in Christ's sacrifice and resurrection: and thus they are born of water and the Spirit, and constituted citizens of the kingdom of heaven.   *To as many as thus receive him, he gives privilege to become the children of God;* for they are *"born of God"*—born of God, when born of water and the Spirit, because this is the institution of God.

In these days of apostasy men have sought out many inventions.   Some have attempted to get into the kingdom of heaven without being born at all.   Others imagine that they can be born of the Spirit, without water, and that the king is as well pleased with them who have been born without a mother, as those who are lawfully born of father and mother.   Others think that neither Spirit nor water is necessary; but if they are politically born of the flesh, they can enter the kingdom as rightfully as the Jewish circumcised infants enter the

---

[1] John 3:5; Titus 3:5.

earthly kingdom of Israel. But as we have no faith in any modern improvements of the gospel, change or amendment of the constitution of the kingdom of heaven, we must leave them to account to the king himself, who *"have transgressed the law, changed the ordinance, and broken the everlasting covenant;"*[1] and proceed to the question,

THE COMING OF THE KINGDOM

When did the kingdom of heaven commence? "With the ministry of John," says one: "With the ministry of Jesus," says another: "With the first sending out of the twelve apostles," says a third: "At the resurrection of Jesus," says a fourth: "At none of them; but by degrees from the baptism of John till the fall of Jerusalem," says a fifth.

The reader will please remember that there are at least *five elements* essential to a perfectly-organized kingdom, and that it may be contemplated in reference to one or more of these component parts. Hence the numerous and various parables of the Saviour. Sometimes he speaks of the administration of its affairs—of its principles in the heart—of its subjects—of its king—of its territory—of its progress—of various incidents in its history. Hence the parable of the sower—of wheat and darnel—of the leaven—of the merchant seeking goodly pearls—of the grain of mustard-seed—of the sweep-net—of the marriage of a king's son—of a nobleman going into a far country—of the ten virgins—of the talents—of the sheep and goats—present to our view the kingdom of heaven in different attitudes, either in its elements or in its history—its commencement or its close.

The approaching or the coming of the reign of heaven can properly have respect only to one or two of the elements of a kingdom; or to the formal exhibition of that whole organization of society which we call *a kingdom*. It can have no proper allusion to its territory; for that was created and located before man was created. It can not allude either to the persons who were constituted subjects, for they too were in existence before the kingdom commenced. It can not allude to the birth or baptism of the king, for it was not till after these that Jesus *began* to proclaim its coming or approach. It can not have reference to the ministry of John or of Jesus, any more than to the patriarchal or Jewish dispensations; because Jesus did not begin to proclaim the coming of this reign *till after John was cast into prison*. This is a fact of so much importance, that Matthew, Mark, and Luke distinctly and substantially declare, that, in conformity to ancient predictions, Jesus was to begin to proclaim in *Galilee*, and

---

[1] Isaiah 24:5.

that he did not commence to proclaim the doctrine of the gospel of the coming of the reign, till after John's ministry ceased and he was cast into prison. In this assertion the evangelists agree: "Now Jesus [after his baptism and temptation in the wilderness], hearing that John was imprisoned, retired into Galilee; and, having left Nazareth, resided at Capernaum. For thus saith the Prophet," etc. From that time Jesus *began* to proclaim, saying, "*Reform, for the reign of heaven approaches*"; or, "the kingdom of heaven is at hand," as says the common version.[1]

Some Baptists, for the sake of *immersion,* and some of our brethren in the Reformation, for the sake of *immersion for the remission of sins,* seem desirous to have John in the kingdom of heaven, and to date the commencement of the Christian dispensation with the first appearance of John the Immerser. They allege in support of this hypothesis that Jesus said, "The law and the prophets continued till John" (the only instructors of men); "since that time the kingdom of God is preached, and every man presses into it." "Publicans and harlots show you the way into the kingdom of heaven," said Jesus to the Pharisees. Again, "Alas for you, scribes and Pharisees! for you shut the kingdom of heaven against men, and will neither enter yourselves, nor permit others that would to enter." "The kingdom of God is within you." "The kingdom of heaven has overtaken you." From these premises they infer that the kingdom of heaven was actually set up by John the Baptist: "for," say they, "how could men and women *enter into a kingdom* which was not set up? And did not John immerse for the remission of sins, and call upon men to repent and reform in order to baptism?"

The Pedobaptists, too, will have Abraham, Isaac, and Jacob, Moses, David, and all the circumcised Jews, in the kingdom of heaven, because Jesus said, "Before Abraham was, I am"; "Abraham saw my day and was glad"; and Paul says Moses esteemed the reproach of Christ greater riches than all the treasures of Eygpt, and forsook Egypt in faith of the Christian recompense of reward. Yes, and Paul affirms that Abraham, Isaac, Jacob, and their families, who dwelt in tents in the promised land, looked not only to the rest in Canaan, but they sought a heavenly country, and expected the city of foundations, whose builder and maker is God. Thus the Jews had Christ in the manna and in the rock, and baptism in the cloud and in the sea.

The mistake is specifically the same. Christ was promised and prefigured before he came, and the kingdom of heaven was promised and preached by John, by Jesus, the twelve, and the seventy (who

---

[1] Matthew 4:12; Mark 1:14; Luke 3:30; 4:14.

went about proclaiming the glad tidings of the reign), before the reign of Christ or kingdom of heaven commenced. Because Christ was promised and prefigured in the patriarchal and Jewish ages, the Pedobaptists will have the kingdom of heaven on earth since the days of Abel; and because the glad tidings of the reign and kingdom of heaven and the principles of the new and heavenly order of society were promulgated by John, the Baptists will have John the Baptist in the kingdom of heaven, and the very person who set it up.

Let us, then, examine this matter with all candor: and first, we shall place the passages above quoted out of the testimonies of the evangelists on one side, and the following passages on the other side; and then see if we can reconcile them. John says, "Reform, for the reign of God approaches." Jesus began to proclaim, saying, "Reform, for the reign or kingdom of heaven is at hand." He also commanded the twelve and the Seventy to peregrinate all Judea, making the same proclamation.[1] Of John the Baptist he said, though greater than all the prophets, "The least in the kingdom of heaven is greater than he."

Thus, after John was beheaded, we had some eighty-four preachers daily proclaiming the nigh approach of the reign of God; and Jesus often assuring his disciples that the kingdom of God was soon to appear, and that some of his companions would see him enter upon his reign before they died,—and yet the kingdom was set up by John! Scribes and Pharisees were shutting the kingdom against men, when Jesus had only given the keys to Peter! John the Baptist was in the kingdom, and the least in the kingdom is greater than he! More than eighty preachers say, "Reform, for the reign of heaven is at hand"; and John the Baptist, before he died, introduced all Judea and Jerusalem into it! How, then, shall we reconcile these apparent contradictions? Make both sides figurative, and it may be done. Regard both sides literally, and it can not be done! To say that the kingdom came in one point of view at one time, and in another point of view at another time, is only to say that it came in different senses —literally and figuratively. For our part, we must believe that the kingdom of heaven began, or the reign of heaven literally and truly commenced, in one day.

Many of its principles were developed by the ancient prophets; David, Isaiah, and others wrote much concerning it; John the Baptist proclaimed its immediate and near approach, and more fully developed its spiritual design; therefore he was superior to them. Jesus often unfolded its character and design in various similitudes; and

---

[1] Matthew 10:8; Luke 1:1-11. When eating the last supper he distinctly said that the reign of God was then future. Luke 22:18.

every one who understood and received these *principles* was said to "press into the kingdom," or to have "the kingdom within them"; and wherever these principles were promulgated, "the kingdom of heaven" was said to "come nigh" to that people, or to have "overtaken them"; and those who opposed these principles, and interposed their authority to prevent others from receiving them, were said to "shut the kingdom of heaven against men"; and thus all these scriptures must of necessity be understood from the contexts in which they stand: for it is impossible that the reign of heaven could literally commence "*till Jesus was glorified,*" "received the promise of the Holy Spirit," was "made Lord and Christ," and "sat down with his Father upon the throne"—for he left the earth *to receive a kingdom.*[1]

To make this, if possible, still more evident, we ask, *When did the kingdom of God, established by Moses among the seed of Abraham, cease?* This question penetrates the whole nature and necessity of the case; for will any one suppose that there were two kingdoms of God on earth at one and the same time? Certainly the one ceased before the other began.

Now, that the kingdom of God, ministered by Moses, had not ceased during the personal ministry of the Messiah on earth, is, we think, abundantly evident from the following facts and documents:—

First. Jesus was to have appeared, and did appear, "*in the end of the world,*" or last days of the first kingdom of God. "In the conclusion of the age has he appeared, to put away sin by the sacrifice of himself." The "world to come" was one of the names of the gospel age. He has not subjected "the world to come" to angels, as he did the world past, says Paul to the Hebrews. He appeared, then, not in the beginning of the gospel age, but in the end of the Jewish age.

Second. The temple was the house of God to the very close of the life of Jesus. For it was not till the Jewish ministry conspired to kill him that he deserted it. At the last festival of his life, and immediately before he fell into their hands, on walking out of the temple, he said, "Behold, your house is deserted, for you shall not see me henceforth till you shall say, Blessed be he that comes in the name of the Lord!" It was his Father's house, the house of God, till that moment. Then, indeed, the glory departed.

Third. The Jewish offerings and service, as a divine institution, continued till the condemnation of Jesus. He sent the cleansed leper to the priest to make the offering commanded in the law. He commanded the people to hear the doctors of the law who sat in Moses' chair. He paid the didrachma. He was a minister of the circumci-

---

[1] Luke 19:11-15.

sion. He lived *under*, not *after*, the law. He kept all its ordinances, and caused all his disciples to regard it in its primitive import and authority to the last passover. *Indeed, it could not be disannulled, for it was not consummated till on the cross he said, "It is finished."*

Fourth. When he visited Jerusalem the last time, and in the last parable pronounced to them, he told them plainly that "the kingdom of God should be taken from them" and given to a nation who should make a better use of the honors of the kingdom; consequently at that time the Jews had the kingdom of God.

Fifth. It was not until his death that the veil of the temple was rent; that the things "which could be shaken were shaken." It was then, and not till then, that he nailed the legal institution to the cross. Then, and not till then, was the middle wall of partition broken down. The last sabbath he slept in the grave. *From the moment of his death there was no life in the old kingdom of God.* The temple was deserted, its veil rent, its foundations shaken, the city devoted, the ritual abolished, and as after death the judgment—the temple, city, and nation waited for the day of his vengeance.

The kingdom of God was evidently in the Jewish institution till Jesus died. Hence the kingdom of heaven came not while Jesus lived. In anticipation, they who believed the gospel of the kingdom received the kingdom of God, just as in anticipation, he said, "I have finished the work which thou gavest me to do," before he began to suffer; and as he said, "This cup is the new testament in my blood, shed for the remission of the sins of many," before it was shed. So while the doctrines of this reign—faith, repentance, baptism, and a new principle of sonship to Abraham—were promulging by John, the twelve, the seventy, and by himself, the kingdom of heaven was approaching; and those who received these principles by anticipation were said to enter into the kingdom, or to have the kingdom within them.

The principles of any reign or revolution are always promulged, debated, and canvassed before a new order of things is set up. A party is formed upon these principles before strength is acquired, or a leader obtained competent to the commencement of a new order of things. In society, as in nature, we have first the blade, then the stem, and then the ripe corn in the ear. We call it wheat, or we call it corn, when we have only the promise in the blade. By such a figure of speech the kingdom of God was spoken of, while as yet only its principles were promulging.

When these American states were colonial subjects of the king of England, and long before the setting up of a republic, republican doctrines were promulged and debated. The believers and advocates of these doctrines were called republicans, while as yet there was not a republic on this continent. He who dates the commencement of the kingdom of heaven from the ministry of John the Baptist sympathizes with him who dates the American republics from the first promulgation of the republican principles, or from the formation of a republican party in the British colonies. But, as a faithful and intelligent historian, in writing the history of the American republics, commences with the history of the first promulgation of these principles, and records the sayings and deeds of the first promulgers of the new doctrines; so the sacred historians began their history of the kingdom of heaven with the appearance of John in the wilderness of Judea, preaching the Messiah, faith, repentance, a holy life, and *raising up a new race of Israelites on the principle of faith rather than of flesh;* for this, in truth, was the "blade" of the kingdom of heaven.

Having from all these considerations seen that until the death of the Messiah his kingdom *could not* commence; and having seen from the record itself that it *did not* commence before his resurrection, we proceed to the development of things after his resurrection, to ascertain the day on which this kingdom was set up, or the reign of heaven began.

The writer to whom we are most indebted for an orderly and continued narrative of the affairs of the kingdom of heaven is the evangelist Luke. His history begins with the angelic annunciations of the nativity of John and Jesus, and ends with the appearance of the great standard-bearer of the cross in Imperial Rome, A. D. 64. That part of the history to which we now look as a guide to the affairs of the commencement of the reign is the notice which he makes of the *forty days* which the Lord spent in his crucified body, previous to his ascension. The reader ought not to be told (for he ought to know) that Jesus rose in the same body in which he was crucified, and in the reanimated fleshly body did eat, drink, and converse with his apostles and friends for forty days. That body was not changed till, like the living saints who shall be on the earth at his second personal coming, it was made spiritual, incorruptible, and glorious at the instant of his ascension. So that the man Christ Jesus was made like to all his brethren in his death, burial, resurrection, transfiguration, ascension, and glorification; or, rather, they shall be made to resemble him in all these respects.

The apostles testify that they saw him ascend—that a cloud received him out of their sight—that angels descended to inform them that he was taken up into heaven, not to return for a long time—that he ascended far above all the visible heavens, and now fills all things. Stephen, when dying, saw him standing on the right hand of God.

Much attention is due to all the incidents of these forty days,—as much, at least as to the forty days spent by Moses in the mount with God in the affairs of the preceding kingdom of God. For the risen Messiah makes the affairs of his approaching kingdom the principal topic of these forty days.[1] Towards the close of these days, and immediately before his ascension, he gave the commission to his apostles concerning the setting up of this kingdom. "All authority in heaven and in earth is given to me: go, *therefore*," said he, "convert the nations" (announce the gospel to every creature), "immersing them into the name of the Father, and of the Son, and of the Holy Spirit, teaching them to observe *all the things* which I have commanded you; and, behold! I am with you always, even to the conclusion of this state."[2] "But continue in the city of Jerusalem until you be invested with power from on high." Thus, according to his promise and the ancient prophecy, it was to "*begin at Jerusalem.*"[3]

The risen Saviour thus directs our attention to Jerusalem as the *place*, and to a period distant "not many days" as the *time*, of the beginning of his reign. The great facts of the death, burial, and resurrection of Jesus, not being yet fully developed to his apostles, they were not qualified to take any steps to the setting up of a kingdom which was to be *founded upon Christ crucified*. They needed an interpreter of these facts, and a supernatural advocate of the pretensions of the king, before they could lay the foundation of his kingdom.

Again, the king himself must be glorified before his authority could be established on earth; for till he received the promise of the Spirit from his Father, and was placed on his throne, the apostles could not receive it; so that Christ's ascension to heaven, and coronation, were indispensable to the commencement of this reign of heaven.

Here let us pause for a moment,—leave the earth, and on the wings of faith in the testimony of prophets and apostles, the two witnesses for Jesus, let us follow him to heaven and ascertain his reception into the heaven of heavens, and exaltation to the right hand of God.

THE ASCENSION OF THE MESSIAH

Prophets and apostles must now be heard. David, by the Spirit, says, "The chariots of God are twenty thousand, even thousands of angels; the Lord is among them as in Sinai in the holy place. Thou hast ascended on high; thou hast led captivity captive; thou hast re-

---

[1] Acts 1:3.
[2] Matthew 28:18-20; Mark 16:15; Luke 24:47, 48.
[3] Isaiah 2:3; Micah 4:2.

ceived gifts for men; yea, for the rebellious, that the Lord God might dwell among them."[1] The same prophet, in speaking of the solemn and joyful procession at the carrying up of the ark of the ancient constitution to Mount Zion, turns his eyes from the type to the antitype, and thus describes the entrance of the Messiah into heaven:— "Who shall ascend into the hill of God?" The attendant angels in the train of the Messiah, approaching the heaven of heavens, shout, "Lift up your hands, O you gates! be lifted up, you everlasting doors, and the King of glory shall come in." Those within, filled with astonishment that any one should so confidently demand admission into those gates so long barred against the sons of men, responsive shout, "Who is the King of glory?" The angels in attendance upon the Messiah reply, in strains as triumphant, "The Lord, strong and mighty! the Lord, mighty in battle!" and, still more exultingly triumphant, shout, "Lift up your heads, O you gates! even lift them up, you everlasting doors, and the King of glory shall come in. Who is the King of glory? He is the Lord of hosts! he is the King of glory!"[2]

CORONATION OF THE MESSIAH

Every thing in its proper order. He that ascended first descended. Jesus died, was buried, raised from the dead, ascended, and was crowned Lord of all. In the presence of all the heavenly hierarchs, the four living creatures, the twenty-four seniors, and ten thousands times ten thousand angels, he presents himself before the throne. So soon as the First-Born from the dead appears in the palace-royal of the universe, his Father and his God, in his inaugural address, when anointing him Lord of all, says, "Let all the angels of God worship him." "Sit thou at my right hand, till I make thy enemies thy footstool." "Jehovah shall send out of Zion [Jerusalem] the rod of thy strength: rule thou in the midst of thine enemies, [the city of thy strongest foes]." "Thy people, willing in the day of thy power, shall come to thee. In the beauty of holiness, more than the womb of the morning, shalt thou have the dew of thy progeny. The Lord hath sworn, and will not repent. Thou art a priest forever, after the order of Melchizedek. The Lord at thy right hand shall strike through kings [that oppose thee] in the day of his wrath." "Thy throne, O God, endures forever: the scepter of thy kingdom is a scepter of rectitude. Thou hast loved righteousness and hated iniquity; therefore God, thy God, hast anointed thee with the oil of joy above thy fellows. Thou, Lord, in the beginning hast laid the foundations of the earth, and the heavens are the works of thy hand: they shall perish,

---

[1] Psalm 68:17, 18.   [2] Psalm 24:9, 10.

but thou remainest; and they shall all grow old as does a garment, and as a vesture shalt thou fold them up, and they shall be changed: but thou art the same, and thy years shall not fail."[1]

Thus God highly exalted him, and did set him over all the works of his hands, and gave him a name and an honor above every name in heaven and on earth, that at the name of Jesus glorified every knee shall bow, and every tongue confess, to the glory of God.

"Now we see Jesus, who was made a little lower than the angels, that he might taste death for all, on account of the sufferings of death, crowned with glory and honor." Now "angels, authorities, principalities, and powers are subjected to him." "His enemies will I clothe with shame, but upon himself shall his crown flourish."

The Holy Spirit sent down by Jesus from heaven, on the Pentecost after his resurrection, to the disciples in attendance in Jerusalem, informs the apostles of all that had been transacted in heaven during the week after his ascension, and till that day. Peter now, filled with that promised Spirit, informs the immense concourse assembled on the great day of Pentecost, that God had made that Jesus whom they had crucified both Lord and Christ—exalted him a Prince and a Saviour to grant repentance to Israel and remission of sins.

The first act of his reign was the bestowment of the Holy Spirit, according to the prophecy of Joel and his own promise. So soon as he received the kingdom from God his Father, he poured out the blessings of his favor upon his friends; he fulfilled all his promises to the apostles, and *forgave three thousand of his fiercest enemies.* He received pardons and gifts for them that did rebel, and shed forth abundantly all spiritual gifts on the little flock to whom it pleased the Father to give the kingdom. Thus commenced the reign of Heaven, on the day of Pentecost, in the person of the Messiah, the Son of God, and the anointed Monarch of the universe. Under him his people, saved from their sins, have received a kingdom which can not be shaken or removed.

But, as the erection of the Jewish tabernacle, after the commencement of the first kingdom of God, was the work of some time, and of united and combined effort on the part of those raised up and qualified for the work; so was the complete erection of the new temple of God. The apostles, as wise masterbuilders, laid the foundation—promulged the constitution, laws, and institutions of the king, and raised the standard of the kingdom in many towns, cities, and countries, for the space of forty years. Some of them not only saw "the Son of Man enter upon his reign," and the kingdom of God commence on

---

[1] Psalm 90 and Hebrews.

Pentecost, and carry his conquests over Judea, Samaria, and the uttermost parts of the earth; but they saw the Lord "come with power
and awful glory," and accomplish all his predictions on the deserted
and devoted temple. Thus they saw a bright display of the golden
scepter of his grace in forgiving those who bowed to his authority,
and an appalling exhibition of the iron rod of his wrath in taking vengeance on his enemies who would not have him to reign over them.

PRESENT ADMINISTRATION OF THE KINGDOM OF HEAVEN

During the personal absence of the king, he has committed the
management of this kingdom to stewards. These were, first, apostles;
next to them, prophets; next, teachers; then, assistants or helpers;
then, directors or presidents, all furnished with gifts, knowledge, and
character, suited to their respective functions. Besides these, many
persons possessed of miraculous powers—gifts of healing and speaking foreign languages—were employed in setting up and putting in
order the communities composing the kingdom of heaven. Angels
also were employed, and are still employed, under the great king in
administering to them who are heirs of salvation. For Jesus now, as
Lord of all, has the Holy Spirit at his disposal, and all the angels of
God; and these are employed by him in the affairs of his kingdom.[1]

The apostles were plenipotentiaries and ambassadors for Jesus,
and had all authority delegated to them from the king. Hence every
thing was first taught and enjoined by them. They were the first
preachers, teachers, pastors, overseers, and ministers in the kingdom,
and had the direction and management of all its affairs.[2]

The communities collected and set in order by the apostles were
called the *congregations of Christ,* and all these taken together are
sometimes called *the kingdom of God.* But the phrases "church of
God," or "congregation of Christ," and the phrases "kingdom of
heaven," or "kingdom of God," do not always nor exactly represent
the same thing. The elements of the kingdom of heaven, it will be
remembered, are not simply its subjects, and therefore not simply the
congregation of disciples of Christ. But as these communities possess the oracles of God, are under the laws and institutions of the
king, and therefore enjoy the blessings of the present salvation, they
are in the records of the kingdom regarded as the only constitutional
citizens of the kingdom of heaven; and to them exclusively belongs
all the present salvation. Their king is now in heaven, but present

---

[1] Corinthians 12:28; Ephesians 4:11; Hebrews 1:14.   [2] 2 Corinthians
3:6; 5:18-20.

with them by his Spirit in their hearts and in all the institutions of his kingdom.

Every immersed believer, of good behavior, is by the constitution a free and full citizen of the kingdom of heaven, and entitled to all the social privileges and honors of that kingdom. Such of these as meet together statedly in one place in obedience to the king, or his ambassadors the apostles, for the observance of all the institutions of the king, compose a family, or house, or congregation of Christ; and all these families or congregations, thus organized, constitute the present kingdom of God in this world. So far the phrases *kingdom of heaven* and *the congregation* or *body of Christ* are equivalent in signification.[1]

Now, in gathering these communities, and in setting them in order, the apostles had when alive, and when dead, by their writings still have, the sole right of legislating, ordering, and disposing of all things. But it is not the will of Jesus Christ, because it is not adapted to human nature, nor to the present state of his kingdom as administered in his absence, that the church should be governed by a written document alone. Hence, in every city, town, and country where the apostles gathered a community by their own personal labors, or by their assistants, in setting them in order, for their edification, and for their usefulness and influence in this world, they uniformly appointed elders, or overseers, to labor in the word and teaching, and to preside over the whole affairs of the community. To these, also, were added *deacons*, or public *ministers* of the congregation, who, under the direction of the overseers, were to manage all the affairs of these individual families of God. This the very names *bishop* and *deacon*, and all qualifications enjoyed, fairly and fully import.

But, as all the citizens of the kingdom are free men under Christ, they all have a voice in the selection of the persons whom the apostles appoint to the offices. The apostles still appoint all persons so elected, possessing the qualifications which they *by the Holy Spirit* prescribed. *And if a congregation will not elect to these offices the persons possessing these qualifications; or if, by a waywardness and selfishness of their own, they should elect those unqualified, and thus disparage those marked out by the possession of those gifts; in either case, they despise the authority of the Ambassadors of Christ and must suffer for it.* It is indeed the Holy Spirit, and not the congregations, which creates bishops and deacons. The Spirit gives the qualifications, both natura land acquired; and speaking to the congrega-

---

[1] Romans 12:4-8; 1 Corinthians 12:27; Hebrews 3:6.

tions in the written oracles, commands their ordination or appointment to the work.[1]

In the present administration of the kingdom of God, *faith is the principle, and ordinances the means of all spiritual enjoyment.* Without faith in the testimony of God, a person is without God, without Christ, and without hope in the world. A Christless universe, as respects spiritual life and joy, is the most perfect blank which fancy can create. Without faith, nothing in the Bible can be enjoyed; and without it there is to man no kingdom of heaven in all the dominions of God.

In the kingdom of nature *sense* is the *principle,* and *ordinances* the *means,* of enjoyment. Without sense, or sensation, nothing in nature can be known or enjoyed. All the creative, recuperative, and renovating power, wisdom, and goodness of God, exhibited in nature, are contained in ordinances. The sun, moon, and stars, the clouds, the air, the water, the seasons, day and night, are therefore denominated the *ordinances* of heaven, because God's power, wisdom, and goodness are *in* them, and felt by us only *through* them.[2]   Now, sense without the ordinances of nature, like faith without the ordinances of religion, would be no *principle* of enjoyment; and the ordinances of nature, without sense, would be no *means* of enjoyment. These are the unalterable decrees of God. There is no exception to them; and there is no reversion of them. To illustrate and enforce the doctrine of this single paragraph is worthy of a volume. The essence, the whole essence, of that reformation for which we contend, is wrapped up in this decree as above expressed. If it be true, the ground on which we stand is firm and unchangeable as the Rock of Ages; if it be false, we build upon the sand. *Reader, examine it well!*

In the kingdom of heaven, faith is, then, the *principle,* and ordinances the *means,* of enjoyment; because all the wisdom, power, love, mercy, compassion, or *grace of God* is in the ordinances of the kingdom of heaven; and if all grace be in them it can only be enjoined through them. What, then, under the present administration of the kingdom of heaven, are the ordinances which contain the grace of God?   They are preaching the gospel—immersion in the name of Jesus into the name of the Father, and of the Son, and of the Holy Spirit—the reading and teaching the living oracles—the Lord's day—the Lord's supper—fasting—prayer—confession of sins—and praise. To these may be added other appointments of God,

---

[1] Acts 6:2-7; 16:23; 20:17; 1 Timothy 3:1-16; Titus 1:5-10; Hebrews 13:7, 17, 24.
[2] Jeremiah 31:35, 36; Job 38:31, 33; Jeremiah 33:25.

such as exhortation, admonition, discipline, etc.; for these also are ordinances of God; and, indeed, all statutes and commandments are ordinances:[1] but we speak not at present of those ordinances which concern the good order of the kingdom, but of those which are primary means of enjoyment. These primary and sacred ordinances of the kingdom of heaven are the means of our individual enjoyment of the present salvation of God.

Without the sun, there is no solar influence; without the moon, there is no lunar influence; without the stars, there is so sidereal influence; without the clouds, there can be no rain; and without the ordinances of the kingdom of heaven, there can be no heavenly influence exhibited or felt. There is a peculiar and distinctive influence exerted by the sun, moon, and stars; and yet they all give light. So in the ordinances of the kingdom of heaven: although they all agree in producing certain similar effects on the subjects of the kingdom, there is something distinctive and peculiar in each of them, so that no one of them can be substituted for another. Not one of them can be dispensed with; they are all necessary to the full enjoyment of the reign of heaven.

In nature and in religion, all the blessings of God bestowed on man are properly classed under two heads. These may be called, for illustration, *antecedent* and *consequent*. The antecedent include all those blessings bestowed on man to prepare him for action and to induce him to action. The consequent are those which God bestows on man through a course of action correspondent to these antecedent blessings. For example, all that God did for Adam in creating for him the earth and all that it contains, animal, vegetable, mineral; in forming him in his own image; giving him for all his physical, intellectual, and moral powers, and investing him with all the personal and real estate which elevated him above all sublunary beings, were antecedent to any act of Adam; and these furnished him with inducements to love, honor, and obey his creator and benefactor. All that God did for Abraham in promises and precepts before his obedience —all that he did for the Israelites in bringing them up out of Egypt and redeeming them from the tyranny of Pharaoh—was antecedent to the duties and observances which he enjoined upon them. And all the blessings which Adam, Abraham, the Israelites, enjoyed through conformity to the institutions under which they were placed, were consequent upon that state of mind and course of action which the antecedent favors demanded and occasioned. *God never commanded a being to do any thing but the power and motive were derived from something God had done for him.*

---

[1] James 1:25.

In the kingdom of heaven the antecedent blessings are the constitution of grace, the king, and all that he did, suffered, and sustained for our redemption. These were finished before we came upon the stage of action. This is all favor, pure favor, sovereign favor: for there can be no favor that is not free and sovereign. But the remission of our sins, our adoption into the family of God, our being made heirs and inheritors of the kingdom of glory, are consequent upon faith and the obedience of faith.

Organization and life of any sort are of necessity the gifts of God; but health and the continued enjoyment of life, and all its various and numerous blessings, are consequent upon the proper exercise of these. He that will not breathe, eat, drink, sleep, exercise, can not enjoy animal life. God has bestowed animal organization and life antecedent to any action of the living creature; but the creature may throw away that life by refusing to sustain it by the means essential to its preservation and comfort.

God made but one man out of the earth, and one earthly *nature* of every sort, by a positive, direct, and immediate agency of wisdom, power, and goodness. He gave these the power, according to his own constitution or *system* of nature, of reproducing and multiplying to an indefinite extent. But still this life is transmitted, diffused, and sustained by God operating through the system of nature. So Jesus in the new creation, by his Spirit sent down from heaven after his glorification, did, by a positive, direct, and immediate agency, create one congregation, one mystical or spiritual body; and, according to the constitution or system of the kingdom of heaven, did give to that mystical body, created in Jerusalem out of the more ancient earthly kingdom of God, the power of reproducing and multiplying to an indefinite extent. But still this new and spiritual life is transmitted, diffused, and sustained by the Spirit of God, operating through the constitution, or system of grace, ordained in the kingdom of heaven.

Hence, in setting up the kingdom of heaven, as in setting up the kingdom of nature, there was a display of divinity, compared with every thing subsequent, properly supernatural. Hence the array of apostles, prophets, extraordinary teachers, gifts, powers, miracles, etc., etc. But after this new mystical body of Christ was created and made, it had, and yet has, according to the system of grace under the present administration of the kingdom of heaven, the power of multiplying and replenishing the whole earth, *and will do it;* for as God breathed into the nostrils of Adam the spirit of life, after he had raised him out of the dust; and as he bestowed on his beloved Son Jesus, after he rose out of the water, of the Holy Spirit without measure; so on the formation of the first congregation, figuratively called the *body of Christ*, Jesus did breathe into it the Holy Spirit to inhabit and animate it till he come again. The only temple and habitation on earth since Jesus pronounced desolation on that in Jerusalem, is the body of Christ.

Now, this first congregation of Christ, thus filled with the Spirit of God, had the power of raising other congregations of Christ; or, what is the same thing, of causing the body of Christ to grow and increase. Thus we see that other congregations were soon raised up in Judea and Samaria by the members of the Jerusalem body. Many were begotten to God by the Spirit of God, through the members of the first congregation. And since the Spirit himself ceased to operate in all those splendid displays of supernatural grandeur, by still keeping the disciples of Christ always in remembrance of the things spoken by the holy apostles, and by all the arguments derived from the antecedent blessings bestowed, working in them both to will and do according to the benevolence of God, he is still causing the body of Christ to grow and increase in *stature,* as well as in knowledge and favor of God. Thus the church of Christ, inspired with his Spirit, and having the oracles and ordinances of the reign of heaven, is fully adequate to the conversion of the whole world, if she prove not recreant to her Lord.

In the work of conversion, her evangelists, or those whom she sends beyond the precincts of her weekly meetings, have, under the influence of the Spirit of God, simply to propose the constitution, or the glad tidings of the reign, to those without; and, by all the arguments which the oracles of God and the times and occasions suggest, to beseech and persuade men to be reconciled to God, to kiss the Son, to accept the constitution, to bow to him who is ordained a prince and a saviour to grant repentance and remission of sins to all who submit to his government. Thus they and the congregation who sends them forth and sustains them in the work beget children to God by the gospel, and enlarge the body of Christ.

With all these documents before us, may we not say, that, as Eve was the mother of all living, so "Jerusalem is the mother of us all"? And thus, to use the language of Paul, "Men are begotten to God by the gospel" through the instrumentality of the congregations of Christ.

Under the present administration of the kingdom of heaven, a great apostasy has occurred, as foretold by the apostles. As the church, compared to a city, is called "Mount Zion," the apostate church is called "Babylon the Great." Like Babylon the type, "Mystery Babylon" the antitype is to be destroyed by a Cyrus that knows not God. She is to fall by the sword of infidels, supported by the fierce judgments of God. "The Holy City" is still trodden under foot, and the sanctuary is filled with corruptions. It is, indeed, a den of thieves; but strong is the Lord that judges the apostate city. Till that great and notable day of the Lord come, we can not, from the prophetic word, anticipate a universal return to the original gospel, nor a general restoration of all the institutions of the kingdom of heaven in their primitive character; and, consequently, we can not promise to ourselves the universal subjugation of the nations to the scepter of Jesus.

But were we to enter upon the consideration of the administration of the affairs of the kingdom after the fall and overthrow of the apostate city and the conversion of the Jews, we should have to launch upon a wide and tempestuous ocean, for which our slender bark is not at this time sufficiently equipped. This may yet deserve the construction of a large vessel in a more propitious season. Meanwhile the original gospel is extensively proclaimed and many thousands are preparing for the day of the Lord; and these are taught by the "faithful and true witness" that the day of the Lord will come as a thief in the night, and that their happiness and safety alike consist in being prepared for his second advent.

REMISSION OF SINS

Luther said that the doctrine of justification, or forgiveness, was the test of a standing or falling church. If right in this, she could not be very far wrong in any thing else; but if wrong here, it was not easy to suppose her right in any thing. I quote from memory, but this was the idea of that great reformer.[1] We agree with him in this as well as in many other sentiments. Emerging from the smoke of the great city of mystical Babylon, he saw as clearly and as far into these matters as any person could in such a hazy atmosphere. Many of his views only require to be carried out to their legitimate issue, and we should have the ancient gospel as the result.

The doctrine of remission is the doctrine of salvation; for to talk of salvation without the knowledge of the remission of sins is to talk without meaning. To give to the Jews "a knowledge of salvation by the remission of their sins," was the mission of John the Immerser, as said the Holy Spirit. In this way he prepared a people for the Lord. This doctrine of forgiveness was gradually opened to the people during the ministry of John and Jesus, but was not fully developed until Pentecost, when the secrets of the reign of heaven were fully opened to men.

From Abel to the resurrection of Jesus, transgressors obtained remission at the altar, through priests and sin-offerings; but it was an *imperfect* remission as respected the conscience. "For the law," says Paul (more perfect in this respect than the preceding economy), "containing a shadow only of the good things to come, and not even the very image of these things, never can, with the same sacrifices which they offer yearly forever, make those who come to them perfect. Since, being offered, would they not have ceased? because the worshipers, being once purified, should have no longer conscience of sins."

The *good things* to come were future during the reign of Moses and his institution. They have come; and a clear, and full, and perfect remission of sins is the great result of the new economy in the consciences of all the citizens of the kingdom of Jesus. The perfection of the conscience of the worshipers of God under Christ is the grand distinguishing peculiarity in them compared with those under Moses. They have not only clearer views of God, of his love, of his

---

[1] The reformer also said: "If the article of justification be once lost, then is all true Christian doctrine lost."—Preface to the Ephesians, Galatians, Philippians, Ed. 1800.

character, and of immortality; but they have consciences which the Jewish and patriarchal ages could not produce.

If faith only were the means of this superior perfection and enjoyment, and if striking symbols or types were all that were necessary to afford this assurance and experience of pardon, the Jewish people might have been as happy as the Christian people. They had as true testimony, as strong faith, and as striking emblems as we have. Many of them through faith obtained a high reputation, were approved by God, and admired by men for their wonderful achievements.

The difference is in the constitution. They lived under a constitution of *law*—we under a constitution of *favor*. Before the law their privileges were still more circumscribed. Under the government of the Lord Jesus there is an institution for the forgiveness of sins, like which there was no institution since the world began. It was owing to this institution that Christians were so much distinguished at first from the subjects of every former institution.

Our political happiness in these United States is not owing to any other cause than to our political institutions. If we are politically the happiest people in the world, it is because we have the happiest political institutions in the world. So it is in the Christian institution. If Christians were and may be the happiest people that ever lived, it is because they live under the most gracious institution ever bestowed on men. The meaning of this institution has been buried under the rubbish of human traditions for hundreds of years. It was lost in the dark ages, and has never been, till recently, disinterred. Various efforts have been made, and considerable progress attended them; but since the grand apostasy was completed, till the present generation, the gospel of Jesus Christ has not been laid open to mankind in its original plainness, simplicity, and majesty. A veil in reading the new institution has been on the hearts of Christians, as Paul declares it was upon the hearts of the Jews in reading the old institution towards the close of that economy.

The object of this essay is to open to the consideration of the reader the Christian institution for the remission of sins; to show by what means a person may enjoy the assurance of a personal and plenary remission of all his sins. This we shall attempt to do by stating, illustrating, and proving the following *twelve* propositions:—

PROP. I.—*The apostles taught their disciples, or converts, that their sins were forgiven, and uniformly addressed them as pardoned or justified persons.*

John testifies that the youngest disciples were pardoned. "I write to you, little children, because your sins *are forgiven you* on account of his name."[1] The young men strong in the Lord, and the old men steadfast in the Lord, he commends for their attainments: but the *little children* he addressed as possessing this blessing as one common to all disciples:—"Your sins are forgiven you, *on account of his name.*"

Paul, in his letter to the Hebrews, asserts, that one of the provisions of the new institution is *the remission of the sins of all under it.* "*Their sins* and iniquities I will remember no more."[2] From this he argues, as a first principle, in the Christian economy, "Now where remission of these is, no more offering for sin is needed."[3] The reason assigned by the apostles why *Christians* have no *sin-offering* is, because they have obtained remission of sins as a standing provision in the new institution.

The same apostle testifies that the Ephesian disciples had obtained remission. "Be to one another kind, tender-hearted, forgiving each other, even as God for Christ's sake *has forgiven you.*"[4] Here, also, in the enumeration of Christian privileges and immunities under Christ, he asserts forgiveness of sins as the common lot of all disciples. "In whom we have redemption through his blood, even *the forgiveness of sins,* according to the riches of favor."[5] In his letter to the Colossians, he uses the same words:—"By whom we have *the forgiveness of sins.*"[6]

Figurative expressions are used by the same apostle, expressive of the same forgiveness common to all Christians. "And such [guilty characters] were some of you; but *you are washed;* but *you are sanctified;* but *you are justified* by the name of the Lord Jesus, and by the Spirit of our God."[7] Peter also is a witness here. "Seeing *you have purified your souls* by obeying the truth through the Spirit.[8]

But there is no need of foreign, or remote, or figurative expressions, when so literally and repeatedly the apostles asserted it as one of the adjuncts of being a disciple of Jesus. Had we no other testimony than that found in a single letter to the Colossians, it would be sufficient to sustain this position. The command given in chapter 3, verse 13 assumes it as a principle, "*As Christ forgave you, so also do you.*" But in the second chapter he makes this an inseparable adjunct of being in Christ. "You are *complete* in him—circumcised—buried with him—raised with him—made alive with him—*having forgiven you all trespasses.*"

These explicit testimonies from the most illustrious witnesses sus-

[1] 1 John 2:13.
[2] Hebrews 10:17. [3] Hebrews 10:18. [4] Ephesians 4:32. [5] Ephesians 1:7.
[6] Colossians 1:14. [7] 1 Corinthians 6:11. [8] 1 Peter 1:22.

tain my first proposition. On these evidences I rely, and I shall henceforth speak of it as a truth not to be questioned, viz.: that all the disciples of Christ converted in the apostolic age were taught by the apostles to consider themselves as pardoned persons.

PROP. II.—*The apostolic converts were addressed by their teachers as justified persons.*

We know that none but innocent persons can be legally justified; but it is not in the forensic sense this term is used by the apostles. Amongst the Jews it imported no more than *pardoned,* and when applied to Christians it denoted that they were acquitted from guilt,—discharged from condemnation, and accounted as righteous persons in the sight of God.

Paul, in Antioch in Pisidia, assured the Jews, that *in* or *by* Jesus all that believed were justified from all things (certainly here it is equivalent to pardoned from all sins) from which they could not be justified by the law of Moses. The disciples are said to be justified by faith.[1] By favor or grace.[2] *In* or *by* the blood of Christ.[3] By the name of the Lord Jesus.[4] By works.[5] It is God who justifies.[6]

Christians are said to be justified by God, by Christ, by favor, by faith, by the blood of Jesus, by the *name* of the Lord Jesus, and by the Spirit of God—also by works. Pardon and acquittal are the prominent ideas in every application of the term. God is the justifier. Jesus also, as his Messiah, justifies, and the Spirit declares it. As an act of favor it is done, by *the blood of Jesus* as the rightful and efficient cause—by *the faith* as the instrumental cause—by *the name* of Jesus the Lord as the immediate and connecting cause—and by *works* as the demonstrative and conclusive cause. Nothing is more plain from the above testimonies than that all Christians are declared to be justified under the reign of Jesus Christ.

PROP. III.—*The ancient Christians were addressed by the apostles as sanctified persons.*

Paul addressed all the disciples in Rome as saints or sanctified persons. In his first letter to the Corinthians he addresses them all as the *sanctified* under Christ Jesus. "To the congregation of God which is at Corinth, to *the sanctified* under Christ Jesus." Paul argues with the Hebrews that "by the will of God we are sanctified by the offering of Jesus Christ once only." "For by this one offering he has forever *perfected* [the conscience of] the *sanctified*." So usual was it for the apostles to address their disciples as sanctified

---

[1] Romans 5:1. [2] Romans 3:24. [3] Romans 5:9. [4] 1 Corinthians 6:11.
[5] James 2:24. [6] Romans 8:33.

persons, that occasionally they are thus designated in the inscription upon their epistles. Thus, Jude, addressing indiscriminately the whole Christian community, inscribes his catholic epistle "To *the* *sanctified* by God our Father and to the preserved [or saved] by Jesus Christ; to the called." "The sanctifier and the sanctified are all of one family," says the apostle to the Gentiles. And therefore the sanctifier addressed the sanctified as his brethren, and the brethren the disciples as sanctified. But once more we must hear Paul, and hear him connecting his sanctification with the *name* of the Lord Jesus. He says, "But now you are sanctified by *the name* of the Lord Jesus and by the Spirit of our God."[1]

PROP. IV.—*The ancient Christians, the apostolic converts, were addressed as "reconciled to God."*

Paul repeatedly declares that the disciples were reconciled to God. "When enemies, we were reconciled to God by the death of his Son."[2] To the Corinthians he says, "God has reconciled us to himself by Jesus Christ";[3] and to the Colossians he asserts, "It pleased the Father by him to *reconcile* all things to him, having made peace by the blood of his cross; I say whether they be things on the earth or things in the heavens. Even you [Gentiles] who were formerly alienated in mind, and enemies by works which are wicked, *he has now, indeed, reconciled* in the body of his flesh through death."[4] To the Ephesians he declares, that though "once they were without God and without hope in the world, far off, they are now, through the blood of Christ, *made nigh.*" He has made the believing Jews and Gentiles one, that he might, under Christ, *reconcile both in one body to God,* through the cross, having slain the enmity between both thereby. Indeed, he represents God as in Christ *reconciling a world to himself;* and so all under Christ are frequently said to be reconciled to God through him; which was the point to be proved.

PROP. V.—*The first disciples were considered and addressed by the apostles as "adopted into the family of God."*

This adoption is presented by the apostles as the great reason which called forth the Son of God. "God," he says, "sent forth his Son, born of a woman, born under the law, that he might buy off those under the law, that we might receive the adoption of sons." "And because you *are sons,* he has sent forth the spirit of his Son into your hearts, crying *Abba Father.*"[5] "You are, therefore, now sons of God."

[1] 1 Corinthians 6:11, 16. [2] Romans 5:10. [3] 2 Corinthians 5:18. [4] Colossians 1:19-22. [5] Galatians 4:6.

Indeed, the same writer, in his letter to the Ephesians, goes still further, and represents this adoption of Jews and Gentiles into the rank and dignity of the sons and daughters of the Lord Almighty as the great object contemplated in God's predestination. "Having," says he, "predestinated, or beforehand determinately pointed us out, for an *adoption* into the number of children by Jesus Christ, *for himself,* according to the good pleasure of his will."[1] Another testimony must suffice on this point. "Beloved," says the apostle John, "*now* are we *the sons of God;* and what manner of love God has bestowed upon us, that we should be called *sons of God!* If sons, then we are heirs of God—joint heirs with Christ."

PROP. VI.—*My sixth proposition is, that the first Christians were taught by the inspired teachers to consider themselves as saved persons.*

Because of some ambiguity in the popular import of the term *saved,* when applied to the disciples of Christ, we shall define it as used in this proposition. I need not here descant upon the temporal saviours and temporal salvations which are so conspicuous in sacred history. I need not state that Noah and his family were saved from the judgment inflicted upon the Old World; the Israelites from the Egyptians, and from all their enemies; that Paul's companions were saved from the deep, and God's people in all ages, in common with all mankind, from ten thousand perils to which their persons, their families, and their property have been exposed. It is not the present salvation of our bodies from the ills of this life; but it is *the salvation of the soul* from the guilt, pollution, and dominion of sin. "Thou shalt call his name Jesus, for he will save his people from their sins." It is the salvation of the soul in the present life of which we speak. And here it ought to be clearly and distinctly stated that there is a *present* and *future* salvation, of which all Christians are to be partakers The former is properly the *salvation of the soul,* and the latter is the *salvation of the body,* at the resurrection of the just. There are few professing Christianity, perhaps none, who do not expect a future salvation—the glory of salvation to be revealed in us at the last time. Peter, who uses this expression in the beginning of his first epistle, and who invites the saints to look forward to the salvation yet future, in the same connection reminds them that they have *now* received the salvation of the soul. Indeed, the salvation of the soul is but the *first-fruit* of the Spirit, and but an earnest until the adoption, "the redemption of the body" from the bondage of corruption. It was in this sense of the word that salvation was announced to all who sub-

---

[1] Ephesians 1:5.

mitted to the Lord Jesus, and hence it is in this connection equivalent to a deliverance of the soul from the guilt, pollution, and dominion of sin. Having thus defined the present salvation of the soul, I proceed to the proof of my sixth proposition, viz.: that the first Christians were taught by their inspired teachers to consider themselves as *saved persons.*

Peter, on Pentecost, exhorted the Jews to *save themselves* from that untoward generation, by reforming and being "immersed for the remission of their sins, in the name of the Lord Jesus." Luke, in recording the success attendant on Peter's labors, expresses himself thus:—"And the Lord added, daily, *the saved* to the congregation."[1] Those who obeyed the gospel were recorded by Luke as *"the saved."* The king's translators supplied out of their own system the words *"should be."* They are not in any copy of the Greek Scriptures. Such is the first application of the words *"the saved"* in the Christian Scriptures.

Paul uses the same words in the first letter to the Corinthians, and applies them to all the disciples of Jesus. "To the destroyed, the doctrine of the cross is foolishness; but to us *the saved,* it is the power of God."[2] In the same letter, he says of the Gospel, "By which *you are saved,* if you retain in your memory the word which I announce to you."[3] In his second letter he uses the same style, and distinguishes the disciples by the same designation:—"We are through God a fragrant odor of Christ among *the saved,* and among the destroyed." The Ephesians, he declares, *are saved* through favor; and to Titus he says, "God has *saved* us, not by works of righteousness which we have done, but according to his own mercy,"—by what means we shall soon hear Paul affirm. Promises of salvation to the obedient are to be found in almost every public address pronounced by the apostles and first preachers. For the Saviour commanded them to assure mankind that every one who believed the gospel, and was immersed, should be saved. And, connecting faith with immersion, Peter averred that immersion *saved* us, purifying the conscience through the resurrection of Jesus.[4]

While the Christians are taught to expect and hope for a *future* salvation—a salvation from the power of death and the grave—a salvation to be revealed in the last time—they receive the first-fruit of the Spirit, the salvation of the soul from guilt, pollution, and the dominion of sin, and come under the dominion of righteousness, peace, and joy. This is what Peter affirms of all the Christians in Pontus, Galatia, Cappadocia, Asia Minor, and Bithynia, to whom he thus

---

[1] Acts 2:47.   [2] 1 Corinthians 1:18.   [3] 1 Corinthians 15:2.
[4] 1 Peter 3:21.

speaks:—"Jesus, having not seen, you love; on whom, not now looking, but believing, you rejoice with joy unspeakable and full of glory,
receiving the reward of your faith, *the salvation of your souls.*"[1]

These six propositions being each and everyone of them clearly sustained by the unequivocal testimony of God, now adduced, and, as is
well known to the intelligent disciple, by many more passages,
equally plain and forcible, not adduced; we shall now engross them
into one leading proposition, which we shall in this essay consider as
not to be questioned—as irrefragably proved.

*The converts made to Jesus Christ by the apostles were taught to
consider themselves pardoned, justified, sanctified, reconciled,
adopted, and saved; and were addressed as pardoned, justified, sanctified, reconciled, adopted, and saved persons, by all who first
preached the gospel of Christ.*

While this proposition is before us, it may be expedient to remark
that all these terms are expressive not of any quality of mind—not of
any personal attribute of body, soul or spirit; but each of them represents, and all of them together represent *a state* or *condition.* But,
though these terms represent state and not character, there is a relation between state and character, or an influence which state has
upon character, which makes the state of immense importance in a
moral and religious point of view.

Indeed, the strongest arguments which the apostles use with the
Christians to urge them forward in the cultivation and display of all
the moral and religious excellencies of character are drawn from the
meaning and value of the *state* in which they are placed. Because
forgiven, they should forgive; because justified, they should live righteously; because sanctified, they should live holy and unblamably;
because reconciled to God, they should cultivate peace with all men,
and act benevolently towards all; because adopted, they should walk
in the dignity and purity of sons of God; because saved, they should
abound in thanksgivings, praises, and rejoicings, living soberly, righteously, and godly, looking forward to the blessed hope.

As this essay is designated for readers of the most common capacity and most superficial education, I trust I may be permitted to
speak still more plainly upon the difference between *state* and *character.* Childhood is a state; so is manhood. Now, a person in the
state of childhood may act sometimes like a person in the state of
manhood, and those arrived at the state of manhood may in character
or behavior resemble those in a state of childhood. A person in the
state of a son may have the character of a servant; and a person in

---

[1] 1 Peter 1:8, 9.

the state of a servant may have the character of a son. This is not generally to be expected, though it sometimes happens. Parents and children, masters and servants, husbands and wives, are terms denoting relations or states. To act in accordance with these states or relations is quite a different thing from being in any one of these states. Many persons enter into the state of matrimony, and yet act unworthily of it. This is true of many other states. Enough, we presume, is said to contradistinguish state and character, relations and moral qualities.

It is scarcely necessary to remark here, that as the disciples of Christ are declared to be in a pardoned, justified, sanctified, reconciled, adopted, and saved state, they are the only persons in such a state; and all others are in an unpardoned, unjustified, unsanctified, unreconciled, unadopted, and lost state.

When, then, is a change of state effected, and by what means?— This is the great question soon to be discussed.

We are constrained to admit that a change in any one of these states necessarily implies, because it involves, a change in all the others. Every one who is *pardoned* is justified, sanctified, reconciled, adopted, and saved, and so every one that is *saved* is adopted, reconciled, sanctified, justified, and pardoned.

To illustrate what has already been proved, let us turn to some of the changes which take place in society as at present constituted. A female changes her state. She enters into the state of matrimony. So soon as she has surrendered herself to the affectionate government and control of him who has become her husband, she has not only become a wife, but a daughter, a sister, an aunt, a niece, etc.; and may stand in many other relations in which she before stood not. All these are connected with her becoming the wife of a person who stands in many relations. So when a person becomes Christ's, he is a son of Abraham, an heir, a brother, or is pardoned, justified, sanctified, reconciled, adopted, and saved.

To be *in* Christ, or *under* Christ, then, is to stand in these new relations to God, angels, and men; and to be out of him, or not under his mediatorship or government, is to be in or under Adam only. It is to be in what is called "the state of nature," unpardoned, unjustified, unsanctified, unreconciled, and an alien from the family of God, lost in trespasses and sins.

These things premised, the question presents itself, *When are persons in Christ?* I choose this phrase in accommodation to the familiar style of this day. No person *in* a house, *in* a ship, *in* a state, *in* a kingdom, but he that has gone or is introduced *into* a state, *into* a kingdom; so no person is *in* Christ but he who has been introduced *into* Christ. The Scripture style is most religiously accurate. We have the words *"in Christ,"* and the words *"into Christ,"* often repeated in the Christian Scriptures; but in no one place can the one phrase be substituted for the other. Hence, in all places where any person is said to be *in Christ*, it refers not to his conversion, regeneration, or putting on Christ, but to a state of rest or privilege subsequent to conversion, regeneration, or putting on Christ. But the phrase *into Christ* is always connected with conversion, regeneration, immersion, or putting on Christ. Before we are justified in Christ, live in Christ, or fall asleep in Christ, we must come, be introduced, or immersed into Christ. *Into* belongs only to verbs implying motion towards; and *in* to verbs implying rest or motion in. He eats, sleeps, sits in the house. He walks into the field; he rides into the city. "Into Christ" is a phrase only applicable to conversion, immersion, or regeneration, or what is called putting on Christ, translation into his kingdom, or submission to his government.[1]

---

[1] To prevent mistakes, I shall here transcribe a part of a note found in the Appendix to the second edition of the *new version* of the Christian Scriptures, p. 452.

"I am not desirous of diminishing the difference of meaning between immersing a person *in the name* of the Father, and *into the name* of the Father. They are quite different ideas. But it will be asked, Is this a correct translation? To which I answer, most undoubtedly it is. For the preposition *eis* is that used in this place, and not *en*. By what *inadvertency* the king's translators gave it *in* instead of *into* in this passage, and elsewhere gave it *into* when speaking of the same ordinance, I presume not to say. But they have been followed by most modern translators, and with them they translate it *into* in other places where it occurs, in relation *to this institution*. For example:—1 Corinthians 12:13: For by one spirit we are all immersed *into* one body. Romans 6:3: Don't you know that so many of you as were immersed *into* Christ were immersed *into* his death? Galatians 3:27: As many of you as have been immersed *into* Christ have put on Christ. Now, for the same reason they ought to have rendered the following passages the same way:—Acts 8:16: Only they were immersed *into* the name of the Lord Jesus. 19:3: *Into* what name were you then immersed? When they heard this, they were immersed *into* the name of the Lord Jesus. 1 Corinthians 1:13. Were you immersed *into* the name of Paul? Lest any should say I had immersed *into* my own name. 1 Corinthians 10:1: Our fathers were all immersed *into* Moses in the cloud and in the sea. Now, in all these places it is *eis*, and *en* is clearly marked in the last quotation. They were immersed *into* Moses—not *into* the cloud and *into* the sea, but *in* the cloud and in the sea. To be immersed *into* Moses is one thing, and *in* the sea is another. To be immersed *into* the name of the Father, and *in* the name of the Father, are just as distinct. "*In the name*" is equivalent to "*by the authority of*." In the name of the king or commonwealth, is by the authority of the king or commonwealth. Now the question is, Did the Saviour mean that the disciples were to be immersed by the authority of the Father, Son, and Holy Spirit? If by the authority of the Father, for what purpose were they immersed? The authority by which any action is done is one thing, and the object for which it is done is another. Now, who that can discriminate can think that it is one and the same thing to be immersed

Presuming on the intelligence of our readers so far as to suppose them assured that this is no mere verbal criticism, but a discrimination that detects one of the pillars of an apostate church, I proceed to another preliminary proposition, which I choose to submit in the following word, *to-wit:*—

PROP. VII.—*A change of views, though it necessarily precedes, is in no case equivalent to, and never to be identified, with a change of state.*

In all the relations of his life, in all states or conditions of men, we feel the truth of this; and I would to heaven that our readers could see as plainly what is of infinitely more importance to them,—that no change of heart is equivalent to or can be substituted for a change of state! A change of heart is the result of a change of views, and whatever can accomplish a change of views may accomplish a change of heart or feeling; but a change of state always calls for something more.[1]

---

in the name of the Lord, and to be immersed *into* the name of the Lord Jesus? The former denotes the authority by which the action is performed —the latter the object for which it is performed. Persons are said to enter *into* matrimony, to enter *into* an alliance, to get *into* debt, to run *into* danger. Now, to be immersed *into* the name of the Lord Jesus was a form of speech in ancient usage, as familiar and significant as any of the preceding. And when we analyze these expressions, we find they all import that the persons are either under the obligations or influence of those things into which they are said to enter, or into which they are introduced. Hence, those immersed into one body were under the influence and obligations of that body. Those immersed into Moses assumed Moses as their lawgiver, guide, and protector, and risked every thing upon his authority, wisdom, power, and goodness. Those who were immersed into Christ put him on, and acknowledged his authority and laws, and were governed by his will; and those who were immersed into the name of the Father, Son, and Holy Spirit, regarded the Father as the fountain of all authority—the Son as the only Saviour—and the Holy Spirit as the only advocate of the truth, and teacher of Christianity. Hence, such persons as were immersed into the name of the Father acknowledged him as the only living and true God —Jesus Christ as his only begotten Son, the Saviour of the world—and the Holy Spirit as the only successful advocate of the truth of Christianity upon earth."

[1] *State* here has respect to the whole person. It may be argued that state is as pertinently applied to the mind or heart as to the whole person; and that when the state of the mind is changed by a belief of God's testimony, the subject of that change is brought into as near a relation to God as he can be in this life; and, as the kingdom of Jesus is a spiritual kingdom, he is as fit for admission into it, and for the enjoyment of its blessings, whenever his heart is changed from enmity to love, as he ever can be: nay, in truth, is actually initiated into the kingdom of Jesus the moment his mind is changed—and that to insist upon any personal act as necessary to admission, because such acts are necessary to admission into all the social and political relations in society, is an overstraining the analogies between things earthly and things heavenly. Not one of our opponents, as far as we remember, has thus argued. We have sometimes thought that they

Lavinia was the servant of Palemon, and once thought him a hard master. She changed her views of him; and her feelings were also changed towards him; still, however, she continued in the state of a handmaid. Palemon offered her first his heart, and then his hand, and she accepted them. He vowed and she vowed before witnesses, and she became his wife. Then, and not till then, was her state changed. She is no longer a *servant;* she is now a *wife.* A change of views and of feelings led to this change in state; but let it be noted that this might not have issued in a change of state; for Maria, who was another handmaid of Palemon, and changed her views of him and her feelings towards him as much—nay, more than did Lavinia; yet Maria lived and died the servant-maid of Palemon and Lavinia.

William Agricola and his brother Thomas, both Canadians, were once much opposed to the constituted government of New England. They both changed their views, and, as a matter of course, their feelings were changed. William became a citizen of Rhode Island; but Thomas, notwithstanding his change of heart, lived and died a colonial subject of a British king.

John and James Superbus became great enemies to each other. They continued irreconciled for many years. At length a change of views brought about a change of heart; but this change for more than a year was concealed in the heart, and by no overt act appeared. They were not reconciled until mutual concessions were made and pledges of a change of feeling were tendered and reciprocated. From enemies they became friends.

A thousand analogies might be adduced, to show that though a change of state often—nay, generally—results from a change of feelings, and this from a change of views, yet a change of state does not generally follow, and is something quite different from, and can not be identified with, a change of heart. So in religion, a man may change his views of Jesus, and his heart may be changed towards him; but, unless a change of state ensures, he is still unpardoned, un-

---

might have thus argued with incomparably more speciosity than appears in any of their objections.

But, without pausing to inquire whether the state of the heart can be perfectly changed from enmity to love, without an assurance of remission on some ground, or in consequence of some *act of the mind* prerequisite thereunto;—without being at pains to show that the truth of this proposition is not at all essential to our argument, but only *illustrative* of it; we may say, that as Christ has redeemed the whole man, body, soul, and spirit, by his obedience even to death—so in coming into his kingdom on earth, and in order to the *enjoyment* of all the present salvation, the *state of the whole person* must be changed; and this is what we apprehend Jesus meant by his saying, "Unless a *man* is born of *water* and spirit, he can not enter into the Kingdom of God," and what we mean in distinguishing a change of heart, or of views and feelings, from a change of state.

justified, unsanctified, unreconciled, unadopted, and lost to all Christian life and enjoyable. For it has been proved that these terms represent states and not feelings, condition and not character; and that a change of views or of heart is not a change of state. To change a state is to pass into a new relation, and relation is not sentiment nor feeling. Some *act*, then, constitutional, by stipulation proposed, sensible and manifest, must be performed by one or both the parties before such a change can be accomplished. Hence, always, in ancient times, the proclamation of the gospel was accompanied by some instituted act proposed to those whose views were changed, by which their state was to be changed, and by which they were to stand in a new relation to Jesus Christ.

This brings us to *"the obedience of faith."* From the time the proclamation of God's philanthropy was first made, there was an act of obedience proposed in it by which the believers in the proclamation were put in actual possession of its blessings, and by conformity to which act a change of state ensued.

To perceive what this act of faith is, it must be remarked that where there is no *command* there can be no *obedience*. These are correlate terms. A message or proclamation which has not a command in it can not be obeyed. But the gospel can be obeyed or disobeyed, and therefore in it there is a command. Lest any person should hesitate in a matter of such importance, we will prove—

PROP. VIII.—*The gospel has in it a command, and as such must be obeyed.*

And here I need only ask, Who are they who shall be punished with everlasting destruction from the presence of the Lord? Paul replies, "They who know not God, and *obey not the gospel of his Son*."[1] To "obey the gospel," and to "become obedient to the faith," were common phrases in the apostolic discourses and writings. "By whom we have received apostleship, in order to the *obedience of faith* in all nations, on account of his name."[2] "By the commandment of the everlasting God, the gospel is made known to all nations for the *obedience of faith*."[3] "A great company of the priest became obedient to the faith,"[4] "But they have not all obeyed the gospel";[5] and "What shall be the end of them who *obey not the gospel?*"[6] From these sayings it is unquestionably plain, that either the gospel itself, taken as a whole, is a command, or that in it there is a command through the obedience of which salvation is enjoyed.

---

[1] 2 Thessalonians 1:8.   [2] Romans 1:5.   [3] Romans 16:26.
[4] Acts 6:7.   [5] Romans 10:16.   [6] 1 Peter 4:17.

The obedience of the gospel is called the obedience of faith, compared with the obedience of the law,—faith in God's promise through Jesus Christ being the principle from which obedience flows. To present the gospel in the form of a command is an act of favor, because it engages the will and affections of men, and puts it in their power to have an assurance of their salvation from which they would be necessarily excluded if no such act of obedience were enjoyed.

Whatever the act of faith may be, it necessarily becomes the line of discrimination between the two states before described. On this side and on that mankind are in quite different states. On the one side they are pardoned, justified, sanctified, reconciled, adopted and saved; on the other, they are in a state of condemnation. This act is sometimes called immersion, regeneration, conversion; and, that this act may appear obvious to all, we shall be at some pains to confirm and illustrate it.

That a relation or a state can be changed by an act, I need scarcely at this time attempt to prove; especially to those who know that the act of marriage, of naturalization, adoption, and their being born, changes the state of the subject of such acts. But, rather than attempt to prove that a state is or may be changed by an act, I should rather ask if any person has heard, knows, or can conceive, of a state being changed without some act. This point, being conceded to us by all the rational, we presume not to prove. But a question may arise whether *faith* itself, or an act of obedience to some command or institution, is that act by which our state is changed.

PROP. IX.—*That it is not faith, but an act resulting from faith, which changes our state, we shall now attempt to prove.*

No relation in which we stand to the material world—no political relation, or relation to society—can be changed by believing, apart from the acts to which that belief or faith induces us. Faith never made an American citizen, though it may have been the cause of many thousands migrating to this continent and ultimately becoming citizens of these United States. Faith never made a man a husband, a father, a son, a brother, a master, a servant, though it may have been essentially necessary to all these relations, as a cause or principle preparatory or tending thereunto. Thus, when in Scripture men are said to be justified by faith, or to receive any blessing through faith, it is because faith is the principle of action, and, as such, the cause of those acts by which such blessings are enjoyed. But the principle without those acts is nothing; and it is only by the acts which it induces to perform that it becomes the instrument of any blessings to man.

Many blessings are metonymically ascribed to faith in the sacred writings. We are said to be justified, sanctified, and purified by faith —to walk by faith, and to live by faith, etc., etc. But these sayings, as qualified by the apostles, mean no more than by believing the truth of God *we have access* into all these blessings. So that, as Paul explains, "by faith *we have access* into the favor in which we stand." These words he uses on two occasions,[1] when speaking of the value of this principle, contrasted with the principle of law; and in his letter to the Hebrews, when he brings up his cloud of witnesses to the excellency of this principle, he shows that *by it* the ancients obtained a high reputation—that is, as he explains, by their acts of faith in obedience to God's commands.

That faith by itself neither justifies, sanctifies, nor purifies, is admitted by those who oppose immersion for the forgiveness of sins. They all include the idea of *the blood of Christ.* And yet they seem not to perceive that, in objecting to immersion as necessary to forgiveness in connection with faith, their own arguments preclude them from connecting the blood of Christ with faith. If they admit that faith, apart from the blood of Christ, can not obtain pardon, they admit all that is necessary to prove them inconsistent with themselves in opposing immersion for the remission of sins; or remission as that act by which our state is changed.

The apostle Peter, when first publishing the gospel to the Jews, taught them that they were not forgiven their sins by faith; but by an act of faith, by a believing immersion into the Lord Jesus. That this may appear evident to all, we shall examine his Pentecostian address, and his Pentecostian hearers.

Peter—now holding the keys of the kingdom of Jesus, and speaking under the commission for converting the world, and by the authority of the Lord Jesus; guided, inspired, and accompanied by the Spirit—may be expected to speak the truth, the whole truth, plainly and intelligibly, to his brethren the Jews. He had that day declared the gospel facts, and proved the resurrection and ascension of Jesus to the conviction of thousands. They believed and repented—believed that Jesus was the Messiah, had died as a sin-offering, was risen from the dead, and crowned Lord of all. Being full of this faith, they inquired of Peter and the other apostles *what they ought to do* to obtain remission. They were informed that, though they now believed and repented, they were not pardoned, but must *"reform and be immersed for the remission of sins."* Immersion for the forgiveness of sins was *the command* addressed to these believers, to

---

[1] Romans 5:2; Ephesians 3:12.

these penitents, in answer to the most earnest question; and by one of the most sincere, candid, and honest speakers ever heard. This act of faith was presented as that act by which a change in their state could be affected; or, in other words, by which alone they could be pardoned. They "who gladly received this word were that day immersed"; or, in other words, the same day were converted, or regenerated, or obeyed the gospel. Those expressions, in the apostle's style, when applied to persons coming into the kingdom, denote the same act, as will be perceived from the various passages in the writings of Luke and Paul. This testimony, when the speaker, the occasion, and the congregations are all taken into view, is itself alone sufficient to establish the point in support of which we have adduced it.

But the second discourse, recorded by Luke from the lips of the same Peter, pronounced in Solomon's Portico, is equally pointed, clear, and full in support of this position. After he had explained the miracle which he had wrought in the name of the Lord Jesus, and stated the same gospel facts, he proclaims the same command:—"Reform and be converted, that your sins may be blotted out"; or, "Reform and turn to God, that so your sins may be blotted out; that seasons of refreshment from the presence of the Lord may come, and that he may send Jesus, whom the heavens must receive till the accomplishment of all the things which God has foretold," etc. Peter, in substituting other terms in this proclamation for those used on Pentecost, does not preach a *new* gospel, but *the same* gospel in terms equally strong. He uses the same word, in the first part of the command, which he used on Pentecost. Instead of *"be immersed,"* he has here *"be converted,"* or, *"turn to God"*; instead of *"for the remission of your sins,"* here it is, *"that your sins may be blotted out"*; and instead of *"you shall receive the gift of the Holy Spirit,"* here it is, *"that seasons of refreshment from the presence of the Lord may come."*[1] On Pentecost, it was—First, "Reform"; Second, "Be immersed"; Third, "For the remission of sins"; and Fourth, "You shall receive the gift of the Holy Spirit." In Solomon's Portico, it was—First, "Reform"; Second, "Be converted"; Third, "That your sins may be blotted out"; and Fourth, "That seasons of refreshment from the presence of the Lord may come"; that "you may have righteousness,

---

[1] There is no propriety in the common version of this member of the sentence—*when,* instead of *that* "seasons of refreshment." Some make modern *revivals* "seasons of refreshment," such as these here alluded to. Then it would read—"That your sins may be blotted out in times of revivals"—when revivals shall come! The term is *opos,* which, in this construction, as various critics have contended, is equivalent to *"that"* in our tongue. To promise a future remission is no part of the gospel, nor of the apostolic proclamation. All Christians experience seasons of refreshment in cordially obeying the gospel.

peace, and joy in a holy spirit." So read the different clauses in those two discourses to the Jews, expressive of the same acts.

There is yet, in this discourse in the Portico, a very strong expression, declarative of the same gracious connection between immersion and remission. It is the last period of his discourse. "Unto you first, brethren of the Jews, God, having raised up his Son Jesus, sent him to *bless you,* every one of you, in the act of turning from your iniquities"; or, as we would say, in the act of conversion. Why the apostle Peter should have used "converted," or "turning to God," instead of "be immersed," is, to the candid and unprejudiced reader of this narrative, very plain. After Pentecost, the disciples immersed on that day, *having turned to God* through Jesus, were spoken of by their brethren as *discipled* or *converted* to Jesus. The unbelieving Jews, soon after Pentecost, knew the disciples called the immersed "*converted*"; and, immersion being the act of faith which drew the line of demarcation between Christians and Jews, nothing could be more natural than to call the act of immersion the converting of a Jew. The time intervening between these discourses was long enough to introduce and familiarize this style in the metropolis; so that when a Christian said, *"Be converted,"* or *"Turn to God,"* every Jew knew the act of putting on the Messiah to be that intended. After the immersion of some Gentiles into the faith, in the house and neighborhood of Cornelius, it was reported that the Gentiles were converted to God. Thus, the apostles, in passing through the country, gave great joy to the disciples from among the Jews, "telling them of the conversion" or immersion of the Gentiles.[1] Indeed, in a short time it was a summary way of representing the faith, reformation, and immersion of disciples, by using one word for all. Thus, "All the inhabitants of Sharon and Lydda turned," or "were converted, ·to the Lord."[2]

While on the subject of conversion, we shall adduce, as a fourth testimony, the words of the Lord Jesus to Paul, when he called him. Paul is introduced by Luke in the Acts, telling what the Lord said to him when he received his apostleship. "I send you Paul, by the faith that respects me, to open their eyes; to *turn* or *convert* them from darkness to light, and from the power of Satan to God; that they may receive forgiveness of sins, and an inheritance among the saved."[3] Every thing to be accomplished among the Gentiles was to be effected by the faith or truth in Christ. The Saviour connected that with opening their eyes; their conversion from the ignorance and tyranny of sin and Satan; their forgiveness of sins; and finally, an inheritance among the saved or sanctified. First, faith or illumination;

---

[1] Acts 15:3.   [2] Acts 9:35.   [3] Acts 24:17, 18.

then, conversion; then, remission of sins; then, the inheritance. All these testimonies concur with each other in presenting the act of faith —Christian immersion, frequently called *conversion*—as that act, inseparably connected with the remission of sins; or that change of state of which we have already spoken.

One reason why we would arrest the attention of the reader to the substitution of the terms *convert* and *conversion*, for *immerse* and *immersion*, in the apostolic discourses and in the sacred writings, is not so much for the purpose of proving that the forgiveness of sins, or a change of state, is necessarily connected with the act of faith called "Christian immersion," as it is to fix the minds of the biblical students upon a very important fact, viz.: that no person is altogether discipled to Christ until he is immersed. It is true that this view of the matter bears strongly upon the question; but it bears upon other great matters pertaining to the present and ancient order of things.

Discovering that much depends upon having correct views on this point, we have carefully examined all those passages where "conversion," either in the common version, or in the new version, or in the original, occurs; and have found a uniformity in the use of this term, and its compounds and derivatives, which warrants the conclusion that no person was said to be converted until he was immersed; and that all persons who were immersed were said to be converted. If any apostatized, they were again converted; it was in that sense in which our Lord applied the word to Peter, "When you are *converted*, strengthen your brethren," or as James used it in his letter when he said, "If any of you err from the truth, and one convert him, let him know that he who converts a transgressor from the error of his way shall save a soul from death and hide a multitude of sins."

The commission of converting the world teaches that immersion was necessary to discipleship; for Jesus said, "Convert the nations, immersing them into the name," etc., and "teaching them to observe," etc. The construction of the sentence fairly indicates that no person can be a disciple, according to the commission, who has not been immersed; *for the active participle in connection with an imperative either declares the manner in which the imperative shall be obeyed, or explains the meaning of the command.*

To this I have not found an exception. For example:—"Cleanse the house, sweeping it"; "Cleanse the garment, washing it," shows the manner in which the command is to be obeyed, or explains the meaning of it. Thus, "Convert [or disciple] the nations, immersing them, and teaching them to observe," etc., expresses the manner in which the command is to be obeyed.

If the apostles had only preached and not immersed, they would not have converted the hearers according to the commission: and if they had immersed, and not taught them to observe the commands of the Saviour, they would have been transgressors. A disciple, then, according to the commission, is one that has heard the gospel, believed it, and has been immersed. A disciple, indeed, is one that continues in keeping the commandments of Jesus.[1]

PROP X.—*I now proceed to show that immersion and washing of regeneration are two Bible names for the same act, contemplated in two different points of view.*

The term *regeneration* occurs but twice in the common version of the New Testament, and not once in the Old Testament. The first is Matthew 19:28: "You that have followed me in the regeneration, when the Son of Man shall sit on the throne of his glory, you also shall sit upon twelve thrones, judging the twelve tribes of Israel." Dr. George Campbell, following the punctuation adopted by Griesbach, and substituting the word *renovation* instead of *regeneration*, renders it, "That, at the *renovation*, when the Son of Man shall be seated on his glorious throne, you, my followers, sitting also upon twelve thrones," etc. *Genesis*, being the term used for *creation*, *palingenesia*, denotes the new creation—either literally at the resurrection of the dead, or figuratively at the commencement of the Christian era, or at the commencement of the millennium. Josephus, the Jew, called the return of Israel to their own land and institution the "regeneration" or "palingenesia."

---

[1] The following examples of the above general rule illustrate its value and certainly:—"Let us offer up the sacrifice of praise to God, *confessing* to his name." (Heb. 13:10.) "Let us go forth to him out of the camp, *bearing* his reproach." (Heb. 13:13.) "Be an approved workman, *rightly* dividing the word of truth." (2 Tim. 2:15.) "Guard the precious deposit, *avoiding* profane babblings." (1 Tim. 6:20.) "Observe these things without prejudice, *doing* nothing by partiality." (1 Tim. 5:21.) "Pray everywhere, *lifting* up holy hands." (1 Tim. 2:8.) "Walk in wisdom to them that are without, *gaining* time." (Col. 4:5.) "Do all in the name of the Lord Jesus, *giving* thanks to God." (Col. 3:17.) "Speak the truth, *putting* away lying." (Eph. 4:25.) "Be not vainglorious, *provoking* one another." (Gal. 5:26.) "Convert the nations, *baptizing* them," etc., etc. Now, do not all these participles define their respective imperatives, or show the way and manner in which this command should be obeyed? Many similar examples may be found in all the sacred writings.

This rule has passed through a fiery trial. I have only been more fully convinced of its generality and value. There is no rule in the English syntax more general in its application. I would only add, that the participle does not always express every thing in the command: but it always points out something emphatically in the intention of the imperative, and without which the injunction can not be suitably and fully performed.

We have, however, no need of this rule, nor of any thing not generally conceded, to establish the point before us; for the New Testament and all antiquity teach that, so long as the apostles lived, no one was regarded as a disciple of Christ who had not confessed his faith and was immersed.

No writer of any note, critic or expositor, supposes that *regeneration* in Matthew 19 applies to what is, in theology, called the *new birth*, or *regeneration of the soul,*—not even the Presbyterian Matthew Henry, nor Dr. Whitby, Campbell, Macknight, Thompson; nor, indeed, any writer we recollect ever to have read. Regeneration in this passage denotes a state, a new state of things. In the same sense we often use the term. The American Revolution was the regeneration of the country or the government. The commencement of the Christian era was a regeneration; so will be the creation of the new heavens and new earth. As this is so plain a matter, and so generally admitted, we proceed to the second occurrence of this term.

"God saved us by *the washing of regeneration*, and renewing of the Holy Spirit."[1] God has saved us though the *bath of regeneration*, and the renewing of the Holy Spirit. This is the second time the word *regeneration* is found in the New Testament; and here it is conceded, by the most learned Pedobaptists and Baptists, that it refers to immersion. Though I have been led to this conclusion from my views of the Christian religion, yet I neither hold it myself, nor justify it to others on this account. I choose rather to establish it by other testimonies than by those who agree with me in the import of this institution. Among these I shall place Dr. James Macknight, formerly prolocutor or moderator of the Presbyterian church of Scotland, and translator of the Apostolic Epistles. One of his notes upon Titus 3:5 is in the following words: "Through the bath of regeneration," "Through *baptism*, called the bath of regeneration, not because any change in the nature" (but I would not say in the *state*) "of the baptized person is produced by baptism; but because it is an emblem of the purification of his soul from sin." He then quotes in proof, (Acts 22:16), "Arise, and be immersed, and wash thee from thy sins."—*Paul*. He supports his view also from Ephesians 5:26, and John 3:5. "The bath of regeneration" is, then, according to this learned Pedobaptist, Christian immersion.

Parkhurst, in his Lexicon, upon the word *loutron,* connects the same *phrase,* the washing or bath of regeneration, with Ephesians 5:26, and John 3:5, as alluding to immersion. So say all the critics, one by one, as far as I know. Even Matthew Henry, the good and venerable Presbyterian commentator, concedes this point also, and quotes Ephesians 5:26; Acts 22:16; and Matthew 28:19, 20, in support of the conclusion that the *washing of regeneration* refers to baptism.

Our opponents themselves being judges, we have gained this

---

[1] Titus 3:5.

point, viz.: that the only time that the phrase *washing of regenera-tion* occurs in the New Testament, with reference to a personal change, it means, or is equivalent to, immersion. *Washing of re-generation and immersion are therefore only two names of the same thing.* Although I might be justified in proceeding to another topic and supposing this point to be fully established, I choose rather, for the sake of *the slow to apprehend,* to fortify this conclusion by some other testimonies and arguments.

As regeneration is taught to be equivalent to *"being born again,"* and understood to be of the same import with a new birth, we shall examine it under this metaphor. For if immersion be equivalent to regeneration, and regeneration be of the same import with being born again, then being born again and being immersed are the same thing; for this plain reason, that things which are equal to the same thing are equal to one another. *All must admit that no person can be born again of that which he receives.* For as no person is born naturally, so no person can be born again—or born metaphorically—of that which he receives. It destroys the idea, the figure, the allusion, and every thing else which authorizes the application of these words to any change which takes place in man, to suppose that the subject of the new birth, or regeneration, is born again of something which he has received. This single remark shows the impropriety and inaccu-racy of thought; or, perhaps, the popular notions of regeneration sanction and sanctify.

In being born naturally there is the begetter, and that which is begotten. These are not the same. The act of being born is differ-ent from that which is born. Now, the Scriptures carry this figure through every prominent point of coincidence. There is the beget-ter. "Of his own will be hath begotten or impregnated us," says James the apostle. *"By the word of truth,"* as the incorruptible seed; or, as Peter says, "We are born again, not from corruptible, but from incorruptible seed, the word of God which endureth forever." But when the act of being born is spoken of, then the water is intro-duced. Hence, before we come into the kingdom we are born of water.

The Spirit of God is the begetter, the gospel is the seed; and, being thus begotten and quickened, we are born of the water. A child is alive before it is born, and the act of being born only changes its state, not its life. Just so in the metaphorical birth. Persons are begotten by the Spirit of God, impregnated by the word, and born of the water.

In one sense a person is born of his father; but not until he is first born of his mother. So in every place where water and the Spirit, or water and the word, are spoken of, *the water stands first.* Every child is born of its father when it is born of its mother. Hence, the Saviour put the mother first, and the apostles follow him. No other reason can be assigned for placing the water first. How uniform this style! Jesus says to Nicodemus, "You must be born again, or you can not discern the reign of God." *Born again!* What means this? "Nicodemus, unless you are born of water and the Spirit you can not enter into the kingdom of God." So Paul speaks to the Ephesians (5:26), "He cleansed the church [or the disciples] by *a bath of water, and the word.*" And to Titus he says, "He saved the disciples *by the bath* of regeneration, and renewing of the Holy Spirit." Now, as soon as, and not before, a disciple, who has been begotten of God, is born of water, he is born of God, or of the Spirit. *Regeneration is, therefore, the act of being born.*[1] Hence its connection always with water. Reader, reflect—what a jargon, what a confusion, have the mystic doctors made of this metaphorical expression, and of this topic of regeneration. To call the receiving of any spirit or any influence, or energy, or any operation upon the heart of man, regeneration, is an abuse of all speech, as well as a departure from the diction of the Holy Spirit, *who calls nothing personal regeneration except the act of immersion.*[2]

Some curious criticisms have been offered, to escape the force of the plain declaration of Jesus and his apostles upon this subject. Some say that the words, "Except a man be born of water and Spirit," are not to be understood literally. Surely, then, if to be born of water does not mean to be born of water, to be born of the Spirit

---

[1] See the following essay on Regeneration.

[2] That John 3:5 and Titus 3:5 refer to immersion is the judgment of all the learned Catholics and Protestants of every name under heaven.

The authors and finishers of the Westminster creed—one hundred and twenty-one Divines, ten Lords, and twenty Commissioners of the Parliament of England—under the question 165, *"What is baptism?"* quote John 3:5, Titus 3:5, to prove that baptism is a washing with water and a *"sign of remission of sins."*

Michaelis, Horne, Lightfoot, Geveridge, Taylor, Jones of Nayland, Bp. Mant, Whitby, Burkit, Bp. Hall, Dr. Wells, Hooker, Dr. C. Ridley, Bp. Ryder —but why attempt a list of great names? There are a thousand more who assert it.

Bp. White says, that "regeneration, as detached from baptism, never entered into any creed before the seventeenth century."

Whitby, on John 3:5, says, "That our Lord here speaks of baptismal regeneration, *the whole Christian church* from its *earliest times* has invariably taught."

Our modern "great divines," even in America, have taught the same. Timothy Dwight, the greatest Rabbi of Presbyterians the New World has produced, says, vol. 4, pp. 300, 301, *"to be born again* is precisely the same thing as to be born of water and the Spirit."—"To be born of water is to be baptized." And how uncharitable! He adds, "He who, understanding the nature and authority of this institution, refuses to be baptized, will never

must mean something else than to be born of the Spirit. This is so fanatical and extravagant as to need no other exposure. He who can not see the propriety of calling immersion a being born again can see no propriety in any metaphor in common use. A resurrection is a new birth. Jesus is said to be the *first-born* from the dead, because the first who rose from the dead to die no more. And, surely, there is no abuse of speech, but the greatest propriety, in saying that he who has died to sin, and been buried in water, when raised up again out of that element, is born again or regenerated. If Jesus was born again when he came out of a sepulchre, surely he is born again who is raised up out of the grave of waters.

Those who are thus begotten and born of God are children of God. It would be monstrous supposition that such persons are not freed from their sins. *To be born of God and born in sin is inconceivable.* Remission of sins is as certainly granted to *"the born of God,"* as life eternal and deliverance from corruption will be granted to the *children of the resurrection* when born from the grave.

To illustrate what has (we presume to say) been now proved, we shall consider *political regeneration.* Though the term *regeneration* is laxly employed in this association, yet by such a license of speech we may illustrate this subject to the apprehension of all. Yes, the whole subject of faith, change of heart, regeneration, and character.

All the civilized nations and kingdoms have constitutions, and in their constitutions they have declared who are members of the social compact. Besides those who compose the community at the time a constitution is adopted, they say who shall participate its blessings in

---

enter into the visible nor invisible kingdom of God." Vol. 4, p. 302. So preached the President of Yale.

George Whitefield, writing on John 3:5, says, "Does not this verse urge the *absolute necessity of water baptism?* Yes, when it is to be had. But how God will deal with persons unbaptized, *we can not tell.*" Vol. 4, p. 355. I say with him, *We can not tell with certainty.* But I am of the opinion that when a neglect proceeds from a simple mistake or shear ignorance, and when there is no aversion, but a will to do everything the Lord commands, the Lord will admit into the everlasting kingdom those who by reason of this mistake never had the testimony of God assuring them of pardon or justification here, and consequently never did fully enjoy the salvation of God on earth. But I will say with the renowned President of Yale, that "he who, understanding the nature and authority of this institution, refuses to be baptized will never enter the visible nor invisible kingdom of God." By the "visible and invisible kingdom" he means the kingdom of grace and glory. He adds on the same page, "He who persists in this act of rebellion against the authority of Christ will never belong to his kingdom." Vol. 4, p. 302.

John Wesley asserts, that "by baptism we enter into *covenant with God,* an everlasting covenant, are admitted into the church, made members of Christ, made the children of God. By *water* as the *means,* the water of baptism, we are regenerated or born again." (Preservative, pp. 146, 150.)

all time coming; that is, who shall be admitted into it, and by what means they shall become members of it. They have always decreed that their own posterity shall inherit their political rights and immunities; but they have also ordained that foreigners—that is, members of other communities—may become, by adoption or naturalization, citizens or fellow-members of the same community. But they have, in their wisdom and benevolence, instituted a rite or form of adoption, which form has much meaning; and which, when submitted to, changes the state of the subject of it. Now, as the Saviour consented to be called a *king*, and to call the community over which he presides a *kingdom*, it was because of the analogy between these human institutions and his institution; and for the purpose not of confounding but of aiding the human mind in apprehending and comprehending the great object of his mission to the world. And it is worthy of the most emphatic attention that it was *when speaking of a kingdom he spoke of being born again.* Yes; on that occasion, and on that occasion only, when he spoke of *entering into his kingdom*, did he speak of the necessity of *being born again.* And had he not chosen that figure he would not have chosen the figure of a *new birth.* With these facts and circumstances before us, let us examine political regeneration as the best conceivable illustration of religious regeneration.

A B was born on the island of Great Britain, a native subject of George III, King of Great Britain. He was much attached to his native island, to the people, the manners and customs of his ancestors and kinsmen. With all these attachments still increasing, he grew up to manhood. Then he heard the report of this good land—of this large, fertile, and most desirable country. The country, the people, and the government were represented to him in the most favorable light. Sometimes these representations were exaggerated; but still he could separate the truth from the fable, and was fully persuaded not only of the existence of these United States, but also of the eligibility of being a citizen thereof. He believed the testimony which he heard, resolved to expatriate himself from the land of his nativity, to imperil life and property, putting himself aboard of a ship, and bidding adieu to all the companions of his youth, his kinsmen, and dear friends. So full was his conviction, and so strong his faith, that old Neptune and King Eolus, with all their terrors, could not appal him. He sailed from his native shores, and landed on this continent. He was, however, ignorant of many things pertaining to this new country and government; and on his arrival asked for the rights and immunities of a citizen. He was told that the civil rights of hospitality to a *stranger* could be extended to him as a *friendly alien;* but not one of the rights or immunities of a *citizen* could be his, unless he were born again. *"Born again!"* said he, in a disappointed tone, to Columbus, with whom he had his first conversation on the subject. "What do you mean by being born again?"

Columbus. You must be *naturalized,* or adopted as a citizen; or, what we call *born again.*

A B. I do not understand you. How can a man be born when he is grown?

Col. That which is born of Great Britain is British, and that which is born of America is American. If, then, you would be an American citizen, you must be born of America.

A B. Born of America! You astonish me. I have come to America, well disposed towards the people and the country. I was once attached to England, but I became attached to the United States; and because of my faith and attachments I have come here: and will you not receive me into your kingdom because I could not help being born in England?

Col. Well disposed as I am, and we are, to receive you, most assuredly I say to you, unless you are regenerated in a court-house, and been franchised by and before the judges, you can never become a citizen of these United States.

A B. Yours is an arbitrary and despotic government. What airs of sovereignty you have assumed!

Col. By no means. Right, reason, wisdom, policy, and benevolence for you, as well as the safety, dignity, and happiness of the whole community, require that every alien shall be naturalized, or made a citizen, before he exercise or enjoy the rights of a citizen.

A B. You are certainly arbitrary—if not in the thing itself, of regeneration—in the place and manner in which it shall be done. Why, for instance, say that it must be done in a *court-house?*

Col. I will tell you; because there are the *judges,* the *records,* and the *seal* of the government.

A B. I understand you. Well, tell me, how is a man born again? Tell me plainly and without a figure.

Col. With pleasure. You were born of your mother and of your father when you were born in England; and you were born *legitimately,* according to the institutions of England. Well, then, you were born *of* England, as well as born *in* it; and were, therefore, wholly English. This was your first birth. But you have expatriated yourself, as your application here proves—I say *sentimentally* you have expatriated yourself; but we must have a formal *solemn pledge* of your renunciation; and we will give you a formal solemn pledge of your adoption. You must, *ex animo,* in the presence of the judges and the records, renounce all allegiance to every foreign prince and potentate, and especially to his majesty the King of Great Britain.

A B. Is that the thing? I can, with all my heart, renounce all *political* allegiance to every foreign prince and government. Is that all? I have, then, no objection to that.

Col. There is this also:—You are not only to renounce all political allegiance, but you must also, from the soul, solemnly vow in the presence of the same judges and recorders, that you will adopt and submit to the constitution and government of these United States.

A B. I can do that also. I can renounce, and can adopt; nor do I object to the place where it shall be done. But, pray, what solemn pledge will *you give me?*

Col. So soon as you have vowed renunciation, and adopted, in the presence of the judges and recorders, we will give you a certificate, with a *red seal,* the *seal of state,* attached to it; stating that you, having now been naturalized, or born according to our institutions, are born *of* America; and are now a son, an adopted son, of America. And that *red* seal indicates that the blood, the best blood, of this government will be shed for you, to protect you and defend you; and that your life will, when called for, be cheerfully given up for your mother, *of* whom you have been politically born; as it would have been for your own natural political mother, of whom you were first born.

A B. To this I must subscribe. In my mother-tongue, it all means that I give myself up politically to this government, and it gives itself up to me, before witnesses too. How soon, pray, after this new birth may I exercise and enjoy all the rights of a citizen?

Col. They are yours the first breath you breathe under your new mother. It is true, we have not, in these United States, any *symbol* through which a person is politically regenerated. We only ask a solemn pledge, and give one. Some nations have symbols. But we understand that, the moment the vow is taken, the person is politically born again. And, as every other child has all the rights of a child which it can exercise so soon as it inhales the air, so have all our political children all political rights, so soon as the form of naturalization is consummated. But, remember, *not till then.*

A B. You say some nations had their symbols. What do you mean by these?

Col. I mean that the naturalized had to submit to some emblematic rite, by which they were symbolically detached from every other people and introduced among those who adopted them and whom they adopted. The Indian nations wash all whom they adopt in a running stream, and impose this task upon their females. The Jews circumcised and washed all whom they admitted to the rights of their institutions. Other customs and forms have obtained in other nations; but we regard simply the meaning of the thing, and have no symbol.

A B. In this I fell but little interested. I wish to become a citizen of these United States; especially as I am informed I can have no inheritance among you, nor a *voice* in the nation, nor any immunity, unless I am born again.

Col. You must, then, submit to the institution; and I know that so soon as you are politically born again, you will feel more of the importance and utility of this institution than you now can; and will be just as anxious as I am to see others submit to this wise, wholesome, and benevolent institution.

A B. As my faith brought me to your shores, and as I approve your constitution and government, I will not (now that I understand your institutions) suffer an opportunity to pass. I will direct my course to the place where I can be born again.

I ought here to offer an apology for a phrase occuring frequently in this essay and in this dialogue. When we represent the subject of immersion as active, either in so many words or impliedly, we so far depart from that style which comports with the figure of *"being born."* For all persons are passive in being born. So, in immersion, the subject buries not himself, raises not himself; but is buried and raised by another. So that in the act the subject is always passive. And it is of that act alone of which we thus speak.

From all that has been said on *regeneration,* and from the illustration just now adduced, the following conclusions must, we think, be apparent to all:—

First. Begetting and quickening necessarily precede being born.

Second. Being born imparts no new life; but is simply *a change of state,* and introduces into *a new mode of living.*

Third. Regeneration or immersion—the former referring to the import of the act, and the latter term to the act itself—denote only the act of being born.

Fourth. God, or the Spirit of God, being the author of the whole institution, imparting to it its life and efficiency, is the *begetter,* in the fullest sense of that term. Yet, in a subordinate sense, every one skilful in the word of God, who converts another, may be said to have begotten him whom he enlightens. So Paul says, "I have begotten Onesimus in my bonds"; and "I have begotten you, Corinthians, through the gospel."

Fifth. The gospel is declared to be *the seed,*—the power and strength of the Holy Spirit to impart life.

Sixth. And the great argument, pertinent to our object, in this long examination of conversion and regeneration, is that which we conceive to be the most apparent of all other conclusions, viz.: that remission of sins, or coming into a state of acceptance, being one of the present immunities of the kingdom of heaven, can not be scripturally enjoyed by any person before immersion. As soon can a person be a citizen before he is born, or have the immunities of an American citizen while an alien, as one enjoy the privileges of a son of God before he is born again. For Jesus expressly declares, that he has not given the privilege of sons to any but those born of God.[1] If, then, the present forgiveness of sins be a privilege, and a right of those under the new constitution, in the kingdom of Jesus; and if being born again, or being born of *water* and of the Spirit, is necessary to admission, and if being born of *water* means *immersion,* as clearly proved by all witnesses; then, remission of sins can not, in this life, be constitutionally enjoyed previous to immersion. If there be any proposition regarding any item of the Christian institution, whch admits a clearer proof or fuller illustration than this one, I have yet to learn where it may be found.

But, before we dismiss the sixth evidence, which embraces so many items, I beg leave to make a remark or two on the propriety of considering the term "immersion" as equivalent to the term "conversion."

Conversion is, on all sides, understood to be a turning to God. Not a thinking favorably of God, nor a repenting for former misdeeds; but an actual turning to God, in word and in deed. It is true, that no person can be said to turn to God, whose mind is not enlightened, and whose heart is not well disposed towards God. All human actions, not resulting from previous thought or determination, are rather the actions of a machine, than the action of a rational being. "He that comes to God," or turns to him, "must believe that God exists, and that he is a rewarder of every one who diligently seeks him." Then he will seek and find the Lord. An "external conversion" is no conversion at all. A turning to God with the lips, while the heart is far from him, is mere pretence and mockery. But, though I never thought any thing else since I thought upon religion, I understand the "turning to God" taught in the new institution to be a coming to the Lord Jesus, not a *thinking* about doing it, nor a *repenting* that we have not done it; but an *actual coming* to him. The question then is, Where shall we find him? Where shall we meet him? Nowhere on

[1] John 1:12.

earth but in his institutions. "Where he records his name," there alone can he be found; for there alone has he promised to be found. I affirm, then, that the first institution, in which we can meet with God, is the institution for remission. And here it is worthy of notice, that the apostles, in all their speeches and replies to interrogatories, never commanded an inquirer to pray, read, or sing, *as preliminary to his coming; but always commanded and proclaimed immersion as the first duty, or the first thing to be done, after a belief of testimony.* Hence, either praying, singing, reading, repenting, sorrowing, resolving, nor waiting to be better, was the converting act. Immersion *alone* was the act of turning to God. Hence, in the commission to convert the nations, the only institution mentioned after proclaiming the gospel was the immersion of the believers, as the divinely authorized way of carrying out and completing the work. And from the day of Pentecost to the final *Amen* in the revelation of Jesus Christ, no person was said to be converted, or to turn to God, until he was buried in and raised up out of the water.

If it were not to treat this subject as one of doubtful disputation, I would say, that had there not been some act, such as immersion, agreed on all hands to be the medium of remission and the act of conversion and regeneration, the apostles could not, with any regard to truth and consistency, have addressed the disciples as pardoned, justified, sanctified, reconciled, adopted, and saved persons. If all this had depended upon some mental change, as faith, they could never have addressed their congregations in any other way than as the moderns do: and that is always in the language of doubt and uncertainty,—hoping a little, and fearing much. This mode of address and the modern compared is proof positive that they viewed the immersed through one medium, and we through another. They taught all the disciples to consider not only themselves as saved persons, but all whom they saw or knew to be immersed into the Lord Jesus. They saluted every one of his coming out of the water, as *saved,* and recorded him as such. Luke writes, "The Lord added *the saved* daily to the congregation."[1]

Whenever a child is born into a family, it is a brother or a sister to all the other children of the family; and its being born of the same parents is the act causative and declarative of its fraternity. All is mental and invisible before coming out of the water; and as immersion is the first act commanded, and the first constitutional act; so it was, in the commission, *the act* by which the apostles were commanded to turn or convert those to God who believed their testimony. In this sense, then, it is the converting act. No man can, scripturally,

---

[1] Acts 2:47.

be said to be converted to God until he is immersed. How ecclesiastics interpret their own language is no concern of ours. We contend for the pure speech, and for the apostolic ideas attached to it.

To resume the direct testimonies declarative of the remission of sins by immersion, we turn to the Gentiles. Peter was sent to the house of Cornelius to tell him and his family "words by which they might be saved." He tells these words. He was interrupted by the miraculous descent of the Holy Spirit. But it is to be noticed, that the testimony, to which the Holy Spirit there affixed its seal, was the following words:—"To him gave all the prophets witness, that every one who believes on him *shall receive remission of sins by his name."* While speaking these words, concerning remission of sins by or through his name, the Holy Spirit, in its marvellous gifts of tongues, fell upon them.

Many, seeing so much stress laid upon faith or belief, suppose that all blessings flow from it *immediately.* This is a great mistake. Faith, indeed, is the principle, and the distinguishing principle, of this economy: but it is only the principle of action. Hence, we find the name or person of Christ always interposed between faith and the cure, mental or corporeal. The woman who touched the tuft of the mantle of Jesus had as much faith before as after; but, though her faith was the cause of her putting forth her hand, and accompanied it, *she was not cured until the touch.* That great type of Christ, the brazen serpent, cured no Israelite simply by faith. The Israelites, as soon as they were bitten, believed it would cure them. But yet they were not cured as soon as bitten; nor until *they looked* to the serpent. It was one thing to believe that looking at the serpent would cure them; and another to look at it. It was *the faith* remotely; but *immediately, the look,* which cured them. It was not faith in the waters of Jordan that healed the leprosy of Naaman the Syrian. It was immersing himself in it, according to the commandment. It was not faith in the pool of Siloam that cured the blind man whose eyes Jesus anointed with clay. It was his washing his eyes in Siloam's water. Hence, the imposition of hands, or a word, or a touch, or a shadow, or something from the persons of those anointed with the Holy Spirit, was the *immediate* cause of all the cures recorded in the New Testament. It is true, also, that without faith it is impossible to be healed; for in some places Jesus could not work many miracles, because of their unbelief. It is so in all the moral remedies and cures. It is impossible to receive the remission of sins without faith. In this world of means (however it may be in a world where there are no means), it is as impossible to receive any blessing through faith without the appointed means. *Both are indis-*

pensable. Hence *the name* of the Lord Jesus is interposed between faith and forgiveness, justification, and sanctification, even where immersion into that *name* is not detailed. It would have been unprecedented in the annals of the world for the historian always to have recorded all the circumstances of the same institution, on every allusion to it; and it would have been equally so for the apostles to have mentioned it always in the same words. Thus, in the passage before us, the *name* of the Lord is only mentioned. So in the first letter to the Corinthians, the disciples are represented as saved, as washed, as justified, sanctified *by the name* of the Lord Jesus, and by the Spirit of our God. The frequent interposition of the name of the Lord between faith and forgiveness, justification, sanctification, etc., is explained in a remark in James's speech in Jerusalem.[1] It is the application of an ancient prophecy, concerning the conversion of the Gentiles. The Gentiles are spoken of as turning to, or seeking the Lord. But who of them are thus converted? "Even all the Gentiles *upon whom* my name is called." It is, then, to those *upon whom* the name of the Lord is called, that the name of the Lord communicates remission, justification, etc.

Some captious spirits need to be reminded that, as they sometimes find forgiveness, justification, sanctification, etc., ascribed to grace, to the blood of Christ, to the name of the Lord, without an allusion to faith; so we sometimes find faith, and grace, and the blood of Christ, without an allusion to water. Now, if they have any reason and right to say, that faith is understood in the one case; we have the same reason and right to say, that water or immersion is understood in the other. For their argument is, that in sundry places this matter is made plain enough. This single remark cuts off all their objections drawn from the fact that immersion is not always found in every place where *the name* of the Lord, or *faith*, is found connected with forgiveness. Neither is grace, the blood of Christ, nor faith, always mentioned with forgiveness. When they find a passage where remission of sins is mentioned without immersion, it is weak or unfair in the extreme, to argue from that, that forgiveness can be enjoyed without immersion. IF THEIR LOGIC BE WORTH ANY THING, IT WILL PROVE, THAT A MAN MAY BE FORGIVEN WITHOUT GRACE, THE BLOOD OF JESUS, AND WITHOUT FAITH: FOR WE CAN FIND PASSAGES, MANY PASSAGES, WHERE REMISSION, OR JUSTIFICATION, SANCTIFICATION, OR SOME SIMILAR TERM, OCCURS, AND NO MENTION OF EITHER GRACE, FAITH, OR THE BLOOD OF JESUS.

As this is the pith, the marrow and fatness, of all the logic of our most ingenious opponents on this subject, I wish I could make it

---

[1] Acts 15:17.

more emphatic than by printing it in capitals. I know some editors, some of our doctors of divinity, some of our most learned declaimers, who make this argument, which we unhesitatingly call a genuine sophism, the Alpha and the Omega of their speeches against the meaning and indispensable importance of Christian immersion.

The New Testament would have been a curious book, if, every time *remission of sins* was mentioned or alluded to, it had been preceded by *grace, faith, the blood of Jesus, immersion, etc., etc.* But now the question comes, which, to the rational, is the emphatic question:—WHETHER DO THEY THINK, BELIEVE, TEACH, AND PRACTICE MORE WISELY AND MORE SAFELY, WHO THINK, BELIEVE, AND TEACH THAT GRACE, FAITH, THE BLOOD OF JESUS, THE NAME OF THE LORD, AND IMMERSION, ARE ALL ESSENTIAL TO IMMEDIATE PARDON AND ACCEPTANCE;—OR THEY WHO SAY, THAT FAITH ONLY, GRACE ONLY, THE BLOOD OF CHRIST ONLY, THE NAME OF THE LORD ONLY—AND IMMERSION NOT AT ALL? To all men, women, and children of common sense, this question is submitted.

It is, however, to me admirable, that the remission of sins should be, not merely unequivocally, but so repeatedly declared through *immersion*, as it is in the apostolic writings. And here I would ask the whole thinking community, one by one, whether if the whole race of men had been assembled on Pentecost, or in Solomon's Portico, and had asked Peter the same question which the convicted proposed, would he, or would he not, have given them the same answer? Would he not have told the whole race to reform, and be immersed for the remission of their sins? or to reform and be *converted*, that their sins might be blotted out?—to arise and be immersed, and wash away their sins? If he would not, let them give a reason; and if they say he would, let them assign a reason why they do not go and do likewise.

Some have objected against the "seasons of refreshment," or the comforts of the Holy Spirit, being placed subsequent to "conversion," or "regeneration" or "immersion" (for when we speak scripturally we must use these terms as all referring to the same thing), because the gifts of the Holy Spirit were poured out upon the Gentiles before immersion. They see not the design of thus welcoming the Gentiles into the kingdom. They forget the comparison of the Gentiles to a returning prodigal, and his father going out to meet him, even while he was yet a good way off. God had welcomed the first-fruits of the Jews into his kingdom by a stupendous display of spiritual gifts, called the *baptism of the Holy Spirit,* before any one of the Jews had been immersed into the Lord Jesus. And, as Peter explains this matter in Cornelius's case, it appears that God determined to make no difference between the Jews and Gentiles in receiving them into his kingdom. Hence, says Peter, "he gave them the *same gift* which he gave to us Jews *at the beginning*" (never since Pentecost). Thus Peter was authorized to command those Gentiles to be immersed by the authority of the Lord, no man daring to forbid it. But these gifts of the Holy Spirit differed exceedingly from the seasons of refreshment, from the righteousness, peace, and joy in the Holy Spirit, the common enjoyment of all who were immersed into the name of the Lord Jesus for the remission of sins.[1]

Let it be noted here, as pertinent to our present purpose, that as the apostle Peter was interrupted by the baptism of the Holy Spirit, when he began to speak of the forgiveness by *the name* of the Lord Jesus; so soon as he saw the Lord had received them, he commanded them to be immersed by the authority of the Lord. And here I must propose another question to the learned and the unlearned. How comes it to pass that, though once, and only once, it is commanded that the nations who believe should be immersed into the name of the Father, and of the Son, and of the Holy Spirit; and though we read of no person being immersed into this name in this way, I say, how comes it to pass that all sects use these words without a scruple, and baptize or sprinkle in this name; when more than once persons are commanded to be immersed *for the remission of sins,* and but few of the proclaimers can be induced to immerse for the remission of sins, though so repeatedly taught and proclaimed by the apostles? Is one command, unsupported by a single precedent, sufficient to justify this practice of Christians; and sundry commands and precedents from the same authority insufficient to authorize or justify us in immersing for the remission of sins? Answer this who can: I can not upon any other principle than that the tyrant Custom, who gives no account of his doings, has so decreed.

I come now to another of the direct and positive testimonies of the apostles, showing that immersion for the remission of sins is an institution of Jesus Christ. It is the address of Ananias to Saul:— "Arise and be immersed, and wash away your sins, calling upon the name of the Lord." On this testimony we have not as yet descanted in this essay. It has been mentioned, but not examined.

Paul, like the Pentecostian hearers, when convinced of the truth of the pretensions of the Messiah, asked what *he* should do. He was commanded to go into Damascus, and it should be told him there what to do. It was told him in the words now before us. But, say some, this can not be understood literally.

---

[1] See *Christian Baptist,* vol. 6, p. 268.

For experiment, then, take it figuratively. Of what was it figurative? Of something already received? Of pardon formerly bestowed? A figure of the past!? This is anomalous. I find one writer, and but one, who converts this into a *commemorative* baptism, like Israel's commemorating the escape from Egypt, or Christians commemorating the Lord's death. And, if I do not mistake, some preacher said it was a figurative expression, similar to "This is my body"! One, whom I pressed out of all refuges, was candid enough to say, he really did not know what it meant; but it could not mean that Paul was to "be baptized for the remission of his sins"!

"To wash away sins" is a figurative expression. Like other metaphoric expressions, it puts the resemblance in place of the proper word. It necessarily means something analogous to what it said. But we are said to be washed from our sins in or by the blood of Christ. But even *"washed in blood"* is a figurative expression, and means something analogous to washing in water. Perhaps we may find in another expression a means of reconciling these strong metaphors. Revelation 7:14: "They have washed their robes, and made them white in the blood of the Lamb." Here are two things equally incomprehensible—to wash garments *white* in *blood,* and to *wash away* sins in water! An efficacy is ascribed to water which it does not possess, and, as certainly, an efficacy is ascribed to blood which it does not possess. If blood can *whiten* or cleanse garments, certainly water can *wash away* sins. There is, then, a transferring of the efficacy of blood to water, and a transferring of the efficacy of water to blood. This is a plain solution of the whole matter. God has transferred, in some way, the whitening efficacy or cleansing power of water to blood, and the absolving or pardoning power of blood to water. This is done upon the same principle as that of accounting faith for righteousness. What a gracious institution! God has opened a fountain for sin, for moral pollution. He has given it an extension far and wide as sin has spread—far and wide as water flows. Wherever water, faith, and the name of the Father, Son, and Holy Spirit are, there will be found the efficacy of the blood of Jesus. Yes, as God first gave the efficacy of water to blood, he has now given the efficacy of blood to water. This, as was said, is figurative; but it is not a figure which misleads, for the meaning is given without a figure, viz.: immersion for the remission of sins. And to him that made the washing of clay from the eyes the washing away of blindness, it is competent to make the immersion of the body in water efficacious to the washing away of sin *from the conscience.*

From the conscience, I say; for there its malignity is felt; and it is only in releasing the conscience from guilt, and its consequences—

fear and shame, that we are released from the dominion of sin, or washed from its pollution in this world. Thus immersion, says Peter, *saves* us, not by cleansing the body from its filth, but the conscience from its guilt; yes, immersion saves us by burying us with Christ, raising us with him, and so our consciences are purified from dead works to serve the living God. Hence our Lord gave so much importance to immersion in giving the commission to convert the world:— *"He that believes and is immersed shall be saved."*

But, while viewing the water and blood as made to unite their powers, as certainly as Jesus came by water and blood, we ought to consider another testimony given to this gracious combination of powers, by Paul the apostle:—"Being sprinkled in heart from an evil conscience, and being washed in body with clear water."[1] The application of water, the cleansing element, to the body, is made in this gracious institution to reach the conscience, as did the blood of sprinkling under the law.

Some ask, How can water, which penetrates not the skin, reach the conscience? They boast of such an objection, as exhibiting great intellect and good sense. But little do they think, that, in so talking, they laugh at and mock the whole Divine Economy, under the old and new institutions: for, I ask, did not the sacrifices, and Jewish purifications, some way reach the conscience of that people? If they did not, it was all mere frivolity throughout. And can eating bread, and drinking wine, not influence nor affect the soul? And can not *the breath* of one man pierce the heart of another, and so move his blood, as to make his head a fountain of tears? He who thus objects to water, and the import of immersion, objects to the whole remedial institution, as taught by Moses and by Christ, and insults the wisdom and goodness of God in the whole scheme of salvation. And he who objects to water, because it can only take away the filth of the flesh, ought rather to object to blood; because it rather besmears and pollutes than cleanses the body, and can not touch the soul. But all such reasoners are foolish talkers. To submit to God's institution is our wisdom, and our happiness. The experience of the myriads who were immersed for the remission of their sins, detailed in the Christian Scriptures, to say nothing of those immersed in our times, is worth more than volumes of arguments from the lips and pens of those who can only regard and venerate the traditions of their fathers; because it is presumed their fathers were wiser and more able to judge correctly than their sons.

But as it is not our object to quote and expatiate upon all the sacred testimonies, direct and allusive, to immersion for the remission

---

[1] Hebrews 10:24.

of sins, we shall close the proof and illustration of this proposition with an incidental allusion to the cleansing efficacy of this institution, found in the Second Epistle of Peter.[1] After enumerating the additions to faith necessary to secure our calling and election, of which *courage* is the first, and charity, or universal love, the last; the apostle says, that "he who has not these things is blind, shutting his eyes, and forgetting that he was *purified from his old sins.*" I need not here say, that this is, perhaps (and certainly as far as I know), universally understood to refer to Christian immersion. The *"old sins,"* or *"former sins,"* can, we presume, mean no other sins than those washed away in immersion. No person has yet attempted to show that these words can import any thing else. It is one of the most unequivocal, and, because incidental, one of the most decisive proofs, that, in Peter's judgment, all former sins were remitted in immersion. With Peter we began our proof of this position, and with Peter we shall end our proof of it. He first proclaimed reformation for the remission of sins; and in his last and farewell letters to the Christian communities he reminds them of that purification from sin, received in and through immersion; and in the strongest terms cautions them against forgetting that they were so purified.

Were any person to reason upon the simple import of the action commanded by Jesus, I think it might be made apparent from the action itself, in its two parts, *the burial and the resurrection,* that it must import every thing which we have heard the apostles ascribe to it. Corruption goes down into the grave literally, but does corruption come forth out of it? Is there no change of state in the grave? Who is it that expects to come forth from the grave in the same state in which he descends into it? The first-born from the dead did not; nor shall any of them who fall asleep in him. How, then, can it be, that any person buried with Christ in immersion can rise with Christ, and not rise in a new state?! Surely the apostle exhorts to a new life from the change of state effected in immersion. "Since, indeed, you have risen with Christ, set your affections on things above." Walk in a new life.

Again, and in the last place here,—Is a child in the same state after as before its birth? Is not its state changed? And does it not live a new life, compared with its former mode of living? As newborn babes desire the milk of the breast, so let the newly regenerate desire the unadulterated milk of the word, that they may grow thereby. Call immersion, then, a new birth, a washing of regeneration, or a resurrection, and its meaning is the same. And when so denominated, it must import that change of state which is imported

---

[1] 2 Peter 1:9.

in putting on Christ, in being pardoned, justified, sanctified, adopted, reconciled, saved, which was the great proposition to be proved and illustrated, and which we think has been proved and illustrated by the preceding testimonies and reflections.

Though no article of Christian faith, nor item of Christian practice, can, legitimately, rest upon any testimony, reasoning or authority, out of the sacred writings of the apostles, were it only one day after their decease; yet the views and practices of those who were the contemporaries or the pupils of the apostles and their immediate successors may be adduced as corroborating evidence of the truths taught, and the practices enjoined, by the apostles; and, as such, may be cited; still bearing in mind, that where the testimony of apostles ends, Christian faith necessarily terminates. After this preliminary remark, I proceed to sustain the following proposition:—

PROP. XI.—*All the apostolical Fathers, as they are called; all the pupils of the apostles; and all the ecclesiastical writers of note, of the first four Christian centuries, whose writings have come down to us; allude to, and speak of, Christian immersion, as the "regeneration" and "remission of sins" spoken of in the New Testament.*

This proposition I shall sustain by the testimony of those who have examined all Christian antiquity, and by citing the words of those usually called the Apostolic Fathers, and other distinguished writers of the first four hundred years. We shall first summon one whose name is familiar throughout Christendom. Whether the writing be genuine or spurious, it is on all hands admitted to be a fragment of the highest antiquity:—

BARNABAS

In his catholic Epistle, chapter 11, says, "Let us now inquire whether the Lord took care to manifest any thing beforehand, concerning water and the cross. Now, for the former of these, it is written to the people of Israel, how they shall not receive that baptism which brings to forgiveness of sins; but shall institute another to themselves that can not. For thus saith the prophet, 'Be astonished, O Heavens! and let the earth tremble at it; because these people have done two great and wicked things: They have left me, the fountain of living waters, and have digged for themselves broken cisterns that can hold no water. Is my holy mountain Zion a desolate wilderness? For she shall be as a young bird when its nest is taken away.' "—"Consider how he hath joined both the *cross* and the *water* together. For this he saith, 'Blessed are they who, putting their trust in the cross, de-

scend into the water; for they shall have their reward in due time; then, saith he, will I give it them.' But as concerning the present time, he saith, 'Their leaves shall not fail.' Meaning thereby that every word that shall go out of your mouth shall through faith and charity be to the conversion and hope of many. In like manner does another prophet speak: 'And the land of Jacob was the praise of all the earth;' magnifying thereby the vessels of his Spirit. And what follows? 'And there was a river running on the right hand, and beautiful trees grew up by it; and he that shall eat of them shall live forever.' The significance of which is this:—*that we go down into the river full of sins and pollution; but come up again bringing forth fruit; having in our hearts the fear and hope which are in Jesus by the Spirit:* 'And whosoever shall eat of them shall live forever.' That is, whosoever shall hearken to those that call them, and shall believe, shall live forever."

CLEMENT AND HERMAS

The former gives no testimony on the subject. The latter deposes as follows.[1]

In speaking of a tower built upon the water, by which he signified the building of Christ's church, he thus speaks:—"Hear, therefore, why the tower is built on the waters: because your life is saved, and shall be saved, by water." In answer to the question, "Why did the stones come up into this tower out of the deep?" he says it was necessary for them to come up by (or *through*) water, that they might be at rest; for they could not otherwise enter the kingdom of God: for before any one *receives the name of the Son of God*, he is liable to death; but when he receives that *seal*, he is delivered from death and assigned to life. Now, that seal is *water*, into which persons go down liable to death, but come out of it assigned to life; for which reason to these also was this seal preached; and they made use of it that they might enter the kingdom of God."

Both Clement and Hermas wrote about the end of the first or beginning of the second century.

Hermas, moreover, deposes as follows, in another work of his called "The Commands of Hermas."[2]

"And I said to him, I have even now heard, from certain teachers, that there is no other repentance besides that of *baptism*, when we

---

[1] Book of Similitudes, chap. 16.
[2] Com. 4, chap. 3.

go down into the water, and *receive the forgiveness of sins,* and after that we should sin no more, but live in purity. And he said to me, *Thou hast been rightly informed.*"

Having closely and repeatedly examined the Epistles of Clement; of Polycarp, to the Philippians; of Ignatius, to the Ephesians; that to the Magnesians; that to the Trallians, the Romans, the Philadelphians, the Smyrnians, and his Epistle to Polycarp; together with the catholic Epistle of Barnabas, and the genuine works of Hermas, I can affirm that the preceding extracts are the only passages in all these writings that speak of immersion.

Having heard the Apostolic Fathers, as they are called, depose to the views of the pupils of the apostles, down to A. D. 140; I will summon a very learned Pedobaptist antiquarian, who can bring forward every writer and Father, down to the fifth century; and, before we hear any of his witnesses, we shall interrogate him concerning his own convictions after he had spent many years in rummaging all Christian antiquity:—

TESTIMONY OF DR. W. WALL, AUTHOR OF "THE HISTORY OF INFANT BAPTISM."[1]

Pray, Doctor, have you examined all the primitive writers from the death of John down to the fifth century?

W. Wall.—"I have."

And will you explicitly avow what was the established and universal view of all Christians, public and private, for four hundred years from the nativity of the Messiah, on the import of the saying (John 3:5), "Except a man be born of water and the Spirit, he can not enter into the kingdom of God"?

W. Wall.—"There is not any one Christian writer of any antiquity in any language, but who understands it of *baptism;* and, if it be not so understood, it is difficult to give an account how a person is born of *water,* any more than born of *wood.*"

Did all the Christians, public and private, and all the Christian writers from Barnabas to the times of Pelagius (419), as far as you know, continue to use the term *regenerate* as only applicable to immersion?

W. Wall.—"The Christians did, in all ancient times, continue the use of this name 'regeneration,' for *baptism;* so that they *never* use the word 'regenerate,' or 'born again,' but they mean or denote by it

---

[1] 4th London edition, p. 116, vol. 1, A. D. 1829.

baptism. And almost all the quotations which I shall bring in this book shall be instances of it."[1]

Did they also substitute for *"baptism"* and *"baptize,"* the words *renewed, sanctified, sealed, enlightened, initiated,* as well as *regenerated?*

W. Wall.—"For to *baptize,* they used the following words:— Most commonly, *anagennao,* to regenerate; sometimes, *kainopoico,* to renew; frequently, *agiazo,* to sanctify. Sometimes they call it the *seal;* and frequently, *illumination,* as it is also called, Hebrews 6:4; and sometimes, *teliosis,* initiation."[2] "St. Austin, not less than a hundred times, expresses *baptized* by the word *sanctified.*"[3]

We shall now see some of Mr. Wall's witnesses; and I choose rather to introduce them from his own pen, as he can not be supposed partial to the views I have presented in this essay:—

JUSTIN MARTYR

Justin Martyr wrote about forty years after John the apostle died and stands most conspicuous among the primitive Fathers. He addressed an apology to the Emperor Antoninus Pius. In this apology he narrates the *practices* of the Christians, and the reasons of them. Concerning those who are persuaded and believe the things which are taught, and who promise to live according to them, he writes:—

"Then we bring them to some place where there is water, and they are *regenerated* by the same way of *regeneration* by which we were *regenerated:* for they are washed in water (*en to udati*) in the name of God the Father and Lord of all things, and of our Saviour Jesus Christ, and of the Holy Spirit; for Christ says, Unless you be regenerated you can not enter into the kingdom of heaven; and everybody knows it is impossible for those who are once generated (or born) to enter again into their mother's womb."

"It was foretold by Isaiah, as I said, by what means they who should repent of their sins might escape them; and was written in these words, 'Wash you, make you clean, put away the evil,' " etc.

"And we have been taught by the apostles this reason for this thing. Because we, being ignorant of our first birth, were generated by necessity (or course of nature) and have been brought up in all customs and conversation; that we should not continue children of that necessity and ignorance, but of will (or choice) and knowledge, and should obtain *forgiveness of the sins* in which they have lived, by water (or in water). Then is invoked over him that has a mind

---

[1] Vol. 1, p. 24. [2] Vol. 1, p. 8. [3] Page 194.

to be *regenerated,* the name of God the Father, etc. And this washing is called *the enlightening.*"

As you trace the history of infant baptism, Mr. Wall, as nigh the
apostolic times as possible, pray, why do you quote Justin Martyr,
who never mentions it?

W. *Wall.*—"Because his is the most ancient account of the *way of
baptizing,* next the Scripture; and shows the plain and simple manner
of administering it. Because it shows that the Christians of those
times (many of whom lived in the days of the apostles) used the
word '*regeneration*' (or '*being born again*') for *baptism;* and that
they were taught to do so by the apostles. And because we see by it
that they understood John 3:5, of water baptism; and so did all the
writers of these four hundred years, *not one man excepted.*" (p. 54.)

Did any of the ancients use the word *matheteueo* (to disciple) as
it is used in the commission; or did they call the baptized *discipled?*

W. *Wall.*—"Justin Martyr, in his second apology to Antoninus,
uses it. His words are, 'Several persons among us, of sixty and seventy years old, of both sexes, *who were discipled (matheteueo)* to
Christ, in or from their childhood, do continue uncorrupted." (p.
54.)

So soon as they began to mysticize, they began to teach that immersion *without faith* would obtain remission of sins, and that immersion *without faith* was regeneration. Then came the debates about
original sin: and so soon as original sin was proved, then came the
necessity of infant immersion for the remission of original sin. And
so undisputed was the import of baptism for remission, that when the
Pelagians denied original sin, pressed with difficulty, "why immerse
those who have no sins?" they were pushed to invent *actual sins* for
infants; such as their crying, peevishness, restlessness, etc., on account of which sins they supposed that infants might with propriety
be immersed, though they had no original sin.

TERTULLIAN

Tertullian, the first who mentions infant baptism, flourished about
A. D. 216. He writes against the practice; and among his most conclusive arguments against infant immersion (for then there was no
sprinkling), he assumes, as a fundamental principle not to be questioned, that immersion was for the remission of sins; and, this being
universally conceded, he argues as follows:—

"Our Lord says, indeed, 'Do not forbid them to come to me';
therefore, let them come when they are grown up—let them come
when they understand—when they are instructed whither it is that

they come. Let them be made Christians when they can know Christ. What need their *guiltless* age make such haste to *the forgiveness of sins?* Men will proceed more warily in worldly goods; and he that should not have earthly goods committed to him yet shall have heavenly! Let them know how to desire this salvation, that you may appear to have given to one that asketh." (p. 74.)

ORIGEN

Origen, though so great a visionary, is, nevertheless, a competent witness in any question of fact. And here I would again remind the reader, that it is as witnesses in a question of *fact,* and not of *opinion,* we summon these ancients. It is not to tell their own opinions, nor the reasons of them, but to depose what were the views of Christians on this institution in their times. There was no controversy on this subject for more than four hundred years, and therefore we expect only to find incidental allusions to it; but these are numerous, and of the most unquestionable character. Origen, in his homily upon Luke, says,—

"Infants are baptized for the forgiveness of their sins. Of what sins? Or when have they sinned? Or how can any reason of the law, in their case, hold good, but according to that sense that we mentioned even now? (that is) none is free from pollution, though his life be but the length of one day upon the earth."

And in another place he says, that

"The baptism of the church is given for the forgiveness of sins."

And again—

"If there were nothing in infants that wanted forgiveness and mercy, the grace of baptism would be needless to them."

In another place he says,—

"But in the *regeneration* (or new birth), by the laver (or baptism), every one that is born again of water and the Spirit is clear from pollution: clear (as I may venture to say) as by a glass darkly." (p. 82.)

But now let me ask Dr. Wall,—Do Gregory Nazianzen, Basil, Ambrose, Chrysostom, and St. Austin, concur with all their predecessors in those views of regeneration and remission?

W. Wall.—"Yes, exactly. I have observed, among the several names which the ancients give to *baptism,* they often by this phrase, '*the forgiveness of sins,*' do mean the sacrament of baptism." (p. 179.) And as for Chrysostom, he expressly says, "In baptism, or the spiritual circumcision, there is no trouble to be undergone but to throw off the load of sins, and to receive pardon for all foregoing offences." (p. 182.) And again: "There is no receiving or having the bequeathed inheritance before one is baptized; and none can be called *a son* till he is baptized." (p. 183.)

The controversies about infant baptism and original sin were contemporaneous; and just so soon as they decided the nature and extent of original sin, baptism for the remission of sins was given to infants because of this pollution, and defended because of the necessity of regeneration and forgiveness to salvation; and because immersion was universally admitted to be the scriptural regeneration and remission. In this way, there is no reasonable doubt but infant baptism began; and for convenience' sake, as Dr. Wall contends, it was substituted by infant sprinkling.

Unless we were to transcribe all the testimonies of antiquity, one by one, no greater assurance can be given, that, for more than four hundred years after Christ, all writers, orthodox and heterodox, Pelagius and Austin not excepted, concurred in the preceding views. Were I to summon others—Eusebius, Dupin, Lightfoot, and Hammond, *cum multis aliis*, will depose the same.

This proposition we will dismiss with the testimony of the most renowned of the bishops of Africa. I extract it from a work now generally read, called the "History of Martyrs." It is from the account Cyprian gives of his conversion. (p. 317.)

CYPRIAN

"While (says he) I lay in darkness and uncertainty, I thought on what I had heard of a second birth, proposed by the divine goodness; but could not comprehend how a man could receive a new life from his being immersed in water, cease to be what he was before, and still remain the same body. How, said I, can such a change be possible? How can he who is grown old in a worldly way of living strip himself of his former inclinations and inveterate habits? Can he who has spent his whole time in plenty, and indulged his appetite without restraint, ever be transformed into an example of frugality and sobriety? Or he who has always appeared in splendid apparel stoop to the plain, simple, and unornamented dress of the common people? It is impossible for a man who has borne the most honorable posts ever to submit to lead a private and obscure life; or that he who was never seen in public without a crowd of attendants, and persons who endeavored to make their fortunes by attending him, should ever bear to be alone. This (continues he) was my way of arguing: I thought it was impossible for me to leave my former course of life, and the habits I was then engaged in and accustomed to: but no sooner did the life-giving water wash the spots off my soul, than my heart received the heavenly light of the Holy Spirit, which transformed me into a new creature; all my difficulties were cleared, my doubts dissolved, and my darkness dispelled. I was then able to do what before seemed impossible; could discern that my former life was earthly and sinful, according to the impurity of my birth; but that my spiritual birth gave me new ideas and inclinations, and directed all my views to God."

Cyprian flourished A. D. 250.

PROP. XII.—*But even the reformed creeds, Episcopalian, Presbyterian, Methodist, and Baptist, substantially avow the same views of immersion, though apparently afraid to carry them out in faith and practice.*

This proposition will be sustained by an extract from the creed of each of these sects.

EPISCOPALIAN

The clergy are ordered, before proceeding to baptize, to make the following prayer.[1]

"Almighty and everlasting God, who of thy great mercy didst save Noah and his family in the ark from perishing by water; and also didst safely lead the children of Israel thy people through the Red Sea: figuring thereby the holy baptism; and, by the baptism of thy well-beloved Son Jesus Christ in the river Jordan, didst sanctify the element of water, in the mystical washing away of sin; we beseech thee, for thine infinite mercies, that thou wilt mercifully look upon *these thy servants;* wash *them* and sanctify *them* with the Holy Ghost; that *they,* being delivered from thy wrath, may be received into the ark of Christ's church; and, being steadfast in faith, joyful through hope, and rooted in charity, may so pass the waves of this troublesome world, that finally *they* may come to the land of everlasting life; there to reign with thee, world without end, through Jesus Christ our Lord. *Amen.*"

After reading a part of the discourse with Nicodemus, they are ordered to make the following exhortation.[2]

"Beloved, ye hear in this gospel the express words of our Saviour Christ, that except a man be born of water and the Spirit he can not enter into the kingdom of God. Whereby ye may perceive the great necessity of this sacrament, where it may be had. Likewise immediately before his ascension into heaven (as we read in the last chapter of St. Mark's Gospel), he gave command to his disciples, saying, Go

---

[1] Common Prayer, p. 165. [2] Page 165.

ye into all the world and preach the gospel to every creature. He that believeth and is baptized shall be saved; but he that believeth not shall be damned. Which also showeth unto us the great benefit we reap thereby. For which cause St. Peter, the apostle, when, upon his first preaching of the gospel, many were pricked at the heart, and said to him and the rest of the apostles, Men and brethren, what shall we do? replied, and said unto them, Repent, and be baptized every one of you for the remission of sins, and ye shall receive the gift of the Holy Ghost: for the promise is to you and your children, and to all that are afar off, even as many as the Lord our God shall call. And with many other words exhorted he them, saying, Save yourselves from this untoward generation. For, as the same apostle testifieth in another place, even baptism doth also now save us (not the putting away the filth of the flesh, but the answer of a good conscience towards God), by the resurrection of Jesus Christ. Doubt ye not, therefore, but earnestly believe, that he will favorably receive *these* present *persons*, truly repenting and coming unto him by faith; that he will grant *them* remission of *their* sins, and bestow upon *them* the Holy Ghost; that he will give *them* the blessings of eternal life, and *make them partakers* of his everlasting kingdom."

This, I need not add, is in accordance with the sentiments advanced in this essay. What a pity that the Episcopal church does not believe and practice her own creed!

PRESBYTERIAN

The Presbyterian Confession, on Baptism, xxviii., sec. 1, declares that—

"Baptism is a sacrament of the New Testament, ordained by Jesus Christ, not only for the solemn admission of the party baptized into the visible church; but also to be unto him a sign and seal of the covenant of grace, of his engrafting into Christ, of regeneration, of remission of sins, and of his giving up unto God, through Jesus Christ, to walk in newness of life: which sacrament is, by Christ's own appointment, to be continued in his church until the end of the world."

"*A sign and seal of remission of sin!*" This is much nigher the truth than this church seems to be apprized of. However, she can not believe her own creed; for she does not believe that baptism is a sign and a seal of remission of sins, nor of regeneration in her own sense of it, to her baptized or sprinkled infants; but in paying any regard to the Scriptures, she could not say less than she has said. It is no wonder that many sectaries can not be persuaded to think that the Scriptures mean what they say: for they are so much accustomed to say what they do not mean, that they can not think God does mean what he says.

METHODIST

The Methodist Creed says—

"Dearly beloved, forasmuch as all men are conceived and born in sin (and that which is born of the flesh is flesh, and they that are in the flesh can not please God, but live in sin, committing many actual transgressions): and that our Saviour Christ saith, None shall enter into the kingdom of God, except he be regenerate and born anew of water and of the Holy Ghost; I beseech you to call upon God the Father, through our Lord Jesus Christ, that of his bounteous goodness he will grant to *these persons* that which by nature *they* can not have; that *they* may be baptized with water and the Holy Ghost, and received into Christ's holy church, and made lively members of the same."

Then it is ordained that the minister say, or repeat, the following prayer:—

"Almighty and immortal God, the aid of all that need, the helper of all that flee to thee for succor, the life of them that believe, and the resurrection of the dead: We call upon thee for *these persons;* that *they,* coming to thy holy baptism, may receive remission of *their* sins by spiritual regeneration. Receive *them,* O Lord, as thou hast promised by thy well-beloved Son, saying, Ask, and ye shall receive; seek, and ye shall find; knock, and it shall be opened unto you; so give unto us that ask; let us that seek, find; open the gate unto us that knock; that *these persons* may enjoy the everlasting benediction of the heavenly washing, and may come to the eternal kingdom which thou hast promised by Christ our Lord. Amen." (*Dis.*, p. 105.)

Thus the Methodist creed and church are nearly as scriptural as the church from which they sprang. She prays for those to be baptized, that in baptism they may receive the remission of sins! Does she believe what she says?

BAPTIST

Chapter XXX, Section 1.—"Baptism is an ordinance of the New Testament, ordained by Jesus Christ, to be unto the party baptized a sign of his fellowship with him in his death and resurrection; of his being engrafted into him; of remission of sins, and of his giving up unto God, through Jesus Christ, to live and walk in newness of life."

The Baptist follows the Presbyterian church as servilely as the Methodist church follows the English hierarchy. But she avows her faith that immersion is a *sign* of remission. A sign of the past, the present, or the future! A sign accompanying!

The Confession of Bohemia.—"We believe that whatsoever by baptism is in the outward ceremony signified and witnessed, all that doth the Lord God perform inwardly. That is, he washeth away sin, begetteth a man again, and bestoweth salvation upon him; for the bestowing of these excellent fruits was holy baptism given and granted to the church."

The Confession of Augsburg.—"Concerning baptism, they teach that it is necessary to salvation, as a ceremony ordained of Christ, also by baptism the grace of God is offered."

The Confession of Saxony.—"I baptize thee—that is, I do witness that by this dipping thy sins be washed away, and that thou art now received of the true God."

The Confession of Wittenberg.—"We believe and confess that baptism is that sea, into the bottom whereof, as the prophet saith, God doth cast all our sins."

The Confession of Helvetia.—"To be baptized in the name of Christ, is to be enrolled, entered, and received into the covenant and family, and so into the inheritance, of the sons of God; that is to say, to be called the sons of God, to be purged also from the filthiness of sins, and to be endued with the manifold grace of God, and to lead a new and innocent life."

The confession of Sueveland.—"As touching baptism, we confess that it is the font of regeneration washeth away sins, and saveth us. But all these things we do understand as St. Peter doth interpret them. (1 Peter 3:21.)"

Westminster Assembly.—"Before baptism the minister is to use some words of instruction—showing that it is instituted by our Lord Jesus Christ; that it is a seal of the covenant of grace, of our engrafting into Christ, and of our union with him, of remission of sins, regeneration, and life eternal."

The Roman Catholic and the Greek churches say, "We believe in one baptism for the remission of sins."

Calvin makes remission the principal thing in baptism.[1]

"Baptism," says he, "resembles a legal instrument properly attested, by which he assures us that all our sins are cancelled, effaced, and obliterated, so that they will never appear in his sight, or come into his remembrance, or be imputed to us. For he commands all who believe, to be baptized for the remission of their sins.

---

[1] Inst. 1. 4, 115. p. 327.

Therefore, those who have imagined that baptism is nothing more than a mark or sign by which we profess our religion before men, as soldiers wear the insignia of their sovereign as a mark of their profession, have not considered that which was the *principal* thing in baptism; which is, that we ought to receive it with this promise—He that believeth and is baptized shall be saved."

"The ancient Christian church, from the highest antiquity, after the apostolic times, appears generally to have thought that baptism is absolutely necessary for all that would be saved by the grace of Jesus Christ."[1]

"Most of the ancients concluded that baptism was no less necessary unto salvation than faith or repentance itself."[2]

John Wesley, in his comment on the New Testament (p. 250), speaks plainer than either the Methodist Discipline, or the Regular Baptist Confession. His words are:—"Baptism, administered to real penitents, is both a *means* and a *seal* of pardon. Nor did God ordinarily in the primitive church bestow this (pardon) on any, unless through this means." This is almost, if not altogether, as much as we have said on the forgiveness of sins through immersion.

May we not say that we have sustained this last proposition to the full extent of the terms thereof?

With the testimony of John Wesley, the last of the reformers, I close my list of human vouchers for the import of Christian immersion. This list I could swell greatly; for, indeed, I have been quite disappointed in looking back into creeds, councils, commentators, and reformers, ancient and modern. I begin to fear that I shall be suspected to have come to the conclusions which I have exhibited, from consulting human writings, creeds, and reformers. My fears are not that we, who plead for reformation, may appear to have nothing *original* to offer in this reformation; that we are mere gleaners in the fields which other minds have cultivated. It is not on this account our fears are excited, for the reformation we plead is not characterized by new and original ideas and institutions developed in the new institution. But we fear lest any should suspect the views offered to be a human invention or tradition; because we have found so much countenance for them in the works of the most ancient and renowned Christian writers, and the creeds of ancient and modern reformers. We can assure our readers, however, that we have been led to these conclusions by the simple perusal, the unprejudiced and impartial examination, of the New Testament alone. And we may add, that we

---

[1] Vitrings, tom. 1. 50, 2. c. 6, 9.
[2] Owen on Justification, c. 2. p. 183.

are as much astonished as any reader of this essay can be, to find such a cloud of witnesses to the truth and importance of the views offered.

The propositions now proved and illustrated must convince all that there is *some connection* between immersion and the forgiveness of sins. What that connection is, may be disputed by some: but that such a connection exists, none can dispute, who acknowledge the New Testament to contain a divine communication to man. With John Wesley, we say it is "to the believing the *means* and *seal* of pardon for all previous offences"; and we not only say we *think* so, but we preach it as such, and practise it as such. Those who think of any other connection would do well to attempt to form clear ideas of what they mean; for we are assured there is no meaning in any other connection. To make it a commemorative sign of past remission is an outrage upon all rules of interpretation, and a perfect anomaly in all the revelation of God. To make it, prospectively, the sign of a future remission, is liable to the same exceptions. Nothing remains but that it be considered—what it is in truth—the accompanying sign of an accompanying remission; the sign and the seal, or the means and the seal, of remission then granted through the water, connected with the blood of Jesus, by the divine appointment, and through our faith in it.

We have heard some objections, and we can conceive of others which may be presented, to *conversion for the remission of sins.* There can be objections made to any person, doctrine, sentiment, or practice, natural, moral, political, or religious, that ever existed. But, notwithstanding all the objections made to every thing, there are thousands of matters and things we hold to be facts and truths indubitable. Among these certain and sure things, not to be shaken, is the Christian institution.

We will state and examine some objections partially noticed already; but, because they are the most common, or may become common, we will bestow upon them a formal statement and a formal refutation.

Objection 1.—"To make the attainment and the enjoyment of *present salvation*, pardon, justification, sanctification, reconciliation, adoption, dependent upon the contingency of water being present, or accessible, is beneath the dignity and character of a salvation from God."

And to make the attainment and the enjoyment of present salvation, pardon, etc., dependent upon the contingency of faith being present or accessible—upon the blood of Jesus Christ being heard of, or known—is equally objectionable; for what is faith but the belief of testimony? Or what is it in the most popular sense but something wrought in the heart, a compound of knowledge and feeling, of assent and consent? And are not both blood and faith less accessible to mankind than the element of water? How much more water than faith, or than candidates for immersion! And is there not as much power, wisdom, and goodness of God in creating water, as in creating air, words, letters, faith, etc.? Is not water more universal than language, words, books, preachers, faith, etc.? This objection lies as much against any one means of salvation as another; nay, against all means of salvation. Whenever a case shall occur of much faith and little water; or of a little faith and no water, we will repel it by other arguments than these.

Objection 2.—"It makes void the value, excellency, and importance of both faith and grace."

By no means. If a man say, with Paul, we are justified by faith, does it follow that grace is made void? Or if one say we are justified by grace, does it make the blood of Christ of non-effect? Or if, with Paul, a man say we are justified by his blood, does it make faith, repentance, and grace of no effect? Nay, indeed, this gives to faith its proper place and its due value. It makes it the principle of action. It brings us to the water, to Christ, and to heaven. *But it is a principle of action only.* It was not Abel's faith in his head or heart, but Abel's faith at *the altar,* which obtained such reputation. It was not Enoch's faith in principle, but Enoch's faith in his *walk with* God, which translated him to heaven. It was not Noah's faith in God's promise and threatening, but his faith exhibited in *building an ark,* which saved himself and family from the deluge, and made him an heir of a new world, an heir of righteousness. It was not Abraham's faith in God's call, but his *going out* in obedience to that call, that first distinguished him as a pilgrim, and began his reputation. It was not faith in God's promise that Jericho should fall, but that faith carried out in the *blowing of rams' horns,* which laid its walls in ruins, etc. It is not our faith in God's promise of remission, but our *going down* into the water, that obtains the remission of sins. But any one may see why faith has so much praise, and is of so much value. Because, without it, Abel would not have offered more sacrifices than Cain; Enoch would not have walked with God; Noah would not have built an ark; Abraham would not have left Ur of the Chaldees, nor offered his son upon the altar. Without it, Israel would not have passed through the wilderness, nor crossed the Jordan; and without it none receive the remission of their sins in immersion. And again, we would remind the reader that, when he talks of being saved by faith, he should bear in mind that grace is not lost sight of; nor blood, nor water, nor reformation discarded.

We enter the kingdom of nature by being born of the flesh. We enter the kingdom of heaven, or come under the reign of Jesus Christ, in this life, by being born of water and the Spirit. We enter the kingdom of eternal glory by being born again from the earth, and neither by faith, nor the first regeneration. Neither by faith, nor baptism; but by being counted worthy of the resurrection of the just. "I was hungry, and you fed me." Not because you believed, or were born of water; but because "I was hungry, and you fed me," etc.

There are three births, three kingdoms, and three salvations:— one from the grave. We enter a new world on, and not before, each birth. The present animal life, at the first birth; the spiritual, or the life of God in our souls, at the second birth; and the life eternal in the presence of God, at the third birth. And he who dreams of entering the second kingdom, or coming under the dominion of Jesus, without the second birth, may, to complete his error, dream of entering the kingdom of glory without a resurrection from the dead.

Grace precedes all these births—shines in all the kingdoms; but will be glorified in the third. Sense is the principle of action in the first kingdom; faith, in the second; and sight spiritual, in the third. The first salvation is that of the body from the dangers and ills of life; and God is thus "the Saviour of all men." The second salvation is that of the soul from sin. The third is that of both soul and body united, delivered from moral and natural corruption, and introduced into the presence of God, when God shall be all in all.

Objection 3.—"It is so uncharitable to the Protestant Pedobaptists!"

And how uncharitable are the Pedobaptists to the Jews, Turks, and Pagans. Will they promise present salvation from the guilt, pollution, and dominion of sin, with the well-grounded hope of heaven, to Jews, Turks, Pagans, or even Roman Catholics? Or will the Roman Catholics to them? How uncharitable are they who cry "*uncharitable*" to us! Infants, idiots, deaf and dumb persons, innocent Pagans wherever they can be found, with all the pious Pedobaptists, we commend to the mercy of God. But such of them as wilfully *despise* this salvation, and who, having the opportunity to be immersed for the remission of their sins, wilfully *despise* or refuse, we have as little hope for them as they have for all who refuse salvation *on their own terms of the gospel*. While they inveigh against us for laying a scriptural and natural stress upon immersion, do we not see that they lay as great, though an unscriptural and irrational, stress upon their baptism or sprinkling; so much so as to give it, *without faith*, even to infants, so soon as they are born of the flesh?

Objection 4.—"But do not many of them enjoy the present salvation of God?"

How far they may be happy in the peace of God, and the hope of heaven, I presume not to say. And we know so much of human nature as to say, that he that *imagines* himself pardoned will feel as happy as he that is really so. But one thing we do know, that none can *rationally* and with *certainty* enjoy the peace of God, and the hope of heaven, but they who intelligently and in full faith are born of water, or immersed for the remission of their sins. And as the testimony of God, and not conceit, imagination, nor our reasoning upon what passes in our minds, is the ground of our certainty, we see and feel that we have an assurance which they can not have. And we have this advantage over them; we once stood upon their ground, had their hopes, felt their assurance; but they have not stood upon our ground, nor felt our assurance. Moreover, the experience of the first converts shows the difference between their immersion, and the immersion, or sprinklings, of modern gospels.

Objection 5.—"This has been so long concealed from the people, and so lately brought to our view, that we can not acquiesce in it."

This objection would have made unavailing every attempt at reformation, or illumination, of the mind, or change in the condition and enjoyments of society, ever attempted. Besides, do not the experience of all the religious—the observation of the intelligent—the practical result of all creeds, reformations, and improvements—and the expectations and longings of society—warrant the conclusion that either some new revelation, or some new development of the revelation of God, must be made, before the hopes and expectations of all true Christians can be realized, or Christianity save and reform the nations of this world? We want the old gospel back, and sustained by the ancient order of things: and this alone, by the blessing of the Divine Spirit, is all that we do want, or can expect, to reform and save the world. And if this gospel, as proclaimed and enforced on Pentecost, can not do this, vain are the hopes, and disappointed must be the expectations, of the so-called Christian world.

RECAPITULATION

As Christian faith rests upon, and Christian practice proceeds from, *the testimony of God*, and not from the reasonings of men, I will, in this recapitulation, only call up the evidences on one single proposition, assumed, sustained, and illustrated in the preceding pages; and that is the *ninth proposition,* as sustained by the apostolic testimony. We wish to leave before the mind of the intelligent reader the great importance attached to Christian immersion, as presented in the Evangelists, the Acts, and the Epistles.

1. *In the Evangelists*—it is called *the forgiveness of sins.* Matthew and Mark introduce the Messiah in his own person in giving the commission. Luke does not. Matthew presents Jesus saying, "Go, convert the nations, immersing them into the name of the Father, the Son, and the Holy Spirit, teaching them to observe all things which I have commanded you." This, of course, in order to salvation. Mark presents him saying, "Go into all the world, proclaim the glad tidings to the whole creation; and he who believes, and is immersed, shall be saved; but he who believes not shall be condemned." Luke, however, does not introduce the Lord in his own person in giving the charge; but records it, in his own conception of it, in the following words:—that "reformation and forgiveness of sins should be announced in his name to all nations, beginning at Jerusalem." No person, we presume, will question but that Luke thus records the commission; and, if so, then it is indisputable that, as Luke neither mentions faith nor immersion, he substitutes for them the received import of both, when and where he wrote. Metonymically he places repentance, or rather *reformation,* for faith; and *remission of sins,* for immersion. In Luke's acceptation and time forgiveness of sins stood for immersion, and reformation for faith,—the effect for the means or cause. The only reference to the commission found in John occurs 20:21:—"As the Father hath sent me, so send I you; whose sins soever you remit are remitted to them; and whose sins soever you retain are retained." Here is neither faith, repentance, nor baptism; but the object, *remission of sins,* is literally proposed. In the commission, salvation is attached by the Lord Jesus to faith and immersion into his name. He that believes, and is immersed, shall be saved. Thus immersion is taught in the testimonies of Matthew, Mark, Luke, and John.

2. *In the Acts of the Apostles*—Sermon 1, Peter says, "Reform and be immersed, every one of you, in the name of the Lord Jesus, for the remission of your sins, and you shall receive the gift of the Holy Spirit." Sermon 2, he says, "Reform and be converted, that your sins may be blotted out; that seasons of refreshment from the presence of the Lord may come, and that he may send Jesus," etc. In the same discourse he says, "God having raised up his Son Jesus, has sent him to bless you, every one of you, turning from his iniquities." In his third Sermon, recorded Acts 10, he says, "To him all the prophets bear witness, that every one who believes in him shall

receive remission of sins *by his name.*" Paul at Antioch, in Pisidia, declares, that through Jesus was proclaimed the remission of sins; and by him all that believe are justified from all things. Ananias commanded Paul to arise and be immersed, and to wash away his sins, calling upon the name of the Lord. Thus it is spoken of in the Acts of the Apostles.

3. *In the Epistles*—The Romans are said to have been immersed into Christ Jesus—into his death; to have been buried with him, and consequently to have risen with him, and to walk in a new life. The Corinthians are said to have been washed, justified, and sanctified by the name of the Lord Jesus and by the Spirit of our God. The Galatians "were immersed into Christ, and had put him on." The Ephesians were married to Christ, by immersion, as brides were wont to be washed in order to their nuptials. The assembly of the disciples, called *the congregation of the Lord,* making the bride of Christ, were said to be *cleansed* by *the bath of water* and *the word.* The Colossians were *buried with Christ, raised with him,* and are said to have been *forgiven all trespasses,* when they were raised with him, where their resurrection with Jesus and their having all sins forgiven are connected.[1] All the saints are said to be saved by immersion, or "the washing of regeneration and the renewing of the Holy Spirit."[2] The believing Jews had their hearts sprinkled from an evil conscience, and their bodies washed with clean water, or water which made clean. Peter taught all the saints in Pontus, Galatia, Cappadocia, Asia, and Bithynia, that the water of baptism saved them, as the water of the deluge saved Noah in the ark, and that in immersion a person was purged from all his former sins. And John the apostle represents the saved as having "washed their robes and made them white in the blood of the Lamb," and all the baptized little children "as having their sins forgiven." Such are the evidences found in the Epistles. How numerous! how clear! and how unequivocal! Are we not, then, warranted to say, Except a man be regenerated of water, and of the Spirit, he can not enter into the kingdom of God? and that all who, believing, are immersed for the remission of their sins, have the remission of their sins in and through immersion?

CONCLUSION

A word to the regenerated. You have experienced the truth of the promise; and, being introduced by that promise, you have become, like Isaac, children of promise. You heard the testimony of God concerning Jesus of Nazareth, and you believed it. You were,

---

[1] Colossians 2: 11, 13, 14.   [2] Titus 3:5.

in consequence of your faith, so disposed towards the person of Jesus, as to be willing to put yourselves under his guidance. This faith, and this will, brought you to the water. You were not ashamed nor afraid to confess him before men. You solemnly declared you regarded him as God's only Son, and the Saviour of men. You vowed allegiance to him. Down into the water you were led. Then the name of the Holy One upon your faith, and upon your person, was pronounced. You were then buried in the water under that name. It closed itself upon you. In its womb you were concealed. Into the Lord, as in the water, you were immersed. But in the water you continued not. Of it you were born, and from it you came forth, raised with Jesus, and rising in his strength. There your consciences were released; for there your old sins were washed away. And, although you received not the gifts of the Holy Spirit, which confirmed the testimony of the first disciples, you felt the powers of the world to come, were enlightened, and tasted the bounty of God: for seasons of refreshment from the presence of God came upon you. Your hearts were sprinkled from evil consciences, when your bodies were washed in the cleansing water. Then into the kingdom of Jesus you entered. The king of righteousness, of peace and joy, extended his sceptre over you, and sanctified in state and in your whole person, you rejoiced in the Lord with joy unspeakable and full of glory. Being washed, you were sanctified, as well as acquitted. And now you find yourselves under the great advocate, so that sin can not lord it over you; for you always look to the great advocate to intercede for you; and thus, if sin should overtake you, you confess and forsake it, and always find mercy. Adopted thus into the family of God, you have not only received the name, the rank, and the dignity, but also the spirit of a son of God, and find, as such, that you are kings, priests, and heirs of God. You now feel that all things are yours, because you are Christ's and Christ is God's. The hope of the coming regeneration of the heavens and the earth, at the resurrection of the just, animates you. You look for the redemption, the adoption of your bodies, and their transfiguration. For this reason, you purify yourselves even as he is pure. Be zealous, then, children of God; publish the excellencies of him who has called you into this marvellous light and bliss. Be diligent, that you may receive the crown that never fades, and that you may eat of the tree of life, which grows in the midst of the paradise of God. If you suffer with Jesus, you will reign with him. If you should deny him, he will deny you. Add, then, to your faith, courage, knowledge, temperance, patience, brotherly kindness, and universal benevolence; for, if you continue in these things and abound, you shall not be barren nor unfruitful in the knowledge of our Lord and Saviour Jesus Christ. But, should you be deficient in these things, your light will be obscured, and a forgetfulness that you have been purified from your old sins will come upon you. Do, then, brethren, labor to make your calling and election sure; for thus practising you shall never fall, but shall have an easy and abundant entrance into the everlasting kingdom of our Lord and Saviour Jesus Christ.

A word to the unregenerate. Among you are sundry classes of character. Some of you who believe the gospel and are changed in heart, quickened by the Spirit, are not generally ranked among the unregenerate. In the popular sense of this term, you are regenerate. But we use it in its scriptural acceptation. Like Nicodemus, and like Joseph of Arimathea, you believe in Jesus, and are willing to take lessons from him in the chambers. You have confidence in his mission, respect and venerate, and even love, his person; and would desire to be under his government. Marvel not that I say to you, *You must be born again.* Pious as you are supposed to be, and as you may think yourselves to be, unless you are born again you can not enter the kingdom of God. Cornelius and his family were as devout and pious as any of you. "He feared God, gave much alms to the people, and prayed to God continually." Yet, mark it well, I beseech you, it was necessary "to *tell him words* by which himself and his house *might be saved.*" These words were told him: he believed them, and received the Holy Spirit; yet still he must be born again. For a person can not be said to be born again *of any thing which he receives;* and still less of miraculous gifts of the Holy Spirit. He was immersed, and into the kingdom of God he came. He was then saved. You need not ask how or why these things are so. Do as Cornelius did, and then you will think of it in another light,—then you would not for the world be unregenerate. To have the pledge, the promise and seal of God, of the remission of all your sins; to be adopted into his family, and to receive the spirit of a son of God, be assured, my pious friends, are matters of no everyday occurrence; and when you feel yourselves constitutionally invested with all these blessings, in God's own way, you will say "that his ways are not as our ways, nor his thoughts as our thoughts; for as the heavens are higher than the earth, so are his ways higher than our ways, and his thoughts than our thoughts." It is hard to make a slave feel and act as a freeman. As difficult we often find it to make the unregenerate feel and know the value and importance of regeneration. But the regenerate would not be unregenerate for the universe.

God has one way of bestowing every thing. We can not gather grapes off thorns, nor figs off thistles. The reason is, there they do not grow. We can tell no other person why they do not grow there, but that they do not grow there. We can not have any blessing, but in God's own way of giving it. We can not find wool save on the back of the sheep, nor silk save from the worm which spins it from itself. Corn and wheat can not be obtained save from the plants which yield them. Without the plant we can not have the fruit. This is the economy of the whole material system. And in the world of spirits, and spiritual influences, is it not the same? Moral law is as unchangeable as the laws of nature. Moral means and ends are as inseparable as natural means and ends. God can not bestow grace upon the proud, and can not withold it from the humble. He does not do it, and that is enough. He could shower down wheat and corn, and give us rivers of milk and wine, were it a question of mere power. But taking all together, his wisdom, power, and goodness, he can not do it. So neither can he give us faith without testimony, hope without a promise, love without an amiable object, peace without purity, nor heaven without holiness. He can not give to the unborn infant the light of the sun, the vivacity which the air imparts, nor the agility and activity which liberty bestows. He does not do it, and therefore we say, he can not do it. Neither can he bestow the blessings of the reign of heaven upon those who are children of disobedience.

I know how reluctant men are to submit to God's government; and yet they must all bow to it at last. "To Jesus every knee shall bow, and to him every tongue confess." But they will object to bowing *now,* and torture invention for excuses. They will tell me, all that I have said is true of natural and moral means and ends; but immersion is not a moral means, because God forgave sins and saved men before immersion was appointed. "It is a *positive* and not a *moral* institution." And is there no moral influence connected with positive institutions? A written law is a positive institution; for moral law existed before written. But because it has become a positive institution, has its moral power ceased? *The moral influence of all positive institutions is God's will expressed in them.* And it matters not whether it be the *eating* or *not eating* of an apple; the building of an altar, or the building it with or without the aid of iron tools; the offering of a kid, a lamb, a bullock, or a pigeon: it is just as morally binding and has the same moral influence, as "You shall honor your father and mother"; or "You shall not kill." It is *the will of God* in any institution, which gives it all its moral and physical power. No man could now be pardoned as Abel was—as Enoch was—as David was—as the thief upon the cross was. These all lived before the *second* will of God was declared. He took away *"the first will,"* says

Paul, "that he might establish the *second will*," by which we are sanctified! We are not pardoned as were the Jews or the patriarchs. It was not till Jesus was buried and rose again, that an acceptable offering for sin was presented in the heavens. By one offering up of himself, he has perfected the conscience of the immersed or sanctified. Since his oblation, a new institution for remission has been appointed. You need not flatter yourselves that God will save or pardon you except for Christ's sake; and if his name is not assumed by you, if you have not put him on, if you have not come under his advocacy, you have not the name of Christ to plead, nor his intercession on your behalf—and, therefore, for Christ's sake you can not be forgiven. Could Abel, Enoch, Noah, Abraham, Moses, Aaron, think you, if living now,—could they, I ask, find forgiveness at the altar? And will you imagine that he, who honored every institution by Moses, by connecting rewards and punishments with the obedience or disobedience of his commands, will be less jealous for the honor of the institution of his Son? And will that Son, who, for no other purpose than to honor his Father's institution, was immersed in the Jordan, bestow pardon or salvation upon any who refuses to honor him, and him that sent him? He has been graciously pleased to adapt means to ends. He has commanded immersion for the remission of sins; and think you that he will change his institution, because of your stubborn, intractable dispositions? As well, as reasonably, might you pray for loaves from heaven, or manna, because Israel ate in the desert, as to pray for pardon while you refuse the remission of sins by immersion.

Demur not because of the simplicity of the thing. Remember how simple was the eating of the fruit of that tree "whose mortal taste brought death into the world and all our woe." How simple was the rod in the hand of Moses, when stretched over Egypt and the Red Sea! How simple was looking at the brazen serpent! And how simple are all God's institutions! How simple the aliments of nature!—the poisons, too, and their remedies! Where the will of God is, there is omnipotence. It was simple to speak the universe into existence. But God's will gives efficacy to every thing. And obedience ever was, and ever will be, the happiness of man. It is the happiness of heaven. It is God's philanthropy which has given us something to obey. To the angels who sinned he has given no command. It was gracious to give us a command to live—a command to reform—a command to be born again—to live forever. Remember, light and life first came by obedience. If God's voice had not been obeyed, the water would not have brought forth the earth, nor would the sun have blessed it with his rays. The obedience of law was goodness and mercy; but the obedience of faith is favor, and life, and glory everlasting. None to whom this gospel is announced will perish, except those who know not God, and obey not the gospel of his Son. Kiss, then, the Son, lest he be angry, and you perish forever.

To the unregenerate of all classes, whose education and prejudices compel them to assent to the testimony of Matthew, Mark, Luke, John, Paul, Peter, James, and Jude.—You own the mission of Jesus from the bosom of the Eternal—and that is *all* you do! Each of you is living without God, and without hope in the world—aliens from the family of God—of various ranks and grades among men; but all involved in one condemnation, because light has come into the world, and you love darkness, and the works of darkness, rather than light. To live without hope is bad enough; but to live in constant dread of the venegeance of heaven is still worse. But do you not tremble at the word of God?

If you can be saved here or hereafter, then there is no meaning in language, no pain in the universe, no truth in God: death, the grave, and destruction, have no meaning. The frowns of heaven are all smiles, if you perish not in your ways.

But you purpose to bow to Jesus, and to throw yourselves upon his mercy at last. Impious thought! When you have given the strength of your intellect, the vigor of your constitution, the warmth of your affections, the best energies of your life, to the world, the flesh, and the devil, you will stretch out your palsied hand and turn your dim eyes to the Lord, and say, "Lord, have mercy upon me!" The first-fruits and fatlings for the devil, the lame and the blind for God, is the purpose of your heart, and the best resolution you can form!

The thief upon the cross, had he done so, could not have found mercy. It is one thing to have known the way of salvation, assented to it, and to have in deliberate resolution rejected it for the present, with a promise of obeying it at some future period; and to have never known it, nor assented to it, to the end of life. Promise not, then, to yourselves, what has never happened to others. The devil has always said, "You may give *to-morrow* to the Lord—only give me *to-day*." This has been all that he has asked, and this is what you are disposed to give. Promise not *to-morrow* to the Lord, for you will be still less disposed to give it when it comes; and the Lord has not asked you for *to-morrow*. He says, *to-day*, when you shall hear his voice, harden not your hearts. But you say, you are willing to come to the Lord *to-day* if you knew the way, or if you were *prepared!* Well, what does the Lord require of you as *preparation?* He once said, "Let the wicked man forsake his ways, and the unrighteous man his thoughts; and let him turn to the Lord, and he will have mercy upon him; and to our God, for he will abundantly pardon." He says also, "Draw nigh to me, and I will draw nigh to you." "Cleanse your hands, you sinners; and purify your hearts, you men of two souls"; "Wash you, make you clean; put away the evil of your doing"; "Reform and be converted"; "Turn to the Lord"; "Be immersed for the remission of your sins"; and "Submit to the government of Jesus." "What! just as I am?" Pray, how are you? Have you such a persuasion in your heart of the mission of Jesus, as God's own Son and the only Saviour; and have you so much confidence in his personal character, as to be willing to surrender yourself to him for the present and future—for time and eternity? "I have," you say. As one that has heard his voice, I say then, Come and be regenerated, and seasons of refreshment from the Lord will come to you.

"But I thought I ought to feel like a Christian first, and to have the experience of a Christian before I come to the Lord." Indeed! Did the Lord tell you so? "His ministers taught me so." It is hard knowing who are his ministers nowadays. His *commissioned* ministers taught you not so. They were not taught to say so. The Master knew that to wait for health before we went to the physician—to seek for warmth before we approach the fire—to wait till we ceased to be hungry before we approached the table—was not reasonable. And therefore he never asked, as he never expected, any one to feel like a Christian before he was immersed and began to live like a Christian. None but the citizens of any country can experience the good or evil of the government which presides over it. None but the married can experience the conjugal relation and feelings. None but sons and daughters can have the experience of sons and daughters; and none but those who obey the gospel can experience the sweets of obedience. I need not add, that none but the disobedient can experience the pains, the fears, the terrors of the Lord—the shame and remorse which are the first-fruits of the anguish and misery which await them in another world. As the disobedient, who stumble at the word, have the first-fruits of the awful destruction from the presence of the Lord which awaits them, so the obedient have the first-fruits of the Spirit—the salvation of their souls, as an earnest of the salvation to be revealed at the coming of the Lord.

And now let me ask all the unregenerate, What do you propose to yourselves by either delaying or refusing to come to the Lord? Will delaying have any tendency to fit you or prepare you for his salvation? Will your lusts have less power, or sin have less dominion over you, by continuing under their control? Has the intoxicating cup, by indulgence, diminished a taste for it? Has the avarice of the miser been weakened, or cured, by yielding to it? Has any propensity been destroyed by gratifying it, in any other way than as it destroyed the animal system? Can you, then, promise yourselves that, by continuing in disobedience, you will love obedience and be more inclined to submit when you have longer resisted the Spirit of God? Presume not on the mercy of God, but in the way that mercy flows. Grace has its channels, as the waters have their courses; and its path, as the lightning of the clouds. Each has its law, as fixed as the throne of God; and think not God will work a miracle for your salvation.

Think you that the family of Noah could have been saved, if they had refused to enter into the ark? Could the first-born of Israel have escaped the destroying angel, but in houses sprinkled with blood? Or could Israel have escaped the wrath of Pharaoh, but by being immersed into Moses in the cloud and in the sea? These things are written for our admonition, upon whom the consummation of past ages has come. Arise, then, and be immersed and wash away your sins, calling upon the name of the Lord. The *many who refuse grace* will neither prove you wise nor safe in disobedience.

> "Multitudes are no mark
> That you will right be found;
> A few were saved in the ark,
> For many millions drown'd.
> Obey the gospel call,
> And enter while you may;
> Christ's flock have long been small,
> Yet none are safe but they."

EFFECTS OF MODERN CHRISTIANITY[1]

Our greatest objection to the systems which we oppose is their impotency on the heart. Alas! what multitudes of prayerless, saintless, Christless, joyless hearts have crowded Christianity out of the congregations by their experiences before baptism! They seem to have had all their religion before they professed it. They can relate no experience since baptism, comparable to that professed before the "mutual pledge" was tendered and received.

It was the indubitable proofs of the superabundance of this fruit, which caused me first to suspect the far-famed tree of evangelical or-

---

[1] A second essay, called the *"Extra Defended,"* on this same subject, in reply to a pamphlet from Elder Andrew Broaddus, of Virginia, titled the "Extra Examined," appeared in October, 1831. From our Defence, we here insert only four extracts—the subject, as defended, being fully expressed in the preceding essay.

thodoxy. That cold-heartedness—that stiff and mercenary formality —that tithing of mint, anise, and dill—that negligence of mercy, justice, truth, and the love of God, which stalked through the communions of sectarian altars—that apathy and indifference about *"thus saith the Lord"*—that zeal for human prescriptions, and, above all, that willing ignorance of the sayings and doings of Jesus Christ and his apostles, which so generally appeared—first of all created, fostered, and matured my distrust in the reformed systems of evangelical sectaries. Communion, with me, was communion of kindred souls, immersed into one God, that celestial magnet which turns our aspirations and adorations to him who washed us from our sins in his own blood, and made us kings and priests to God.

To sit in the same pew; to gather round the same pulpit; to put our names to the same covenant, or subscription-list; to contribute for a weekly sermon; to lisp the same opinions, extracted from the same creed—always appeared to me unworthy bonds of union or communion, and therefore my soul abhorred them as substitutes for the love of God shed abroad in the heart, for the communion of the Holy Spirit. "If a man would give all the substance of his house as a substitute for love, it should be utterly contemned."

The Divine Philosopher preached reformation by addressing himself to the *heart*. We begin with the heart. "Make the tree good," and then good fruit may be expected. But this appears to be the error of all sects in a greater or less degree; they set about *mending* the heart, as preliminary to that which alone can *create a new heart*. Jesus gives us the philosophy of his scheme in an address to a sinner of that time:—"Your sins," says he, "are forgiven you: go, and sin no more." He first changes the sinner's state, not external, but internal, and then says, *"Go, and sin no more."* He frankly forgave the debt. The sinner loved him.

There was much of this philosophy in the question, *"Who loves most*—he that was forgiven five hundred pence, or he that was forgiven fifty?"* How much does he love who is not forgiven at all? Aye, that question brings us onward a little to the reason why the first act of obedience to Jesus Christ should be baptism into his name, and that for the remission of sins.

But now we speak of the exercises of the heart. While any man believes the words of Jesus, "Out of the heart proceed the actions which defile the man," he can never lose sight of the heart, as the object on which all evangelical arguments are to terminate, and as the *fons et principium*, the fountain and origin, of all piety and humanity.

Once for all, let it be distinctly noted, that we appreciate nothing in religion which tends not directly and immediately, proximately and remotely, to the purification and perfection of the heart. Paul acts the philosopher fully once, and, if we recollect right, but once, in all his writings upon this subject. It has been for many years a favorite topic with me. It is in his first epistle to Timothy:—"Now the end of the commandment [or gospel] is love out of a pure heart —out of a good conscience—out of faith unfeigned." Faith unfeigned brings a person to remission, or to a good conscience; a good conscience precedes, in the order of nature, a pure heart; and that is the only soil in which love, that plant of celestial origin, can grow. This is our philosophy of Christianity—of the gospel. And thus it is the wisdom and power of God to salvation. We proceed upon these as our axiomata in all our reasonings, preachings, writings:—first, unfeigned faith; second, a good conscience; third, a pure heart; fourth, love. The testimony of God, apprehended, produces unfeigned or genuine faith; faith, obeyed, produces a good conscience. This Peter defines to be the use of baptism, the answer of a good conscience. This produces a pure heart, and then the consummation is love—love to God and man.

Paul's order or arrangement is adopted by us as infallible. Testimony—faith unfeigned—remission, or a good conscience—a pure heart—love. Preaching, praying singing, commemorating, meditating, all issue here. "Happy the pure in heart, for they shall see God."

IMMERSION NOT A MERE BODILY ACT

Views of baptism, as a mere external and bodily act, exert a very injurious influence on the understanding and practice of men. Hence many ascribe to it so little importance in the Christian economy. "Bodily exercise," says Paul, "profits little." We have been taught to regard immersion in water, into the name of the Father, the Son, and the Holy Spirit, as an act of the whole man,—body, soul, and spirit. The soul of the intelligent subject is as fully immersed *into the Lord Jesus*, as his body is immersed *in the water*. His soul rises with the Lord Jesus, as his body rises out of the water; and into one spirit with all the family of God is he immersed. It is not like circumcising a Hebrew infant or proselyting to Moses a Gentile adult. The candidate, believing in the person, mission, and character of the Son of God, and willing to submit to him, immediately, upon recognizing him, hastens to be buried with the Lord, and to rise with him, not corporeally, but spiritually, with his whole soul.

Reader, be admonished how you speak of bodily acts in obedience to divine institutions. Remember Eve, Adam, and all transgressors on the one hand. Remember Abel, Noah, Enoch, Moses, Abraham, down to the harlot Rahab, on the other; and be cautious how you speak of bodily acts! Rather remember the sacrifice of a body on Mount Calvary, and talk not lightly of bodily acts. There is no such thing as outward bodily acts in the Christian institution; and less than in all others, in the act of immersion. Then it is that the spirit, soul, and body of man become one with the Lord. Then it is that the power of the Father, Son, and Holy Spirit comes upon us. Then it is that we are enrolled among the children of God, and enter the ark, which will, if we abide in it, transport us to the Mount of God.

JUSTIFICATION ASCRIBED TO SEVEN CAUSES

In examining the New Testament, we find that a man is said to be *"justified by faith* (Rom. 5:1; Gal. 2:16; 3:24); *"justified freely by his grace."* (Rom. 3:24; Titus 3:7); *"justified by his blood"* (Rom. 5:9); *"justified by works"* (James 2:21, 24, 25); *"justified in or by the name of the Lord Jesus"* (1 Cor. 6:11); *"justified by Christ"* (Gal. 2:16); *"justified by knowledge"* (Isa. 53:11). "It is God that justifies" (Rom. 3:33), viz.: by these *seven* means,—by Christ, his name, his blood, by knowledge, grace, faith, and by works. Are these all literal? Is there no room for interpretation here? He that selects *faith* out of *seven* must either act arbitrarily or show his reason; but the reason does not appear in the text. He must reason it out; he must infer it. Why, then, assume that faith *alone* is the reason of our justification? Why not assume that the *name* of the Lord alone is the great matter, seeing his name "is the only name given under heaven by which any man can be saved"; and men "who believe receive *the remission of sins by his name"*;[1] and, especially, because the name of Jesus, or of the Lord, is more frequently mentioned in the New Testament, in reference to all spiritual blessings, than any thing else! Call all these *causes* or *means* of justification, and what then? We have the grace of God for the *moving* cause, Jesus Christ for the *efficient* cause, his blood the *procuring* cause, knowledge the *disposing* cause, the name of the Lord the *immediate* cause, faith the *formal* cause, and works for the *concurring* cause. For example: a gentleman on the seashore describes the wreck of a vessel at some distance from land, driving out into the ocean, and covered with a miserable and perishing sea-drenched crew. Moved by pure philanthropy, he sends his son in a boat to save them. When the boat arrives at the wreck, he invites them in, upon this condition, that they submit to his guidance. A number of the crew stretch out their arms, and, seizing the

---

[1] Acts 10:43.

boat with their hands, spring into it, take hold of the oars, and row to land, while some, from cowardice, and others because of some difficulty in coming to the boat, wait the expectation of a second trip; but before it returned, the wreck went to pieces, and they all perished. The *moving* cause of their salvation who escaped was the good will of the gentleman on the shore; the son, who took the boat, was the *efficient* cause; the boat itself, the *procuring* cause; the knowledge of their perishing condition and his invitation, the *disposing* cause; the seizing the boat with their hands, and springing into it, the *immediate* cause; their consenting to his condition, the *formal* cause; and their rowing to shore, under the guidance of his son, was the *concurring* cause of their salvation. Thus men are justified or saved by grace, by Christ, by his blood, by faith, by knowledge, by the name of the Lord, and by works. But of the *seven* causes, *three* of which are purely instrumental, why choose *one* of the instrumental, and emphasize upon it as the justifying or saving cause, to the exclusion of, or in preference to, the others? Every one in its own place is essentially necessary.

If we examine the word *saved* in the New Testament, we shall find that we are said to be saved by as many causes, though some of them differently denominated, as those by which we are said to be justified. Let us see: we are said to be "saved by grace" (Eph. 2:5); "saved through his life" (Rom. 5:9, 10); "saved through faith" (Eph. 2:8; Acts 16:31); "saved by baptism" (1 Pet. 3:21); or "by faith and baptism" (Mark 16:16; or "by the washing of regeneration and renewal of the Holy Spirit" (Titus 3:5); or "by the gospel" (1 Cor. 15:1); or "by calling upon the Lord," and by "enduring to the end" (Acts 2:21; Rom. 10:13; Matt. 10:22). Here we have salvation ascribed to grace, to Jesus Christ, to his death and resurrection—*three* times to baptism, either by itself or in conjunction, once with faith, and once with the Holy Spirit; to works, or to calling upon the Lord, or to enduring to the end. To these we might add other phrases nearly similar, but these include all the causes to which we have just now alluded. Saved by grace, the *moving* cause; by Jesus, the *efficient* cause; by his death, and resurrection, and life, the *procuring* cause; by the gospel, the *disposing* cause; by faith, the *formal* cause; by baptism, the *immediate* cause; and by enduring to the end, or persevering in the Lord, the *concurring* cause.

PETER IN JERUSALEM, AND PAUL IN PHILIPPI, RECONCILED

Thousands ask Peter, *What shall we do?* The jailer asks Paul, *What shall I do? to be saved,* if the reader pleases. Peter says, "Reform, and be baptized every one of you," etc. Paul answers, "Believe

in the Lord Jesus Christ, and thou shalt be saved, with thy family."
How is this, Paul and Peter? Why do you not preach the same gospel, and answer the same question in the same or similar terms?
Paul, do you preach another gospel to the Gentiles than that Peter
preached to the Jews? What sayest thou, Paul? Paul replies—
"Strike, but hear me. Had I been in Jerusalem on the day of Pentecost, I would have spoken as Peter did. Peter spoke to believing and
penitent Jews; I spoke to an ignorant Roman jailer. I arrested his
attention after the earthquake, by simply announcing that there was
salvation to him and all his family through belief in Jesus."—But why
did you not mention repentance, baptism, the Holy Spirit? "Who told
you I did not?" Luke says nothing about it; and I concluded you
said nothing about them. Luke was a faithful historian, was he not?
"Yes, very faithful; and why did you not faithfully hearken to his account? Does he not immediately subjoin that as soon as I got the
jailer's ear, I *spoke the word of the Lord to him, and to all that were
in his house?*" Why, you reason like a Pedobaptist. You think, do
you, that the jailer's children were saved by his faith! "I spoke the
whole gospel, or word of the Lord, to the jailer and to his family. In
speaking *the word of the Lord,* I mentioned repentance, baptism, remission, the Holy Spirit, the resurrection, judgment, and eternal life:
else why should I have baptized him an all his house, and why
should he have rejoiced afterwards with all his family?" Paul, I beg
your pardon. I will not now interrogate Peter, for I know how he
will answer me: he would say, "Had I been in Philippi, I would have
spoken to an ignorant pagan as Paul did, to show that salvation
flowed through faith in Jesus; and when he believed this and repented, I would *then* have said, Be baptized for the remission of your
sins."

REGENERATION

"I create new heavens and a new earth." (Isa. 65:18.)
"Behold, I make all things new." (Rev. 21:5.)

We intend an essay full of "the seeds of things." The topic is a common one, a familiar one, and yet it is an interesting one. Much has been said, much has been written upon it; and yet it is no better understood than it ought to be. Few give themselves the trouble of thinking much on the things which they think they understand; and many would rather follow the thoughts of others than think for themselves. Suspense is painful, much study is a weariness of the flesh; and, therefore, the majority are content with the views and opinions handed to them from those who have gone before.

We wish to treat this subject as if it were a new one; and to examine it now as if we had never examined it before. It is worthy of it. Generation is full of wonders, for it is full of God's physical grandeur; yet regeneration is still more admirable, for in it the moral attributes of Jehovah are displayed. But we aim not at a development of its wonders, but at a plain, common-sense, scriptural exposition of its import.

We have not learned our theology from Athanasius, nor our morality from Seneca; and, therefore, we shall not call upon them for illustration, argument, or proof. To the Sacred Records, in which alone Christianity yet remains in all its freshness, we look for light; and thither would we direct the eyes of our readers. It is not the regeneration of the schools— in which Christianity has been lowered, misapprehended, obscured, and adulterated—of which we are to write; but that regeneration of which Jesus spoke, and the apostles wrote.

A few things must be premised—a few general views expressed —before we, or our readers, are prepared for the more minute details: and, to approach the subject with all unceremonious despatch, we observe, that—

Man unregenerate is ruined in body, soul, and spirit; a frail and mortal creature. From Adam his father he inherits a shattered constitution. He is the child of a fallen progenitor, a scion from a degenerate stock.

Superior to Adam, the exile from Eden, in physical, intellectual, and moral nature, none of his descendants can rise. It is not in nature to improve itself; for above its fountain the stream can not rise.

Cain, the first-born of Eve, was in nature the image and likeness of him that begat him. Education failed to improve him, while Abel, his younger brother, obtained the excellency which faith in God's promise alone bestows. The first-born, it will be conceded, was at least equal to his younger brother; and who can plead that in nature he excels Eve's eldest son?

Man in his ruins is, however, a proper subject of a remedial system. He is susceptible of renovation. Therefore God has placed him under a regenerating economy. This economy contemplates the regeneration of the whole human constitution, and proposes as its consummation the transformation of spirit, soul, and body. The destiny of the regenerate is described by Paul in one sentence:—"As we now bear the image of the earthly Adam, we shall then bear the image of the heavenly Adam."

God's own Son is proposed as a model. Conformity to him in glory, honor, and immortality, as the perfection of the regenerate, is the predestination of him who speaks of things that are not, as though they were.

Regeneration is, therefore, moral and physical: or, in other words, there is now a renovation of the mind—of the understanding, will, and affections—and there will hereafter be a renovation of the body: —"For this corruptible body shall put on incorruption, and this mortal body shall put on immortality."

The renovation of the mind and character is, therefore, that moral regeneration which is to be effected in this life; for which the remedial system, or kingdom of heaven, was set up on earth; and this, therefore, first of all, demands our attention.

Before we attempt an answer in detail to the question, *How is this moral regeneration effected?* we shall attend to the principle on which the whole remedial system proceeds. The grand principle, or means which God has adopted for the accomplishment of this moral regeneration, is the full demonstration and proof of a single proposition addressed to the reason of man. This sublime proposition is *that God is love.*

The reason and wisdom of this procedure will suggest itself to every one who can understand the views and feelings of all unregenerated men. Man, in a state of alienation and rebellion, naturally suspects, that if he be a sinner, and if God hate sin, he must hate him. As love begets love, so hatred begets hatred; and if a sinner suspects that God hates him, he can not love God. He must know that God loves him, before he can begin to love God. "We," says an apostle, "love God because he first loved us." While alienated in heart, through the native darkness of his understanding, the sinner misinterprets every restraint which God has placed in his way to prevent his total ruin as indications of the wrath of Heaven. His transgression of these restraints, and his consciousness of having defied the veracity and power of God, only increase his enmity, and urged him onward to his apostasy and wanderings from his Creator. The goodness of God, being misunderstood, furnishes to him no incentive to repentance and reformation. Guilt, and fear, and shame, the fruits of his apostasy, becloud his understanding, and veil from his eyes all the demonstrations of benevolence and goodness with which the creation abounds. Adam, under a tree, hiding from God, trembling with fear, suspicious of the movements of every leaf, and covered with shame as with a garment, is both an illustration and proof of these views of the state of mind which obtains in the unregenerate.

Neither the volume of creation, nor that of God's providence, is sufficient to remove from the natural man these misconceptions and the consequent alienation of heart. The best proof that these two volumes can not do this is, that they never have, in any one instance, yet done it. From the nature of things it is indeed evident that they can not do it. The elements are too often at war with the happiness of man. The ever-changing attitude of the natural world, in reference to health, and life, and comfort, render it at best doubtful whether the laws of nature, which ultimately bring man down to the grave, are the effect of benevolence or of malevolence towards mankind. A third volume explanatory of both, and replete also with supernatural developments, is wanting, to furnish the most diligent student of nature and providence with the means of learning the true and full character of him against whom we have rebelled.

That volume is the Bible. Holy prophets and apostles spake as they were moved by the Spirit of knowledge and revelation. Its records, its history, its prophecy, its precepts, its laws, its ordinances, and its examples, all develop and reveal God to man and man to himself.

But it is in the person and mission of the Incarnate Word that we learn that *God is love.* That God gave his Son for us, and yet gives his Spirit to us—and thus gives us himself—are the mysterious and transcendent proofs of the most august proposition in the universe. The gospel, heaven's wisdom and power combined, God's own expedient for the renovation of human nature, is neither more nor less than the illustration and proof of this regenerating proposition.

Thus we hasten to our subject. Having glanced at the great landmarks of the plantations of nature and grace, now that we may, in the light of truth, ascertain the true and heaven-taught doctrine of regeneration, we shall cautiously survey the whole process, as developed by the commissioned teachers of the deep counsels of the only true God.

That certain things, parts of this great progress, may be well understood, certain terms, which we are wont to use to represent them, must be well defined, and accurately apprehended. These terms are *Fact, Testimony, Faith, Repentance, Reformation, Bath of Regeneration, New Birth, Renewing of the Holy Spirit, Newness of Life.*[1]

"All things are of God" in the regeneration of man, is our motto; because our apostle affirmed this as a cardinal truth. He is the author of the *facts* and of the *testimony* which declares them; and, being the author of these, he is the author of all the effects produced by these facts. The Christian is a new *creation*, of which God is the *Creator*. The change of heart and of character, which constitutes moral regeneration, is the legitimate impression of the facts or things which God has wrought. The facts constitute the moral seal which stamps the image of God upon man. In the natural order, we must place them first, and, therefore, we must first define the term

REPENTANCE

Repentance is usually defined "*sorrow for any thing that is past*"; and in the religious vocabulary it is simply "*sorrow for sin.*" This is one, but it is only one, of the natural effects of the belief of the testimony of God. The gospel facts, testimony, and faith contemplate more than this. But yet it is necessary that this point of faith should be distinctly apprehended, especially in this age, when it occupies so large a space in the systems of theology.

Repentance, in our current acceptation, is sorrow for sin; and certainly there is no man who believes the revealed facts found in the testimony of God, who will not be sorry for his sins. But simple sorrow for the past is but a feeling of the heart; which, unless it excite to reformation or the abandonment of sin, is of no more use than the regrets of Judas after he had sold his Master for fifteen dollars. Repentance must, however, precede reformation; for unless we are sorry for the past, and grieved with ourselves, we will not think of a change of conduct. Repentance is to reformation what motive is to action, or resolution to any undertaking. It was well for David to resolve to build the temple; and so it is well to form any good design; but much better to execute it. To feel sorry for the poor and the afflicted, and to resolve to assist and comfort them, is well; but to go

---

[1] For Fact, Testimony and Faith, see pp. 89-105.

and do it is better; and, indeed, unless our sorrow for the past terminate in reformation for the future, it is useless in the estimation of heaven and earth; as useless as to say to the hungry, Be filled; or to the naked, Be clothed.

Genuine repentance does not always issue in reformation. Judas was sorrowful even to death, but could not reform. Many have been so genuinely sorry for their sins as to become suicides. Speak we of "a godly sorrow"? No: this is not to be expected from unconverted and ungodly persons. Christians, Paul teaches, when they err, may repent with a godly sorrow; but this is not to be expected from the unregenerate, or from those who have not reformed. It is not, then, the genuineness of repentance that is to be appreciated, unless by genuine repentance is meant more than simple sorrow for the past— unless by genuine repentance is meant reformation. Yet without sincere or unfeigned repentance, there can not be real or genuine reformation.

This leads us to observe, that the only unequivocal evidence of sincere repentance is the actual redress of the injury done; not only a cessation from the sin, but a restitution for the sin, as far as restitution can possibly be made. *No restitution, no repentance—provided restitution can be made.* And I may be permitted to add, *that without repentance and restitution, when possible, there can be no remission.*

The preachers of repentance—of the necessity of repentance in order to remission—ought to set this matter fairly and fully before sinners. Do they represent repentance as sorrow for the past, and a determination to reform? How, then, will the sinner know that he is sorry for his sins against men, or how will the community know that he has repented of such sins, unless full restitution was made? It is impossible that either the sinner himself, or the community who know his sins against man, can have any certain evidence that he is penitent, unless by making all possible restitution.

Peccator wounded the reputation of his neighbor Hermas, and on another occasion defrauded him of ten pounds. Some of the neighborhood were apprized that he had done both. Peccator was converted under the preaching of Paulinus, and, on giving in a relation of his sorrow for his sins, spoke of the depth of his convictions, and of his abhorrence of his transgressions. He was received into the congregation, and sat down with the faithful to commemorate the great sin-offering. Hermas and his neighbors were witnesses of all this. They saw that Peccator was penitent, and much reformed in his behavior; but they could not believe him sincere, because he had made no restitution. They regarded him either as a hypocrite or self-de-

ceived; because, having it in his power, he repaid not the ten
pounds, nor once contradicted the slanders he had propagated.
Peccator, however, felt little enjoyment in his profession, and soon
fell back into his former habits. He became again penitent, and, on
examining the grounds of his falling off, discovered that he had never
cordially turned away from his sins. Overwhelmed in sorrow for the
past, he resolved on giving himself up to the Lord; and, reflecting on
his past life, set about the work of reformation in earnest. He called
on Hermas, paid him his ten pounds, and the interest for every day
he had kept it back; went to all the persons to whom he had slan-
dered him, told them what injustice he had done him, and begged
them, if they had told it to any other persons, to contradict it.
Several other persons whom he had wronged in his dealings with
them he also visited; and fully redressed all these wrongs against his
neighbors. He also confessed them to the Lord, and asked him to forgive him. Peccator was then restored to the church; and, better still,
he enjoyed a peace of mind, and a confidence in God, which was a
continual feast. His example, moreover, did more to enlarge the congregation at the Cross-roads than did the preaching of Paulinus in a
whole year. This was, unequivocally, *sincere* repentance.

This is the repentance which Moses preached, and which Jesus
approbated. Under the law, confession to the priest, and the presenting of a trespass-offering, availed nothing to forgiveness without
restitution. But the law went into details still more minute than
these; for provision is made for the case in which the sinner could
not find the person against whom he had sinned. In such a case, the
penitent sinner was to seek out the kindred of the injured party, and
if he could find any kinsman he was to recompense this kinsman; but
if he could not find a kinsman, he must recompense it to the Lord,
besides offering his trespass-offering. It was to go into the Lord's
treasury.[1] The principle uniformly, in all cases of sin against man,
was, the sinner "shall make amends for the harm he has done, and
shall add the fifth part thereto."[2]

If any one suppose that repentance is to be less sincere or unequivocal under the gospel, let him remember that Zaccheus proposed
more than adding a fifth; he would restore fourfold; and that Jesus
approbated him for so doing. Indeed, John the Immerser demanded
fruits worthy of repentance or reformation, and Paul proclaimed that
those who turned to God should do works meet for, or worthy of, repentance.[3]

"Works worthy of repentance" is a phrase which can be under-

---

[1] Numbers 5:7, 8.   [2] Leviticus 5:16.   [3] Acts 26:20.

stood in no other sense than those works which make amends for the harm done to men and the dishonor done to God, as far as both are possible. Can any man think that he is sorry for that sin or wrong which he has done, when he makes no effort to make amends to him who was injured in person, character, or property, by it? Works worthy of his professed repentance are wanting, so long as any being whom he has injured in person, property, or reputation, is unredressed to the utmost extent of his ability.

One of our most popular commentators says—and with much truth—"No man should expect mercy at the hand of God, who, having wronged his neighbor, refuses, when he has it in his power, to make *restitution*. Were he to weep tears of blood, both the justice and mercy of God would shut out his prayer, if he make not his neighbor amends for the injury he has done him. He is a dishonest man who illegally holds the property of another in his hands."[1]

Every preacher of repentance should insist upon these evidences of sincerity, both for the satisfaction of the penitent himself, and for the good of the community. "Many that believed came and confessed, and showed their deeds; many of them, also, who used curious arts, bringing their books together, burnt them before all; and they computed the value of them and found it fifty thousand pieces of silver."[2] This was making restitution, in their case, as far as possible; and the principle here evinced is applicable in every other case.

But, in pursuing this subject so far, we have passed over the boundaries of repentance, and sometimes confounded it with reformation. This is owing to the licentious use of language, to which modern theology has so richly contributed. We shall, however, redress this wrong, as far as practicable, by a few remarks on

REFORMATION

The word *metanoia*, used by the sacred writers and heaven-taught preachers of the new economy, as indicative of the first effect of faith, as has been often shown, is different from that which our word *repentance* fitly represents. It literally imports *a change of mind;* but, as Parkhurst, Campbell, and many others say, "such a change of mind as influences one's subsequent behavior for the better." "It has been observed by some, and I think with reason, that the former (*metanoeo*) denotes properly a change to the better; the latter (*metamelomai*) barely a change, whether to the better or to the worse; that the former marks a change of mind that is durable,

---

[1] Adam Clarke on Genesis 11:2.   [2] Acts 19:18-20.

and produces consequences; the latter expresses only a present uneasy feeling of regret, without regard to duration or effects: in fine, that the first may be translated into English *I reform;* the second, *I repent,* in the familiar acceptation of the words. Now as every one who reforms *repents,* but as every one who repents does *not reform,* this distinction is necessary and proper, and there is nothing hazarded, nothing lost, by translating the former, *I reform,* and the latter, *I repent.* There is something gained, especially in all places where we have the word in the imperative mood, because then it is of importance to know precisely what is intended. If we are commanded only to change our mind, or to be sorry for the past, we have obeyed when we feel regret; but if more than mere change of mind or regret is intended, we have not obeyed the commandment, until we change for the better. Now, it is we think, very evident from various passages of the sacred writings of the apostles, and from their speeches, that they commanded more than a simple change of mind as respected past conduct, or mere sorrow for the past. Peter commanded the thousands assembled on the day of Pentecost, who had changed their minds, and who were sorry for the past, to do something which they had not yet done; and that something is in the common version rendered *repent;* and in the new version, *reform;* and in the old English Bible, *amend your lives.* The word here used is the imperaive of *metanoeo.* Judas repented, and many like him, who never reformed; and, therefore, it is of importance that this distinction should be kept in view.[1]

Repentance is not reformation, but it is necessary to it; for whoever reforms must first repent. Reformation is, indeed, the carrying out of the purpose into our conduct. But, as reformation belongs rather to another part of our essay than the present, we shall, on the premises already before us, pause and offer a few reflections.

In the preceding definition of words and ideas, it would appear that we have a literal and unfigurative representation of the whole process of what is figuratively called *regeneration.* For, as we shall soon see, the term *regeneration* is a figure of speech which very appropriately, though analogically, represents the reformation or renovation of life of which we have now spoken.

That the preceding arrangement is not arbitrary, but natural and necessary, the reader will perceive, when he reflects, that the thing done, or the fact, must precede the report or testimony concerning it; that the testimony concerning it must precede the belief of it; that belief of the testimony must precede any feeling correspondence with

---

[1] See Family Testament, Note 30, page 74.

the fact testified; and that feeling must precede action in conformity to it. Fact, testimony, faith, feeling, action, are therefore bound together by a natural and gracious necessity, which no ingenuity can separate. And will not every Christian say, that when a person *feels* and *acts* according to the faith, or the testimony of God, he is a new creature—regenerate—truly converted to God? He that believes that facts testified in the record of God understands them feels according to their nature and meaning, and acts in correspondence with them—has undergone a change of heart and of life which makes him a new man.

This is that moral change of heart and life which is figuratively called *regeneration.* We are not to suppose that regeneration is something which must be added to the faith, the feeling, and the action or behavior, which are the effects of the testimony of God understood and embraced; or which are the impress of the divine facts attested by prophets and apostles. It is only another name for the same process in all its parts.

It may also be observed, that numerous figures and analogies are used by the inspired writers to set forth this change, as well as other leading truths and lessons in the Bible. In their collective capacity Christians are called a kingdom, a nation, a generation, a family, a house, a flock, a city, a temple, a priesthood, etc. In their individual capacity, they are called kings, priests, soldiers, citizens, children, sheep, branches, stones, etc. They are said to be begotten, born, regenerated, builded, engrafted, converted, created, planted. Now, under whatever figure they are considered or introduced, reason argues that everything said of them should be expressed in conformity with the figure under which they are presented. Are they called *sheep?*—then he that presides over them is called a *Shepherd;* their enemies are *wolves* and *dogs;* their sustenance is the *green pasture;* their place of safety and repose, the *sheepfold;* their errors are *wanderings* and *strayings;* their conversion, a *return;* and their good behavior, a *hearing of the voice,* or a *following,* of the Shepherd. Are they called *children?*—then collectively they are a *family;* they are *begotten* and *born again; God is their Father;* their separation is an *adoption;* Jesus is their *elder brother;* they are *heirs* of God; they *live* and *walk* with God. Are they *priests?*—Jesus is their *High-Priest;* the church, their *temple;* the Saviour is their *altar;* their songs, their praises, are *incense* ascending to heaven; and their oblations to the poor, their works of love, are *sacrifices* most acceptable to God. Are they called *citizens?*—the church is then *the kingdom of heaven; Jerusalem is the mother of them all;* formerly they were *aliens,* and their naturalization is *regeneration.* Are they called *branches?*—then

Jesus is the *true vine;* his Father, the *vine-dressser;* their union with Christ, an *engrafting;* the discipline of the gospel, a *pruning;* and their good works are *fruits of righteousness.*

Thus there is no confusion of metaphor in the Scriptures of truth —in the dialect of heaven. It is the language of Ashdod, it belongs to the confusion of Babel, to mingle and confound all figures and analogies. Hence we so often hear of *being born again,* without any allusion to a family or a kingdom! Had a modern assembly of divines been employed to accommodate the Scripture style to their orthodox sentiments, we should not have had to read all the Old Testament and all the historic books of the New, to find the subject of regeneration but once proposed to an alien, as the fact is; but then we should have found it in the history of Abel, of Enoch, of Noah, and of Abraham, if not in every section of the law of Moses, in the Prophets, and in the Psalms. John the Baptist, Jesus, and the holy twelve, would have had it in every sermon; and true faith would have been always defined as the fruit of regeneration.

But Jesus had a *kingdom* in his eye in his discourse, before he ever mentioned being "born again" to Nicodemus; for unless there was a family, a state, or a kingdom to be born into, it is impossible for any one to be born into it. And if the kingdom of heaven only began to be after Jesus entered into heaven; or if it was only approaching from the ministry of John to the day of Pentecost, then it would have been preposterous indeed—an incongruity of which no inspired man was ever guilty—to call any change of heart or life *a regeneration,* or *a new birth.* It is true that good men in all ages were made such by facts, testimony, faith, and feeling, by a change of heart, by the Spirit of God; but the *analogy,* or *figure* of being *born,* or of being *regenerated,* only began to be preached, when the kingdom of heaven began to be preached and men began to press into it.

We are now, perhaps, better prepared to consider the proper import and meaning of *"regeneration"* in general, and of *"the bath of regeneration"* in particular.

REGENERATION

This word is found but twice in all the oracles of God—once in Matthew 19:28, and once in Titus 3:5. In the former it is almost universally understood to mean *a new state of things,* not of *persons* —a peculiar era, in which all things are to be made new:—such as the formation of a new church on the day of Pentecost, or the commencement of the milennium, or the general resurrection. The biblical critics of eminence have assigned it to one or other of these great changes in the state of things. So we use the word *revolution*, and the phrase *the Revolution*, to express a change in the political state of things. The most approved punctuation and version of this passage renders it altogether evident that a new era is alluded to. "Jesus answered, Indeed, I say unto you, that at the renovation [regeneration] when the Son of Man shall be seated on his glorious throne, you, my followers, sitting also upon twelve thrones, shall judge the twelve tribes of Israel." This being so evident, and so often alluded to in our former writings, we shall proceed to the remaining occurrence, Titus 3:5.

All the new light which we propose to throw on this passage will be gathered from an examination of the acceptation of the word *generation* in the sacred writings. Our reason for this is, that we object to a peremptory decision of the meaning of a word which occurs only in the passage under discussion, from our reasonings upon the isolated passages in which it is found. In such a case, if we can not find the whole word in any parallel passages, the proper substitute is the root or branches of that word, so far as they are employed by the same writers. Moreover, we think it will be granted, that, whatever may be the scriptural acceptation of the word *generation*, regeneration is only the repetition of that act or process.

After a close examination of the passages in which *generation* occurs in the writings of the Hebrew prophets and apostles, we find it used only in two acceptations—as descriptive of the whole process of creation and of the thing created. A race of men, or a particular class of men, is called a *generation;* but this is its figurative rather than its literal meaning. Its literal meaning is the formation or creation of anything. Thus it is first used in the Holy Scriptures. Moses calls the creation, or whole process of formation of the heavens and the earth, "The *generations* of the heavens and the earth."[1] The account of the formation of Adam and Eve, and also the account of the creations of Adam and Eve, are, by the same writer, called "The book or record of the *generations* of Adam."[2] This is the literal import of the word; consequently, *regeneration* literally indicates the whole process of renovating or new-creating man.

This process may consist of numerous distinct acts; but it is in accordance with the general usage to give to the beginning or consummating act the name of the whole process. For the most part, however, the name of the whole process is given to the consummating act, because the process is always supposed incomplete until that act

---

[1] Genesis 2:4.   [2] Genesis 5:1.

is performed. For example: In the process of tanning, fulling, forging, etc., the subject of these operations is not supposed to be tanned, fulled, forged, until the last act is performed. So in all the processes of nature—in the animal, vegetable, and mineral kingdoms—the last act consummates the process. To all acquainted with the process of animalization, germination, crystallization, etc., no further argument is needed. But in the style of our American husbandmen, no crop or animal is *made,* until it come to maturity. We often hear them say of a good shower, or a few clear days, "This is the *making* of the wheat or corn." In the same sense it is, that most Christians call *regeneration* the *new birth;* though *being born* is only the last act in natural generation, and the last act in regeneration.

In this way the *new birth* and *regeneration* are used indiscriminately by commentators and writers on theology, and, by a figure of speech, it is justified on well-established principles of rhetoric. This leads us to speak particularly of

THE BATH OF REGENERATION

By "the bath of regeneration" is not meant the first, second, or third act; but the last act of regeneration, which completes the whole, and is, therefore, used to denote the new birth. This is the reason why our Lord and his apostles unite this act with water. Being *born of water,* in the Saviour's style, and *the bath of regeneration,* in the apostles' style, in the judgment of all writers and critics of eminence, refer to one and the same act—viz.: Christian baptism. Hence it came to pass, that *all the ancients* (as fully proved in our first Extra on Remission) used the word *regeneration* as synonymous in signification with *immersion.* In addition to the numerous quotations made in our Essay on Remission, from the creeds and liturgies of Protestant churches, we shall add another from the Common Prayer (?) of the Church of England, showing unequivocally that the learned doctors of that church used the words *regeneration* and *baptism* as synonymous. In the address and prayer of the minister after the baptism of the child, he is commanded to say,—

"Seeing now, dearly beloved brethren, that this child is regenerate, and grafted into the body of Christ's church, let us give thanks unto Almighty God for these benefits, and with one accord make our prayer unto him that this child may lead the rest of his life according to this beginning."

"Then shall be said, all kneeling,—

"We yield thee hearty thanks, most merciful Father, that it hath pleased thee to regenerate this infant with thy Holy Spirit, to receive him for thine own child by adoption, and to incorporate him into thy holy church. And humbly we beseech thee to grant that he, being dead unto sin, and living unto righteousness, and being buried with Christ in his death, may crucify the old man, and utterly abolish the whole body of sin; and that as he is made partaker of the death of thy Son, he may also be partaker of his resurrection; so that finally, with the residue of the holy church, he may be an inheritor of thine everlasting kingdom, through Christ our Lord. Amen."

Eusebius, in his life of Constantine, page 628, shows that St. Cyprian, St. Athanasius, and, indeed, all the Greek Fathers, did regard baptism as the consummating act; and therefore they call it *teliosis*, the consummation. These authorities weigh nothing with us; but, as they weigh with our opponents, we think it expedient to remind them on which side the Fathers depose in the case before us. By these quotations we would prove no more than that the ancients *understood* the washing of regeneration, and indeed used the term *regeneration*, as synonymous with baptism.

But were we asked for the precise import of the phrase *washing* or *bath* of *regeneration*, either on philological principles, or as explained by the apostles, we would give it as our judgment, that the phrase is a circumlocution or periphrasis for water. It is *loutron*, a word which more properly signifies the vessel that contains the water, than the water itself; and is, therefore, by the most learned critics and translators, rendered *bath*, as indicative either of the vessel containing the fluid, or of the use made of the fluid in the vessel. It is, therefore, by a metonymy, that water of baptism, or the water in which we are regenerated. Paul was a Hebrew, and spoke in the Hebrew style. We must learn that style before we fully understand the apostle's style. In other words, we must studiously read the Old Testament before we can accurately understand the New. What more natural for a Jew accustomed to speak of "the water of purification," of "the water of separation,"[1] than to speak of "the bath of regeneration"? If the phrase "water of purification" meant water used for the purpose of purifying a person—if "the water of separation" meant water used for separating a person—what more natural than that "the bath of regeneration" should mean water for regenerating a person?

But the New Testament itself confirms this exposition of the phrase. We find the word *loutron* once more used by the same apostle, in the same connection of thought. In his letter to the Ephesians, he affirms that Jesus has sanctified (separated, purifed with the

---

[1] See Numbers 8:7; 19:9, 13, 20, 21; 31:23.

water of purification) the church by a *loutron* of water—"a bath of water, with the word"—"having cleansed it by a bath of water, with the word."[1] This is still more decisive. The king's translators, so fully aware that the sense of this passage agrees with Titus 3:5, have, in both places, used the word *washing*, and Macknight the term *bath*, as the import of *loutron*. What is called the *washing* or *bath of regeneration*, in the one passage, is in the other, called "the washing" or "bath of water." What is called *saved* in one is called *cleansed* in the other; and what is called *the renewal of the Holy Spirit* in the one is called *the word* in the other; because the Holy Spirit consecrates or cleanses through the word. For thus prayed the Messiah, "Consecrate them through the truth: thy word is the truth." And again, "You are clean through the word that I have spoken unto you."

To the same effect, Paul to the Hebrew Christians, says, "Having your hearts sprinkled from a guilty conscience, and your bodies washed with pure water"—the water of purification, the water of regeneration: (for the phrase "pure water" must be understood, not of the quality of the water, but metonymically of the effect, the cleansing, the washing, or the purifying of the person)—"having your bodies or persons *washed* with pure water," or water that purifies or cleanses.

No one, acquainted with Peter's style, will think it strange that Paul represents persons as *saved*, *cleansed*, or *sanctified* by water; seeing Peter unequivocally asserts that "we are saved" through water, or through baptism, as was Noah and his family through water and faith in God's promise. "The antitype immersion does also now save us."

Finally, our great prophet, the Messiah, gives to water the same place and power in the work of regeneration. For when speaking of being *born again*—when explaining to Nicodemus *the new birth*, he says, "Except a man be *born of water* and of the Spirit, he can not enter into the kingdom of God." May not we, then, supported by such high authorities, call that water of which a person is born again, the water or bath of regeneration?

NEW BIRTH

We have already seen that the consummation of the process of generation or creation is in the birth of the creature formed. So it is in the moral generation, or in the great process of regeneration. There is a state of existence from which he that is born passes; and there is a state of existence into which he enters after birth. This is true of the whole animal creation whether oviparous or viviparous.

---

[1] Ephesians 5:26.

Now the manner of existence, or the mode of life, is wholly changed; and he is, in reference to the former state, dead, and to the new state, alive. So in moral regeneration. The subject of this great change, before his new birth, existed in one state; but after it he exists in another. He stands in a new relation to God, angels, and men. He is now born of God, and has the privilege of being a son of God, and is consequently pardoned, justified, sanctified, adopted, saved. The state which he left was a state of condemnation, what some call "the state of nature." The state into which he enters is a state of favor, in which he enjoys all the heavenly blessings through Christ: therefore, it is called "the kingdom of heaven." All this is signified in his death, burial, and resurrection with Christ; or in his being born of water. Hence the necessity of being buried with Christ in water, that he may be born of water, that he may enjoy the renewal of the Holy Spirit, and be placed under the reign of favor.

All the means of salvation are means of enjoyment, not of procurement. Birth itself is not for procuring, but for enjoying, the life possessed before birth. So in the analogy:—no one is to be baptized, or to be buried with Christ; no one is to be put under the water of regeneration for the purpose of *procuring* life, but for the purpose of *enjoying* the life of which he is possessed. If the child is never born, all its sensitive powers and faculties can not be enjoyed; for it is after birth that these are fully developed and feasted upon all the aliments and objects of sense in nature. Hence all that is *now* promised in the gospel can only be *enjoyed* by those who are born again and placed in the kingdom of heaven under all its influences. Hence the philosophy of that necessity which Jesus preached:—"Unless a man be born again, he can not discern the kingdom of heaven," —unless a man be born of water and the Spirit, he can not enter into it.

But let no man think that in the act of being born, either naturally or metaphorically, the child purchases, procures, or merits either life or its enjoyments. He is only by his birth placed in circumstances favorable to the enjoyment of life, and all that makes life a blessing. "To as many as receive him, believing in his name, he grants the privilege of being children of God, who derive their birth not from blood, nor from the desire of the flesh, nor from the will of man, but from God."

RENEWING OF THE HOLY SPIRIT

"He has saved us," says the apostle Paul, "by the bath of regeneration and the *renewing of the Holy Spirit,* which he poured on us richly through Jesus Christ our Saviour; that, being justified by his favor [in the bath of regeneration] we might be made heirs according to the hope of eternal life." Thus, and not by works of righteousness, he has saved us. Consequently, being born of water and the renewing of the Holy Spirit are not works of merit or of righteousness, but only the means of enjoyment. But this pouring out of the influences, this renewing of the Holy Spirit, is as necessary as the bath of regeneration to the salvation of the soul, and to the enjoyment of the hope of heaven, of which the apostle speaks. In the kingdom into which we are born of water, the Holy Spirit is as the atmosphere in the kingdom of nature; we mean that the influences of the Holy Spirit are as necessary to *the new life,* as the atmosphere is to our animal life in the kingdom of nature. All that is done in us before regeneration, God our Father effects by *the word,* or the gospel as dictated and confirmed by his Holy Spirit. But after we are thus begotten and born by the Spirit of God—after our new birth—the Holy Spirit is shed on us richly through Jesus Christ our Saviour; of which the peace of mind, the love, the joy, and the hope of the regenerate is full proof; for these are among the fruits of that Holy Spirit of promise of which we speak. Thus commences

THE NEW LIFE

Newness of life is a Hebraism for a *new life.* The new birth brings us into a new state. "Old things have passed away; all things have become new," says an apostle: "for if any one be in Christ, he is a new creature." A new spirit, a new heart, and an outward character, corresponding to this change, are the effects of the regenerating process: "for the end of the change," the grand results of the remedial system, is "love out of a pure heart, a good conscience, and faith unfeigned." "Love is the fulfilling of the whole law," and the fruit of the whole gospel. It is the cardinal principle of all Christian behavior, the soul of the new man, the breath of the new life. Faith works by no other rule. It is a working principle, and love is the rule by which it operates. The Spirit of God is the spirit of love and the health of a sound mind. Every pulsation of the new heart is the impulse of the spirit of love. Hence the brotherhood is beloved, and all mankind embraced in unbounded good will. When the tongue speaks, the hands and the feet move and operate, under the unrestrained guidance of this principle, we have the Christian character drawn to the life. For meekness, humility, mercy, sympathy, and active benevolence are only the names of the various workings of this all renovating, invigorating, sanctifying, and happifying principle. "He that dwells in love dwells in God, and God in him."

The Christian, or the new man, is then a philanthropist to the utmost meaning of that word. Truth and love have made him free from all the tyrannies of passion, from guilt and fear and shame; have filled him with courage, active and passive. Therefore, his enterprise, his capital enterprise, to which all others minister, is to take part with our Saviour in the salvation of the world. "If by any means I may save some" are not the words of Paul only, but of every *new man.* Are they merchants, mechanics, husbandmen?—are they magistrates, lawyers, judges, or unofficial citizens?—are they masters, servants, fathers, sons, brothers, neighbors?—whatever or wherever they may be, they live for God and his city, for the King and his empire. They associate not with the children of wrath—the miser, the selfish, the prodigal, the gay, the proud, the slanderer, the tattler, the rake, the libertine, the drunkard, the thief, the murderer. Every new man has left these precincts; has broken his league with Satan and his slaves, and has joined himself to the family of God. These he complacently loves—those he pities—and does good to all.

The character of the new man is an elevated character. Feeling himself a son and heir of God, he cultivates the temper, spirit, and behavior which correspond with so exalted a relation. He despises every thing mean, grovelling, earthly, sensual, devilish. As the only begotten and well-beloved Son of God is to be the model of his future personal glory, so the character which Jesus sustained among men is the model of his daily imitation. His everyday aspiration is—

> "Thy fair example will I trace,
>   To teach me what I ought to be;
> Make me by thy transforming grace,
>   Lord Jesus, daily more like thee."

The law of God is hid in his heart. The living oracles dwell in his mind, and he grows in favor with God as he grows in the knowledge of God and of Jesus Christ his Lord. As a newborn babe he desires the unadulterated milk of the word of God, that he may grow by it; for as the thirsty hart pants after the brooks of water, so pants his soul after God. Thus he lives to God, and walks with him. This is the character of the regenerate—of him that is born of God—of the new man in Christ Jesus. This is that change of heart, of life, and of character, which is the tendency and the fruit of the process of regeneration, as taught and exemplified by the apostles, and those commended by God, in their writings.

We now proceed to offer a few remarks on physical regeneration, the second part of our subject.

PHYSICAL REGENERATION

Our mortal bodies are apt to feel the regenerating power of the son of God. This is emphatically called *"the glory of his power."* "The redemption of the body" from the bondage of corruption is the consummation of the new-creating energy of him who has immortality. Life and incorruptibility were displayed in and by his resurrection from the dead. It was great to create man in the image of God —greater to redeem his soul from general corruption; but greatest of all to give to his mortal frame incorruptible and immortal vigor. The power displayed in the giving to the dead body of the Son of God incorruptible glory and endless life is set forth by the apostle Paul as incomparably surpassing every other divine work within the reach of human knowledge. He prays that the minds of Christians may be enlarged to apprehend this mighty power—that the Father of glory would open their minds, "that they might know the exceeding greatness of his power in relation to us who believe—according to the working of his mighty power, which he wrought in Christ when he raised him from the dead and set him at his own right hand in the heavenly places." Faith in this wonderful operation of God—and hope for the riches of the glory of the inheritance of the saints in light —are in the most powerful principles of action which God has ever planted in the human breast. This is the transcendent hope of the Christian calling, which imparted such heroic courage to all the saints of eternal renown. This better resurrection in prospect has produced heroes which make cowards of all the boasted chiefs of worldly glory. As the magnetic needle ever points to the pole, so the mind, influenced by this hope, ever rises to the skies, and terminates in the fulness of joy, and the pleasures for evermore in the presence and at the right hand of God.

To raise a dead body to life again is not set forth as more glorious than by a touch to give new vigor to the palsied arm, to impart sight to the blind, or hearing to the deaf; but to give that raised body the deathless vigor of incorruptibility, to renovate and transform it in all its parts, and to make every spirit feel that it reanimates its own body, that it is as insusceptible of decay, as immortal as the Father of eternity, is a thought overwhelming to every mind; a development which will glorify the power of God, as the sacrifice of his Son now displays his righteousness, faithfulness, and love to the heavens and to the earth.

This new birth from the dark prison of the grave is fitly styled "the redemption of the body" from bondage, "the glorious liberty of the sons of God." As in our watery grave, the old man is figuratively buried to rise no more, so in the literal grave, the prison of the body, we leave all that is corrupt; for he that makes all things new will raise us up in his own likeness, and present us before his Father's face in all the glory of immortality. Then will regeneration be complete. Then will be the full revelation of the sons of God.

Immortality, in the sacred writings, is never applied to the spirit of man. It is not the doctrine of Plato which the resurrection of Jesus proposes. It is the *immortality of the body* of which his resurrection is a proof and pledge. This was never developed till he became the first-born from the dead, and in a human body entered the heavens. Jesus was not a spirit when he returned to God. He is not made the head of the new creation as a Spirit, but as the Son of Man. Our nature in his person is glorified; and when he appears to our salvation, we shall be made like him, we shall see him as he is. This is the Christian hope.

> "A hope so great and so divine,
>   May trials well endure,
> And purge the soul from sense and sin
>   As Christ himself is pure."

Thus matters stand in the economy of redemption. Thus the divine scheme of regeneration is consummated: the moral part by the operation of moral means; the physical part, by the mighty power of God operating through physical means. By the word of his power he created the heavens and the earth; by the word of his grace he reanimates the soul of man; and by the word of his power he will again form our bodies anew, and reunite the spirit and the body in the bonds of an incorruptible and everlasting union. Then shall death "be swallowed up forever."—"*Where now thy victory, boasting grave?*" But for this we must wait. "We know not what we shall be." We only know, that when he appears, we shall be like him; that we shall see him as he is.

THE USE OF THE THEORY OF REGENERATION

One would imagine, from the voluminous arguments, debates, and sermons upon the theory of regeneration, that a sound theory was essential to salvation: that it must be preached in every sermon, in order to regenerate the hearers. Nothing can be more preposterous. Who can think that any theory of the resurrection or regeneration of the body can affect the body in the grave? As little can any theory affect the unregenerate, or those dead in trespasses and in sins. A sermon upon regeneration, or upon natural birth, would be as efficacious upon those unborn, in bringing them into this life, as a sermon upon moral or physical regeneration. This explains the fact, that in all the accounts of apostolical preaching to Jew and Gentile —in the extracts of their sermons and speeches found in the New Testament—the subject of regeneration is not once mentioned. It is, in all the historic books of the New Testament, but once propounded, but once named; and that only in a private conference with a Jewish senator, on the affairs of Christ's kingdom. No theory understood or believed by the unregenerate, no theory proposed to them for their acceptance, can avail any thing to their regeneration. We might as reasonably deliver a theory of digestion to a dyspeptic, to cure his stomach—or a theory of vegetation to a scion, to hasten its growth— as to preach any view of regeneration to a sinner to make him a Christian.

Of what use, then, are the previous remarks on this subject? I will first candidly inform the reader, that they were not written for his regeneration, either of mind or body; but for the benefit of those who are employed in the work of regenerating others, and for the conviction of such Christians as may have been induced to regard us as aiming at nothing but the mere immersion of persons, as alone necessary to the whole process of conversion or regeneration, in their acceptation of these words.[1]   The use of this theory, if it have any, is

---

[1] It may again be necessary, in this fastidious age, to remark, that in this essay, in order to disabuse the public mind on our use and acceptation of the term *regeneration,* we have taken the widest range which a supreme regard for the apostolic style could, in our judgment, allow. While we argue that the phrase *bath of regeneration* (Titus 3:5) is equivalent to *immersion,* as already explained, and as contradistinguished from the *renewing of the Holy Spirit,* of which the immersed believer is a proper subject; we have spoken of the whole process of renovation, not in the strict application of the phrase (Titus 3:5), but rather in the whole latitude of the figure employed by the apostle.   It is not the first act of begetting, nor the last act of being born, but the whole process of conversion alluded to in the figure of *generation,* to which we have directed the attention of our readers.   For, as often before stated, our opponents deceive themselves and their hearers, by representing us as ascribing to the word *immersion,* and the act of immersion, all that they call *regeneration.*   While, therefore, we contend that being "born again," and being immersed, are, in the apostle's style, two names for the same action, we are far from supposing or teaching that, in forming the new man, there is nothing necessary but to be born.

If any ask why this matter was not fully developed in our first essays on this subject, our answer is, Because we could not anticipate that our opponents would have so represented or misrepresented our views.   Were a general asked why he did not arrange all his troops in the beginning of the action as he had them arranged when he triumphed over his enemy, he would reply, That the manoeuvres and assaults of the enemy directed the disposition of his forces.

Our opponents contend for a regeneration begun and perfected before faith or baptism—a spiritual change of mind by the Holy Spirit, antecedent to either knowledge, faith, or repentance, of which infants are as susceptible as adults; and, therefore, as we contend, make the gospel of no

as a guide to those who are laboring publicly or privately for the regeneration of sinners. If we have assigned a proper place for facts, testimony, faith, feeling, action, the bath of regeneration, the renewing of the Holy Spirit, and a new life, the course is fairly marked out. They are to present the great facts, to declare the whole testimony of God to sinners, in order to their conversion or regeneration. Like Paul, in his account of his labors in Corinth, they must go out, not in the strength of human philosophy, "*but declaring the testimony of God,*" and laying before their hearers "the wonderful works of God."

This is the use, and the only proper use, of sound theory on any subject. It is to guide the operator, not the thing operated upon. I would hope, under the Divine blessing, to be the means of regenerating one person in one year, never once naming regeneration, nor speculating upon the subject, by stating and enforcing the testimony of God, than by preaching daily the most approved theory of regeneration ever sanctioned by any sanhedrin on earth.[1] With these views, we have, then, offered the preceding remarks; and shall now briefly turn our attention to—

---

effect. By way of reprisals, they would have their converts think that we go for nothing but water, and sacrastically call us the advocates of "water regeneration." They think there is something more sublime and divine in "spirit regeneration"; and therefore claim the title of orthodox. This calumny has been one occasion of the present essay, and it has occasioned that part of it which gives the fullest latitude to the term *regeneration*, which analogy gives to the figure used by the apostle. But when we speak in the exact style of the living oracles on this subject, we must represent *being born again* (John 3:5) and *regeneration* (Titus 3:5) as relating to the act of immersion alone. See *Extra Defended*, pp. 24-36.

[1] *August 1.*—I have just now opened the Cincinnati *Baptist Journal* of 26th July, from which I read an approved definition of regeneration. It is orthodox, spiritual, physical, mystical, and metaphysical regeneration. It is quoted from the "Standard." Regeneration, in the *Evangelical Standard*, is thus defined:

"Is the sinner active in regeneration? Certainly he is. His mind is thinking, rational principle, which never ceases to act; and, therefore, when the word passive is applied to it, by Old Divines, or by Calvinists, they do not mean that it is *literally* dead, like inert matter, which requires a physical impulse to put it in motion. They only mean to convey the scriptural idea, that the Holy Spirit is the *sole* agent in regeneration, and that the sinner has *no more efficient agency* in accomplishing it, than Lazarus had in becoming alive from the dead. Still, they grant that his mind is most active, but unhappily its activity is all *against* the divine influence; as the Scriptures assure us, unregenerated persons 'do always resist' the strivings of the Spirit. 'Every imagination of the thoughts of man's heart is only evil continually.' 'There is none that doeth good; no, not one.' The sinner, therefore, instead of voluntarily co-operating with the Holy Spirit, does all he can to *resist* his divine influence, and prevent his own regeneration, until he is *made* willing by almighty power."

What a comfortable thing is this theory of regeneration! The sinner's to be regenerated when actively striving against the divine influence. At the moment of regeneration, "he has," in one sense, "no more efficient

THE REGENERATION OF THE CHURCH

The word *regeneration* we have found once used in the sense of a new state of things, or of the introduction of a new state of things.[1] In this application of the word, we would turn the attention of our readers to the necessity of the regeneration of the church.

I speak not of the regeneration of any sectarian establishment. They are built upon another foundation—upon the foundation of decrees of councils, creeds, formularies, or acts of Parliament. But we speak of those societies that professedly build upon the foundation of apostles and prophets, without any human bond of union, or rule of life—our brethren of the reformation, now in process.

Should any one imagine that the state of things to which we have attained is the sole or ultimate object of our aspirations or our efforts, he would do us the greatest injury. Societies, indeed, may be found among us, far in advance of others, in their progress towards the ancient order of things; but we know of none that has fully attained to that model. It is, however, most acceptable to see so many societies formed and forming, under the banners of reformation, with the determination to move onwards in conformity to the sacred oracles, till they stand perfect and complete in all the will of God.

Our opponents can not, or will not, understand how any society can be in progress to a better order of things than that under which they may have commenced their pilgrimage. Their sectarian policies were soon formed, and the limits of their reformation were soon fixed; beyond which it soon became heretical to move. The founders of all new schisms not only saw through a glass darkly, but their horizon was so circumscribed with human traditions, that they only aimed at moving a few paces from the hive in which they were gen-

---

agency in accomplishing it than Lazarus had in becoming alive from the dead"; and in another sense, he is not passive, but "does all he can to *resist* the divine influence, and *prevent* his own regeneration, until he is *made* willing by almighty power." This is *Standard* divinity; and he that preaches this divinity is a pious, regenerated, Regular Orthodox Baptist Christian Minister! Of how much value, on this theory, is all the preaching in Christendom? The Holy Spirit may be busily at work upon some drunken sot, or some vile debauchee, who is as dead as Lazarus on one side, and on the other resisting the Spirit with all his moral and physical energy, up to the moment that the Almighty arm pierces him to the heart with a sword, and makes him alive by killing him!

The absurdity and licentiousness of such a view of the great work of removation we had thought so glaring that no editor in the West would have had boldness to have published it. This is proof of the necessity of our present essay, and will explain to the intelligent reader why we have given to the whole process of renovation the name of regeneration, which properly belongs to the last act.

[1] Matthew 19:28.

erated. A new creed was soon adopted, and then their stature was complete. They bounded from infancy to manhood in a few days, and decided, if any presumed further to advance, they should be treated as those who had refused to move from the old hive. Hence it became as censurable to grow beyond a certain standard, as not to grow at all. This never was our proposition, and never can be our object. We have no new creed to form, no rules of discipline to adopt. We have taken the Living Oracles as our creed, our rules and measures of faith and practice; and, in this department, have no additions, alternations, or amendments to propose. But in coming up to this standard of knowledge, faith, and behavior, we have something yet before us, to which we have not attained.

That we may be distinctly understood on this subject, we shall speak particularly on the things wanting in our individual characters, and of the things wanting in our church order, to give to our meetings that interest and influence which they ought to exert on the brotherhood and on society at large.

It will be understood, that our remarks on the things which are wanting in the disciples are applicable not to every individual, but to the general mass. And, first of all, there is wanting a more general and particular knowledge of the Holy Scriptures than is possessed by a great majority of the reformers. There is, perhaps, wanting a taste or disposition for that private devotional reading of the oracles of God, which is essential to a growth in that knowledge of God and of Jesus Christ which constitutes the most striking attributes in Christian character. We thus reason from the proficiency which is discoverable in the bounds of our acquaintance, which is large enough to afford data for every general conclusion.

To read the Scriptures for the sake of carrying out into practice all that we learn, and to read them for the sake of knowing what is written, are very different objects, and will produce very different results. Their influence on the temper and behavior, in the former case, will very soon become manifest to all with whom we associate; while, in the latter case, there is no visible improvement. David said that he "hid the word of God in his heart," or laid it up in his mind, "that he might not sin against God"; and that he had "more understanding than all his teachers, because God's testimonies were his meditation." It will be admitted that the sacred writings of the apostles and evangelists of Jesus Christ ought to be as precious and as delightful to the Christian, as were the ancient oracles to the most pious Jew. Now, as an example of what we mean by a private devotional reading and study of the oracles of Christ, we shall permit a Jew to tell his experience:—

"The law of thy mouth is better to me than thousands of gold and silver. With my whole heart have I sought thee; my soul breaketh for the longing that it has to thy judgments at all times. Thy testimonies are my delight and my counsellors. Teach me, O Lord, the way of thy statutes, and I will keep it to the end. Give me understanding, and I shall keep thy law; yes, I will observe it with my whole heart. Make me to go in the path of thy commandments, for in it do I delight. Thy statutes have been my songs in the house of my pilgrimage. At midnight I will rise to give thanks to thee, because of thy righteous judgments. Oh, how I love thy law; it is my meditation all the day! How sweet are thy words to my taste; sweeter than honey to my mouth! Thy testimonies have I taken as a heritage forever, for they are the rejoicing of my heart. Great peace have they that love thy law—nothing shall cause them to stumble."

These are only a few extracts from one piece, written by a king three thousand years ago. On another occasion he pronounced the following encomium on the testimony of God:—

"The law [doctrine] of the Lord is perfect, converting [restoring] the soul; the testimony of the Lord is sure, making wise the simple; the statutes of the Lord are right, rejoicing the heart; the commandment of the Lord is pure, enlightening the eyes. The fear of the Lord is clean, enduring forever; the judgments of the Lord are true and righteous altogether. More to be desired are they than gold —yea, than much fine gold: sweeter also than honey, and the honeycomb. By them is thy servant warned, and in keeping of them there is great reward."

This fully reveals all that we mean by a devotional private study of the Holy Scriptures. Every Christian who can read may every day thus refresh, strengthen, and comfort his heart, by reading or committing to memory, and afterwards reflecting upon, some portion of the book. He may carry in his pocket the blessed volume, and many a time through the day take a peep into it. This will preserve him from temptation, impart courage to his heart, give fluency to his tongue, and the graces of Christianity to his life.

In this age, when ignorance of the Christian Scriptures is so characteristic, and the rage for human opinions and traditions so rampant, it is a duty doubly imperative on our brethren, to give themselves much more to the study of the book; and then one of them will put a host of the aliens to flight; and, what is still more desirable, he will have communion with God all the day, and ever rejoice in his salvation.

In the second place, there is wanting among disciples, who are heads of families, more attention, much more effort, to bring up their children "in the correction and instruction of the Lord." The children of all disciples should be taught the oracles of God from the first dawning of reason. The good seed should be sown in their hearts, before the strong seeds of vice can take root. *From a child* Timothy knew the Holy Scriptures, and they were able to make him wise to salvation, through the Christian faith. How many more Timothys might we have, if we had a few more of the daughters of Lois, and a few more mothers like Eunice! Most saints, in this generation, appear more zealous that their children should shine on earth, than in heaven—and that they may be rich here, at the hazard of eternal bankruptcy. They labor to make them rich and genteel, rather than pure and holy: and spend more time in fashioning them to the foolish and wicked taste of *polished* society, than in teaching them by precept and example the word that is better than gold, and more precious than rubies. Well, they sow darnel, and can not reap wheat. They may have a mournful harvest, and years of bitterness and sorrow may reward them for their negligence and error. If only a tithe of the time, and the labor and expense, that it costs to fit a son or a daughter to shine in the middle or front ranks of genteel society, were spent in teaching them to fear God and to keep his commandments, how many more virtuous, solid, and useful citizens—how many more valuable members of the family of God—how many more faithful and able witnesses for the truth of God—would be found in all corners of the land!

Every Christian family ought to be a nursery for God. Their offspring should be trained for the skies. For such are the promises of God, such are the facts on record, and such is the experience of Christians, that every parent who does his duty to his children may expect to see them inherit the blessing. Their didactic labors, aided by their example and their constant prayers, will seldom or never fail of success in influencing their descendants to walk in their ways. The very command to bring up their children in the Lord implies its practicability. And both Testaments furnish us with all assurance that such labors will not be in vain. The men of high renown in sacred history were generally the sons of such parentage. The sons of God were found among the sons of Seth, while the daughters of men were of the progeny of Cain. Abraham was the descendant of Shem; Moses and Aaron were the sons of believing parents; Samuel was the son of Hannah, and David was the son of Jesse. John the Harbinger was the son of Zachariah and Elizabeth; and it pleased the heavenly Father that his Son should be the child of a pious virgin.

But it is under Christ that the faithful are furnished with all the necessary means of bringing up their offspring for the Lord. The numerous failures which we witness are to be traced either to great neglect, or to some fatal notion which paralyzes all effort; for some think that the salvation or damnation of their offspring was a matter settled for all eternity, irrespective of any agency on their part: that some are born "vessels of wrath," and others "vessels of mercy"; and hence the instructions, examples, and prayers of parents are of no avail. Among the descendants of such, it will no doubt often happen that some *become* vessels of wrath, fitted for destruction, while others *become* vessels of mercy predestined to glory.

When God gave a revelation to Jacob, and commanded a law to Israel, he gave it in charge that they should "teach it to their children, that they might *put their trust in God*, and might not be, like their fathers, a rebellious race." The apostles of Christ have also taught the Christians the same lesson. This is our guide, and not our own reasonings. Now, let the disciples make this their business, morning, noon, and evening, and then we shall see its effects.

We are sorry to see this great duty, to which nature, reason, revelation alike direct, so much neglected by many of our brethren—to find among their children those who are no better acquainted with the Scriptures than the children of their neighbors, who believe in miraculous conversions, or think it is a sin to attempt what they imagine to be the work of God alone—never suspecting that God works by human means, and employs human agency in his works of providence and redemption.

I never knew but of a very few families that made it their daily business to train up their children in the knowledge of the Holy Scriptures, to cause them every day to commit to memory a portion of the living oracles; but these few instances authorize me to think, and to say, that such a course, persisted in and sustained by the good example of parents, will very generally, if not universally, issue in the salvation of their children. And before any one says, I have found an exception to the proverb of Solomon, which says, "Train up a child in the way it should go, and when he is old he will not depart from it,"—let him show that his child was *trained up in the way he should go.*

In the third place, there is wanting, among the disciples, a stricter regard to relative duties; we mean, not only the duties which justice, truth, and moderation claim; but *all* relative duties. So long as Christians live after the manner of men in the flesh, according to the fashion of this world, they must, like other men, contract debts which they can not promptly pay, make covenants and bargains, give promises which they can not fulfil, and stake pledges which they are unable to redeem. All this is wholly incompatible with our profession. Such were not the primitive disciples. Skeptics of every name, men of the world, who have ever read the New Testament, know that such behavior is utterly incompatible with the letter and spirit of Christianity. A Christian's word or promise ought to be, and is, if Christ be honored, as solemn and obligatory as any bond. And as for breach of bargain or covenant, even where it is greatly or wholly to the disadvantage of the Christian, it is not even to be thought of—"he changes not, though to his hurt he covenants." How much has the gospel lost of its influence, because of the faithlessness of its professors! Oh, when shall it be again said of Christians in general that "they bind themselves, as with a solemn oath, not to commit any kind of wickedness—to be guilty neither of theft, robbery, nor adultery—*never to break a promise*, or to keep back a deposit when called upon?" Pliny writes to the Emperor Trajan that such was the character of Christians A.D. 106-7, as far as he could learn it from those who were not Christians. Were all the common (nowadays rather *uncommon*) virtues of justice, truth, fidelity, honesty, practiced by all Christians, how many mouths would be stopped, and how many new arguments in favor of Jesus Christ could all parties find! But, even were these common virtues as general as the Christian profession, there are the other finer virtues of benevolence, goodness, mercy, sympathy, which belong to the profession, expressed in taking care of the sick, the orphan, the widow—in alleviating all the afflictions of our fellow-creatures. Add these virtues, or *graces,* as we sometimes call them, to the others, and then how irresistible the argument for the divine authenticity of the gospel! Let industry, frugality, temperance, honesty, justice, truth, fidelity, humility, mercy, sympathy, appear conspicuous in the lives of the disciples, and the contrast between them and other professors will plead their cause more successfully than a hundred preachers.

In the last place there is wanting a more elevated piety to bring up the Christian character to the standard of primitive times. We want not fine speeches nor eloquent orations on the excellencies of Christian piety and devotion. These are generally acknowledged. But we need to be roused from our supineness, from our worldly-mindedness, from our sinful conformities to an apostate generation, to the exhibition of that holiness in speech, in behavior, without which no one shall please the Lord. What mean the numerous exhortations of the apostles to watchfulness and prayer, if these are not essential to our devotion to God and consecration to his service?

If our affections are not placed on things above, we are unfit for the kingdom of glory. To see the folly of a profession of Christianity

without the power of godliness, we have only to put the question,
How is that person fit for the enjoyment of God and Christ, whose
heart is filled with the cares, anxieties, and concerns of this life—
whose whole life is a life of labor and care for the body—a life of
devotion to the objects of time and sense? No man can serve God
and Mammon. Where the treasure is, the heart must also be.
Thither the affections turn their course. There is no room for the
residence of the Spirit of God in a mind devoted to the affairs of this
life. The spirit of the policies of this world, and the Spirit of God,
can not dwell in the same heart. If Jesus or his apostles taught any
one doctrine clearly, fully, and unequivocally, it is this doctrine:—
that "the cares of this world, the lusts of other things, and the deceitfulness of riches, stifle the word, and render it unfruitful."

If any one would enjoy the power of godliness, he must give up
his whole soul to it. The business of this life will be performed religiously, as a duty subordinate to the will of God. While his hands
are engaged in that business which his own wants or those of this
household make necessary, his affections are above. He delights in
God, and communes with him all the day. A Christian is not one
who is pious by fits and starts, who is religious or devout one day of
the week, or for one hour of the day. It is the whole bent of his soul
—it is the beginning, middle, and the end of every day. To make
his calling and election sure is the business of his life. His mind
rests only in God. He places the Lord always before him. This is
his joy and delight. He would not for the world have it otherwise. He
would not enjoy eternal life, if he had it at his option, in any other
way than that which God himself has proposed. He accedes to
God's arrangements, not of necessity, but of choice. His religious
services are perfect freedom. He is free indeed. The Lord's commandments are not grievous, but joyful. The yoke of Christ is to
him easy, and his burden light. He will sing, with David,—

"The love that to thy laws I bear
  No language can display;
They with fresh wonders entertain
  My ravish'd thoughts all day.

"The law that from thy mouth proceeds,
  Of more esteem I hold
Than untouch'd stores, than thousand mines
  Of silver and of gold.

"Whilst in the way of thy commands,
  More solid joy I found
Than had I been with vast increase
  Of envied riches crown'd.

> "Thy testimonies I have kept,
> And constantly obey'd;
> Because the love I bore to them
> Thy service easy made."

In the same ratio as Christians devoutly study the oracles of God, teach them to their children, practice all relative duties to society at large, and rise to a more elevated piety, they will increase their influence in the great and heavenly work of regenerating the world.

A few remarks on the things wanting in the order of Christian assemblies, to give to their public meetings that influence on themselves, and on society at large, will finish this section of our essay.

Our heavenly Father wills our happiness in all its institutions. His ordinances are, therefore, the surest, the simplest, and the most direct means of promoting our happiness. The Lord Jesus gave himself for the church that he might purify and bless it; and therefore, in the church are all the institutions which can promote the individual and social good of the Christian community. In attending upon these institutions on the Lord's day, much depends upon the preparation of heart in all who unite to commemorate the death and resurrection of the Son of God.

In adverting to the most scriptural and rational manner of celebrating or observing the day to the Lord, both for their own comfort and the regeneration of the world, we would first of all remark, that much depends upon the frame of mind, or preparation of heart, in which we visit the assemblies of the saints.

Suppose two persons, A and B, if you please, members of the same church, take their seats together at the Lord's table. A, from the time he opened his eyes in the morning, was filled with the recollections of the Saviour's life, death, and resurrection. In his closet, in his family, and along the way, he was meditating or conversing on the wonders of redemption, and renewing his recollections of the sayings and doings of the Messiah. B, on the other hand, arose as on other days, and finding himself free from all obligations arising from the holiness of the time, talks about the common affairs of every day, and allows his thoughts to roam over the business of the last week, or, perhaps, to project the business of the next. If he meet with a neighbor, friend, or brother, the news of the day is inquired after, expatiated upon, discussed; the crops, the markets, the public health, or the weather—the affairs of Europe, or the doings of Congress, or the prospects of some candidate for political honor—become the theme of conversation. As he rides or walks to the church, he chats upon all, or any of these topics, till he enters the door of the meeting-house. Now, as A and B enter the house in very different states of mind, may it not be supposed that they will differ as much in their enjoyments as in their morning thoughts? Or can B by a single effort, unburden his mind, call in the wanderings of his thoughts, and in a moment transport himself from the contemplation of things on earth to things in heaven? If this can be imagined, then meditation and preparation of heart are wholly unnecessary to the acceptable worship of God, and to the comfortable enjoyment of his institutions.

But is it compatible with experience, or is it accordant to reason, that B can delight in God, and rejoice in commemorating the wonders of his redemption, while his thoughts are dissipated upon the mountains of a thousand vanities?—while, like a fool's eyes, his thoughts are roaming to the ends of the earth? Can he say, with a pious Jew, "How amiable are thy tabernacles, O Lord of hosts! My soul longs—yes, even faints—for the courts of the Lord! My heart and my flesh cry out for the living God. Happy they who dwell in thy house; they will be still praising thee! A day in thy courts is better than a thousand. I had rather be a doorkeeper in the house of my God, than to dwell in the tents of wickedness." "One thing have I desired of the Lord, and that I will seek after, that I may dwell in the house of the Lord all the days of my life, to behold the beauty of the Lord, and to inquire in his temple. Oh, send out thy light and thy truth! Let them lead me, let them bring me to thy holy hill and to thy tabernacles. Then will I go to the altar of God, to God my exceeding joy; yes, I will praise thee, O God, my God!"

Or had the Jew a sublimer worship, more exalted views of God's salvation, and more piety, than a Christian? Or were the ordinances of the Jewish sanctuary more entertaining and refreshing than the ordinances of the Christian church? This will not be alleged; consequently B, and all of that school, are utterly at fault when they approach the house of God in such a state of mind as they approach the market-place, the forum, or the common resorts of this present world.

Christians need not say, in excuse for themselves, that all days are alike, that all places and times are alike holy, and that they ought to be in the best frame of mind all the time. For even concede them all their own positions: they will not contend that a man ought to speak to God, or to come into the presence of God, as they approach men. They will not say that they ought to have the same thoughts or feelings in approaching the Lord's table, as in approaching a common table; or on entering a court of political justice, as in coming into the house of God. There is, in the words of Solomon the Wise, a season and time for every object and for every work: here is the Lord's day, the Lord's table, the Lord's house, and the Lord's people;

and there are thoughts, and frames of mind, and behavior compatible and incompatible with all these.

In the public assembly the whole order of worship ought to do justice to what is passing in the minds of all the worshippers. That joy in the Lord, that peace and serenity of mind, that affection for the brethren, that reverence for the institutions of God's house, which all feel, should be manifest in all the business of the day. Nothing that would do injustice to all or any of these ought ever to appear in the congregation of Jesus Christ our Lord. No levity, irreverence, no gloom, no sadness, no pride, no unkindness, no severity of behavior towards any, no coldness, nothing but love, and peace, and joy, and humility, and reverence, should appear in the face, in the word or action, of any disciple.

These are not little matters. They all exert a salutary influence on the brethren and the strangers. These are visible and sensible displays of the temper and spirit of Christians; and if Paul thought it expedient to write of *evils* and *long hair* when admonishing a church "to do all things decently and in order," we, in this day of degeneracy, may be allowed to notice matters and things as minute as those before us.

We intend not now to go into details of church order or Christian discipline, nor to expatiate on the necessity of devoting a part of the time to singing, praying, reading, teaching, exhorting, commemorating, communicating; nor on how much of this or that is expedient. Times and circumstances must decide how much time shall be taken up in these exercises, and when it shall be most fitting to meet, to adjourn, etc. Nor is it necessary now to say, that there must be scriptural order, and presidency, and proper discipline, and due subordination to one another in the fear of God. We now speak rather of the *manner* in which all things are to be done, than of the things themselves, their necessity or value.

After noticing what in some instances appears to be wanting in the manner of coming together on the Lord's day, we proceed to notice in order the things wanting in many congregations, for the purposes already specified.

And, first of all, be it observed, that in some churches there appears to be wanting *a proper method of handling the Scriptures to the edification of the brethren.* It is admitted by all the holy brethren, that the Scriptures of truth, called *the living oracles,* are the great instrument of God for all his purposes in the saints on earth. Through them they are converted to God, comforted, consecrated, made meet for an inheritance among the sanctified, and qualified for every good word and work. Every thing, then, depends upon the proper understanding of these volumes of inspiration. They can only operate as far as they are understood.

The system of sermonizing on a text is now almost universally abandoned by all who intend that their hearers should understand the testimony of God. Orators and exhorters may select a word, a phrase, or a verse; but all who feed the flock of God with knowledge and understanding know that this method is wholly absurd. Philological lectures upon a chapter are only a little better. The discussion of any particular topic, such as faith, repentance, election, the Christian calling, may sometimes be expedient: but in a congregation of Christians, the reading and examining the different books in regular succession, every disciple having the volume in his hand, following up the connection of things, examining parallel passages, interrogating and being interrogated, fixing the meaning of particular words and phrases by comparison with the style of that writer or speaker, or with that of others; intermingling these exercises with prayer and praises, and keeping the narrative, the epistle, the speech, so long as is necessary for the youngest disciple in the congregation to understand it, and to become deeply interested in it, will do more in one year than is done in many on the plan of the popular meetings of the day.

Great attention should be paid to all the allusions, in any composition, to the particularities of time, place, and circumstance, to the geographical, historical, and chronological particulars of all questions of fact connected with all persons of note in the narratives: for these are often the best interpreters of style, and expositors of the meaning of what is written.

This searching, examining, comparing, and ruminating upon the Holy Scriptures in private, in the family, in the congregation, can not fail to make us learned in the knowledge of God and in the knowledge of man. The Bible contains more real learning than all the volumes of men. It instructs us in all our natural, moral, political, and religious relations. Though it teaches us not astronomy, medicine, chemistry, mathematics, architecture, it gives us all that knowledge which adorns and dignifies our moral nature and fits us for happiness. Happy the person who meditates upon it day and night! He grows and flourishes in moral health and vigor, as the trees upon the watercourses. His leaf never fades—his fruit never fails.

The congregations of the saints want system in furthering the knowledge of this book. The simple reading of large portions in a desultory manner is not without some good effect; for there is light, and majesty, and life, in all the oracles of God; no man can listen to them without edification. But the profit accruing from such readings is not a tithe of that which might be obtained in the proper systematic reading and examination of them. The congregation is the school of Christ, and every pupil there should feel that he has learned something every day he waits upon his Master. He must take the Master's book with him, and, like every other good and orderly pupil, he must open it and study it, with all the helps that the brotherhood, his school-fellows, can furnish for his more comprehensive knowledge of all its salutary communications.

A Christian scribe, well instructed in its contents, or a plurality of such, who can bring out of their intellectual treasury things new and old, will greatly advance the students in this heavenly science; but, in the absence of such, the students must be self-taught; and self-taught scholars are generally the best taught; for they can not progress, unless they study with diligence, and carefully learn the rudiments of every science.

To give some idea of the diligence and attention to the minutest matters which are necessary to proficiency in the knowledge of all that is written in the New Testament, we shall suppose that the disciples have for their lesson, on some particular day, the Nativity of the Messiah. The second chapter of Matthew is read. After reading this chapter, or the whole of the first section of Matthew's Testimony, the elder or president for the day asks some brother, a good reader, to read what the other evangelists have testified on this subject. Mark and John being silent on the nativity, he reads Luke, second section, second chapter, from the first to the forty-first verse. After the reading of this chapter, the following points are the subjects of inquiry, and most of them are proposed to the brethren for solution:—

1. Who was Caesar Augustus, and over what people did he reign?

2. At what period of his reign was the edict of enrolment issued, or when did the first register take effect?

3. What did Syria include, and what were its boundaries?

4. Who presided over Syria at the time of the first register?

5. Who was king in Judea at this time?

6. How far did Judea extend, or in what part of the Holy Land was it situated?

7. In what country was Jerusalem, where situated, and by what other names was it known?

8. What was the native city of Joseph?

9. Where was Nazareth situated, and in what district?

10. What was the boundary of Galilee, and what were its principal towns?

11. In what canton or district was Bethlehem, and how far from Jerusalem?

12. Who were the magians?

13. Why was "Herod alarmed, and all Jerusalem with him," when the magians reported the star in the east?

14. What were the scribes and chief priests assembled by Herod, and why were they called together?

15. By what means did they decide the questions referred to them?

16. On what prophet do they rely, and where shall the quotation be found?

17. Of what family and lineage were Joseph and Mary?

18. By what means did the magians find the house in which the Messiah was born?

19. Why did the magians not return to Herod?

20. Whither did the shepherds of Bethlehem, or the eastern magians, first pay their respects to the Messiah?

21. In what quarter of the globe does Egypt lie?

22. How far from Bethlehem?

23. How long was the Messiah kept in Egypt?

24. He predicted his return from Egypt, and where shall it be found?

25. Who foretold the slaughter of the male infants in Bethlehem, and what instigated Herod to this cruel massacre?

26. Who succeeded Herod in the throne of Judea?

27. Why did Joseph retire to Nazareth?

28. What prophet foretold this circumstance, and where shall it be found?

These matters being all ascertained, to which the maps, geographical and chronological indexes, and the appendix to the Family Testament, will greatly contribute, some moral reflections will naturally occur; for in all these incidents are manifest the wisdom, care, and economy of our heavenly Father, his faithfulness, condescension, and love; the great variety of his instruments and agents; the ease with which he frustrates the evil counsels and machinations of his enemies; the infallible certainty of his foreknowledge; the perfect free agency of men, good and evil; the deep humiliation of his only-begotten Son, in all the circumstances of his nativity. Irresistible arguments in favor of his pretensions may be drawn from these ancient prophecies, from their minuteness of time, place, and circumstance;

many eloquent and powerful lessons on human pride, vanity, and arrogance may be deduced from the birthplace, cradle, and family connections of the heir of the universe; and many other touching appeals to the heart, which the birth, circumcision, and dedication of the Messiah, with all the incidents in Bethlehem, Jerusalem, and the temple, connected with his first appearance on earth, furnish, will present themselves, with unfading freshness and beauty, to the brotherhood of Christ.

A hint to the wise is sufficient. Were this method pursued only two hours every Lord's day, every disciple giving his heart to the work, and were the results then compared with the products of the scrap-doctors or sermonizers to sleeping and dreaming hearers, no man, having any regard for his reputation for good sense, could give his vote for the popular system.

A reformation in the manner of handling the Living Oracles is much wanting; and the sooner and more generally it is attempted, the greater will be the regenerating influence of the brotherhood on the world. Intelligent in the Holy Scriptures, clothed with the armor of light, every disciple going forth will be a David against the Philistines—a host against the armies of the aliens. And, better still, the words of heavenly favor dwelling in his heart, he will carry with him into every society a fragrance like the rose of Sharon—a sweetness of perfume like a garden which the Lord has blessed.

There appears to be wanting in some congregations a proper attention to discipline, and a due regard to decorum in the management of such cases as occur. In every family, and in every congregation, there is occasional need of discipline. Offences, delinquencies, and apostasies did occur in the congregations over which the apostles either were, or had been, presidents; and they will happen again in this state of discipline and trial in which we are all placed. They must be expected; and every congregation ought to be prepared to act upon the emergency with intelligence and decorum. Much injury has been done to the progress of churches, by a remissness in attention to such cases, and in the manner they have been disposed of when taken up.

Nothing can be more preposterous and revolting to every sentiment of good order and decorum, than that every offender and offence should, at the very offset, be dragged into the public assembly. Persons who have the care of a congregation, the seniors whose age and experience have taught them prudence, ought to be first informed of such cases; and they ought to present the matter to the congregation. Every novice is not to feel himself at liberty to disturb the congregation by presenting, on his own responsibility, and at his own discretion, a complaint against a brother, whether it be of a public or private nature.

But we are now speaking of the *manner* of procedure in such cases. The most tender regard for the feelings of all, the utmost sympathy for the offender, the most unyielding firmness in applying the correctives which the head of the church has commanded, and the necessity of acting promptly in accordance with the law in the case, are matters of much importance.

No passion, no partiality, no bad feeling—nothing but love and piety, but faithfulness and truth; nothing but courtesy and gentleness —should ever appear in the house of God. And when any one is found guilty and excluded from the society, it should be done with all solemnity, and with prayer that the institution of Christ may be a blessing to the transgressor.

But evil-doers, or those that act not honorably according to the law of Christ, ought not to be tolerated in the professed family of God. Such persons are a dead weight on the whole society—spots in every feast of love, and blemishes upon the whole profession. One sinner destroys much good; yet separation or abscission, like amputation, is only to be used in the last stage, when all other remedies, of remonstrance and admonition, expostulation and entreaty, have failed. To prevent gangrene, or an injury to the whole body, amputation is necessary, an indispensable remedy. More strictness, more firmness, and more tenderness in such cases would add greatly to the moral influence of every society. A few persons walking together in the bonds of Christian affection, and under the discipline of Christ, is better than the largest assembly in which there are visibly and manifestly many who fear not God and keep not his commandments.

In the house of God all should be purity, reverence, meekness, brotherly kindness, and love. Confidence in the honesty and sincerity of our brethren is the life of communion. To feel ourselves united with them who are determined for eternal life, and resolved to seek first of all, chief of all, above all, the kingdom of heaven, and the righteousness required in it, is most animating, comforting, exhilarating. But to be doubtful whether we are uniting with a mass of ignorance, corruption, and apathy, is as rottenness in the bones; love waxes cold, and then we have the form without the power of godliness.

That the church may have a regenerating influence upon society at large, there is wanting a fuller display of Christian philanthropy in all her public meeings; care for the poor, manifested in the liberality of her contributions; the expression of the most unfeigned sympathy for the distresses of mankind, not only among the brotherhood, but among all men; and an ardent zeal for the conversion of sinners, proportioned to her professed appreciation of the value of her own salvation, and to her resources and means of enlightening the world on the things unseen and eternal. The full display of these attributes is the most efficient means of causing the gospel to sound abroad, and to achieve new conquests among our fellow-citizens. The Christian health and vigor of every church is to be estimated more by her exertions and success in bringing sinners home to God, than by all her other attainments. Too long has it been considered the duty, the almost exclusive duty, of the preacher, to convert the world. He must spend his time and wear out his constitution in journeyings and preachings, while the individual members of the church are to mind their own business, seek their own wealth and domestic comfort. He must endure the heat and the cold, forsake his wife and family, and commit the management of his affairs to others, while they have only to look on and pray for his success. Strange infatuation! Has he received a commission from the skies—has he been drafted out of the ranks to go to war, and they all left at home to take care of their wives and children? Some may believe this—some may imagine that it is his duty alone to spend his time and his talents in this work, and theirs daily to labor for their own interest and behoof; but surely such are not the views and feelings of our brethren!

The work of the Lord will never progress—or, in other words, the regenerating influence of the church will amount to little or nothing —so long as it is thought to be not equally the duty of every member, or the special duty of one or two, denominated preachers, to labor for the Lord.

There is either a special call, a general call, or no call at all, to labor for the conversion of the world. If there be a few specially called, the rest have nothing to do but to mind their own concerns; "to seek their own things, and not the things of Jesus Christ." If none be called, then it is the duty of none, and the Lord has nothing for his people to do—no world to convert; or, at least, nothing for them to do in that work. None of us are prepared for the consequences of either of these assumptions. It follows, then, that it is the duty of all to labor according to their respective abilities in this work. All are called to labor for the Lord. I hold that every citizen in Christ's kingdom is bound to take up arms for the king, as much as I am; and, if he can not go to fight the battles of the Lord, he must take care of the wives and children of those who can and who will fight for their king and country. But the expense of the war must be borne by the subjects of the crown; and, as the Lord will not have any taxgatherers in his kingdom, but accepts only voluntary contributions, he makes a mark over against the names of those who do nothing, and he will settle with them at his return. He calls even the contributions for the gospel, made by those at home, "a fragrant odor, a sacrifice acceptable, well pleasing to God."

But we are afraid of doing any thing of this sort, lest we should be like some other people, who we think have acted imprudently. Strange, indeed, that when any thing has been once abused, it is never again to be used! But I have inadvertently strayed off from my purpose. The manner in which the brethren labor for the salvation of the world is all that comes within our prescribed limits. On this, enough has been said. Let the brethren solemnly consider the things that are wanting to give to their meetings that influence which they ought to exert upon themselves and upon society at large.

We are as susceptible of receiving moral and religious advantages, from our own good order and decorum in the congregation, as those who attend our meetings as spectators. And in this instance, as well as in all the variety of doing good, he that waters others is again watered in return; for he that blesses others is always blessed in blessing them. None enjoys the blessings of the gospel more fully than they who are most active and influential in blessing others. What happy seasons are those in which we see many turning to the Lord! Now, if we would have a perpetual feast, we must be perpetually devoted to the promotion of the happiness of others. We must live for God, as well as live to God.

In filling up these outlines, other matters still more minute, but, perhaps, equally important, will present themselves to the attention of the brethren. Now, we can not set about these matters too soon. The time has again come, when judgment must begin at the house of God. The people who have long enjoyed the word of life and the Christian institutions must soon come to a reckoning. They must give an account of their stewardship, for the Lord has promised to call them to a judgment. An era is just at the door, which will be known as *the regeneration* for a thousand years to come. The Lord Jesus will judge that adulterous brood, and give them over to the burning flame, who have broken the covenant, and formed alliances with the governments of the earth. Now the cry is heard in our land, "Come out of her, my people, that you partake not of her sins, and that you may not receive of her plagues." The Lord Jesus will soon rebuild Jerusalem, and raise up the tabernacle of David which has so long been in ruins. Let the church prepare herself for the return of her Lord, and see that she make herself ready for his appearance.

THE REGENERATION OF THE WORLD

All the kingdoms of this world shall soon become the kingdoms of our Lord the king. He will hurl all the present potentates from their thrones. He will grind to powder the despotisms, civil and ecclesiastic; and, with the blast of his mouth, give them to the four winds of heaven. The antichristian power, whether it be called Papistical, Mohammedan, Pagan, or Atheistic, will as certainly be destroyed, as Jesus reigns in heaven. No trace of them shall remain. The best government on earth, call it English or American, has within it the seeds of its own destruction—carries in its constitution a millstone, which will sink it to the bottom of the sea. They acknowledge not that God has set his Christ upon his throne. They will not kiss the Son. Society under their economy is not blessed. The land mourns through the wickedness of those that sit in high places. Ignorance, poverty, and crime abound, because of the injustice and iniquities of those who guide the destinies of nations. Men that fear not God, and love not his Son, and that regard not the maxims of his government, yet wear the sword and sway the sceptre in all lands.

This is wholly adverse to the peace and happiness of the world. Therefore he will break them in pieces like a potter's vessel, and set up an order of society in which justice, inflexible justice, shall have uncontrolled dominion. Jesus will be universally acknowledged by all the race of living men, and all nations shall do him homage. This state of society will be the consummation of the Christian religion, in all its moral influences and tendencies upon mankind.

How far this change is to be effected by moral and how far by physical means, is not the subject of our present inquiry. But the preparation of a people for the coming of the Lord must be the result of the restoration of the ancient gospel and order of things. And, come when it may, the day of the regeneration of the world will be a day as wonderful and terrible as was the day of the deluge, of Sodom's judgment, or of Jerusalem's catastrophe. Who shall stand when the Lord does this? But all the regenerations, physical and moral, individual, congregational, or national, are but types and shadows, or means of preparation, for the—

REGENERATION OF THE HEAVENS AND THE EARTH

The Bible begins with the generations of the heavens and the earth; but the Christian revelation ends with the regenerations or new creation of the heavens and the earth. This the ancient promise of God confirmed to us by the Christian apostles. The present elements are to be changed by fire. The old or antediluvian earth was purified by water; but the present earth is reserved for fire, with all the works of man that are upon it. It shall be converted into a lake of liquid fire. But the dead in Christ will have been regenerated in body before the old earth is regenerated by fire. The bodies of the saints will be as homogeneous with the new earth and heavens as their present bodies are with the present heavens and earth. God re-creates, regenerates, but annihilates nothing; and, therefore the present earth is not to be annihilated. The best description we can give of this regeneration is in the words of one who had a vision of it on the island of Patmos. He describes it as far as it is connected with the New Jerusalem, which is to stand upon the new earth, under the canopy of the new heaven:

"And I saw a new heaven and a new earth: for the former heaven and the former earth were passed away; and the sea was no more. And I, John, saw the holy city, the New Jerusalem, descending from God out of heaven, prepared like a bride adorned for her husband. And I heard a great voice out of heaven, saying, Behold, the tabernacle of God is with men, and he shall pitch his tent among them, and they shall be his people, and God himself shall be among them— their God. And he shall wipe away every tear from their eyes; and death shall be no more, nor grief, nor crying; nor shall there be any more pain: for the former things are passed away."

A WORD TO THE MORAL REGENERATORS OF THE AGE

God, our heavenly Father, works by means, as we all confess. His means are wisely adapted to the ends he has in view. His agents are the best agents for the work he has to accomplish. He employs not physical means nor agents for moral ends and purposes. Nor does he produce physical effects by moral means and agents. He has been pleased to employ not angels, but men, in the work of regenerating the world. Men have written, printed, and published the gospel for nearly two thousand years. They have perpetuated it from generation to generation. They have translated it from language to language, and carried it from country to country. They have preached it in word and in deed, and thus it has come down to our days.

During the present administration of the reign of heaven, no change is to be expected; no new mission is to be originated, no new order of preachers is to be instituted. The king has gone to a far country; and, before his departure, he called together his servants, and committed to them the management of his estate till he return. He has not yet come to reckon with them. They were commanded first to proclaim the doctrine of his reign; then to write it in a book, and to commit it to faithful men, who should be able to teach it correctly to others. By these faithful men the records have been kept; and through their vigilance and industry they have been guarded from corruption, interpolation, and change. One generation handed them over to the next; and, if ignorance and unfaithful copyists neglected their duty, others more faithful have corrected them; and now we are able to hear the words which Jesus spake, and to read the very periods penned by the apostles.

Thus, whatever the prophets and the apostles have achieved since their death, has been accomplished by human agents like ourselves. Where men have not carried this intelligence in speech or writing, not one of our race knows God or his anointed Saviour. No angel nor Holy Spirit has been sent to the pagan nations: and God has exerted no power out of his word to enlighten or reclaim savage nations. These indisputable facts and truths have much moral meaning, and ought to give a strong impulse to our efforts to regenerate the world.

The best means of doing this is the object now before us; and this is one the importance of which can not be easily exaggerated. There are three ways of proceeding in this case, which now seem to occupy a considerable share of public attention. These are properly called *theorizing, declaiming,* and *preaching;* on each of which we may offer a remark or two in passing.

The *theorizers* are those who are always speculating upon correct notions, or the true theory of conversion. They are great masters of method, and with some of them it is a ruinous error to place faith before regeneration, or repentance after faith. Heresy, with these, is the derangement of the method which these have proposed for God to work by in converting the sinner. And the true faith which is connected with salvation is an apprehension of this theory and acquiescense in it. These are all theorists, heady or speculative Christians; and with them the whole *scheme* of redemption is a splendid theory.

Our maxim is, *Theory for the doctors, and medicine for the sick.* Doctors fatten on theories, but patients die who depend on theory for a cure. A few grains of practice is worth a pound of theory. The mason and the carpenter *build* the house by *rule;* but he that inhabits it *lives* by *eating* and *drinking.* No man ever was cured physically, politically, morally, or religiously, by learning a correct theory of his physical, political, moral, or religious malady. As soon might we expect to heal an ulcer on the liver by a discourse upon that organ, its functions, its diseases, and their cure, as to restore a sinner by means of the theory of faith, repentance, regeneration, or effectual calling. But on this enough has already been said and more than is necessary to convince those who can think, and who dare to reason on such themes.

The declaimers are not those only who eulogize virtue and reprobate vice; but that large and respectable class who address themselves to the passions, to the hopes and fears of men. They are those who are so rhetorical upon the joys of heaven, and the terrors of hell: who horrify, terrify, and allure by the strength of their descriptions, the flexions of their voices, the violence of their gestures, and their touching anecdotes. Their hearers are either dissolved in tears, or frantic with terror. These talk much about the heart; and, on their theory, if man's heart was extracted, all his religion would be extracted with it. The religion of their converts flows in their blood, and has its foundation in their passions.

The preachers, properly so called, first address themselves to the understanding, by a declaration or narrative of the wonderful works of God. They state, illustrate, and prove the great facts of the gospel; they lay the whole record before their hearers; and when they have testified what God has done, what he has promised and threatened, they exhort their hearers on these premises and persuade them to obey the gospel, to surrender themselves to the guidance and direction of the Son of God. They address themselves to the whole man, his understanding, will, and affections, and approach the heart by taking the citadel of the understanding.

The accomplished and wise proclaimer of the word will find it always expedient to address his audience in their proper character; to approach them through their prejudices, and never to find fault with these prepossessions which are not directly opposed to the import and design of the ministry of reconciliation. He will set before them the models found in the sacred history, which show that the same discourse is not to be preached in every place and to every assembly, even when it is necessary to proclaim the same gospel. Paul's addresses to the Athenians, Lycaonians, Antiochians, to Felix, the Jailer, and King Agrippa, are full of instruction on this topic.

Augustine has written a treatise on preaching which Luther proposed to himself as a model; but it is said that Augustine fell as far short of his own precepts as did any of his contemporaries. We all can with more facility give precepts to others, than conform to them ourselves. In Augustine's treatise, which in some respects influenced and formed the style and plan of Luther, and through him all the Protestants, there is much said on the best rhetorical mode "of exhibiting the truth to others," but it savors more of the art of the schoolmen, than of the wisdom of the apostles. He labors more on the best style and mode of expressing one's self, than on the things to be said.

Our best precepts in this matter are derived rather from the books of Deuteronomy and Nehemiah, than from any other source out of the New Testament. The book of Deuteronomy may be regarded as a series of sermons or discourses, delivered to the Jews by their great teacher, Moses, rather than as a part of the Jewish history. Two things in this book deserve great attention. The first is the simplicity, fulness, and particularity of his narratives of the incidents on the journey through the wilderness:—God's doings and theirs, for the last forty years, are intelligibly laid before them. The next is the use made of these facts; the conclusions deduced, the arguments drawn, and the exhortations tendered, from these facts. For a fair and beautiful specimen of this, let the curious reader take up and carefully read the first four chapters of the book of Deuteronomy. The fact and the application, the argument and the exhortation, after the manner of Moses, can not fail to instruct him.

The writings of the scribes during the captivity teach us how to address a people that have lost the true meaning of the oracles of God. The readings, expositions, exhortations, and prayers of Ezra and Nehemiah are full of instruction to Christians in these days of Babylonish captivity. To address a people long accustomed to hearing the Scriptures, yet ignorant of them, and consequently disobedient, is a matter that requires all the wisdom and prudence which can be acquired from Jewish and Christian records.

The manner of address, next to the matter of it, is most important. The weightiest arguments, the most solemn appeals, the most pathetic expostulations, if not sustained by the gravity, sincerity, and piety of the speaker, will be like water spilled upon the ground. A little levity, a few witticisms, a sarcastic air, a conceited attitude, or a harsh expression, will often neutralize all the excellencies of the most scriptural and edifying discourse. The great work of regenerating men is too solemn, too awfully grave and divine, to allow any thing of the sort. Humility, serenity, devotion, and all benevolence in aspect, as well as in language, are essential to a successful proclamation of the great facts of the Living Oracles. He that can smile in his discourse at the follies, need not weep over the misfortunes of the ignorant and superstitious. He that can, while preaching the gospel, deride and ridicule the errors of his fellow-professors is, for the time being, disqualified to persuade them to accept of truth, or gladly to receive the message of salvation.

Those preachers have been sadly mistaken, who have sought popularity by their eccentricities, and courted smiles rather than souls; —who, by their anecdotes and foolish jests, told with the Bible before them, have thought to make themselves useful by making themselves ridiculous—and to regenerate men by teaching them how to violate the precepts of the gospel, and to disdain the examples of the Great Teacher and his apostles.

It will not do. These are the weapons of this world, and no part of the armor of light. Jesus and his apostles never sanctioned, by precept or example, such a course; and it is condemned by all sensible men, whether Jews or Gentiles, professors or profane.

In attempting to regenerate men, we must place before them the new man, not the old man, in the preacher as well as in the discourse; and, while we seek out arguments to convince and allure them, we must show them, in our speech and behavior, that we believe what we preach. So did the apostles and evangelists. They commended themselves to every man's conscience in the sight of Jesus Christ.

Error must be attacked. It must be opposed by the truth. But it may be asked, whether the darkness may not be more easily dissipated by the introduction of light, than by elaborate discourses upon its nature and attributes. So with moral darkness or error. To dissipate it most effectually, the easiest and most ready way is to introduce the light of truth. No preacher is obliged to learn all the errors of all ages, that he may be able to oppose them; nor is a congregation enlightened in the knowledge of God by such expositions of error. Present opposing errors may require attention; but to attack these most successfully, it is only necessary to enforce the opposing truths.

This is a very grave subject, and requires very grave attention. Much depends upon a rational and scriptural decision of the question, *Which is the most effectual way to oppose and destroy error?* To aid us in such an inquiry, it is necessary to examine how the prophets and apostles opposed the errors of their times. The world was as full of error in those days as it has ever been since. The idolatries of the pagan world, and the various doctrines of the sects of philosophers, in and out of the land of Israel, threw as much labor into their hands, as the various heresies of apostate Christendom have thrown into ours. Their general rule was to turn the artillery of light, and to gather into a focus the arrows of day, upon the dark shades of any particular error. Their philosophy was:—The splendors of light most clearly display the blackness of darkness, and scatter it from its presence. Thus they opposed idolatry, superstition, and error of every name. Going forth in the armor of light, as the sun in the morning, the shades of the night retired from their presence, and the cheering beams of day so gladdened the eyes of their converts, that they loved darkness no more. Let us go and do likewise.

An intimate acquaintance with the Holy Scriptures is the best apparatus for the work of regenerating men. The best piece I have found in the celebrated treatise of Augustine on preaching is the following:—

"He, then, who handles and teaches the word of God should be a defender of the true faith, and a vanquisher of error; and in accomplishing this, the object of preaching, he should conciliate the adverse, excite the remiss, and point out to the ignorant their duty and future prospects. When, however, he finds his audience favorably disposed, attentive, and docile, or succeeds in rendering them so, then other things are to be done, as the case may require. If they are to be instructed, then to make them acquainted with the subject in question, narration must be employed; and, to establish what is doubtful, resort must be had to reasoning and evidence. If they are to be moved rather than instructed, then, to arouse them from stupor in putting their knowledge into practice, and bring them to yield full assent to those things which they confess to be true, there will be need of the higher powers of eloquence; it will be necessary to entreat, reprove, excite, restrain, and do whatsoever else may prove effectual in moving the heart.

"All this, indeed, is what most men constantly do with respect to those things which they undertake to accomplish by speaking. Some, however, in their way of doing it, are blunt, frigid, inelegant; others, ingenious, ornate, vehement. Now, he who engages in the business of which I am treating must be able to speak and dispute with wisdom, even if he can not do so with eloquence, in order that he may profit his audience; although he will profit them less in this case, than if he could combine wisdom and eloquence together. He who abounds in eloquence without wisdom is certainly so much the more to be avoided, from the very fact that the hearer is delighted with what it is useless to hear and thinks what is said to be true, because it is spoken with elegance. Nor did his sentiment escape the notice of those among the ancients, who yet regarded it us important to teach the art of rhetoric; they confessed that wisdom without eloquence profited states but very little, but that eloquence without wisdom profited them not at all, and generally proved highly injurious. If, therefore, those who taught the precepts of eloquence, even though ignorant of the true, that is, the celestial wisdom which cometh down from the Father of lights, were compelled by the instigations of truth to make such a confession, and that too in the very books in which their principles were developed; are we not under far higher obligations to acknowledge the same thing, who are the sons and daughters of this heavenly wisdom? Now, a man speaks with greater or less wisdom according to the proficiency he has made in the sacred Scriptures. I do not mean in reading them and committing them to memory, but in rightly understanding them and diligently searching into their meaning. There are those who read them and yet neglect them; who read them, to remember the words, but neglect to understand them. To these, without any doubt, those persons are to be preferred, who, retaining less the words of the Scriptures, search after their genuine signification with the inmost feelings of the heart. But better than both is he, who can repeat them when he pleases, and at the same time understands them as they ought to be understood."[1]

Luther's favorite maxim was, *"Bonus Textuarius, Bonus Theologu";* or, One well acquainted with the Scriptures, makes a good theologian.

There is one thing, above all others, which must never be lost sight of by him who devotes himself to the work of regeneration. This all-important consideration is, that the end and object of all his labors is *to impress the moral image of God upon the moral nature of man.* To draw this image upon the heart, to transform the mind of man into the likeness of God in all moral feeling, is the end proposed in the remedial system. The mould into which the mind of man is to be cast is the apostles' doctrine; or the seal by which this impression is to be made is the testimony of God. The gospel facts are like so many types, which, when scientifically arranged by an accomplished compositor, make a complete form, upon which, when the mind of man is placed by the power which God has given to the preacher, every type makes its full impression upon the heart. There is written upon the understanding, and engraved upon the heart, the will, or law, or character, of our Father who is in heaven.

The apostles were these accomplished compositors, who gave us a *perfect "form of sound words."* Our instrumentality consists in bringing the minds of men to this form, or impressing it upon their hearts. To do this most effectually the preacher or evangelist must have the word of Christ dwelling in him richly, in all wisdom; and he must "study to show himself an approved workman, irreproachable, rightly dividing the word of truth." He that is most eloquent and wise in the Holy Scriptures, he who has them most at command, will have the most power with men; because, being furnished with the words of the Holy Spirit, he has the very arguments which the Spirit of God chooses to employ in quickening the dead, in converting sinners. For to the efficacy of the living word not only Paul deposes,

---

[1] From the *Biblical Repository,* p. 574. Translated from the Latin by O. A. Taylor, of Andover, Mass.

but James and Peter also bear ample testimony. "Of his own will he has begotten us, *by the word of truth,* that we might be a kind of firstfruits of his creatures."[1] "Having been regenerated, not by corruptible seed, but by incorruptible, *through the word* of the living God which remains."[2] To the fruits of his labors, such a preacher, with Paul, may say, "To Jesus Christ, through the gospel, I have regenerated or begotten you."

Thus, in the midst of numerous interruptions, we have attempted to lay before the minds of our readers the whole doctrine of regeneration, in all its length and breadth, in the hope, that after a more particular attention to its meaning and value, by the blessing of God, they may devote themselves more successfully to this great work; and not only enjoy more of the Holy Spirit themselves, but be more useful in forwarding the moral regeneration of the world.

To God our Father, through the great Author of the Christian faith, who has preserved us in health in this day of affliction and great distress, be everlasting thanks for the renewing of our minds by the Holy Spirit, and for the hope of the regeneration of our bodies, of the heavens and of the earth, at the appearance of the Almighty regenerator, who comes to make all things new!—Amen.

---

[1] James 1:18.   [2] 1 Peter 1:23.

BREAKING THE LOAF

Man was not made for the Christian institution, but the Christian institution for man. None but a master of the human constitution—none but one perfectly skilled in all the animal, intellectual, and moral endowments of men—could perfectly adapt an institution to man in reference to all that he is, and to all that he is destined to become. Such is the Christian institution. Its evidences of a divine origin increase and brighten in the ratio of our progress in the science of man. He who most attentively and profoundly reads himself, and contemplates the picture which the Lord of this institution has drawn of him, will be most willing to confess, that man is wholly incapable of originating it. He is ignorant of himself, and of the race from which he sprang, who can persuade himself that man, in any age, or in any country, was so far superior to himself as to have invented such an institution as the Christian. That development of man in all his natural, moral, and religious relations, which the Great Teacher has given, is not further beyond the intellectual powers of man, than is the creation of the sun, moon, and stars beyond his physical strength.

The eye of man can not see itself; the ear of man can not hear itself; nor the understanding of man discern itself: but there is One who sees the human eye, who hears the human ear, and who discerns the human understanding. He it is who alone is skilled in revealing man to himself and himself to man. He who made the eye of man, can he not see? He who made the ear of man, can he not hear? He who made the heart of man, can he not know?

It is as supernatural to adapt a system to man as it is to create him. He has never thought much upon his own powers, who has not seen as much wisdom on the outside as in the inside of the human head. To suit the outside to the inside required as much wisdom as to suit the inside to the outside, and yet the exterior arrangement exists for the interior. To fashion a casement for the human soul exhibits as many attributes of the Creator, as to fashion a human spirit for its habitation. Man, therefore, could as easily make himself, as a system of religion to suit himself. It will be admitted, that it calls for as much skill to adapt the appendages to the human eye, as the human eye to its appendages. To us it is equally plain, that it requires as much wisdom to adapt a religion to man, circumstanced as he is, as to create him an intellectual and moral being.

But to understand the Christian religion, we must study it; and to enjoy it, we must practice it. To come into the kingdom of Jesus

Christ is one thing, and to live as a wise, a good, and a happy citizen is another. As every human kingdom has its constitution, laws, ordinances, manners, and customs; so has the kingdom of the Great King. He, then, who would be a good and happy citizen of it, must understand and submit to its constitution, laws, ordinances, manners, and customs.

The object of the present essay is to develop one of the institutions or ordinances of this kingdom; and this we shall attempt by stating, illustrating and sustaining the following propositions:—

PROP. I.—*There is a house on earth, called the house of God.*

The most high God dwells not in temples made with human hands; yet he condescended in the age of types to have a temple erected for himself, which he called his house, and glorified it with the symbols of his presence. In allusion to this, the Christian community, organized under the government of his Son, is called his house and temple. "You are God's building," says Paul to a Christian community. This building is said to be "built upon the apostles and prophets—Jesus Christ himself being the chief cornerstone." "Know you not that you are the temple of God? The temple of God is holy, which temple you are."

But in allusion to the Jewish temple, the Christian church occupies the middle space between the outer court and the holiest of all. "The holy places made with hands were figures of the true." The common priests went *always* into the first tabernacle or holy place, and the high priest *once a year* into the *holiest of all.* Thus, our Great High Priest went *once for all* into the true "holiest of all," into the real presence of God, and has permitted us Christians, as a royal priesthood, as a chosen race, to enter always into the only holy place now on earth—the Christian church. "As living stones we are built up into a *spiritual house,* a holy priesthood, to offer up spiritual sacrifices most acceptable to God by Jesus Christ."[1]

But all we aim at here is to show that the community under Christ is called "*the house of God.*" Paul once calls it *a* house of God, and once *the* house of God. An individual or single congregation, he calls "*a house of God.*"[2] I have written to you, "that you may know how to behave yourself in a house of God, which is the congregation of God."[3] And in his letter to the Hebrews,[4] speaking of the whole Christian community, he calls it the house of God.[5] "Having a Great High Priest over the house of God, let us draw near," etc. It is, then, apparent, that there is under the Lord Mes-

---

[1] 1 Peter 2:5.   [2] 1 Timothy 3:15.   [3] Greek, *oikos Theou.*
[4] Hebrews 10:21.   [5] Greek, *ho oikos Theou.*

siah, now on earth, an institution called *the house of God;* and this resembles the *holy place* between the outer court and the holiest of all, which is the position to be proved.

PROP. II.—*In the house of God there is always the table of the Lord.*

As there is an analogy between the Jewish holy place, and the Christian house of God; so there is an analogy between the furniture of the first tabernacle or holy place, and those who officiated in it; and the furniture of the Christian house of God, and those who officiate in it. "In the first tabernacle," said Paul, "which is called *holy,* there were the candlestick, and the table, and the shewbread," or the loaves of the presence. On the golden table every Sabbath day were placed *twelve* loaves, which were exhibited there for one week, and on the next Sabbath they were substituted by twelve fresh loaves sprinkled over with frankincense. The loaves which were removed from the table were eaten by the priests. These were called in the Hebrew *"loaves of the faces,"* or the loaves of the presence. This emblem of the abundance of spiritual food in the presence of God for all who dwell in the holy place stood always upon the golden table furnished by the twelve tribes, even in the wilderness. The light in the first tabernacle was not from *without,* but from the seven lamps placed on the golden candlestick; emblematic of the perfect light, not derived from this world, which is enjoyed in the house of God.

If, then, in the emblematic house of God, to which corresponds the Christian house of God, there was not only a table overlaid with gold, always spread, and on it displayed twelve large loaves, or cakes, sacred memorials and emblems of God's bounty and grace; shall we say that in that house, over which Jesus is a Son, there is not to stand always a table more precious than gold, covered with a richer repast for the holy and royal priesthood which the Lord has instituted, who may always enter into the holy place consecrated by himself?

But we are not dependent on analogies, nor far-fetched inferences, for the proof of this position. Paul, who perfectly understood both the Jewish and Christian institutions, tells us that there is in the Christian temple a table, appropriately called the Lord's table, as a part of its furniture. He informs those who were in danger of being polluted by idolatry, "that they could not be partakers of the Lord's table, and of the table of demons."[1] In all his allusions to this table in this connection, he represents it as continually approached by

---

[1] 1 Corinthians 10:21.

those in the Lord's house. "The cup of the Lord" and "the loaf," for which thanks were continually offered, are the furniture of this table, to which the Christian brotherhood have free access.

The apostle Paul reminds the saints in Corinth of their familiarity with the Lord's table, in speaking of it as being common as the meetings of the brotherhood. "The cup of blessing for which we bless God, is it not the joint participation of the blood of Christ? The loaf which we break, is it not the joint participation of the body of Christ?" In this style we speak of things common and usual, never thus of things uncommon or unusual. It is not the cup which we *have received* with thanks; nor is it the loaf which we have broken; but which we *do* break. But all that we aim at here is now accomplished; for it has been shown that *in the Lord's house there is always the table of the Lord*. It is scarcely necessary to add, that if it be shown that in the Lord's house there is the Lord's table, as a part of the furniture, it must always be there, unless it can be shown that only some occasions require its presence, and others its absence; or that the Lord is poorer or more churlish at one time than at another; that he is not always able to keep a table, or too parsimonious to furnish it for his friends. But this is in anticipation of our subject, and we proceed to the third proposition.

PROP. III.—*On the Lord's table there is of necessity but one loaf.*

The necessity is not that of a positive law enjoining one loaf and only one, as the ritual of Moses enjoined twelve loaves. But it is a necessity arising from the meaning of the institution as explained by the apostles. As there is but one literal body, and but one mystical or figurative body having many members; so there must be but one loaf. The apostle insists upon this, "Because there is one loaf, we, the many, are one body; for we are all partakers of that one loaf."[1] The Greek word, *artos*, especially when joined with words of number, says Dr. Macknight, always signifies *a loaf*, and is so translated in our Bibles:—"Do you not remember the *five loaves?*"[2] There are many instances of the same sort. Dr. Campbell says, "that in the plural number it ought always to be rendered loaves; but when there is a numeral before it, it indispensably must be rendered a loaf or loaves. Thus we say one loaf, seven loaves; not one bread, seven breads."—"Because there is one loaf," says Paul, "we must consider the whole congregation as one body." Here the apostle reasons from what is more plain to what is less plain; from what was established to what was not so fully established in the minds of the Corinthians.

---

[1] 1 Corinthians 10:17. [2] Matthew 16:9.

There was no dispute about the one loaf; therefore, there ought to be none about the one body. This mode of reasoning makes it as certain as a positive law; because that which an apostle reasons from must be an established fact, or an established principle. To have argued from an assumption or a contingency to establish the unity of the body of Christ would have been ridiculous in a logician, and how unworthy of an apostle! It was, then, an established institution, that there is but one loaf, inasmuch as the apostle establishes his argument by a reference to it as an established fact. Our third proposition is, then, sustained, that *on the Lord's table there is of necessity but one loaf.*

PROP. IV.—*All Christians are members of the house or family of God, are called and constituted a holy and royal priesthood, and may, therefore bless God for the Lord's table, its loaf, and cup— approach it without fear, and partake of it with joy as often as they please, in remembrance of the death of their Lord and Saviour.*

The different clauses of this proposition, we shall sustain in order —*"all Christians are members of the family or house of God."*[1] "But Christ is trusted as a Son *over his own family,* whose family we are, provided we maintain our profession and boasted hope unshaken to the end";—*"are called and constituted a holy and a royal priesthood."*[2] You, also, as living stones are built up a spiritual temple, a holy priesthood, to offer spiritual sacrifices most acceptable to God through Jesus Christ." In the ninth verse of the same chapter he says, "But you are an elect race, a chosen generation, a royal priesthood"; and this is addressed to all the brethren dispersed in Pontus, Galatia, Cappadocia, Asia, and Bithynia.

May not, then, holy and royal priests thank God for the Lord's table, its loaf, and cup of wine? May they not, without a *human* priest to consecrate the way for them, approach the Lord's table, and handle the loaf and cup? If the common priests did not fear to approach the golden table, and to place upon it the loaves of the presence; if they feared not to take and eat that consecrated bread, because priests according to the flesh—shall royal priests fear, without the intervention of human hands, to approach the Lord's table and to partake of the one loaf? If they should, they know not how to appreciate the consecration of Jesus, nor how to value their high calling and exalted designation as kings and priests to God. And may we not say, that he who, invested with a little clerical authority, derived only from "the Man of Sin and Son of Perdition," if bor-

---

[1] Hebrews 3:6.   [2] 1 Peter 2:5.

rowed from the Romanists, says to them, "Stand by, I am holier than thou,"—may we not say that such a one is worse than Diotrephes, who affected a pre-eminence, because he desecrates the royal priesthood of Jesus Christ, and calls him common and unclean, who has been consecrated by the blood of the Son of God? Such impiety can only be found among them who worship the beast, and who have covenanted and agreed that none shall buy or sell, save those who receive a mark on their foreheads and letters-patent in their hands. But allow common sense to whisper a word into the ears of preists' "laymen," but Christ's "royal priests." Do you not thank God for the cup while the priest stands by the table; and do you not handle the loaf and cup when they come to you? And would not your thanksgiving have been as acceptable, if the human mediator had not been there, and your participating as well pleasing to God, and as consolatory to yourself, if you had been the first that had handled the loaf or the cup, as when you are the second, or the fifty-second, in order of location? Let reason answer these two questions, and see what comes of the haughty assumptions of your Protestant clergy! But this is only by the way.

I trust it is apparent that the royal priesthood may approach the Lord's table *without fear*, inasmuch as they are consecrated to officiate by a blood, as far superior to that which consecrated the fleshly priesthood, as the Lord's table, covered with the sacred emblems of the sacrifice of the Lord himself, is superior to the table which held only the twelve loaves of the presence; and as they are, to say the least, called by as holy and divine an election, and are as *chosen a race* of priests, as were those sprung from the loins of Levi.

PROP. V.—*The one loaf must be broken before the saints feed upon it, which has obtained for this institution the name of "breaking the loaf."*

But some, doubtless, will ask, "Is it not called *the Lord's supper?*" Some have thought, among whom is Dr. Bell, that 1 Corinthians 11:20 applies to the feasts of love or charity, rather than the showing forth the Lord's death. These may read the passage thus:—"But your coming together into one place is not to eat a Lord's supper; for in eating it every one takes first his own supper; alluding, as they suppose, to a love-feast eaten before *the breaking the loaf.*" But this Lord's supper is contradistinguished from their *own* supper. And might it not as reasonably be said, you can not call *your* showing forth the Lord's death a Lord's supper; for before eating it you have eaten a supper of your own, which prevents you from making a *supper* of it? You do not make it a Lord's supper, if you first eat your own supper.

Nor, indeed, could the Corinthians call any eating the "Lord's supper," conducted as was the eating of their own suppers; for one ate and drank to excess, while another who was poor, or had no supper to bring, was hungry and put to shame. Could this be called a supper in honor of the Lord?

But as the Lord had eaten a religious supper, had partaken of the paschal lamb with his disciples, before he instituted the breaking of the loaf, and drinking of the cup, as commemorative of his death, it seems improper to call it a supper; for, it was instituted and eaten *after a supper.* Not in the sense of one of the meals of the day, can it be called either dinner or supper; for it supplies the place of no meal. *Diepnos,* here rendered *supper,* in the days of Homer represented breakfast.[1] It also signified food in general or a feast. In the times of Demosthenes, it signified a feast or an evening meal. But it is of more importance to observe, that it is in the New Testament used figuratively as well as literally. Hence, we have the gospel blessings compared to a supper. We read of the "marriage-supper of the Lamb," and "supper of the Great God." Jesus says, "If any man open to me, I will [*deipneso*] take supper with him and he with me." When thus used, it neither regards the time of day, nor the quantity eaten. If applied, then, to this institution, it is figuratively, as it is elsewhere called *"the feast."* For not only did the Lord appoint it, but in eating it we have communion with the Lord. The same idiom, with the addition of the article, occurs in Revelation 1:10, *"he kuriake hemera,"* the Lord's day. Upon the whole it appears more probable that the apostle uses the words *kuriakos deipnos,* or Lord's supper, as applicable to the breaking of the loaf for which they gave thanks in honor of the Lord, than to their own supper or the feasts of love, usual among the brethren. If we say, in accordance with the apostle's style, the Lord's day, the Lord's table, the Lord's cup, we may also say the Lord's supper. For in the Lord's house these are all sacred to him.

As the calling of Bible things by Bible names is an important item in the present reformation, we may here take occasion to remark, that both "the Sacrament" and "the Eucharist" are of human origin. The former was a name adopted by the Latin church; because the observance was supposed to be an oath or vow to the Lord; and, as the term *sacramentum* signified an oath taken by a Roman soldier to be true to his general and his country, they presumed to call this institution a sacrament or oath to the Lord. By the Greek church it is called *the Eucharist,* which word imports *the giving of thanks,* be-

---

[1] *Iliad,* Book 2, lines 381-99, and 8, lines 53-66.

cause, before participating, thanks were presented for the loaf and the cup. It is also called the communion, or *"the communion of the saints";* but this might indicate that it is exclusively the communion of saints; and, therefore, it is more consistent to denominate it literally "the breaking of the loaf." But this is the only preliminary to the illustration and proof of our fifth proposition.

We have said that the loaf must be broken before the saints partake of it. Jesus took a loaf from the paschal table and broke it before he gave it to his disciples. They received a broken loaf, emblematic of his body once whole, but by his own consent broken for his disciples. In eating it we then remember that the Lord's body was by his own consent broken or wounded for us. Therefore, he that gives thanks for the loaf should break it not as the representative of the Lord, but after his example; and after the disciples have partaken of this loaf, handing it to one another, or while they are partaking of it, the disciple who brake it partakes with them of the broken loaf: thus they all have communion with the Lord and with one another in eating the broken loaf. And thus they as priests feast upon his sacrifice. For the priests ate of the sacrifices and were thus partakers of the altar. The proof of all this is found in the institution given in Matthew 26, Mark 14, Luke 22, and 1 Corinthians 11. In each of which his breaking of the loaf, *after* giving thanks, and *before* his disciples partook of it, is distinctly stated.

It is not, therefore, strange, that the literal designations of this institution should be what Luke has given it in his Acts of the Apostles thirty years after its institution. The first time he notices it is Acts 2:42, when he calls it emphatically *te klasei tou artou,* the breaking of the loaf, a name at the time of his writing, A.D. 64, universally understood. For, says he, in recording the piety and devotion of the first converts, "they continued steadfast in the teaching· of the apostles, in the fellowship, in *the breaking of the loaf,* in the prayers —praising God." It is true, there is more than breaking a loaf in this institution. But, in accordance with general if not universal usage, either that which is first or most prominent in laws, institutions, and usages, gives a name to them. Thus we have our *Habeas Corpus,* our *Fieri Facias,* our *Nisi Prius,* our *Capias,* our *Venditioni Exponas,* names given from the first words of the law.

But to break a loaf, or *to break bread,* was a phrase common among the Jews to denote ordinary eating for refreshment. For example, Acts 2:46—"Daily, with one accord, they continued in the temple and in breaking bread from house to house. They ate their *food* with gladness, and simplicity of heart." Also, after Paul had restored Eutychus at Troas, we are informed he brake a loaf and ate.

Here it must refer to himself, not only because it is used *indefinitely,* but because he that eats is in the same number with him that breaks a loaf. But when an established usage is referred to, the article or some definite term ascertains what is alluded to. Thus Acts 2:42, it is *"the* breaking of the loaf." And Acts 20:7, it is "They assembled for *the* breaking of the loaf." This loaf is explained by Paul (1 Cor. 10:16), *"The* loaf which we break, is it not the communion of the body of Christ?" This proposition being now, as we judge, sufficiently evident, we shall proceed to state our sixth.

PROP. VI.—*The breaking of the loaf and the drinking of the cup are commemorative of the Lord's death.*

Upon the loaf and upon the cup of the Lord, in letters which speak not to the eye, but to the heart of every disciple, is inscribed, *"When this you see, remember me."* Indeed, the Lord says to each disciple, when he receives the symbols into his hands, "This is my body broken for *you.* This is my blood shed for *you."* The loaf is thus constituted a representation of his body—first whole, then wounded for our sins. The cup is thus instituted a representation of his blood—once his life, but now poured out to cleanse us from our sins. To every disciple he says, "For *you* my body was wounded; for *you* my life was taken." In receiving it the disciple says, "Lord, I believe it. My life sprung from thy suffering; my joy from thy sorrows; and my hope of glory everlasting from thy humiliation and abasement even to death." Each disciple, in handing the symbols to his fellow disciple, says, in effect, "You, my brother, once an alien, are now a citizen of heaven; once a stranger, are now brought home to the family of God. You have owned my Lord as your Lord, my people as your people. Under Jesus the Messiah we are one. Mutually embraced in the everlasting arms, I embrace you in mine; thy sorrows shall be my sorrows, and thy joys my joys. Joint debtors to the favor of God and the love of Jesus, we shall jointly suffer with him, that we may jointly reign with him. Let us, then, renew our strength, remember our King, and hold fast our boasted hope unshaken to the end."

> "Blest be the tie that binds
> Our hearts in Christian love;
> The fellowship of kindred minds
> Is like to that above."

Here he knows no man after the flesh. Ties that spring from eternal love, revealed in blood and addressed to his senses, draw forth all that is within him of complacent affection and feeling to those joint heirs with him of the grace of eternal life. While it represents to him *"the bread of life"*—all the salvation of the Lord—it is the strength of his faith, the joy of his hope, and the life of his love.[1]

This institution commemorates the love which reconciled us to God, and always furnishes us with a new argument to live for him who died for us. Him who feels not the eloquence and power of this argument, all other arguments assail in vain. God's goodness, developed in creation and in his providence, is well designed to lead men to reformation. But the heart on which these fail, and to which Calvary appeals in vain, is past feeling, obdurate, and irreclaimable, beyond the operation of any moral power known to mortal man.

Every time the disciples assemble around the Lord's table, they are furnished with a new argument also against sin, as well as with a new proof of the love of God. It is as well intended to crucify the world in our hearts, as to quicken us to God, and to diffuse his love within us. Hence it must in reason be a stated part of the Christian worship, in all Christian assemblies; which leads us to state, illustrate, and sustain the following capital proposition, to which the preceding six are all preliminary.

PROP. VII.—*The breaking of the one loaf, and the joint participation of the cup of the Lord, in commemoration of the Lord's death, usually called "the Lord's supper," is an instituted part of the worship and edification of all Christian congregations in all their stated meetings.*

Argument 1. The first Christian congregation which met in Jerusalem, and which was constituted by the twelve apostles, did as statedly attend upon the breaking of the loaf in their public meetings, as they did upon any other part of the Christian worship. So Luke records (Acts 2:42), "They continued steadfast in the apostles' doctrine, in the fellowship, in the *breaking of the loaf,* and in the prayers." Ought we not, then, to continue as steadfast in the breaking of the loaf, as in the teaching of the apostles, as in the fellowship, as in the prayers commanded by the apostles?

Argument 2. The apostles taught the churches to do all the Lord commanded. Whatever, then, the churches did by the appointment or concurrence of the apostles, they did by the commandment of Jesus Christ. Whatever acts of religious worship the apostles taught and sanctioned in one Christian congregation, they taught and sanctioned in all Christian congregations, because all are under the same government of one and the same king. But the church in Troas met upon

---

[1] *Christian Baptist,* Vol. 3, No. 1. In that volume, in the fall of 1825, were written four essays on the breaking of bread, which see.

the first day of the week, consequently all the churches met upon the first day of the week for religious purposes.

Among the acts of worship, or the institutions of the Lord, to which the disciples attended in these meetings, the breaking of the loaf was so conspicuous and important, that the churches are said to meet on the first day of the week for this purpose. We are expressly told that the disciples at Troas met for this purpose; and what one church did by the authority of the Lord, as a part of his instituted worship, they all did. That the disciples in Troas met for this purpose is not to be inferred; for Luke says positively (Acts 22:7), "And on the first day of the week, when the disciples came together for the breaking of the loaf, Paul, being about to depart on the morrow, discoursed with them, and lengthened out his discourse till midnight." From the manner in which this meeting of the disciples at Troas is mentioned by the historian, two things are very obvious:—first, that it was an established custom or rule for the disciples to meet on the first day of the week. Second, that the primary object of their meeting was to break the loaf. They who object to breaking the loaf on the first day of every week when the disciples are assembled usually preface their obligations by telling us, that Luke does not say they broke the loaf *every* first day; and yet they contend against the Sabbatarians that they ought to observe *every* first day to the Lord in commemoration of his resurrection. The Sabbatarians raise the same objection to this passage, when adduced by all professors of Christianity to authorize the weekly observance of the first day. They say that Luke does not tell us that they met for any religious purpose on every first day. How inconsistent, then, are they who make this sentence an express precedent for observing every first day, when arguing against the Sabbatarians, and then turn round and tell us that it will not prove that they broke the loaf *every* first day! If it does not prove the one, it is most obvious it will not prove the other; for the weekly observance of this day, as a day of the meeting of the disciples, and the weekly breaking of the loaf in those meetings, stand or fall together. Hear it again:—"And on the first day of the week, when the disciples assembled to break the loaf." Now, all must confess, who regard the meaning of words, that the meeting of the disciples and the breaking of the loaf, as far as these words are concerned, are expressed in the same terms as respects the frequency. If the one was *fifty-two* times in a year, or only *once*, so was the other. If they met every first day, they broke the loaf every first day; and if they did not break the loaf every first day, they did not meet every first day. But we argue from the style of Luke, or from his manner of narrating the fact, that they did both. If he had said that on *a* first day the disciples assembled to break the loaf, then I would admit that both the Sabbatarians, and the semi-annual or septennial communicants, might find some way of explaining this evidence away.

The definite article is, in the Greek and in the English tongue, prefixed to stated fixed times, and its appearance here is not merely definitive of one day, but expressive of a stated or fixed day. This is so in all languages which have a definite article. Let us illustrate this by a very parallel and plain case. Suppose some five hundred or one thousand years hence the annual observance of the Fourth of July should have ceased for several centuries, and that some person or persons devoted to the primitive institutions of this mighty republic were desirous of seeing the fourth of every July observed as did the fathers and founders of the republic during the hale and undegenerate days of primitive republican simplicity. Suppose that none of the records of the first century of this republic had expressly stated, that it was a regular and fixed custom for a certain class of citizens to pay a particular regard to the fourth day of every July; but that a few incidental expressions in the biography of the leading men in the republic spoke of it as Luke has done of the meeting at Troas. How would it be managed? For instance, in the life of John Quincy Adams, it is written, A.D. 1823, "And on the Fourth of July, when the republicans of the city of Washington met to dine, John Q. Adams delivered an oration to them." Would not an American, a thousand years hence, in circumstances such as have been stated, find in these words *one* evidence that it was an established usage, during the first century of this republic, to regard the Fourth of July as aforesaid? He would tell his opponents to mark that it was not said that on *a* fourth of July, as if it were a particular occurrence; but it was, in the fixed meaning of the English language, expressive of a fixed and stated day of peculiar observance. At all events, he could not fail in convincing the most stupid, that the primary intention of that meeting was to dine. Whatever might be the frequency or the intention of that dinner, it must be confessed, from the words above cited, that they *met to dine*.

Another circumstance that must somewhat confound the Sabbatarians, and the lawless observers of the breaking of the loaf, may be easily gathered from Luke's narrative. Paul and his company arrived at Troas either on the evening of the first day, or on Monday morning at an early hour; for he departed on Monday morning, as we term it, at an early hour; and we are positively told that he tarried just seven days at Troas. Now, had the disciples been Sabbatarians, or observed the seventh day as a Sabbath, and broke the loaf on it as the Sabbatarians do, they would not have deferred their meeting till the first day, and kept Paul and his company waiting, as he was evidently in a great haste at this time. But his tarrying *seven* days, and his early departure on Monday morning, corroborates the evidence adduced in proof, that the first day of the week was the *fixed* and *stated* day for the disciples to meet for this purpose.[1]

From the second of the Acts, then, we learn that *the breaking of the loaf* was a stated part of the worship of the disciples in their meetings; and from the twentieth we learn that the first day of the week was the stated time for those meetings; and, above all, we ought to notice that the most prominent object of their meeting was to break the loaf. Other corroborating evidences of the stated meeting of the disciples on the first day for religious purposes are found in the fact, that Paul says he had given order to all the congregations in Galatia, as well as that in Corinth, to attend to the fellowship, or the laying up of contributions for the poor saints on the first day of every week. "On the first day of *every week* let each of you lay somewhat by itself, according as he may have prospered, putting it into the treasury, that when I come there may be no collections" for the saints. *Kata mian Sabbaton* Macknight justly renders *"first day of every week"*; for every linguist will admit that *kata polin* means every city; *kata menan*, every month; *kata ecclesian*, every church; and therefore, in the same usage, *kata mian Sabbaton* means the first day of every week.

Now, this prepares the way for asserting not only that the disciples in Troas assembled on the first day of every week for "the breaking of the loaf," but also for adducing a third argument:—

Argument 3. The congregation in Corinth met every first day, or the first day of every week, for showing forth the Lord's death. Let the reader bear in mind that he has just heard that Paul commanded the church in Corinth, or every saint in Corinth, to contribute according to his ability, by putting into the treasury every first day his contributions to avoid collections when Paul came. This is agreed on all hands to prove the weekly meeting of the saints. Now, with this concession in mind, we have only to notice what is said (11:20). "When you come together in one place, that is, every week at least, *this is not to eat the Lord's supper*. To act thus is unworthy the subject of your meeting. To act thus is not to eat the Lord's supper. It is not to show forth the Lord's death." Thereby declaring that this is the chief object of meeting. When the teacher reproves his pupils for wasting time, he can not remind them more forcibly of the object of coming to school, nor reprove them with more point, than to say,

---

[1] *Christian Baptist,* pp. 211-212.

"When you act thus, this is not to assemble to learn." This is the exact import of the apostle's address:—"When you assemble thus, it is *not* to eat the Lord's supper." We have seen, then, that the saints met every first day in Corinth; and when they assembled in one place is was to eat the Lord's supper, a declaration of the practice of the primitive congregations as explicit as could incidentally be given, differing only from a direct command in the form in which it is expressed. But it is agreed on all hands that whatsoever the congregations did with the approbation of the apostles they did by their authority. For the apostles gave them all the Christian institutions. Now, as the apostle Paul approbated their meeting every week, and their coming together into one place to show forth the Lord's death, and only censured their departure from the meaning of the institution, it is as high authority as we could require for the practice of the weekly meeting of the disciples.

But when Acts 2:42; Acts 20:7; 1 Corinthians 11:20, and 16:1, 2 are compared and added together, it appears that we act under the influence of apostolic teaching and precedent when we meet every Lord's day for the breaking of the loaf. But this is still further demonstrated by a fourth argument drawn from the following fact:—

Argument 4. No argument can be adduced from the New Testament of any Christian congregation assembling on the first day of the week, unless for the breaking of the loaf. Let an example be adduced by those who teach that Christians ought to meet on the first day of the week not to break the loaf, and then, but not till then, can they impugn the above fact. Till this is done, a denial of it must appear futile in the extreme. The argument, then, is, Christians have no authority, nor are under any obligations, to meet on the Lord's day, from any thing which the apostles said or practiced, unless it be to show forth the Lord's death, and to attend to those means of edification and comfort connected with it.

Argument 5. If it be not the duty and privilege of every Christian congregation to assemble on the first day of every week to show forth the Lord's death, it will be difficult, if not impossible, from either Scripture or reason, to show that it is their duty or privilege to meet monthly, quarterly, semi-annually, annually, or indeed at all, for this purpose. For from what premises can any person show that it is a duty or privilege to assemble monthly, which will not prove that it is obligatory to meet weekly. We challenge investigation here, and affirm that no man can produce a single reason why it should or could be a duty or a privilege for a congregation to meet monthly, quarterly, or annually, which will not prove that it is its duty and privilege to assemble every first day for this purpose.

Argument 6. Spiritual health, as well as corporeal health, is dependent on food. It is requisite for corporeal health, that the food not only be salutary in its nature and sufficient in its quantity, but that it be received at proper intervals, and these regular and fixed. Is it otherwise with moral health? Is there no analogy between the bread that perishes, and the bread of life? Is there no analogy between natural and moral life—between natural and moral health? and, if there be, does it not follow, that if the primitive disciples only enjoyed good moral health when they assembled weekly to show forth the Lord's death, they can not enjoy good moral health who only meet quarterly or semi-annually for this purpose?

Argument 7. But in the last place, what *commemorative* institution, in any age, under any religious economy, was ordained by divine authority, which had not a fixed time for its observance? Was it the commemoration of the finishing of creation signified in the weekly Sabbath? Was it the passover, the Pentecost, the feast of tabernacles? Was it the feast of Purim either? What other significant usage was it, the times or occasion of whose observance were not fixed? How often was circumcision to be administered to the same subject? How often Christian immersion? Is there a single institution commemorative of any thing, the meaning or frequency of the observance of which is not distinctly, either by precept or example, laid down in the Holy Scriptures? Not one of a *social* character, and scarcely one of an individual character. The commemoration of the Lord's death must, then, be a weekly institution—an institution in all the meetings of the disciples for Christian worship; or it must be an anomaly—a thing *sui generis*—an institution like no other of divine origin. And can any one tell why Christians should celebrate the Lord's resurrection *fifty-two* times in a year, and his death only *once, twice,* or *twelve times?* He that can do this will not be lacking in a lively imagination, however defective he may be in judgment or in an acquaintance with the New Testament.

Having written so much on this subject formerly, I shall now introduce a few persons out of the many men of renown who, since the Reformation, have pled this cause. We shall not only introduce them to our readers, but we shall let them speak to them.

John Brown, of Haddington, author of the Dictionary of the Bible, and teacher of theology for that branch of the Presbyterian church called the *"Secession,"* has written a treatise on this subject. We shall give him the task of stating and removing the objections to this apostolic institution. The reader will perceive that there are many impurities in his style; and, although his speech betrays that he has been in Ashdod, still, his arguments are weighty and powerful.

He offers various arguments for the weekly observance of this institution, and states and refutes nine objections to the practice. A few of these strongest we shall quote:—

"All the arguments I ever knew advanced in support of the unfrequent administration of the Lord's supper appear to me altogether destitute of force. The following are the principal:—

"*Objection 1.* The frequent administration of this ordinance, in the apostolic and primitive ages of Christianity, was commendable and necessary, because the continual persecutions that then raged gave them ground to fear that every Sabbath might be their last; whereas now we are not in such danger, and therefore need not so frequent use of this ordinance.

"*Answer.* Ought we not still to live as if every Sabbath were to be our last? Have we now a lease on our life more than these had? Did not many Christians in these times live to as great an age as we do now? Indeed, is it not evident, from the best historians, that the church was generally under no persecution above one-third of the time that weekly communion was practiced? But, say they had been constantly exposed to the cruelest persecution, the objection becomes still more absurd. If they attended this ordinance weekly at the peril of their lives does it follow that now, when God gives us greater and better opportunity for it, we ought to omit it? Does God require the greatest work at his people's hands, when he gives least opportunity? Or does he require least work, when he gives the greatest opportunity for it? What kind of a master must God be, if this were the case? Besides, do not men need this ordinance to preserve them from the influence of the world's smiles as much as of its frowns?"—"Let us invert this objection, and try if it has not more force. It would then run thus:—The primitive Christians received the Lord's supper weekly, as their souls were in greater danger from the smiles and allurements of the world, which are usually found more hurtful to men's spiritual concerns than its frowns; and as they had greater opportunity for doing so by their enjoying peace and liberty; yet this frequency of administering and partaking is not requisite now, as we, being under the world's frowns, are in less hazard as to our spiritual concerns; and especially as we can not attend upon it but at the peril of our lives, God having expressly declared that he loves mercy better than sacrifice.

"*Objection 2.* The primitive and reforming times were seasons of great spiritual liveliness, and of large communications of divine influences to the souls of believers; whereas it is quite otherwise now. Therefore, though frequent administration was then commendable, yet, in our languishing decayed state, it is unnecessary.

"*Answer.* Ought we to repair seldom to the wells of salvation, because we can bring but little water at once from them? Ought we seldom to endeavor to fill our pitchers at the fountain of living waters, because they are small? Is not this ordinance a cordial for restoring the languishing, strengthening the weak, recovering the sick, and reviving the dying believer? How reasonable, then, is it to argue that languishing, weak, sick, and dying believers must not have it often administered to them, just because they are not in perfect health?"—"Would not the objection inverted read better? The primitive Christians had this ordinance frequently administered to them, because, being decayed and withered, weak and sickly, and receiving only scanty communications of divine influence at once, it was necessary for them to be often taking new meals; whereas, we, being now strong and lively Christians, and receiving on these occasions such large supplies of grace as are sufficient to enable us to walk many days under their powerful influence, have no occasion for so frequently attending on that ordinance, which is especially calculated for strengthening languishing, weak, sickly believers.

"*Objection 3.* If the Lord's supper were frequently administered, it would become less solemn, and, in time, quite contemptible, as we see is the case with baptism, through the frequency of the administration of that ordinance.

"*Answer.* Is this means of keeping up the credit of the Lord's supper, of God's divising or not? If it is, where is that part of his word that warrants it? The contrary I have already proved from Scripture. Since, then, it is only of man's invention, what ground is there to hope it will really maintain the credit and solemnity of the ordinance? Did not the Papists of old pretend to maintain and advance its solemnity, by reduction of the frequency of administration? Did they not take away the cup from the people, which Calvin says was the native consequence of the former? Did they not annex the administration of this ordinance to those seasons which superstition had aggrandized; namely, Easter, Pentecost, and Christmas? Did they not annex a world of ceremonies to it? Did they not pretend that it was a real sacrifice, and that the elements were changed by consecration into the real body and blood of Christ? And did all this tend to the support of the proper credit of this ordinance? On the contrary, did it not destroy it? Though the doctrine of transubstantiation procured a kind of reverence for it, yet, was this reverence divine? or was it not rather devilish, in worshiping the elements? Now, how are we sure that our unfrequent administration of this ordinance will more effectually support its solemnity? Is it not strange that we should have so much encouragement from the practice of the apostles, the primitive Christians, and the whole of the reformed churches, to profane this solemn ordinance; while the most ignorant and abandoned Papists are our original pattern for the course that tends to support its proper honor and credit? What a strange case this must be, in order to support the credit of God's ordinance, we must forsake the footsteps of the flock, and walk in the paths originally chalked out by the most ignorant and wicked antichristians!

"Besides, if our unfrequent administration of this ordinance render it solemn, would it not become much more so, if administered only once in seven, ten, twenty, thirty, sixty, or a hundred years?—Shall we not then find that those who pray once a month or hear a sermon once a year, have their minds far more religiously impressed with solemn views of God, than those who pray seven times a day, and hear a hundred sermons within the year?

"Let us invert this objection, and see how it stands. All human devices to render God's ordinances more solemn are impeachments of his wisdom, and have always tended to bring the ordinances into contempt. But unfrequent administration of the supper is a human device, first invented by the worst of Papists, and therefore it tends to bring contempt on this ordinance, as we see sadly verified in the practice of those who voluntarily communicate seldom."

The means by which the weekly observance of the supper was set aside Mr. Brown states in the following words:—

"The means by which the unfrequent administration of this ordinance appears to me to have been introduced into the church do not savor of the God of truth. The causes that occasioned its introduction appear to have been pride, superstition, covetousness, and carnal complaisance. The Eastern hermits, retiring from the society of men, had taken up their residence in deserts and mountains, and, being far removed from the places of its administration, seldom attended. This, though really the effect of their sloth and distance, they pretend to arise from their regard and reverence for this most solemn ordinance. It being easy to imitate them in this imaginary holiness, which lay in neglecting the ordinances of God, many of the Eastern Christians left off to communicate, except at such times as superstition had rendered solemn, as at Pasch; and contented themselves with being spectators on other occasions. On account of this practice, we find the great and eloquent Chrysostom, once and again, bitterly exclaiming against them as guilty of the highest contempt of God and Christ; and calls their practice a most wicked custom."

An objection not formally stated by Mr. Brown, which I have frequently heard, is drawn from the words, "*as often as you do this,* do it in remembrance of me." From these words it is pled that we are without law in regard to time how often; and consequently can not be condemned for a partial or total neglect; for "where there is no law, there is no transgression." "As *often*" is used not to license the frequency, but to denote the manner. "Always do it in remembrance of me." The connection in which these words occur regarding the manner or design of the observance and not how often it may or may not be celebrated, it is a violation of every rule of interpretation to infer another matter from them, which was not in the eye of the apostle. Besides, if the words "as oft" leave it discretionary with any society how often, they are blameless if they never once, or more than once, in all their lives, show forth the Saviour's death. This interpretation makes an observance without reason, without law, without precedent, and consequently without obligation.

Next to Mr. Brown, we shall introduce a few extracts from *William King*, Archbishop of Dublin. The editors of the *Christian Examiner* presented a very valuable extract from Mr. King, in their seventh of May number of the first volume, from which I quote the following (pp. 163, 165, 166, 167):—

"The following remarks on this institution of our Saviour are copied from a *'Discourse Concerning the Inventions of Men in the Worship of God,'* by William King, of Ireland. He was born at Antrim, 1650; educated at Trinity College, Dublin; and held successively the dignities of Dean of St. Patrick's, Bishop of Derry, and Archbishop of Dublin. He died in 1729. His method in this discourse is to examine and compare the worship of God, as taught in the Scriptures, with the practice of the different religious sects of the day:—

"Christ's positive command to do this in remembrance of him, etc., must oblige us in some times and in some places; and there can be no better way of determining when we are obliged to do it than by observing when God in his goodness gives us opportunity; for either we are then obliged to do it, or else we may choose whether we will ever do it or no; there being no better means of determining the frequency, than this of God's giving us the opportunity. And the same rule holding in all other general positive commands, such as those that oblige us to charity, we may be sure it holds likewise in this. Therefore, whoever slights or neglects any opportunity of receiving which God affords him does sin, as certainly as he who, being enabled by God to perform an act of charity, and invited by a fit object, neglects to relieve him, or shuts up his bowels of compassion against him concerning whom the Scriptures assure us that the love of God dwells not in him. And the argument is rather stronger against him who neglects this holy ordinance; for how can it be supposed *that man* has a true love for his Saviour, or a due sense of his sufferings, who refuses or neglects to remember the greatest of all benefits, in the easiest manner, though commanded to do it by his Redeemer, and invited by a fair opportunity of God's own offering.

"It is manifest that if it be not our own fault, we may have an opportunity every Lord's day when we meet together; and, therefore, that church is guilty of laying aside the command, whose order and worship doth not require and provide for this practice. Christ's command seems to lead us directly to it: for 'Do this in remembrance of me' implies that Christ was to leave them; that they were to meet together after he was gone; and that he required them *to remember him at their meetings whilst he was absent.* The very design of our public meetings on the Lord's day, and not on the Jewish Sabbath, is, to remember and keep in our minds a sense of what Christ did and suffered for us till he come again, and this we are obliged to do, not in such a manner as our own inventions suggest, but by such means as Christ himself has prescribed to us; that is by celebrating this holy ordinance.

"It seems then probable, from the very institution of this ordinance, that our Saviour designed it should be a part of God's service in all the solemn assemblies of Christians, as the passover was in the assembles of the Jews. To know, therefore, how often Christ requires us to celebrate this feast, we have no more to do but to inquire how often Christ requires us to meet together; that is, at least every Lord's day."

We shall next introduce an American Rabbi, of very great celebrity, Dr. John Mason, of New York. The passages which I quote are found in a note attached to page 188 of the New York edition of Fuller's *Strictures on Sandemanianism:*—

"Mr. Fuller does not deny that the Lord's supper was observed by the first Christians every Lord's day (nor will this be denied by any man who has candidly investigated the subject); but he seems to think that Acts 20:7 does not prove that it was so. Others, eminent for piety and depth of research, have considered this passage as affording a complete proof of the weekly observance of the Lord's supper. Dr. Scott, in his valuable *Commentary,* observes on this passage —'*Breaking of bread* or commemorating the death of Christ in the eucharist, was one chief end of their assembling; this ordinance seems to have been *constantly administered every Lord's day,* and probably no professed Christians absented themselves from it, after they had been admitted into the church, unless they lay under some censure, or had some real hindrance.'

"Dr. Mason, of this city, in his *Letters on Frequent Communion,* speaks on this subject with still greater decision. 'It is notorious, that during the first three centuries of the Christian era communions were held, with the frequency of which, among us, we have neither example nor resemblance. It is also notorious, that it has been urged as a weighty duty by the best of men and the best churches, in the best of times.'

"Weekly communions did not die with the apostles and their contemporaries. There is a cloud of witnesses to testify that they were kept up by succeeding Christians, with great care and tenderness, for above two centuries. It is not necessary to swell these pages with quotations. The fact is indisputable.

"Communion every Lord's day was universal, and was preserved in the Greek church till the seventh century; and such as neglected *three weeks* together were excommunicated.

"In this manner did the spirit of ancient piety cherish the memory of the Saviour's love. There was no need of reproof, remonstrance, or entreaty. No trifling excuses for neglect were ever heard from the lips of a Christian; for *such* a neglect had not yet degraded the Christian's name. He carried in his own bosom sufficient inducements to obey, without reluctance, the precepts of his Lord. It was his choice, his consolation, his joy. These were days of life and glory; but days of dishonor and death were shortly to succeed; nor was there a more ominous symptom of their approach, than the decline of frequent communicating. For as the power of religion appears in a solicitude to magnify the Lord Jesus continually, so the decay of it is first detected by the encroachments of indifference. It was in the *fourth* century, that the church began very discernibly to forsake her first love.

"The excellent Calvin complains that in this day professors, conceiting that they had fully discharged their duty by a single communion, resigned themselves for the rest of the year to supineness and sloth. It ought to have been (says he) far otherwise. *Every week,* at least, the table of the Lord should have been spread for Christian assemblies; and the promises declared, by which, partaking of it, we might be spiritually fed."[1]

We shall now hear the celebrated John Wesley. After *fifty-five* years' reflection upon the subject, he decides that Christians should show forth the Lord's death every Lord's day. He prefaces the 106th Sermon (Luke 22:19), with this remark:—

---

[1] Mason's *Letters on Frequent Communion,* pp. 34-38, 52, Edinburgh edition, 1799.

"This discourse was written above five-and-fifty years ago, for the use of my pupils at Oxford. I have added very little, but retrenched much; as I then used more words than I now do. But, I thank God, I have not yet seen cause to alter my sentiments in any point which is therein delivered."

The sermon is entitled "The Duty of Constant Communion," concerning which the refomer says:—

"It is no wonder that men who have no fear of God should never think of doing this. But it is strange that it should be neglected by any that do fear God, and desire to save their souls; and yet nothing is more common. One reason why many neglect it is, they are so much afraid of *eating and drinking unworthily,* that they never think how much greater the danger is when they do not eat or drink at all."

In speaking of *constantly* receiving the supper, Mr. Wesley says:—

"I say *constantly* receiving; for as to the phrase *frequent* communion, it is absurd to the last degree. If it means any thing else but constant, it means more than can be proved to be the duty of any man. For if we are not obliged to communicate *constantly,* by what argument can it be proved that we are obliged to communicate *frequently?* yea, more than once a year? or once in seven years? or once before we die? Every argument brought for this either proves that we ought to do it *constantly,* or proves nothing at all. Therefore, that undeterminate, unmeaning way of speaking ought to be laid aside by all men of understanding. Our power is the only rule of our duty. Whatever we can do, that we ought. With respect either to this or any other command, he that, when he may obey if he will, does not, will have no place in the kingdom of heaven."

Though we may have some objections to the style in which John Wesley speaks of the meaning of this institution, as we have indeed to that of all the others from whom we have quoted, yet we would recommend to the whole Methodistic community the close perusal of the above sermon. It will be found in Vol. 3, pp. 171-197.

The elders among the Methodists, with whom John Wesley is such high authority, we would remind of his *advice,* found in his Letters to America, 1784, lately quoted in the *Gospel Herald,* Lexington, Ky. "I ALSO ADVISE THE ELDERS TO ADMINISTER THE SUPPER OF THE LORD ON EVERY LORD'S DAY."

So much for John Brown, John Mason, and John Wesley, and the authorities which they quoted. While quoting the sayings of the Johns, I am reminded of something said by the great John Milton, the "immortal bard" of England. In his posthumous works, he

says, "The Lord's supper (which the doctrine of transubstantiation, or rather anthropophagy, has well-nigh converted into a ban-
quet of cannibals) is essential to be observed, and may be administered by any one with propriety, as well as by an appointed minister.
There is no order of men which can claim to itself either the right of
distribution, or the power of withholding the sacred elements, seeing
that in the church we are all alike priests." "The master of a family,
or any one appointed by him, is at liberty to celebrate the Lord's
supper from house to house, as was done in the dispensation of the
passover." "All Christians are a royal priesthood: therefore, any believer is competent to act as an ordinary minister according as convenience may require; provided only, he be endowed with the necessary
gifts: these gifts constituting his commission." Thus did the famous
Milton make way for the weekly observance of the supper, by divest-
ing it of the priestly appendages and penances of the dark ages.

A cloud of witnesses to the plainness and evidence of the New
Testament on the subject of the weekly celebration of the Lord's supper might be adduced. But this we think unnecessary; and, as we
would avoid prolixity and tediousness, we shall only add a few extracts from the third volume of the *Christian Baptist*, second ed., p.
254, in proof of the assertion, *"All antiquity is on the side of the disciples meeting every first day to break the loaf."*

All antiquity concurs in evincing that, for the *three first centuries*, all the churches broke bread once a week. Pliny, in his *Epistles*, book 10; Justin Martyr, in his Second Apology for the Christians; and Tertullian, *De Ora.*, page 135, testify that it was the universal practice in all the weekly assemblies of the brethren, after they
had prayed and sung praises. "The bread and wine being brought to
the *chief brother*, he taketh it and offereth praise and thanksgiving to
the Father, in the name of the Son and Holy Spirit. After prayer
and thanksgiving, the whole assembly saith, *Amen!* When thanksgiving is ended by the *chief guide*, and the consent of the whole people, the *deacons* (as we call them) give to every one present part of
the bread and wine, over which thanks are given."

"The weekly communion was prepared in the Greek church till
the *seventh century;* and, by one of their canons, 'such as neglected
three weeks together were excommunicated.'[1]

"In the *fourth century*, when all things began to be changed by
baptized pagans, the practice began to decline. Some of the councils
in the western part of the Roman Empire, by their canons, strove to
keep it up. The councils held at Illiberis in Spain, A.D. 324, decreed

---

[1] Erskine's *Dissertations*, page 271.

that 'no offerings should be received from such as did not receive the Lord's Supper.'[1]

"The council at Antioch, A.D. 341, decreed that 'all who came to church, and heard the Scriptures read, but afterwards joined not in prayer, and receiving the sacrament, should be cast out of the church, till such time as they gave public proof of their repentance.'[2]

"All these canons were unable to keep the carnal crowd of professors in a practice for which they had no spiritual taste; and, indeed, it was likely to get out of use altogether. To prevent this, the Council of Agatha, in Languedoc, A.D. 506, decreed that 'none should be esteemed good Christians who did not *communicate* at least *three times* a year,—at Christmas, Easter, and Whitsunday.'[3] This soon became the standard of a good Christian, and it was judged presumptuous to commune oftener.

"Things went on in this way for more than six hundred years, until they got tired of even *three* communications in one year; and the infamous Council of Lateran, which decreed auricular confession and transubstantiation, decreed that 'an annual communion at Easter was sufficient.' This association of the 'sacrament' with Easter, and the mechanical devotion of the ignorant at this season, greatly contributed to the worship of the Host.[4] Thus the breaking of bread in simplicity and godly sincerity once a week degenerated into a pompous sacrament once a year at Easter.

"At the Reformation this subject was but slightly investigated by the reformers. Some of them, however, paid some attention to it. Even Calvin, in his *Institutes*, lib. 4, chap. 17, sect. 46, says, 'And truly this custom, which enjoins communicating once a year, *is a most evident contrivance of the Devil*, by whose instrumentality soever it may have been determined.'

"And again (*Inst.*, lib. 6, chap. 18, sect. 56), he says, 'It ought to have been far otherwise. *Every week*, at least, the table of the Lord should have been spread for Christian assemblies, and the promises declared by which, in partaking of it, we might be spiritually fed.'

"Martin Chemnitz, Witsius, Calderwood, and others of the reformers and controversialists, concur with Calvin; and, indeed, almost every commentator on the New Testament concurs with the Presbyterian Henry in these remarks on Acts 20:7. 'In the primitive times it was the custom of many churches to receive the Lord's supper every Lord's day.'

"The Belgic reformed church, in 1851, appointed the supper to

[1] Council Illiberis, Can. 28. [2] Council Antioch, Can. 2.
[3] Council Agatha, Can. 18. [4] Bingham's Ori., lib. xv. c. 9.

be received every other month. The reformed churches of France, after saying that they had been too remiss in observing the supper but four times a year, advise a *greater frequency*. The church of Scotland began with *four* sacraments in a year; but some of her ministers got up to *twelve* times. Thus things stood till the close of the last century.

"Since the commencement of the present century, many congregations in England, Scotland, Ireland, and some in the United States and Canada, both Independents and Baptists, have attended upon the supper every Lord's day, and the practice is every day gaining ground.

"These historical notices may be of some use to those who are ever and anon crying out *Innovation! Innovation!* But we advocate the principle and the practice on apostolic grounds alone. Blessed is that servant who, knowing his Master's will, doeth it with expedition and delight!

"Those who would wish to see an able refutation of the Presbyterian mode of observing the sacrament, and a defence of weekly communion, would do well to read Dr. John Mason's *Letters on Frequent Communion*, who is himself a high-toned Presbyterian, and consequently his remarks will be more regarded by his brethren than mine."

Thus our seventh proposition is sustained by the explicit declarations of the New Testament, by the reasonableness of the thing itself when suggested by the apostles, by analogy, by the conclusions of the most eminent reformers, and by the concurrent voice of all Christian antiquity. But on the plain sayings of the Lord and his apostles, we rely for authority and instruction upon *this* and *every other* Christian institution.

It does, indeed, appear somewhat incongruous, that arguments should have to be submitted to urge Christians to convene weekly around the Lord's table. Much more in accordance with the genius of our religion would it be, to see them oversolicitous to be honored with a seat at the King's table, and asking with intense interest, might they be permitted so often to eat in his presence, and in honor of his love. To have to withstand their daily convocations for this purpose would not be a task so unnatural and so unreasonable, as to have to reason and expostulate with them to urge them to assemble for weekly communion.

But, as the want of appetite for our animal sustenance as a symptom of ill health, or approaching disease; so a want of relish for spiritual food is indicative of a want of spiritual health, or of the presence of a moral disease, which, if not healed, must issue in apostasy from the Living Head. Hence, among the most unequivocal prognosis of a spiritual decline, the more decisive is a want of appetite for the nourishment which the Good Physician prepared and prescribed for his family. A healthy and vigorous Christian excluded from the use and enjoyment of all the provisions of the Lord's house can not be found.

But much depends upon the *manner* of celebrating the supper, as well as upon the *frequency*. The simplicity of the Christian institution runs through every part of it. While there is the form of doing every thing, there is all attention to the thing signified. But there is the form as well as the substance, and every thing that is done must be done in some manner. The well-bred Christian is like the well-bred gentleman—his manners are graceful, easy, artless, and simple. All stiffness and forced formality are as graceless in the Christian as in the gentleman. A courteous and polite family differs exceedingly from a soldier's messmates or a ship's crew, in all the ceremonies of the table. There is a Christian decency and a Christian order, as well as political courtesy and complaisance.

Nothing is more disgusting than mimicry. It is hypocrisy in manners, which, like hypocrisy in religion, is more odious than apathy or vulgarity. There is a saintishness in demeanor and appearance, which differs as much from sanctity as foppery from politeness. The appearance of sanctimoniousness is as much to be avoided as actual licentiousness of morals. An austere and rigid pharisaism sits as awkwardly upon a Christian, as a mourning habit upon a bride. Cheerfulness is not mirth—solemnity is not pharisaism—joy is not noise—nor eating, festivity.

But to act right in anything, we must feel right. If we would show love, we must first possess it. If a person would walk humbly, he must be humble: and if one would act the Christian on any occasion, he must always live the Christian. Persons who daily converse with God, and who constantly meditate upon his salvation, will not need to be told how they should demean themselves at the Lord's table.

The following extract from my memorandum-book furnishes the nighest approach to the model which we have in our eye of good order and Christian decency in celebrating this institution. Indeed, the whole order of that congregation was comely:—

"The church in _____ consisted of about fifty members. Not having any person whom they regarded as filling Paul's outlines of a bishop, they had appointed two senior members, of a very grave deportment, to preside in their meetings. These persons were not competent to labor in the word and teaching; but they were qualified to rule well, and to preside with Christian dignity. One of them presided at each meeting. After they had assembled in the morning, which was at eleven o'clock (for they had agreed to meet at eleven and to adjourn at two o'clock during the winter season), and after they had saluted one another in a very familiar and cordial manner, as brethren are wont to do who meet for social purposes; the president for the day arose and said, 'Brethren, being assembled in the name and by the authority of our Lord and Saviour Jesus Christ, on this day of his resurrection, let us unite in celebrating his praise.' He then repeated the following stanza:—

> " 'Christ the Lord is risen to-day!
> Sons of men and angels say;
> Raise your joys and triumphs high,
> Sing, O Heavens! and, earth, reply.'

"The congregation arose and sang this psalm in animating strains. He then called upon a brother, who was a very distinct and emphatic reader, to read a section of the evangelical history. He arose and read, in a very audible voice, the history of the crucifixion of the Messiah. After a pause of a few moments, the president called upon a brother to pray in the name of the congregation. His prayer abounded in thanksgiving to the Father of Mercies, and with supplications for such blessings on themselves and for all men as were promised to those who ask, or for which men were commanded to pray. The language was very appropriate: no unmeaning repetitions, no labor of words, no effort to say any thing and every thing that came into his mind; but to express slowly, distinctly, and emphatically, the desires of the heart. The prayer was comparatively short; and the whole congregation, brethren and sisters, pronounced aloud the final *Amen*.

"After prayer a passage in one of the epistles was read by the president himself, and a song was called for. A brother arose, and, after naming the page, repeated,—

> " ' 'T was on that night when doom'd to know
> That eager rage of every foe;—
> That night in which he was betrayed,—
> The Saviour of the world took bread.'

"He then sat down, and the congregation sang with much feeling.

"I observed that the table was furnished before the disciples met in the morning, and that the disciples occupied a few benches on each side of it, while the strangers sat off on seats more remote. The president arose and said that our Lord had a table for his friends, and that he invited his disciples to sup with him. 'In memory of his death, this monumental table,' said he, 'was instituted; and as the Lord ever lives in heaven, so he ever lives in the hearts of his people. As the first disciples, taught by the apostles in person, came together into one place to eat the Lord's supper, and as they selected the first day of the week in honor of his resurrection, for this purpose; so we, having the same Lord, the same faith, the same hope with them, have vowed to do as they did. We owe as much to the Lord as they; and ought to love, honor, and obey him as much as they.' Thus having spoken, he took a small loaf from the table, and in one or two periods gave thanks for it. After thanksgiving, he raised it in his hand, and significantly brake it, and handed it to the disciples on each side of him, who passed the broken loaf from one to another, until they all partook of it. There was no stiffness, no formality, no pageantry; all was easy, familiar, solemn, cheerful. He then took the cup in a similar manner, and returned thanks for it, and handed it to the disciples sitting next to him, who passed it round; each one waiting upon his brother, until all were served. The thanksgiving before the breaking of the loaf, and the distributing of the cup, were as brief and pertinent to the occasion, as the thanks usually presented at a common table for the ordinary blessings of God's bounty. They then arose, and with one consent sang,—

" 'To him that loved the sons of men,
And wash'd us in his blood;
To royal honors raised our heads,
And made us priests to God!'

"The president of the meeting called upon a brother to remember the poor, and those ignorant of the way of life before the Lord. He kneeled down, and the brethren all united with him in supplicating the Father of Mercies in behalf of all the sons and daughters of affliction, the poor and the destitute, and in behalf of the conversion of the world. After this prayer the fellowship or contribution was attended to; and the whole church proved the sincerity of their desires, by the cheerfulness and liberality which they seemed to evince, in putting into the treasury as the Lord had prospered them.

"A general invitation was tendered to all the brotherhood if they had any thing to propose or inquire, tending to the edification of the body. Several brethren arose in succession, and read several passages in the Old and New Testaments, relative to some matters which had been subjects of former investigation and inquiry. Sundry remarks were made; and after singing several spiritual songs selected by the brethren, the president, on motion of a brother who signified that the hour of adjournment had arrived, concluded the meeting by pronouncing the apostolic benediction.

"I understand that all these items were attended to in all their meetings; yet the order of attendance was not invariably the same. On all the occasions on which I was present with them, no person arose to speak without invitation, or without asking permission of the president, and no person finally left the meeting before the hour of adjournment, without special leave. Nothing appeared to be done in a formal or ceremonious manner. Every thing exhibited the power of godliness as well as the form; and no person could attend to all that passed without being edified and convinced that the Spirit of God was there. The joy, the affection, and the reverence which appeared in this little assembly was the strongest argument in favor of their order, and the best comment on the excellency of the Christian institution."

CONCLUDING ADDRESSES

ADDRESS TO THE CITIZENS OF THE KINGDOM

Fellow-Citizens:—

Your rank and standing under the reign of the Prince of Peace have never been surpassed—indeed, have never been equalled—by any portion of the human race. You have visions and revelations of God—his being and perfection—developments of the depths of his wisdom and knowledge, of the counsels of his grace, and the purposes of his love, which give you an intelllectual and moral superiority above all your predecessors in the patriarchal and Jewish ages of the world. Secrets of God, which were hid from ages and generations, have been revealed to you by the apostles of the great Apostle and High Priest of your confession. What Abraham, Isaac and Jacob— Moses, David, Isaiah, Daniel, and all the prophets down to John the Harbinger, rejoiced to anticipate, you have realized and enjoyed. The intellectual pleasures of the highest and most sublime conceptions of God and of Christ vouchsafed to you so far transcend the attainments of the ancient people of God, that you are comparatively exalted to heaven, and may enjoy the days of heaven upon earth. You have a book which contains not only the charter of your privileges, but which explains a thousand mysteries in the antecedent administrations of God over all the nations of the earth. In it you have such interpretations of God's past providences in the affairs of individuals, families, and nations, as open to you a thousand sources of rational and sentimental enjoyment, from incidents and things which puzzled and perplexed the most intelligent and highly favored of past ages. Mountains are, indeed, levelled; valleys are exalted; rough places are made plain, and crooked ways straight to your apprehension; and, from these data, you are able to form more just conceptions of the present, and more lofty anticipations of the future, than fell to the lot of the most highly favored subjects of preceding dispensations. And, indeed, so inexhaustible are the deep and rich mines of knowledge and understandings in the Christian revelations, that the most comprehensive mind in the kingdom of heaven might labor in them during the age of a Methuselah, constantly enriching itself with all knowledge and spiritual understanding, and yet leave at last vast regions and tracts of thought wholly unexplored.

But this decided superiority over the most gifted saints of former ages you unquestionably enjoy. Among all the living excellencies with which they were acquainted, they wanted a perfect model of all human excellence. Bright as were the virtues and excellencies of an Abraham, a Joseph, a David, there were dark spots, or, at least, some blemishes, in their moral character. They failed to place in living form before their contemporaries, or to leave as a legacy to posterity, every virtue, grace, and excellence that adorn human nature. But you have Jesus, not only as "the image of the invisible God," an "effulgence of his glory and an exact representation of his character"; but as a man, holy, harmless, undefiled, separate from sin, exhibiting in the fullest perfection every excellence which gives amiability, dignity and glory to human character. You have motives to purity and holiness, a stimulus to all that is manly, good, and excellent, from what he said and did, and suffered as the Son of Man, which would have added new charms and beauties to the most exemplary of all the saints of the olden times.

Means and opportunities of the highest intellectual and moral enjoyments are richly bestowed on you, for which they sighed in vain; God having provided some better things for Christians than for Jews and patriarchs. Shall we not, then, fellow-citizens, appreciate and use, as we ought, to our present purity and happiness, to our eternal honor and glory, the light which the Sun of Righteousness has shed so richly and abundantly on us? Remember that we stand upon apostles and prophets, and are sustained by Jesus, the light of the world, and the interpreter and vindicator of all God's ways to man in creation, providence, and redemption. All suns are stars; and he that is now to us in this life "the Sun of Righteousness," in respect of the future is *"the Bright and Morning Star."* Till the day of eternity dawn, and the day-star of immortality arise in our hearts, let us always look to Jesus.

But it is not only the felicity of superior heavenly light, though that is most delectable to our rational nature, which distinguishes you the citizens of this kingdom; but that personal, real, and plenary remission of all sin, which you enjoy through the blood of the Lamb of God, bestowed on you through the ordinances of Christian immersion, and confession of sins.

The Jews, indeed, had sacrifices under the law, which could, and did, take away ceremonial sins; and which so far absolved from the guilt of transgressing that law, as to give them a right to the continued enjoyment of the temporal and political promises of the national compact; but further Jewish sacrifices and ablutions could not reach. This benefit every Jew had from then. But as respected the conscience, Paul, that great commentator on Jewish sacrifice, assures us they had no power. "With respect to the conscience," says he, "they could not make him who did the service perfect."

The entrance of the law gave the knowledge of sin. It gave names to particular sins, and "caused the offence to abound."—The sacrifices appended to it had respect to that institution alone, and not to sin in the general, nor to sin in its true and proper nature. The promise made to the patriarchs, and the sacrificial institution added to it, through faith in that promise, led the believing to anticipate a real sin-offering; but it appears the Jewish sacrifices had only respect to the Jewish institution, and, excepting their typical character, gave no new light to those under that economy on the subject of a true and *proper* remission of sins through the real and bloody sacrifice of Christ.

The patriarch and the believing Jew, as respected a real remission of sins, stood upon the same ground; for, as has been observed, the legal institution, or, as Paul says, "the supervening of the law," made no change in the apprehensions of remission, as respected the conscience. But a new age having come (for "these ordinances for cleansing the flesh were imposed only till the time of reformation"), and Christ having, by a more perfect sacrifice, opened the way into the true holy places, has laid the foundation for perfecting the conscience by a real and full remission of sins, which, by the virtue of his blood, terminates not upon the flesh, but upon the conscience of the sinner.

John, indeed, who lived at the dawn of the reformation, preached reformation with an immersion for the remission of sins; saying that "they should believe in him that was to come after him." Those who believed John's gospel, and reformed, and were immersed into John's reformation, had remission of sins through faith in him that was to come; but you, fellow-citizens, even in respect of the enjoyment of remission, are greatly advanced above the disciples of John. You have been immersed, not only by the authority of Jesus, *as Lord of all,* into the name of the Father, and of the Son, and of the Holy Spirit, but *into the death* or sacrifice of Christ. This no disciple of Moses or of John know anything about. This gives you an insight into sin, and a freedom from it *as respects conscience*—a peace and a joy unutterable and full of glory, to which both the disciples of Moses and of the Harbinger were strangers. So that the light of the risen day of heaven's eternal Sun greatly excels, not only the glimmerings of the stars in the patriarchal age, and the faint light of the moon in the Jewish age, but even the twilight of the morning.

Your new relation to the Father, to the Son, and to the Holy Spirit, into which you have been introduced by faith in the Messiah and immersion into his death, verifies, in respect of the sense and as-surance of remission, all that John and Jesus said concerning the su-periority of privilege vouchsafed to the citizens of the kingdom of heaven. You can see your sins washed away in the blood that was shed on Mount Calvary. That which neither the highly favored John nor any disciple of the Messiah could understand, till Jesus said, *"It is finished,"* you not only clearly perceive, but have cordially em-braced. You can feel, and say with all assurance, that "the blood of Jesus Christ now cleanses you from all sin"; and that by faith you have access to the mediator of the new institution, and to the blood of sprinkling which speaks glad tidings to the heart. You have an advocate with the Father; and, when conscious of any impurity, com-ing to God by him, confessing your sins, and supplicating pardon through his blood, you have the promise of remission. You now know how God is *just* as well as merciful, in forgiving iniquity, trans-gression, and sin.

But superior light and knowledge, and enlarged conceptions of God, with such an assurance of real and personal remission as paci-fies the conscience and introduces the peace of God into the heart, are not the only distinguishing favors which you enjoy in the new relation to the Father, the Son, and the Holy Spirit, into which you are introduced under the reign of heaven; but you are formally *adopted into the family of God,* and constituted the sons and daugh-ters of the Father Almighty.

To be called *"the friend of God,"* was the highest title bestowed on Abraham; to be called *the friends of Christ,* was the peculiar honor of the disciples of Christ, to whom he confided the secrets of his reign; but to be called "the children of God through faith in Jesus Christ" is not only the common honor of all Christians, but the high-est honor which could be vouchsafed to the inhabitants of this earth. Such honor have you, my fellow-citizens, in being related to the only-begotten Son of God: "For to as many as received him he gave the privilege of becoming the sons of God." These, indeed, were not descended from families of noble blood, nor genealogies of high renown: neither are they the offspring of the instincts of the flesh, nor made the sons of God "by the will of man," who sometimes adopts the child of another as his own; but they are "born of God" through the ordinances of his grace. "Behold how great love the Father has bestowed on us, that we should be called the children of God!" "The world, indeed, does not know us, because it did not know him. Beloved, now are we the children of God. It does not yet appear what we shall be."

"Because you are sons, God has sent forth the spirit of his Son into your hearts, crying, Abba, Father." And if sons, it follows you "are heirs of God through Christ"—the heir of all things. Is this, fellow-citizens, a romantic vision, or sober and solemn truth, that you are children of God, possessing the spirit of Christ, and constituted heirs of God, and joint heirs with Christ of the eternal inheritance? What manner of persons, then, ought you to be! How pure, how holy and heavenly in your temper! How just and righteous in all your ways! How humble and devoted to the Lord! How joyful and triumphant in your King!

Permit me, then, to ask, Wherein do you excel?—nay, rather, you will propose this question to yourselves. You will say, How shall we still more successfully promote the interest, the honor, and the triumphs of the gospel of the kingdom? Is there any thing we can do by our behaviour, our morality, our piety, by our influence, by all the earthly means with which God has furnished us? Is there any thing we can do more to strengthen the army of the faith, to invigorate the champions of the kingdom, to make new conquests for our king? Can we not increase the joy of the Lord in converting souls? Can we not furnish occasions of rejoicing to the angels of God? Can we not gladden the hearts of thousands who have never tasted the joys of the children of God?

In the present administration of the kingdom of God, during the absence of the king, he has said to the citizens, "Put on the armor of light"—"Contend earnestly for the faith"—"Convert the world"— "Occupy till I come"—"Let your light shine before men, that they, seeing your good works, may glorify your Father in heaven"—that "the Gentiles may, by your good works which they shall behold, glorify God in the day of visitation." He has thus intrusted to the citizens the great work for which he died,—the salvation of men. Let us, then, brethren, be found faithful to the Lord and to men, that he may address us at his coming with the most acceptable plaudit, "Well done, good and faithful servants; enter into the joy of your Lord!"

Great as the opposition is to truth and salvation, we have no reason to despond. Greater are our friends and allies, and infinitely more powerful, than all our enemies. God is on our side—Jesus Christ is our king—the Holy Spirit is at his disposal—angels are his ministering servants—the prayers of all the prophets, apostles, saints, and martyrs are for our success—our brethren are numerous and strong—they have the sword of the Spirit, the shield of faith, the helmet of salvation, the breastplate of righteousness, the artillery of truth, the arguments of God, the preparation of the gospel of peace —our Commander and Captain is the most successful General that ever entered the field of war—he never lost a battle—he is wonderful in council, excellent in working, valiant in fight—the Lord of *hosts* is his name. He can stultify the machinations of our enemies, control all the powers of nature, and subdue all our foes, terrestrial and infernal. Under his conduct we are like Mount Zion, that can never be moved. Indeed, under him we are come to Mount Zion, the stronghold and fortress of the kingdom, the city of the living God, the heavenly Jerusalem, to myriads of angels, the general assembly and congregation of the first-born, enrolled in heaven—to God, the Judge of all—to the spirits of just men made perfect—to Jesus, the mediator of the new constitution—and to the blood of sprinkling, which speaks such peace, and joy, and courage to the heart. Ought we not, then, brethren, "to be strong in the Lord and in the power of his might"? If, in faith, and courage, and prayer, we put on the heavenly armor, and march under the king, sounding the gospel trumpet, the walls of Jericho will fall to the ground and the banners of the cross will wave over the ruins of paganism, atheism, skepticism, and sectarianism— *Nil desperandum, te duce, Christe.* If a Roman could say, "Nothing is to be feared under the auspices of Caesar," may not the Christian say, "There is no despair under the guardianship of Messiah the king"?

But, fellow-citizens, though clothed with the whole panoply of heaven, and headed by the Captain of Salvation, there is no success in this war to be expected, without constant and incessant prayer. When the apostles began to build up this kingdom, notwithstanding all the gifts they enjoyed, they found it necessary to devote themselves to prayer as well as to the ministry of the word. And when Paul describes all the armor of God, piece by piece, in putting it on he says, "Take the sword of the Spirit—with all supplication and deprecation, pray at all seasons in spirit, watch with all perseverance and supplication for all the saints."

This was most impressively and beautifully pictured in the wars of ancient Israel against their enemies. While Mosees lifted up his holy hands to heaven, Israel prevailed; and when he did not, Amalek prevailed. So is it now. When the disciples of Christ, the heaven-born citizens of the kingdom, continue instant in prayer and watchfulness, the truth triumphs in their hearts and in the world. When they do not, they become cold, timid, and impotent as Samson shorn, and the enemy gains strength over them. Then the good cause of the Lord languishes.

It is not necessary that we should understand how prayer increases our zeal, our wisdom, our strength, our joy, or how it gives success to the cause, any more than that we should understand how our food is converted into flesh, and blood, and bones. It is only nec-essary that we eat; and it is only necessary that we should pray as we are taught and commanded. Experience proves that the outward man is renewed day by day by our daily bread, and experience proves that the inward man is renewed day by day by prayer and thanksgiving. The Lord has promised his Holy Spirit to them that ask him in truth; and is it not necessary to our success? If it be not necessary to give new revelations, it is necessary to keep in mind those already given, and to bring the word written seasonably to our remembrance. Besides, if the Spirit of the Lord was necessary to the success of Gideon and Barak and Samson and David, and all the great warriors of Israel according to the flesh, who fought the battles of the Lord with the sword, the sling, and the bow; who can say that it is not necessary to those who draw the sword of the Spirit and fight the good fight of faith? In my judgment it is as necessary now as then—necessary, I mean, to equal success—necessary to the suc-cess of those who labor in the word and teaching, and necessary to those who would acquit themselves like men, in every department in the ranks of the great army of the Lord of hosts.

Though the weapons of our warfare are not carnal, but spiritual, they are mighty (only, however, *through God,* to the overturning of strongholds) to the overturning of all reasonings against the truth, and every high thing raised up against the knowledge of God, and in leading captive every thought to the obedience of Christ. Let us, then, fellow-citizens, whether as leaders or as private soldiers, abound in prayer and supplications to God night and day. If sincere, and ardent, and incessant prayers to God for every thing that he has promised, for all things for which the apostles prayed, were offered up by all the congregations, and by every disciple in his family and in his closet, for the triumphs of the truth; then would we see the army of the Lord successful in fight against atheism, infidelity, and sectarianism—then would we see disciples growing in knowledge and in favor with God and man. And is not the conversion of the world and our own eternal salvation infinitely worthy of all the effort and enterprise in man, seeing God himself has done so much in the gift of his Son and Holy Spirit, and left for us so little to do—nothing, in-deed, but what is in the compass of our power? And should we withhold that little, especially as he has given us so many and so ex-ceedingly great and precious promises to stimulate us to exertion? Has not Jesus said "The conqueror shall inherit all things"—that he "will not blot his name out of the book of life"—that he "will confess it before his Father and his holy angels"—that he will place him "upon his throne, and give him the crown of life, that shall never fade away"?

Rise up, then, in the strength of Judah's Lion! Be valiant for the truth! Adorn yourselves with all the graces of the Spirit of God! Put on the armor of light; and, with all the gentleness, and meekness, and mildness there is in Christ—with all the courage, and patience, and zeal, and effort, worthy of a cause so salutary, so pure, so holy, and so divine, determine never to faint nor to falter till you enter the pearly gates—never to lay down your arms till, with the triumphant millions, you stand before the throne, and exultingly sing, "Worthy is the Lamb that was slain, to receive power, and riches, and wisdom, and might, and honor, and glory, and blessing!"—"To Him who sits upon the throne, and to the Lamb, be blessing, and honor, and glory, and strength, forever and forever!" Amen.

A WORD TO FRIENDLY ALIENS

Whether to regard you in the light of *Proselytes of the Gate*, who refused circumcision, but wished to live in the land of Israel, to be in the suburbs of the cities of Judah, and to keep some of the institutions of the ancient kingdom of God, without becoming fellow-citizens of that kingdom; or whether to regard you as the Samaritans of old, who built for themselves a temple of God upon Mount Gerizim, held fast a part of the ancient revelation of God, and rejected only such parts of it as did not suit their prejudices—worshipped the God of Israel in common with the idols of the nations from which they sprang—I say, whether to regard you in the light of the one or the other of those ancient professors of religion might require more skill in casuistry than we possess—more leisure than we have at our disposal—and more labor than either of us have patience to endure. One thing, however, is obvious,—that if under the reign of heaven it behooved so good a man as Cornelius ("a man of piety, and one that feared God with all his house, giving also much alms to the people, and praying to God continually") to *"hear words by which he might be saved,"* and to put on Christ by immersion into his death, that he might enter the kingdom of heaven and enjoy the remission of sins, and the hope of an inheritance among all the sanctified—certainly it is both expedient and necessary that you should go also and do likewise.

Every sectarian in the land, how honest and pious soever, ought to bury his sectarianism, and all his other sins of omission and commission, in "the bath of regeneration." It is a high crime and misdemeanor in any man, professing to have received the Messiah in his proper person, character, and office, to refuse allegiance to him in any thing; and to substitute human inventions and traditions in lieu of the ordinances and statutes of Prince Immanuel. Indeed, the keeping up of any dogma, practice, or custom, which directly or indirectly supplants the constitution, laws, and usages of the kingdom over which Jesus presides, is directly opposed to his government; and would ultimate in dethroning him in favor of a rival, and in placing upon his throne the author of that dogma, practice, or usage which supplants the institution of the Saviour of the world.

It is to you, then, who, in the name of the King, are changing his ordinances, and substituting your own expedients for the wisdom and authority of the Judge of all, we now propose the following considerations:

Every kingdom has one uniform law or institution for naturalizing aliens; and that institution, of whatever sort it be, is obligatory, by the authority of the government, upon every one who would become a citizen. We say it is obligatory upon him who desires to be a citizen to submit to that institution. But does not your practice and your dogma positively say that it is not the duty of an alien to be born again, but that it is the duty of his father or guardian to have him naturalized? Now, although many things are in common the duty of brother, father, and child, yet those duties which belong specifically to a father can not belong to his child, either in religion, morality, or society. If it be the father's duty to "offer his child to the Lord," to speak in your own style, it is not the duty of the child to offer himself. It was not Isaac's duty to be circumcised, but Abraham's duty to circumcise him. If, then, it was your father's duty to have made you citizens of the kingdom of heaven, it is not your duty to become citizens, unless you can produce a law saying that in all cases where the father fails to do his duty, then it shall be the duty of the child to do that which his father neglected.

Again—if all fathers, like yours, had, upon their own responsibility, without any command from the Lord, baptized their children, there would not be one in a nation to whom it could be said, "Repent and be baptized"; much less could it be said to every penitent, "Be baptized, every one of you, by the authority of the Lord, for the remission of sins." These remarks are only intended to show that your institutions do, in truth, go to the subversion of the government of Christ, and to the entire abolition of the institutions of his kingdom. On this account alone, if for no other reason, you ought to be constitutionally naturalized, and be legally and honorably inducted into the kingdom of heaven. It is a solemn duty you owe to the King and his government; and if you have a conscience formed by the oracles of

God, you can have no confidence in God, nor real peace of mind, so long as you give your support, your countenance, example, and entire influence to break down the institutions of Jesus Christ, to open his kingdom to all that is born of the flesh, and to prevent, as far as you can, every man from the pleasure of choosing whom he shall obey—of confessing him before men—of taking on his yoke—of dying, being buried, and raised with Christ in his gracious institution. If Jesus himself, for the sake of fulfilling all righteousness, or of honoring every divine institution, though he needed not reformation for remission of sins which John preached, was immersed by John—what have you to say for yourselves—you who would claim the honors and privileges of the kingdom of heaven, refusing to follow the example of Jesus, and who virtually subvert his authority by supporting a system which would, if carried out, not allow a voluntary agent in the race of Adam to do that which all the first converts of Christ did, by authority of the commission which Jesus gave to his apostles?

Again—whatever confidence you may now possess, that you are good citizens of the kingdom of Messiah, that confidence is not founded upon a *"thus saith the Lord,"* but upon your own reasonings, which all men must acknowledge may be in this, as in many other things, fallacious. Jesus has said, "He that believes and is immersed shall be saved"; and Peter commanded every penitent to be immersed for the remission of his sins. Now, he who hears the word, believes it, and is on his own confession immersed, has an assurance, a confidence, which it is impossible for you to have.

Let me add only another consideration, for we are not now arguing the merits of your theory, or that of any party: it is your duty, as you desire the union of (what you call) the church, and the conversion of the world, forthwith to be immersed and to be born constitutionally into the kingdom; because all Protestants, of every name, if sincere believers in Jesus *as the Christ,* irrespective of every opinion found in any human creed, could if they would, honor and obey his institutions, come into one fold, and set down together under the reign of the Messiah. If all would follow your example, this would necessarily follow; if they do not, you have done your duty. In being thus immersed, all the world, Catholic and Protestant, admit that you are truly and scripturally baptized; for all admit that an *immersed* penitent is constitutionally baptized into Christ; but only a part of the professing world can admit that rite of infant affusion on which you rely as introducing you, without previous knowledge, faith, or repentance, into the family of God. Acquit, then, your conscience; follow the example of Jesus; honor and support his authority; promote the union and peace of the family of God; do what in you lies for the conversion of the world; enter into the full enjoyment of the blessings of the kingdom of heaven by confessing the ancient faith, and by being immersed in the name of Jesus, into the name of the Father, and of the Son, and of the Holy Spirit, for the remission of sins. Then you may say, as Jesus said to the Samaritan woman, Although the Samaritans have a temple on Mount Gerizim, a priesthood, and the five books of Moses, "salvation is of the Jews." Although the sects have the oracles of God, human creeds, many altars, priests, and religious usages, *the enjoyment of salvation* is among them who simply believe what the apostles wrote concerning Jesus, and who from the heart obey that mould of doctrine which the apostles delivered to us.

In so doing you will, moreover, most wisely consult your own safety and security from the signal calamities that are every day accumulating, and soon to fall with overwhelming violence on a distracted, divided, alienated, and adulterous generation. If you are *"the people of God,"* as you profess, and as we would fain imagine, then you are commanded by a voice from heaven—"Come out of her, *my people*, that you partake not of the sins of mystic Babylon, and that you receive not a portion of her plagues."[1] If affliction, and shame, and poverty, and reproach, were to be the inalienable lot of the most approved servants of God, it is better, infinitely better, for you to suffer with them, than to enjoy for a season all that a corrupted and apostate society can bestow upon you. Remember who it is that has said, "Happy are they who keep his commandments, for they shall have a right to the tree of life, and they shall enter in through the gates into the city!"

ADDRESS TO BELLIGERENT ALIENS

To him who, through the telescope of faith, surveys your camp, there appears not on the whole map of creation such a motley group, such a heterogeneous and wretched amalgamation of distracted spirits, as are found in actual insurrection and rebellion, in a mad and accursed alliance against the reigning Monarch of creation. In your lines are found every unclean and hateful spirit on this side the fathomless gulf, the dark and rayless receptacle of fallen and ruined intelligences, who, in endless and fruitless wailings, lament their own follies, and through an incessant night of despair anathematize themselves and their coadjutors in the perpetration of their eternal suicide. Yes, in your ranks are found all who willfully reject the Son of God, and will not have him to reign over them; whether they are styled the

[1] Revelation 18:8, 9.

decent moralist, the honest deist, skeptic, atheist, infidel, the speculating Sadducee, the boasting Pharisee, the supercilious Jew, the resentful Samaritan, or the idolatrous Gentile. All ranks and degrees of men in political society—the king and the beggar—the sage philosopher and the uneducated clown—the rich and the poor—who disdain the precepts of the Messiah, unite with you in this unholy alliance against the kingdom of heaven. You may boast of many a decent fellow-soldier in the crusade against Immanuel; many who, when weighed in the balances of the political sanctuary, are not found wanting in all the decencies of this present life; but yet look at the innumerable crowd of every sort of wretches, down to the filthiest, vilest matricide, who in your communion are fighting under your banners—stout-hearted rebels!—leagued with you in your attempts to dethrone the Lord's Anointed. If you boast of one Marcus Aurelius, you must fraternize with many a Nero, Domitian, Caligula, and Heliogabalus. If you rejoice in the virtues of one Seneca, you must own the vices of the ten thousand murderers, robbers, adulterers, drunkards, profane swearers, and lecherous debauchees who have rejected the counsels of heaven because the precepts of righteousness and life forbade their crimes.

If, then, my friends (for I now address the most honorable of your community), you boast that you belong to a very large and respectable synagogue, remember, I pray you, that to this same synagogue in which you have your brotherhood belongs every thing mean, and vile, and wretched, in every land where the name of Jesus has been announced. *What a group!* Have you so much of the reflex light of the gospel falling upon your vision as to flush your cheek with the glow of shame when you look along the lines of your alliance, and survey the horrible faces, the ragged, and tattered, and squalid, and filthy wretches, *your companions in arms—members with you in the synagogue of Satan, and confederates against the Prince of Peace!* If you can not blush at such a spectacle, you are not among them to whom I would tender the pearls of Jesus Christ.

What do you then say? "I am ashamed of such an alliance—of such a brotherhood; and therefore I have joined the Temperance Society—I belong to the Literary Club—and I carry my family regularly to church every Sunday." And do you think O simpleton! that these human inventions, which only divide the kingdom of Satan into castes, and form within it various private communions, honorable and dishonorable associations, learned and unlearned fraternities, moral and immoral conventicles, change the state of a single son of Adam as respects the Son of God! Then may Whig and Tory, Masonic and Antimasonic clubs and conclaves—then may every political cabal, for the sake of elevating some demagogue—change the political relations in the state, and make and unmake American citizens according to fancy, in despite of constitution, law, and established precedents. No, sir; should there be as many parties in the state as there are days in a month, membership in any one of these affects not in the least the standing of any man as a citizen in relation to the United States, or to any foreign power. And by parity of reason, as well as by all that is written in the New Testament, should you join all the benevolent societies on the checkered map of Christendom, and fraternize with every brotherhood born *after the will of man*, this would neither change nor destroy your citizenship in the kingdom of Satan—still you would be an alien from the kingdom of the Messiah—a foreigner as respects all its covenanted blessings—and in the unbiased judgment of the universe, you would stand enrolled among its enemies.

In *character* there are many degrees, as respects any and every attribute which enters into its formation; but as respects *state* there are no degrees. In the nature of things it is impossible. Every man is either married or single, a brother, a master, a citizen, or he is not. Every man is either Christ's or Belial's: there is no middle power, and therefore no neutral state. Hence the King himself, when on the present theatre of war, told his companions to regard every man as his enemy who was not on his side. Among his professed friends, they who in works deny him are even counted as enemies.

What a hopeless struggle is that in which you are engaged! Discomfiture, soon or late, awaits you. Have you counsel and strength to oppose the Sovereign of the Universe? Do you think you can frustrate the counsels of Infinite Wisdom and overcome Omnipotence? Your master is already a prisoner—your chief is in chains. The fire of eternal vengeance is already kindled for Satan and all his subjects. Mad in his disappointed ambition, and implacable in his hatred of him against whom he rebelled, he only seeks to gratify his own malice, by involving with himself in irremediable ruin the unhappy victims of his seduction. He only seeks to desolate the dominions of God, and to ruin forever his fellow-creatures. Will you, then, serve your worst enemy, and war against your best friend?

But your rebellion can effect nothing against God. His arm is too strong for the whole creation. You can not defeat his counsels nor stay his almighty hand. The earth on which you stand trembles at his rebuke; the foundations of the hills and mountains are moved and shaken at his presence. You fight against yourselves. God's detestation of your course arises not from any apprehension that you can injure him; but because you destroy yourselves. Every triumph which your inordinate desires and passions gain over the remonstrances of reason and conscience only precipitates you into deeper and deeper misery, matures you for perdition, and makes it essential, to the good order and happiness of the universe, you should suffer an "everlasting destruction from the presence of the Lord, and from the glory of his power."

What, then, infatuates you, that you should choose death rather than life, and prefer destruction to salvation? "I am not sure that the gospel is true; I love my companions, and can not see any criminality in gratifying those passions and appetites which my Creator has planted in my constitution."

You admit there is a God, your Creator; but you doubt whether the gospel is true! What an abuse of reason and evidence! Can you infer, from any premises in your possession, that he whose creation man is, who has exhibited to the eye and ear of man so much wisdom, power, and goodness, in all his grand designs already accomplished, and daily accomplishing, in the heavens and in the earth, teaching men to sustain the present life, to anticipate the future, and to provide for it, has never intelligibly addressed him on a subject of incomparably more importance—his own ultimate destiny? That God should have been at so much pains to elevate man in nature—to furnish him with such an organization—to bestow on him reason and speech—admirably qualifying him to acquire and communicate instruction, on all things necessary to his present animal enjoyments; and, at the same time to have never communicated to him any thing relative to his intellectual nature—never to have addressed him on the themes which, as a rational creature, he must necessarily most of all desire to know; to have done everything for his body and for the present, and nothing for his mind nor for the future—is, to say the least of it, the most improbable conceit that the most romantic fancy can entertain.

That the Creator could not enlighten him on these topics is wholly inadmissible. That he could, and would not, is directly contrary to every analogy in creation—contradictory to every proof we have of his benevolence, an inexplicable exception to the whole order of his government; for he has provided objects for every sense—objects for every intellectual power—objects for every affection, honorable passion, appetite and propensity, in our constitution; but, on your hypothesis, he has only failed in that which is infinitely more dear to us, more consonant to our whole rational nature, and most essential to our happiness! It is most contrary to reason.

But the folly of your skepticism is still more glaring when we open the book of the gospel of salvation. In the history of Jesus you have the fulfillment of a thousand predictions, experienced by numerous prophets for one thousand five hundred years before he was born. These recorded prophecies were in the possession of his and our most bitter enemies, when he appeared, and are still extant in their hearts. How can you dispose of these? All antiquity confirms the existence of Jesus of Nazareth in the times of Augustus and Tiberius Caesar. No contemporary opponent denied his miracles; they explained them away, but questioned not the wonderful works which he wrought. His character was the only perfect and unexceptionable one the world ever saw, either in print or in real life; and yet you imagine him to have been the greatest liar and most infamous impostor that ever lived. You must admit him to have been the teacher of every thing moral and pure and godlike—to have lived the most exemplary life —to have employed his whole life in doing good, while, to countenance your skepticism, you must imagine him to have been the greatest deceiver and most blasphemous pretender the world ever saw!— Truly, you are fond of paradox!

His apostles, too, for the sake of being accounted the offscourings of the world, and the filth of all society—for the sake of poverty, contumely, stripes, imprisonment, and martyrdom, you imagine travelled over the earth teaching virtue and holiness, discountenancing every species of vice and immorality, while telling the most impudent lies, and that, too, about matters of palpable fact, about which no man having eyes and ears could be mistaken! How great your credulity! How weak your faith!

And to consummate the whole, you admit that in the most enlightened age, and among the most disputatious and discriminating population, both Jewish, Roman, and Grecian, in Jerusalem itself, the very theatre of the crucifixion of Christ, and in all Judea and Samaria, and in all the great towns and cities of the whole ancient Roman Empire, Eastern and Western, these rude and uncultivated Galileans did actually succeed in persuading hundreds of thousands of persons, of all ranks, sexes, ages, and intellects, to renounce their former opinions and practices—to encounter proscription, confiscation of goods, banishment, and even death itself in numerous instances, through faith in their testimony, while every thing was fresh and when the detection of any fiction or fraud was most easy.

Now, if it were possible to place your folly in an attitude still more inexcusable, I would ask you to show what there is in the gospel that is not infinitely worthy of God to bestow and of man to receive. And where under the canopy of the skies, in any country, language, or age of time, is there any thing that confers greater honor on man, or proposes to him any thing more worthy of his acceptance, than the gospel?

Can there have been a more acceptable model proposed, after which to fashion man, than that after which he was originally created? When he was beguiled and apostatized from God, could there have been deputed a more honorable personage to effect his reconciliation to God, than his only-begotten and well-beloved Son? And could there even be imagined a more delectable destiny allotted to man, than an immortality of bliss in the palace of this vast universe, in the presence of his Father and his God forever and ever? Now, with all these premises, will you object to this religion that it requires a man to be pure and holy in order to his enjoyment of this eternal salvation? Then lay your hand upon your face, and blush, and be ashamed forever.

But you say you love your companions. And who are they? Your fellow-rebels, foolish and infatuated like yourselves. The drunkard, the thief, the murderer, love their companions, the partners of their crimes. Conspirators and partisans in any undertaking, kindred spirits in guilty and daring enterprise, confirm each other in their evil machinations, and, either from mutual interest or from some hateful affinity in evil dispositions, coalesce and league together in bands of malicious depredation. A Catiline, a Jugurtha, a Robespierre, had their confederates. The rakes, the libertines, the freebooters of every color, love their own fraternities, and have a liking of some sort for their companions. And wherein does your attachment to your companions differ from theirs? A congeniality of disposition, a similarity of likings and dislikings, all springing from your love of the world and your dislike of the authority of the Messiah. And will not a change of circumstances convert your affections into hatred? Soon or late, if you do not repent and turn to God, you that are leagued in the friendships of the world, these friendships arising from the lusts of the flesh, the lusts of the eye, and the pride of life, will not only become enemies, but mutual tormentors of one another. Your warmest friends in your opposition to the Son of God will become king's evidence against you, and exasperate the flame that will consume you forever and ever. Break off, then, every friendship, alliance, and covenant which you have formed with them that disdain the grace of God and condemn the Saviour of the world, and form an everlasting covenant with the people of God, which shall never be forgotten. Then, indeed, you may love your companions with all the affection of your hearts, and indulge to the utmost every sympathy and social feeling of your nature. Then may you embrace, in all the ardor of fraternal love, those kindred spirits that with you have vowed eternal allegiance to the gracious and rightful Sovereign of all the nations of the redeemed, in heaven and on earth. Such companions are worth possessing, and their friendship worth cultivating and preserving, through all the journey of life; for it will be renewed beyond the Jordan, and flourish with increasing delight through the endless ages of eternity.

But you have said that the gratification of all the impulses and propensities of your nature must be innocent, because they are the creation of God, and were sown in the embryo of your physical constitution. If under the control of that light and reason under which God commanded your affections and appetites to move, your reasoning would be sound and safe; but if they have usurped a tyranny over your judgment, and captivated your reason, they are not to be gratified. They are like successful rebels that have dethroned their sovereign; and because by violence and fraud in possession of the throne, they plead a divine right to wield the sceptre over their dethroned Prince. Such is the meaning of the plea which you urge in favor of your rebellious affections. When man rebelled against his Creator, the beasts of the field, till then under his dominion, rebelled against him; and all his passions, affections, and propensities partook of the general disorder—of that wild and licentious anarchy which ensued upon man's disobedience. And have you not in your daily observation—nay, have you not in your own experience—irrefragable evidence that the uncontrolled indulgence of even the instinctive appetites, as well as the gratification of inordinate passions and affections, necessarily issue in the destruction of the physical constitution of man? Is not the control of reason, is not the exercise of discretion in the license of every animal indulgence, essential to the health and life of man? Then why crave an exemption from the universal law of human existence, in favor of that demoralizing course of indulgence which you would fain call innocent in morals, though in physics evidently destructive to animal organization!

When reconciled to God through the gospel, the peace of God which passes understanding reigning in the heart, all is order and harmony within. Then, under the control of enlightened and sanctified reason, all the passions, appetites, and instincts of our nature, like the planets round the sun, move in their respective orbits in the most perfect order, preserving a perfect balance in all the principles and powers of human action. Pleasures without alloy are then felt and enjoyed from a thousand sources, from which, in the tumult and disorder of rebellion, every transgressor is debarred. It is then found, that there is not a supernumerary passion, affection, nor appetite in man—not one that adds not something to his enjoyment—not one that may not be made an instrument of righteousness, a means of doing good to others, as well as of enjoying good ourselves. Why not, then, lay down the weapons of your rebellion, and be at peace with God, with your fellow-creatures, and with yourselves?

"Admitting, then, that the gospel is true—that in my present state and standing I am an alien from the kingdom of heaven, and that I wished to become a citizen—where shall I find this kingdom of heaven, and how shall I be constituted a citizen thereof?" Well, indeed, may you admit the gospel to be true, both on account of what it is in itself, and the evidence which sustains it. Only suppose it to be false—extinguish all the light which it sheds on the human race —make void all its promises—annul all its hopes—eradicate from the human breast all the motives which it imparts—and what remains to explain the universe, to develop the moral character of God, to dissipate the gloom which envelopes in eternal night the destiny of man, to solace and cheer him during the incessant struggle of life, to soothe the bed of affliction and death, and to counterveil the inward dread and horror of falling into nothing—of being forever lost in the promiscuous wreck of nature—of sinking down into the grave, the food of worms, the prey of an eternal death?

It is like annihilating the sun in the heavens. An eternal night ensues. There is no beauty, form nor comeliness in creation. The universe is in ruins. The world without the Bible is a universe without a sun. The atheist is but an atom of matter in motion, belonging to no system, amenable to none, without a destiny, without an object to live or to die. He boasts there is none to punish him: but then there is none to help him—none to reward him. He has no Father, Proprietor, or Ruler—no filial affection, no sense of obligation, no gratitude, no comfort in reflection, no joy in anticipation. If he can not be blamed, he can not be praised, he can not be honored—and man without honor is more wretched than the beasts that perish. Unenviable mortal!

What an abortion is the system of nature, if man lives not again! It is a creation for the sake of destruction. It is an infinite series of designs, ending in nothing. It is a universe of blanks, without a single prize. It can not be. The Bible is necessary to the interpretation of nature. It is the only comment on nature—on providence—on man. Man without it, and without the hope of immortality, has nothing to rouse him into action. He is a savage, a Hottentot, a cannibal, a worm. You are compelled, then, to admit that the gospel is true, unless you put out the eye of reason, and refuse to hear the voice of nature.

But is it not a happy necessity which compels your belief in God, and in his Son, the renovator of the universe? It opens to you all the mysteries of creation, the arcana of the temple of nature, and inducts you to the fountain of being and of bliss. It inspires you with motives of high and lofty enterprise, stimulates you to manly action, and points out a prize worthy of the best efforts of body, soul, and spirit. Is it not, then, "a credible saying, and worthy of universal acceptance, that Jesus Christ came into the world to save sinners, even the chief"?

But you ask, "Where shall the kingdom of heaven be found, and how may you be constituted a citizen of it?" The prophets and apostles must be your guide in deciding these great questions. Moses in the law, all the prophets, and all the apostles, point you to the Lamb of God that takes away the sin of the world—the Apostle of the Father Almighty—the divinely constituted chief of the kingdom of heaven. He has submitted his claims to your examination—he has invited you to test all his pretensions—and to the humble and docile he has tendered all necessary assistance in deciding upon his person and mission.

His character is so familiar, so condescending, so full of all grace and goodness, that all may approach him. The halt, the maimed, the deaf, the dumb, the blind, found in him a friend and physician indeed. None importune his aid in vain. His ears are always open to the tale of woe. His eye streams with sympathy on every object of distress. He invites all the wretched and repulses none who implore relief. He chides only the proud, and kindly receives and blesses the humble. He invites and beseeches the weary, the heavy-laden, the broken-hearted, the oppressed, and all the sons of want and misfortune, to come to him, and tenders relief to all.

In his official dignity he presides over the universe. He is the High Priest of God and the Prophet and Messenger of Peace. He has the key of David; he opens and shuts the paradise of God. He is the only potentate, and has the power of granting remission of all sins to all who obey him.

To receive him in his personal glory and official dignity and supremacy, as the Messiah of God, the only-begotten of the Father—to know him in his true and proper character—is the only prerequisite to the obedience of faith. He that thus accredits him is not far from the kingdom of heaven. To assume him as your prophet, your high priest, and your king; to submit to him in these relations, being immersed into his death, will translate you into the kingdom of heaven. Why not, then, gladly and immediately yield him the admiration of your understanding and the homage of your heart? Why not now enter into the possession of all the riches, and fulness, and excellence of the kingdom? He commands *all* men to repent—he beseeches every sinner whom he addresses in his word to receive pardon and eternal life as a gracious gift.

Can you doubt his power to save, to instruct, and to sanctify you for heaven? Can you doubt his condescending mercy and compassion? Will not he that pitied the blind Bartimeus, that condoled with the widow of Nain, that wept with Mary and Martha at the grave of Lazarus, that heard the plea of the Syrophenician woman, that cleansed the supplicating leper, that compassionated the famishing multitudes, that looked with pity (even in the agonies of the cross) upon an importuning thief, have pity upon you, and every returning prodigal, who sues for mercy at the gate of his kingdom?

Is there in the universe one whom you can believe with more assurance than the faithful and true witness who, in the presence of Pontius Pilate, witnessed a good confession at the hazard of his life? Is there any person in heaven, on earth, or under the earth, more worthy of your confidence, than the sinner's friend; than he who always, and in all circumstances, bore testimony to the truth? When did he ever violate his word, or suffer his promise to fail? Who ever repented of his confidence in Jesus, or of relying implicitly upon his word? Who ever was put to shame because of confidence in him?

Who can offer such inducements to obedience by his authority as the Saviour of the world? Who has such power to bless? He has all authority in heaven and on earth. He has power to forgive sins, to raise the dead, to bestow immortality and eternal life, and to judge the living and the dead. And has he not tendered a participation of his official authority to every one who submits to his government, and who, by him, is reconciled to God? If he have wisdom and power divine, has he not pledged these to the relief, guidance, and benefit of his people? Who can injure them under his protection—condemn whom he justifies—criminate whom he pardons—or snatch out of his hands those who betake themselves to his mercy?

Was there ever love like his love—compassion like his compassion —or condescension like his condescension? Who ever could—who ever did—humble himself like the Son of God? On whose cheek ever flowed tears of purer sympathy for human woe than those he shed? Whose bowels ever moved with such compassion as that which dissolved his heart in tender mercies for the afflicted sons and daughters of men? Who ever for his friends endured such contradiction of sinners against himself; submitted to such indignities; sustained such accumulated sorrows and griefs; suffered such agonies of mind and body, as those which he endured in giving his life an offering for his enemies? Forsaken by his God, abandoned by his friends, deserted of every stay, surrounded by the fiercest enemies, the most implacable foes whose hearts were harder than adamant, insulting the very pangs which they inflicted, he expired on the accursed tree! The heavens blushed at the sight—the sun covered his face—the earth trembled—the rocks split—the veil of the temple was rent from top to bottom—the graves opened. All nature stood horror-stricken, when Roman soldiers, urged by bloodthirsty priests, nailed him to the cross—when the chief priests, scribes, and elders, in derision said, "He saved others: can not he save himself?" The person who perceives not, who feels not the eloquence of his love consummated in his death—the tenderness of his entreaties and expostulations, is not to be reasoned with—is not to be moved by human power. Will you not, then, honor your reason by honoring the Son of God—by giving up your understanding, your wills, your affections, to the teachings of the good Spirit—to the guidance of his love? Then, and only then, can you feel yourselves safe, secure, and happy.

Need you to be reminded how much you are indebted to his long-suffering patience already—to his benevolence in all the gifts and bounties of his providence vouchsafed to you? How many days and nights has he guarded, sustained and succored you! Has he not saved you from ten thousand dangers—from the pestilence that walks in darkness secretly, and from destruction that wastes at noonday? Who can tell but he has lengthened out your unprofitable existence to this very hour, that you might now repent of all your sins, turn to God with your whole heart, be baptized for the remission of your past transgressions, be adopted into the family of God, and yet receive an inheritance among the sanctified? Arise, then, in the strength of Israel's God—accept salvation at his hands—enter into his kingdom, and be forever blessed. You will not, you can not, repent of such a step, of such a noble surrender of yourself, while life endures; in the hour of death, in the day of judgment, nor during the endless succession of ages in eternity. *To-day*, then, hear his voice: to-morrow may be forever too late! All things are ready—come. Saints on earth, and angels in heaven—apostles, prophets, and martyrs—will rejoice over you, and you will rejoice with them forever and forever. Amen!

THE END